America the Scrivener

Also by Gregory S. Jay

T. S. Eliot and the Poetics of Literary History

*After Strange Texts: The Role of Theory in
the Study of Literature* (coeditor)

Modern American Critics, 1920–1955 (editor)

Modern American Critics since 1955 (editor)

America the Scrivener

DECONSTRUCTION AND THE
SUBJECT OF LITERARY HISTORY

GREGORY S. JAY

Cornell University Press

ITHACA AND LONDON

First published 1990 by Cornell University Press.

International Standard Book Number 0-8014-2386-4 (cloth)
International Standard Book Number 0-8014-9610-1 (paper)
Library of Congress Catalog Card Number 90-1801
Printed in the United States of America
Librarians: Library of Congress cataloging information
appears on the last page of the book.

⊗ The paper used in the text of this publication meets the minimum requirements of the American National Standard for Information Sciences—Permanence of Paper for Printed Library Materials, ANSI Z39.48-1984.

For Hank Lazer and
David Lee Miller

In order to speak of "deconstruction in America," one would have to claim to know what one is talking about, and first of all what is meant or defined by the word "America." Just what is America in this context? Were I not so frequently associated with this adventure of deconstruction, I would risk, with a smile, the following hypothesis: America *is* deconstruction (l'Amérique, mais *c'est* la deconstruction). *In this hypothesis,* America would be the proper name of deconstruction in progress, its family name, its toponymy, its language and its place, its principal residence. And how could we define the United States *today* without integrating the following into the description: It is that historical space which today, in all its dimensions and through all its power plays, reveals itself as being undeniably the most sensitive, receptive, or responsive space of all to the themes and effects of deconstruction. Since such a space represents and stages, in this respect, the greatest concentration *in the world,* one could not define it without at least including this symptom (if we can even speak of symptoms) in its definition. In the war that rages over the subject of deconstruction, there is no front; there are no fronts. But if there were, they would all pass through the United States. They would define the lot, and, in truth, the partition of America. But we have learned from "Deconstruction" to suspend these always hasty attributions of proper names. My *hypothesis* must thus be abandoned. No, "deconstruction" is not a proper name, nor is America the proper name of deconstruction. Let us say instead: deconstruction and America are two open sets which intersect partially according to an allegorico-metonymic figure. In this fiction of truth, "America" would be the title of a new novel on the history of deconstruction and the deconstruction of history.

—Jacques Derrida, *Mémoires*

Contents

Preface

This book contests some of the conventions and restraints of academic criticism, even as it chooses to abide by other no less limiting procedures. Although I am concerned to explore particular issues in contemporary theory—especially as regards literature, history, politics, and subjectivity—I also want to engage in readings of specific works, thus challenging the distinction between "doing theory" and "studying literature." The chapters devoted to such figures as Derrida, Freud, and de Man, moreover, offer readings of *their* texts rather than a series of theoretical propositions that together would constitute a total model for resolving the problems they address. Correspondingly, the readings of such writers as Thoreau, Melville, Poe, Emerson, Douglass, Adams, James, Fitzgerald, and Faulkner do not offer definitive new interpretations of individual works but rather explore some of the ways their texts theorize issues of much contemporary (and historical) interest.

The book's chapters have been arranged around considerations of method, topic, theme, and argument. The methods explored and compared include deconstruction, psychoanalysis, Marxism, the new historicism, and race and gender studies. The topic or place of comparison is American literary history, both as a body of texts and as a discipline with changing boundaries. My title plays off of Melville's "Bartleby, The Scrivener" to suggest figuratively how nations imagine themselves as writers (and vice versa). I discuss that story at some length in my introduction; for me it helps signify a kind of ideology of literary historiography in which the nation represents itself to itself as a writing subject, a single consciousness expressing its history and self-understanding. Melville's story offers a caution against this kind of identification, though in lamenting the artist's estrangement it also expresses the continuing desire for a correspondence between the writer and a community. It is no accident, for Melville's purpose or my own, that the tale of the subject's alienation from writing should be located on Wall Street and focus on the effects of capitalism as a mode of production. This confluence of the problematics of subjectivity, writing, history, and political economy is charted throughout the course of this book.

The theme of the book is "the subject of literary history." My subtitle means to echo that punning use of the phrase "the subject" now so pervasive in cultural studies and invoked by books such as Rosalind Coward and John Ellis's *Language and Materialism: Developments in Semiology and the Theory of the Subject,* Kaja Silverman's *The Subject of Semiotics,* David Carroll's *The Subject in Question,* and Paul Smith's *Discerning the Subject.* My argument focuses on the function of the subject in theories of literature, history, politics, and culture. When I examine how various philosophical, psychoanalytic, and linguistic theories have deconstructed the subject, I attempt to show that these critiques have remained trapped within a specific tradition of metaphysical abstraction for which the name or subject of Hegel can stand as a metaphor as well as a kind of beginning.

The death of the author or of "man" pronounced by commentators on poststructuralism was greatly exaggerated; the return of the subject, however, must be via explicit historical, geographical, political, and social specifications of the location of embodied figures rather than through a reactionary revival of the ideological portrait of a timeless universal humanism. The texts of Derrida exhibit an increasing commitment to remarking the historical location and agency of the body of the writer, and to retracing the borderline between "life" and "work"; thus I take *The Post Card,* which explores the effects of Freud's and Lacan's and Derrida's own desires (libidinal, institutional, theoretical, literary, political) on the structures of their speculations, as my touchstone text of deconstruction. Where my argument arrives is at the dissemination of the position of the subject rather than at its disappearance.

My itinerary from deconstruction to cultural studies, then, is by way of this displacement of a centered subject now deconstructed through the specification of how the partial interests of a group (white, male, middle- or upper-class, heterosexual, Euro-American) are ideologically represented as The Subject of History (and thus of literature, philosophy, and politics as well). A dissemination of the subject means the recognition of the "other" as truly heterogeneous rather than as an artifice constructed to reconfirm the identity of the subject. The political as well as intellectual consequences of this move will entail the theorization of a practice of multicultural social existence which is beyond the scope of this book, but which stands at the horizon of critical thought today.

I resisted the suggestion, and temptation, to divide this project into separate books on critical theory and American literature, respectively. At least since the 1974 publication of Joseph Riddel's *The Inverted Bell: Modernism and the Counterpoetics of William Carlos Williams*, a contentious and rich dialogue has occurred between European theory and the criticism of American literature. The results have taken various forms, but the genres I want to avoid include studies that merely subordinate or domesticate theory by devising ever closer *explications de texte*, and works that simply use literature to illustrate presumed theoretical verities. I do not pretend to have entirely escaped these dual pitfalls. Nevertheless, the structure of the book and the projects of the individual chapters aim to forestall such tendencies as much as possible.

All the chapters engage, to some degree, in what Jacques Derrida has called "speculation," a style of reading and writing which takes chances with texts and theories in a way that both mimes and disrupts their devices, producing kinds of knowledge unaccountable by former philosophies of method. Throughout, I insist that such speculation touches on our concepts of history and politics in ways that ought to be attended to by anyone interested in current efforts to devise innovations in cultural criticism. I also accept as valid, however, the charge that deconstructive criticism has only obliquely addressed itself to historical and political issues. Without erasing the lesson of books like *The Post Card*, I have tried to send my speculations toward that address without assuming I know in advance where (or even if) they ought to arrive. Still the subject of address—in its rhetorical, literary, and psychoanalytic senses—provides various sites in each chapter for speculations on historical and political matters.

This book, then, does not presume to cover comprehensively all the recent theoretical work on literature, history, politics, and subjectivity, preferring to elaborate how deconstruction (now an admittedly indeterminate nominative) has altered our sense of these terms. Nor does it pretend to have discovered a new metanarrative for American literary history. Indeed, in the course of writing this book I have become convinced that we should abandon such stories and the nationalist agenda that they inevitably reinforce. The dialogue among European literature, critical theory, intellectual disciplines, and American writers which this volume enacts represents, however awkwardly, my own idea of the transgressive character future work in literary and cultural studies could take (and by "transgressive" I do not mean "subversive," a word whose political connotations carry values I shall not claim).

My choice of American writers reflects the limits of my theoretical interests, professional training, and personal history and tastes. Each writer offers a powerful example of the interplay among the literary, the historical, the political, and the subjective, and does so in ways different enough to warrant comparison. All are male, and all are, with the exception of Douglass, "white." This selection was intentional. My aim is to deconstruct a dominant tradition from the inside and disclose how the privileged Subject of History conceives and reproduces his story. In so doing I draw upon the critical work of feminists and African-Americanists, as well as poststructuralists, who have taught us how better to read the text of the other. Their work helps me to question the stories of the so-called masters.

The book has been organized to take readers through the respective theoretical meditations on history, subjectivity, and literariness by European theorists into readings of how these terms get theorized by various American texts. Americanists may be tempted to jump right to the latter chapters, whereas theorists may only glance at these after finishing the first three or four. I hope both will resist the temptation to skip around, for I want to bring these two communities of scholarship into greater dialogue with each other. The chapters treating European theorists do so from an American perspective, and the chapters treating American writers read them through frameworks often devised from European theory. One intended consequence is a decentering of the identities of the "theoretical" and the "American," which have often formed an oppositional binary my book displaces whenever possible.

Deconstruction has been not only a matter of reversing binary oppositions but also a matter of disabling the hierarchy of values they enable and of speculating on alternative modes of knowing and of acting. Ultimately it is this discourse on values which connects the chapters that follow, though not in a manner that adds up to a new totality. There would be little value in that and much to be feared. Some readers will be impatient at my reluctance to take sides. In response, I can say that at times I have, with care, made my values known and even advocated them. At other times the choice of sides seemed so problematic that undoing the opposition appeared to be the only responsible activity. In this ethical caution I have kept to the speculative itinerary of the book, recognizing that in theory one can sustain a degree of undecidability which would be impossible, even irresponsible, elsewhere in life.

During the eight years that I was writing this book, I received generous support from three universities and benefited in innumerable ways from my colleagues and students at these institutions. At the University of Alabama I had the great fortune to work with Hank Lazer and David Lee Miller, who over the years have continued to share with me their ideas, imaginations, and honest criticisms. Each read and commented on the manuscript with sympathy and exactitude. I dedicate this book to them as an expression of my abundant gratitude for their extraordinary friendship, tolerance, and support. Elizabeth Meese, Claudia Johnson, William Ulmer, and William Doty also made my years at Alabama rewarding ones. At the University of South Carolina I depended on my friends in the interdepartmental Critical Theory Reading Group, including Meili Steele, Nancy Lane, Gerald Wallulis, Martin Donoghuo, Amitai Avi-Ram, and Chris Schreiner. Each contributed suggestions that improved the book.

Completion of this book was decisively aided by the intellectual stimulation and personal support I have enjoyed since coming to the University of Wisconsin at Milwaukee. Ihab and Sally Hassan went the extra mile to make the transition of our family a happy one. The events they produce, intellectual and social, are always first-rate. James Sappenfield excelled in all his roles—as chair of the English Department, as scholar of American literature, as respected friend—and I deeply appreciate his expressions of confidence in me and my work. Dean William Halloran and the College of Letters and Sciences provided time off from teaching when I had to write. A year-long fellowship at the university's Center for Twentieth Century Studies enabled me to finish and revise the manuscript. I give my profoundest thanks to the center's director, Kathleen Woodward, and its outstanding staff, including Carol Tennessen, Jean Lile, Barbara Obremski, Kate Kramer (who did the index), Thomas Piontek, and Mark Pizzato. My development as a critic has been spurred by many at the university, notably Herbert Blau, Patrice Petro, Andrew Martin, and Cheryl Johnson. Last but certainly not least, the graduate students at Milwaukee contributed a considerable number of insights (with Valerie Ross lending me some puns for the Poe chapter); I am grateful to them for sharing their conversation and work with me.

My appreciation also goes to the many friends and colleagues who have contributed to this book by attending conference presentations, reading drafts, or just sharing their time and thoughts. Paul Jay, brother and professional fellow-traveler, has for over fifteen years been both resource and example; my admiration and affection for him are boundless. As always, Mitchell Breitwieser has been the source of inimitable commentaries, hot tips, and smart rejoinders. Steven Mailloux and Donald Marshall read early drafts and made many important suggestions. Gordon Hutner provided key advice on revisions, as did Thomas Schaub. J. Hillis Miller, John Rowe, Gerald Graff, Neil Schmitz, Joseph Riddel, Eve Bannet, Jonathan Culler, Henry Louis Gates, Jr., Estella Lauter, and Houston Baker each provided advice and support at crucial moments.

I also gratefully acknowledge an NEH fellowship to attend a summer

institute on American Realism at the University of California at Berkeley, conducted by Walter Benn Michaels and Michael Fried.

To my wife, Martha, I owe more than I can begin to say. Her patience,
good cheer, and wise counsel always see me through. The arrival of
my daughter, Lydia, was the greatest event of these years; her joyful
presence has been a blessed relief from the intangible undecidabilities
of theory. Her spirit alleviated many of the strains of the scrivener.

Parts of this book have appeared previously, and I am grateful to
the publishers below for their permission to reprint. Chapter 1 is a
substantially revised version of "Values and Deconstructions: Derrida,
Saussure, Marx," *Cultural Critique* 8 (Winter 1987–88): 153–96; most of
Chapter 2 appeared as "Paul de Man: The Subject of Literary History,"
MLN (December 1988): 969–94; Chapter 3, with some additions, reprints "Freud: The Death of Autobiography," *Genre* 19 (Summer 1986):
103–28; Chapters 4 and 6 incorporate passages from "America the
Scrivener: Economy and Literary History," *Diacritics* 14 (Spring 1984):
36–51; an earlier and much different version of Chapter 5 appeared
as "Poe: Writing and the Unconscious," in *The American Renaissance:
New Dimensions,* ed. Peter Carafiol and Harry Garvin (Lewisburg, Pa.:
Bucknell University Press, 1983), pp. 144–69; Chapter 7 extends and
modifies "American Literature and the New Historicism: The Example
of Frederick Douglass," *boundary 2* 17 (Fall/Winter 1989): 211–42; most
of the first and third sections of Chapter 8 appeared as "Hegel and
Trilling in America," *American Literary History 1* (Winter 1989): 565–
92; Chapter 9 reprints, with new material, "The Subject of Pedagogy:
Lessons in Psychoanalysis and Politics," *College English* 49 (November
1987): 785–800.

GREGORY S. JAY
Milwaukee, Wisconsin

America the Scrivener

Styles of Civil Disobedience

> The movements of deconstruction do not destroy [*ne sollicitent pas*] structures from the outside. They are not possible and effective, nor can they take accurate aim [*n'ajustent leurs coups*], except by inhabiting those structures. Inhabiting them *in a certain way*, because one always inhabits, and all the more when one does not suspect it. Operating necessarily from the inside, borrowing all the strategic and economic resources of subversion from the old structure . . . deconstruction always in a certain way falls prey to its own work.
>
> —Derrida, *Of Grammatology*

> In most books, the *I*, or first person, is omitted; in this it will be retained; that, in respect to egotism, is the main difference. We commonly do not remember that it is, after all, always the first person that is speaking.
>
> —Thoreau, *Walden*

Thoreau's punning passage reminds us that grammar always prescribes the subject. The subject addresses us from a particular syntactic position and from the place of agency and authorship. There, in that site (and self-citation), a subject comes into being, performs, assumes predicates, hazards consequences. It is a public space, historically derived, accessible only through a medium inhabited by others. In this place, perhaps more than any other, the subject is at home, if ever. Thoreau craftily pronounces upon this eccentric subjectivity proper to the writer's vocation. Proper not simply to that of the speaker but to every subject employing language, for this uncanny reverberation is the stamp of the grammatical voice: "it is, after all, always the first person that is speaking." Trained in classical rhetoric and ever ready to exploit the play of syntax or etymology, Thoreau both asserts the primacy of his individual voice and undercuts that assertion by a pragmatic demonstration: this voice appears only courtesy of the grammatical tense it inhabits, on which it depends for its force, its intimacy, and its priority.

The priority of voice over text, however, immediately cancels itself when we read of the "firstness" of the grammatical subject, inherited through the ages, the "person" whose supplementary whispering is essential to the hearing we give "Thoreau." It is this specifying of the location of the speaker which "in respect to egotism, is the main difference" from books written in the third person: the difference of the remembrance of grammar, of history. The figure of Thoreau's "I" cannot be univocally identified with the transparent eyeball, the visionary romantic soul, or the self-reliant ego. His text gives voice to a difference not accountable to an essence—the difference between the assumptions of a subject who forgets language and the premises of a subject who becomes the "first person" by virtue of the play of language. In "a certain way," Thoreau's style delivers a blow against the state of things from within its very borders.

Thoreau's coup, then, provides a small lesson in reading which fore-shadows the concerns and arguments of this book. This moment, and Thoreau's work throughout, epitomizes the triple-play among lan-guage, subjectivity, and history which I intend to explore in the chapters that follow. Much recent literary and critical theory has been dedicated to undoing our definitions of these three terms. The first part of this book discusses their speculative dissemination in the writings of Derrida, de Man, and Freud (with a recurrent turn back to the texts of Marx, Nietzsche, Saussure, and Heidegger). Together such works (especially Derrida's *The Post Card*) argue that theorizing the address of the writing subject—as opposed to the authorial genius or originary self—is crucial to the poststructuralist agenda.[1] Moreover, this subject belongs to any

1. For a balanced and historically sensitive account of how poststructuralists both critique the humanist self and invent various liberating possibilities for the postmodern subject, see Eve Tavor Bannet, *Structuralism and the Logic of Dissent: Barthes, Derrida, Foucault, Lacan* (London: Macmillan, 1989). Bannet rightly insists on contextualizing these theorists in the France of the post–World War II era, in which their attacks on centralization, technology, systematic discipline, the university, and authoritarianism have localizable motives.

Jane Gallop's *Reading Lacan* (Ithaca: Cornell University Press, 1985) also demonstrates the return of the subject (in the reading and in the text). Lacan's "theory and writings lead us," she contends, "not to a dead author, but to something more haunting, more ambiguous and disconcerting, to a fading author, one who is still precariously there, like the father in the dream. The author is dead but does not know it" (177).

Bill Readings believes that the "deconstruction of the subject/object distinction" can be conceived as "the thinking of *political* agency with an *ethical* subject": "To erase the subject is to think its place as an absence, while to subject it to deconstructive work is to displace the subject into indeterminacy, which does not deny the possibility of agency but merely disrupts its status in ways that precisely allow the possibility of a political resistance that might escape confinement to the field of a political real, which is always already defined

effort to rewrite literary history, from challenges to the narratives and contents of literary histories to investigations of the material and political dimensions of literary history as a discursive practice. Literary change and literary history turn on moments of disobedient inhabitation, so that "the subject" provides a theoretical topos for the economy between writing, social history, and the lives of individuals (as the remainder of this introduction will suggest). Part Two of the book takes these theoretical issues into a series of readings of American literary subjects, with a particular eye toward how poststructuralist versions of Marx and Freud can aid in rewriting the subject of American literature. I also examine how various American interpretive strategies have worked to exclude "other subjects" and how the analysis of such repression might alter future pedagogical and institutional practice.

Thoreau's *fort/da* with the personal pronoun appears near the opening of the first chapter of *Walden*, entitled "Economy." The revealing pun of this title may be traced back to the ancient Greek *oikonomia,* or household management. At the literal or referential level the chapter answers his neighbors' practical inquiries about how Thoreau managed his cabin at Walden, and Thoreau so delights in satisfying them that he mockingly includes an account balance sheet with items specified to the quarter cent. This referential hyperbole forms part of the antimaterialist rhetoric of the book, which eternally translates the things of language into the spirits of their possible inferences, allusions, connotations, contradictions, analogies, accidents, etymologies, and prophecies. In this line of work Thoreau produces figures whose value cannot be expressed by the usual coins of the realm.

Thoreau's play with organic and economic metaphors is inseparable from his attitude toward capitalism, society, and the status of the individual subject (for more on Thoreau in this context, see below Chapters 4 and 7). The cabin or household at Walden soon comes to stand for Thoreau's *personal* economy and, beyond that, for his *scriptural* economy. The book describes the way Thoreau inhabits, and defamiliarizes, the structures of the world and of language; indeed, the labor of his

---

by the State as the state (of things)." See "The Deconstruction of Politics," in *Reading de Man Reading,* ed. Lindsay Waters and Wlad Godzich (Minneapolis: University of Minnesota Press, 1989), pp. 234–35.

In contrast, Paul Smith finds no basis for theories of agency, subjectivity, or resistance in deconstruction. Although I sympathize with some of the directions he advocates, I think his analysis of Derrida in particular to be simplistic and inaccurate. See Smith, *Discerning the Subject* (Minneapolis: University of Minnesota Press, 1988), pp. 41–55.

See also "Who Comes after the Subject," ed. Jean-Luc Nancy, special issue of *Topoi: An International Review of Philosophy* 7 (September 1988). This includes an interview with Derrida in which his refusal to "liquidate the subject" is balanced by cautions against any simple return to the humanist subject (113–21).

style becomes the basis for showing their common transactions.[2] "There is a certain class of unbelievers," writes Thoreau, "who sometimes ask me such questions as, if I think I can live on vegetable food alone; and to strike at the root of the matter at once,—for the root is faith,—I am accustomed to answer such, that I can live on board nails. If they cannot understand that, they cannot understand much that I have to say."[3] To take Thoreau at his word is not to take him literally. In one sense Thoreau moves to Walden so that he will have no address (but one wonders if he picked up letters on his daily visits to Concord). Thoreau's principle of stylistic de-composition takes root in the history of language, playing with the values of words, though his faith remains that he can build something different on it, make it, in fact, differ from itself as words lose their singular referential identities.

The making of the cabin stands allegorically for the construction of *Walden* itself, begun in notebook form during those two years by the pond (1845–47) and hammered out during almost seven more years of revision. The subject who comes into being in *Walden,* then, is a "first person" in the additional sense of making his first (and perhaps only) appearance there. As a historical construct this subject works from within the mode of address assigned to it, and reassigns that address by playing seriously with the elements that direct its destination. His will be a style of *civil* disobedience, a dissonant response to the laws of civilization, though one articulated in an artful manner which acknowledges its debts to the state and to history even as it refuses to underwrite the costs of imperialism and tyranny.

Since much contemporary literary theory rests on the revival of the discipline of rhetoric, Thoreau's skill and training as a rhetorician deserve renewed attention. Rhetoric is an antique word for the arts of speech, for the rules and decorum of verbal representation in the public marketplace. This public and thus political (addressed to the *polis*) character of rhetoric cannot be forgotten, and I shall recall it at some length in my chapter on Frederick Douglass. Here I want to note that Thoreau's style causes rhetoric and politics to resound together in a common orchestration that accompanies the subject of language. It will shortly be an overt argument of Thoreau's that his neighbors have ceased to live, that they have been so subjected to the labors of the material economy that the "better part of the man is soon ploughed

2. The pioneering work on Thoreau's language from this perspective was Stanley Cavell's *The Senses of Walden* (1974), now republished with two essays on Emerson (Berkeley: North Point Press, 1981).

3. Henry David Thoreau, *Walden and Civil Disobedience*, ed. Owen Thomas (New York: Norton, 1966), p. 44. Subsequent references to *Walden* and "Civil Disobedience" are to this edition and are given parenthetically in the text.

into the soil for compost." It is to these men (and only rarely to women) that Thoreau addresses his jeremiad, offering *his* subject position as the "first person" of his own domain, in glaring contrast to the third-person obedience concisely imaged in the maxim that "the mass of men lead lives of quiet desperation." Thoreau goes on: "A stereotyped but unconscious despair is concealed even under what are called the games and amusements of mankind. There is no play in them, for this comes after work" (5).

The "play" in Thoreau determines his style as a writer and his way of handling the prescriptions of rhetoric, history, and politics. In his own time, as well as ours, Thoreau was criticized for his failure to take a clearer stand, to occupy a position *unequivocally*. Thoreau writes otherwise, though in later years his texts on Captain John Brown fashioned an extraordinary rhetorical transformation as he identified with that particular historical subject. In *Walden,* however, Thoreau discovers freedom in the difference his writing makes as it responds to the demands made upon it: demands that are economic, social, material, historical, linguistic, perhaps even libidinal. For Thoreau—a man much obsessed with how the ideals of citizenship and virtue ought to underlie the true republic—one's *responsibility* lay precisely in questioning and playing with the *terms* of these demands. Unlike Melville's Bartleby, who eventually refuses to copy the word of the Law (or even to fetch the stamps for posting it), Thoreau in *Walden* makes errant copies of what history dictates.

As Derrida puts it in an essay that much influenced me in the course of writing this book:

> We do not listen in the same way when we are responding to a summons as when we are questioning its meaning, its origin, its possibility, its goal, its limits. . . . Who is more faithful to reason's call, who hears it with a keener ear, who better sees the difference, the one who offers questions in return and tries to think through the possibility of that summons, or the one who does not want to hear any question about the reason of reason?[4]

Derrida's resistance to the "summons" of grounded reason, like Thoreau's "Civil Disobedience" and the refusals of Melville's Bartleby, requires that the Law itself be summoned for an/other hearing, be solicited or tried. In Thoreau the summons of contemporary sociopolitical justice is read by the light of those "Higher Laws" invoked midway through

---

4. Jacques Derrida, "The Principle of Reason: The University in the Eyes of Its Pupils," *Diacritics* 13 (Fall 1983): 9.

Walden. The verdict lies not in the resounding of a univocal revelation, however, but in an apocalypse that reveals the vital inseparability of language, time, and the death of the subject.

A key allegory for Thoreau's decompositional theory of writing occurs during his description of the thawing sandbanks in "Spring." There elaborate etymological speculations on labor, globe, lobe, and leaf produce an organic representation that identifies writing and nature in a manner prescribed by Emerson in *Nature* and repeated by Whitman in *Leaves of Grass*. Emerson's famous formula is: "1. Words are signs of natural facts. 2. Particular natural facts are symbols of particular spiritual facts. 3. Nature is a symbol of Spirit." Relying on the popular etymological historicism of his time, Emerson contends that "every word which is used to express a moral or intellectual fact, if traced to its root, is found to be borrowed from some material appearance."[5] Thus materialism is sub(lim)ated by logocentrism to produce linguistic idealism. In his commentary on "Spring" John Irwin concludes that Thoreau's passage "gives a metaphysical interpretation of what is written in the leaves of the book of nature."[6] While the metaphysical certainly makes up a large portion of Thoreau's compost heap, it would be wrong to conclude that a simple philosophical idealism blossoms here. For one thing, Thoreau's labor with the materiality of the sign returns him to what Emerson, in "The Poet," called "the accidency and fugacity of the symbol" in a way that Emerson's strictures in *Nature* won't allow. The investment in the bank here is speculative because it gives itself over to a process of change and dissemination which generates life at the expense of instituted identities: "You may melt your metals and cast them into the most beautiful moulds you can," writes Thoreau; "they will never excite me like the forms which this molten earth flows out into. And not only it, but the institutions upon it, are plastic like clay in the hands of the potter" (204). On the one hand, the artisanal metaphor of the potter invokes a nostalgic mode of production in contrast to the technological artifice of the molded metal, and this could be read as a romantic naturalism offering a symbolic resolution for the real contradictions of alienated labor under capitalism. On the other hand, nature's processes appear here as a stock of linguistic resources, as tropes for describing culture and its institutions. Nature

5. Ralph Waldo Emerson, *Nature,* in *The Works of Ralph Waldo Emerson,* 14 vols. (Cambridge: Houghton Mifflin, 1883), 1: 31.
6. John Irwin, *American Hieroglyphics: The Symbol of the Egyptian Hieroglyphics in the American Renaissance* (Baltimore: Johns Hopkins University Press, 1980), p. 20. See below, Chap. 1, for a related discussion of etymology, materialism, and the example of the leaf in Nietzsche.

is not an origin to which one could return, but an allegory of the temporal impermanence of human productions.

Walden ends with these words:

> I do not say that John or Jonathan will realize all this; but such is the character of that morrow which mere lapse of time can never make to dawn. The light which puts out our eyes is darkness to us. Only that day dawns to which we are awake. There is more day to dawn. The sun is but a morning star. (221)

The vital terms of this passage now reverberate with all the senses of their previous treatment in the book; each has suffered a decomposition which increases its signifying value in direct correspondence to its growing undecidability. The "lapse of time" echoes the confluence in "Spring" of labor, globe, and leaf, thus reminding us again of writing's circulation through the work of temporality. Thoreau's readers of plain English, "John or Jonathan," British or American literalists, are like those inhabitants of Concord addressed by the book's opening declaration: "I do not propose to write an ode to dejection, but to brag lustily as chanticleer in the morning, standing on his roost, if only to wake my neighbors up" (1). The rhetoric of morning pervades the book, and Thoreau's allusion to Coleridge forms only part of the literary history on which he is banking. It was Emerson, after all, who opened *Nature* by castigating his age for building "the sepulchres of the fathers" and groping "among the dry bones of the past." "The sun shines to-day also," he declared.[7]

Thoreau's dawn, unlike Emerson's, retains the play between darkness and light, mourning and morning, blindness and insight. The density of his language allows for no paraphrasable clarity, and no certainty as to precisely what lies on the horizon. Throughout *Walden*, transformation is a matter of "character," and Thoreau speaks here of the difference between a self that a "mere lapse of time" would bring around, and a subject that dawns in "a light which puts out our eyes" (or I's). The probable allusion here to the blindings of King Lear and Gloucester underscores Thoreau's concern with the transactions between property, inheritance, character, self-knowledge, and death, playing these off the framework of religious resurrection from which the passage obviously borrows. Lear's work of mourning for the dead Cordelia cannot be resolved into Christian dogma, nor can Thoreau's labor in language be simply identified as a transcendentalist gesture (or gestation). This

7. Emerson, *Nature*, 1: 9.

conclusion offers the reader, once more, a space or position or *lapsus* to inhabit, one accessible only by virtue of what the play of language makes possible. This play, however, leaves one's world, and one's self, and the relation between, looking quite different. For Thoreau, the difference is not solely psychological or ontological or aesthetic: from the start, it is practical, economic, political, and historical. These are discourses whose mutual investments in each other Thoreau demonstrates by the intertextuality his allusive and playful language activates. By breaking with the habits of the eye, this irruptive dawn signals the coming into being of the historical per se and of its subject. Thus the outlook here, while not quite that of Emerson's early optimism, is decidedly more hopeful—for the subject and history—than that of Edgar Allan Poe, whose negative sublime and critique of transcendentalism form the topics of the fifth chapter in the present book.

Without turning this Introduction into a full-scale reading of *Walden,* I have meant to suggest the pertinence of the issues its reading raises for us within our current horizon, and I have done so with the explicit intention of sustaining an analogy between Thoreau's texts and those of Derrida.[8] My emphasis on *play* in Thoreau, for example, will readily catch the attention of those who have followed the many attacks on deconstruction. Derrida's *jeu d'esprit* has not been appreciated by the sober gatekeepers of metaphysics, humanism, or aesthetics, or by the various critics who have assigned themselves the task of pronouncing upon the moral, ethical, and political correctness of thinkers today. Defenses of Derrida's play often fail because their appreciations rarely venture beyond the literary, so that what Derrida actually means to gamble, to put at stake, in the games of philosophy and history and politics, goes unpronounced: "One could," he writes, "call *play* the absence of the transcendental signified as limitlessness of play, that is to say as the destruction of onto-theology and the metaphysics of presence. . . . It is therefore *the game of the world* that must be first thought; before attempting to understand all the forms of play in the world."[9] Derrida is quite serious in asking that we think about a mode of writing, of

8. Had I the space, I would pursue this analogy further through a reading of the theoretics of "conscience" as they appear in Derrida's essay on Nelson Mandela, whose civil disobedience belongs to a history stretching back to Thoreau's jail cell in Concord. See Jacques Derrida, "The Laws of Reflection: Nelson Mandela, in Admiration," in *For Nelson Mandela,* ed. Jacques Derrida and Mustafa Tlili (New York: Holt, 1987), pp. 11–42.

9. Jacques Derrida, *Of Grammatology,* trans. Gayatri Chakravorty Spivak (Baltimore: Johns Hopkins University Press, 1976), p. 50. For a fine explication of the play of Derrida's style, see Gregory Ulmer's *Applied Grammatology: Post(e)-Pedagogy from Jacques Derrida to Joseph Beuys* (Baltimore: Johns Hopkins University Press, 1985).

thinking, of being that hazards chance rather than subordinating every play to the ultimate profit of a prescribed Absolute Spirit.[10]

A sophisticated understanding of play—as a mode of thinking engaged in civil disobedience—could counter recent tendencies toward what I call a "New Determinism." The New Determinism may be sighted across the spectrum of the human sciences, from some aspects of the New Historicism and neo-Marxism to the reactionary and ethnocentric prescriptions for cultural engineering espoused by Allan Bloom and E. D. Hirsch. The New Determinism stems from a conventional reading of literary and cultural history, a reading that narrates fragmentation, plurality, difference, and dissemination as variations of the Fall, turning Modernism or Postmodernism or Deconstruction or Feminism into another repetition of our betrayal of the Logos and our seduction by language. Eve Bannet, in explicating the "free play" in the styles of the major poststructuralists, notes: "Implicitly or explicitly, they all tried to present these non-deterministic and non-determining structures as alternatives to the deterministic and determining structures inherent in the society, in the university, in the field of knowledge and in the language they had inherited."[11] In some recent versions of "political" or "historical" criticism, the literary and cultural texts appear once more to be determined, in the last instance, by histories of a totalizing variety. Too little attention is paid to chance and heterogeneity, both within a particular work and within any given historical moment or social entity. The scheme is rather to find the ideology or "power" necessarily determining the coherence of seemingly disparate representational practices. The academic popularity of the New Historicism may stem in part from the mistaken appropriation of its insights by those who wish to use it as an alternative to what they perceive as the ahistorical playfulness of poststructuralism.

Many newly historicized and politicized critics cite the example of Michel Foucault as a model for their work. As Foucault's continuity with the project of the Enlightenment suggests, the exposé of power belongs to a metahistory of liberation whose techniques Foucault's own work forces us to suspect. This metahistory pits an independent self against external forces of oppression, rather than viewing the subject and the social practice as coincident phenomena. Yet such a narrative, however often Foucault wanders into it, does not belong to his theoretical pro-

10. For a cogent defense of the dissemination of art in poststructuralist theory, see David Carroll, *Paraesthetics: Foucault, Lyotard, Derrida* (New York: Methuen, 1987).

11. Bannet, *Structuralism and the Logic of Dissent*, p. 5. For a polemic parallel to my own, see J. Hillis Miller, *The Ethics of Reading* (New York: Columbia University Press, 1987).

gram. "Recent liberation movements," says Foucault, "suffer from the fact that they cannot find any principle on which to base the elaboration of a new ethics. They need an ethics, but they cannot find any other ethics than an ethics founded on so-called scientific knowledge of what the self is, what desire is, what the unconscious is, and so on."[12] An avowed Heideggerean, Foucault resists the determinism of technological thought; his dedication to dismantling the machineries of disciplinary knowledge is deeply rooted in Heidegger's work on the question of technology.[13] Foucault's orientation will not allow, in the final analysis, for a return to empiricism or to a narrative of self-consciousness as freedom. Instead ethics—the subject's mode of being toward other beings in the world—will be thought through in terms of not simply a liberation from discipline but a productive responsibility toward creation:

> From the idea that the self is not given to us, I think that there is only one practical consequence: we have to create ourselves as a work of art. In his analyses of Baudelaire, Flaubert, etc., it is interesting to see that Sartre refers the work of creation to a certain relation to oneself—the author to himself—which has the form of authenticity or of inauthenticity. I would like to say exactly the contrary: we should not have to refer the creative activity of somebody to the kind of relation he has to himself, but should relate the kind of relation one has to oneself to a creative activity.[14]

While Foucault withdraws the self as a centering force, determinism makes a shadowy return as the work of art fabricates the subject. If, however, "creative activity" inherently differs from itself, puts identities at risk in a process whose reverberations, because they are historical, are inevitably interminable, then the "self" yielded by creative activity can never in the traditional sense ground an ethics.

The New Determinism has also played its part in the revival of Marxism, whose academic popularity today is in marked contrast to its demise as the grounds for a political practice (see the final section of Chapter 1 for a discussion of this anomaly). Here too one often discovers polemics against the play, the supposed hedonism or aestheticism of deconstruction, along with charges that poststructuralism has abandoned any

12. Paul Rabinow, ed., *The Foucault Reader* (New York: Pantheon, 1984), p. 343.
13. "For me Heidegger has always been the essential philosopher. . . . My entire philosophical development was determined by my reading of Heidegger." "Final Interview: Michel Foucault," conducted by Gilles Barbadette and Andre Scala, trans. Thomas Levin and Isabelle Lorenz, *Raritan* 5 (Summer 1985): 8–9. See Martin Heidegger, *The Question Concerning Technology and Other Essays*, trans. William Lovitt (New York: Harper and Row, 1977).
14. *The Foucault Reader*, p. 351.

meaningful engagement with the world "outside" the text. Without previewing my detailed response to these indictments, I will point out that a longing for a power of determination often fuels these polemics. I find this particularly poignant in the case of political criticism since I believe I share many of the fundamental attitudes and concerns of those who have stationed themselves on the "left" in cultural criticism. Perhaps the best and most influential book from that quarter, Fredric Jameson's *The Political Unconscious,* begins with a labyrinthine summary of the problem of determination in Marxist theory. Despite the brilliance of its argument, Jameson's chapter finally must take refuge in the assertion that "history" is "the experience of Necessity" *and* an "absent cause": "History is what hurts, it is what refuses desire and sets inexorable limits to individual as well as collective praxis, which its 'ruses' turn into grisly and ironic reversals of their overt intention. But this History can be apprehended only through its effects, and never directly as some reified force."[15] History is a discipline that punishes.

Jameson seems to have abandoned the determinism of "vulgar Marxism," though what we are left with is the puzzling ghost of its machinery. "This is surely a case," comments John Frow, "of having one's referent and eating it too."[16] What have we gained in relegating causation to this *unheimlich* figuration of the "absent cause," especially since it appears to retain the classical outline of the powerfully oppressive origin without sufficiently taking into account the play of indeterminacy in writing, history, or our subjection to them? The one-dimensional view of history here—as simply the narrative of our deprivation—indicates how predetermined Jameson's account still remains by classical Marxism. That narrative depends on logocentric visions of man, matter, history, class, time, and language which all must be given another hearing. (In Chapter 4 I take up these terms in examining the contribution and limits of a Jamesonian approach to literary history.)

Frow's *Marxism and Literary History* offers an illuminating critique of current thinking on both subjects in its title, though the result is to render the possibilities of either rather problematic, to say the least. Frow assimilates the arguments of semiotics and poststructuralism more intelligently than many political critics and uses them against classical Marxist accounts of literature as history's mimetic reflection or expressed truth. These accounts have rested on "acceptance of the metaphor of the determination of the superstructure by the economic base

---

15. Fredric Jameson, *The Political Unconscious: Narrative as a Socially Symbolic Act* (Ithaca: Cornell University Press, 1981), p. 102.
16. John Frow, *Marxism and Literary History* (Cambridge: Harvard University Press, 1986), p. 38.

as an ontological model" (6). Rejecting referentiality, determinism, and representationalism, Frow develops a "descriptive literary history" out of such theorists of production and discourse as Pierre Machery and Foucault. "The conception of literary production as a process," argues Frow,

> implies that on the one hand, as a produced object, the text is seen as a component of the general system of social production, that the 'real' is not its object but its institutional conditions of existence; and on the other hand, as a productive activity, the text is seen as a distinct practice of signification which is related not to a nondiscursive truth but to other practices of signification. In both cases literary discourse is treated as a reality in its own right, a practice which cannot be subordinated to an external reality which in the last instance determines its own representation or expression in discourse. (21)

Nonetheless, this formula leaves the question of literary change, and thus of the "evolution" or series of literary forms, unexplained and does not satisfy Frow's own political agenda. Thus he turns to critiques of the Russian Formalist notion of "defamiliarization," and to contemporary theories of intertextuality, to fashion a scheme wherein the overdetermining motives of intertextual difference are, in the last instance, those of power. The disobedience of the new text vis-à-vis the archive or the surrounding normative discourse is an ultimately political act that belongs to the history of power, and thus to the history of class struggle (59–60). Since symbolic systems and their institutional practices function to realize relations of power, the reading of intertextual differences provides the locus for discerning the historical and political unconscious of the text. In an ingenious revision of Harold Bloom's theses on the anxiety of authority in intertextual struggles, Frow advances the thesis that "the literary canon acts as an exemplary mode of authority and comes to bear a heavy charge of value through which literature comes to 'stand for' (although rarely *completely*) the whole realm of authoritative values. . . . This is to say that literary texts thematize their relation to social power by thematizing their relation to the structure of discursive authority which organizes the linguistic form or the play of languages in their own textual structure" (128–29).[17] Frow's "Marxism" lies in his

---

17. It would be appropriate at this juncture to note that the present book is a kind of sequel to my *T. S. Eliot and the Poetics of Literary History* (Baton Rouge: Louisiana State University Press, 1983), which owed a great deal to Bloom's model. Like many others today, I am interested in rethinking the relation of the subjective and the literary to the historical and the political, though obviously I do not believe we must abandon the texts of Freud and Derrida in the process.

reduction of the play of sign values to the issue of "power" and in his originary postulation of social power as the model (or base) that literature copies. "The text can be defined," he concludes, "as the process of these relations of discursive contradiction; and it is here that ideological value is confirmed or challenged, and textual historicity generated" (169).

But by now surely one senses that the "Marxism" of Frow's theory bears little resemblance to the classical Marxism he has himself dismantled, and his persistence in labeling a sociopolitical reflection on literature "Marxist" only puzzles the reader. Despite the passing uncritical dependence on "class struggle," there is little in this narrative that belongs to the system of materialist dialectic and historiography defined as Marxist. Indeed Frow's recourse to Foucault's writings on power and discourse, themselves offered as Heideggerean revisions of errors in Marxist thought, indicates how far from orthodoxy he has strayed, as does his considerable borrowing from the arguments of Derrida. Marxism in any meaningful sense doesn't survive the cogency of Frow's own theorizing, though admittedly it helps tangentially to give a political orientation to his theses on intertextuality and the description of literary history as a series of breaks from normative values.

Frow's concentration on semiotics and intertextuality produces a descriptive model that eliminates the agency or subject of authorship except as it functions to represent a class's condition. The heterogeneity of the subject and the play of the subject's relation to the archive or discursive norm are not brought into the theory. This, I suspect, is one way that Frow can sneak a manner of determinism back into the scheme of literary history. His concluding chapter, "The Politics of Reading," begins with Foucault's archaeological program for describing the conditions enabling the discourse of the "enunciative subject." This subject quickly gives way, through Derrida's meditations on framing, to Frow's reflections on the institutional power structures determining enunciation.[18] Having abandoned any ontology of the work of art, Frow falls back on a hermeneutically self-reflexive historicism whose object of analysis is its own, or its tradition's, normative interpretations of literature. Like many others today, he advocates pursuing "the possibilities of laying bare the formal and institutional conditions of reading," though even he must admit the relatively innocuous character of this subversion vis-à-vis the grand program of class struggle and revolution

18. Compare Frow's account of theoretical framing with that in Gregory S. Jay and David L. Miller, "The Role of Theory in the Study of Literature?" in Miller and Jay, *After Strange Texts: The Role of Theory in the Study of Literature* (Tuscaloosa: University of Alabama Press, 1985), pp. 3–26.

(224). Struggle in the classroom over literary values and institutions of authority becomes a displaced mimesis of a history that has failed to take place in the "Real." Meanwhile both the play of the literary system and the play of the subject fade from an analysis concerned too exclusively with its own power.

Renouncing interpretation in favor of a subversive archaeology, Frow enables only a partial literary history, since it is one that accounts for only predictable breaks or heterogeneities (those that belong to the history of a certain narrative of power). The kind of reading Derrida performs, both on a text and as a text, is less concerned with description than with production. Taking up the elements of a text into his own speculative rewriting of them, Derrida produces signifying effects that cannot be classified by any notion of correspondence to the original. He does not produce a representation of the text's truth, origin, meaning, or empirical history (though all these may figure in the reading). Rather, by playing along with a text's metaphors, voices, narrative aporias, conceptual ploys, and material devices, Derrida produces knowledge effects that mimic those of the text under analysis, imitating their movements and breaking with their limits (as we shall see in Chapter 3 when considering his reading of Freud). This excess of commentary, by ceaselessly interrupting representation with its other, transgresses toward futurity, and so mimes the way in which the text itself worked toward its own differences. The disobedience of the text before the summons of the literary system can, then, take the form of play rather than negation or contradiction; speculative writing may break with the regime of truth/power, even if this requires occupying a position that has no value either to that regime or to the mirror that is its opposition.

On the other hand, tracing how "deviation" and "erring" can contravene "the laws of destiny," writes Derrida, "introduces the play of necessity and chance into what could be called, by anachronism, the determinism of the universe. Nonetheless, it does not imply a conscious freedom or will, even if for some of us the principle of indeterminism is what makes the conscious freedom of man fathomable."[19] As with Thoreau's "I," the freedom fathomable here comes into being by staking itself in history, which is to say, in a play of necessity and chance that language enacts, but of which language is only a part. Since power is essentially the ability to determine the future, play is that resistance to power which shifts the ground and the terms, differing/deferring the determined future so as to disclose the discourse on values. The indeterminate

19. Jacques Derrida, "My Chances/*Mes Chances:* A Rendezvous with Some Epicurean Stereophanies," in *Taking Chances: Derrida, Psychoanalysis, and Literature,* ed. William Kerrigan and Joseph H. Smith (Baltimore: Johns Hopkins University Press, 1984), pp. 7–8.

subject, the subject for whom the questions of being and ethics coincide, appears here where play suspends the power of determination long enough for there to be a chance that something other may be thought, written, done.

The resistance to play turns out to be the equivalent of the resistance to theory, and a mistaken desire to conflate theory and practice often traps fine minds into wrongful disputes. Theory is the space of play, and it cannot be *solely* judged and evaluated according to the criteria of practice. Practice engages the domain of decisions, of closures, of action that cannot be deferred. Practice requires conclusions. But if practice is to be historically alive, if it is to grow and respond with history, if it is to renounce metaphysical solutions and risk participation in history, it must reserve for itself a space that will allow it to differ from itself. Between theory and practice there must be civil disobedience. The habitation of theory is an outside inside practice. Theory cannot *only* determine practice, and it impoverishes theory to harness its labor to a preconceived agenda. Theory must be free to speculate, to gamble, to play, and it has a responsibility to that freedom which is equal to its responsibility for the consequences of speculation in practice. Theory also takes place *elsewhere* than practice, quite literally, and the difference in their sites and projects should not be cause for alarm. An asymmetry between theory and practice ought to be rigorously maintained, or else both will suffer and wither into determinations without a future. Practice, in its domain, cannot wait for a certificate of theoretical purity, or for a prescription that guarantees the outcome of action. Theory and practice constitute a double bind or antithetical unity that we ought not try to resolve.

Hasty resolutions, like Martin Heidegger's embrace of Nazism as the social movement that would bring us closer to the "mystery of Being," often end tragically. Their lesson is not that the theory is worthless, but that the translation of the theory into a practice, at a specific place and time in history, must be extremely self-critical, as the tradition of Marxist thinking about praxis suggests. However conceived, the notion of praxis involves the subject, for it is through the subject's agency that the play between theory and practice resolves itself. But there is no a priori way of determining the application of a theory or philosophy in practice. Heidegger's diverse philosophical texts did not destine him to Nazism, though we may learn something about Heidegger, his philosophy, and fascism in tracing how he arrived at such an incongruous and terrible conclusion (see below, Chapter 1). Derrida's extensive play on the terms "destiny" and "assignment" (notably in *The Post Card*) is, of course, an elaborate way of taking up Heidegger's themes against Heidegger's history, suggesting that where Heidegger slipped back into the metaphysics of determinism, our own readings must be vigilantly errant. The determination of Dasein as the German Spirit never arrives at its destination when Dasein is read as Da-sign and its correspondence to the real is canceled or stamped "Return to Sender: Address Unknown." Derrida's subjection to Heidegger's philosophical mastery, however, necessitates that this pointedly political postcard lie buried in the Dead Letter (or *l'être*) Office.

The resistance to theory, as de Man argued, turns out to be a resistance to the determined errancy of representation, and so an anxiety about the power of language as it labors to control, know, and alter the world. Misreadings of deconstruction almost always jump to the conclusion that its emphases on play and undecidability yield only paralysis, as if the power of determination in language could be suddenly abolished. Common sense tells us, however, that no deconstruction would have been elicited in the first place except under the conditions of the power of determination in language. That power is exactly what deconstruction attempts to think by means of civil disobedience, answering the summons of the law with questions and experiments that seek other ways of building a world. A responsibility to play, chance, and the accidents of dissemination is simultaneously an attempt to follow rigorously, ethically, the branching paths along which history is made, and to delimit what determination represents.

Derrida, writing in the voice of reason, puts his case this way:

> Language, however, is only one among those systems of *marks* that claim this curious tendency as their property: they *simultaneously* incline toward increasing the reserves of random indetermination *as well as* the capacity for coding and overcoding or, in other words, for control and self-regulation. Such competition between randomness and code disrupts the very systematicity of the system while it also, however, regulates the restless, unstable interplay of the system. Whatever its singularity in this respect, the linguistic system of these traces or marks would merely be, it seems to me, just a particular example of the law of destabilization.[20]

Derrida's unsystematic "law" holds good for the play of the "general text," of which the empirical work of traces or marks is only one "example." History, writing, and the subject all become possible, for Derrida, in the indeterminate economy "between randomness and code." This is why, in part, my analysis of Derrida's relation to Marx in Chapter 1 must proceed by way of Saussure and must involve "close readings" of the plays of signification in their texts. The play's the thing, so to speak,

20. Derrida, "My Chances," pp. 2–3.

where the being of the world and the being of the text obey the "law of destabilization."

The play of a text, however, may be located somewhere besides its puns and allusions. The "law of destabilization" in Thoreau's "Civil Disobedience" concerns the relation between statement and performance, or grammar and trope, so that a de Manian rather than Derridean reading is called for. "Civil Disobedience" (a posthumous title apparently unauthorized by Thoreau, who called his essay "Resistance to Civil Government") is a serious work, a public manifesto designed to declare the individual's independence from the state's laws when those laws violate the dictates of conscience. Developed from lectures first delivered early in 1848, the essay appeared in published form in 1849, five years before *Walden*. The voice of "Civil Disobedience" rarely engages in humor, except sarcasm, and exhibits none of the self-deprecation that helps save *Walden* from self-righteousness. The subject of "Civil Disobedience," in all senses, is the man of moral virtue. Outraged by the twin evils of the imperialistic Mexican War and the ongoing horror of Southern slavery, the speaking subject questions the very terms of his relation to the community or the state. If, as he believes, the ground of political community is the virtue of the individual citizen, what claim can a government make on him when its acts are morally corrupt?

Jefferson's "Declaration of Independence," with its assertion that treason against the king is justified when the king violates the higher laws of nature and of reason, lies behind Thoreau's speech. Jefferson's ploy (not original to him in the eighteenth century) had been to assume and state, a priori, that individual men are *by nature* endowed with equal and inalienable rights, and that governments come into being only through the temporary and willed concession of these rights. Theoretically, as well as anthropologically, Jefferson's thesis is more empowering than persuasive: how "rights" could come into being before the existence of a social community baffles the historical imagination. The individual and the state come into being together, as the child comes into identity only through its accession to the symbolic networks of language and the family. But Thoreau takes up Jefferson's metaphysical notion of a republic constituted by freely associating men of virtue: "I think," says Thoreau, "that we should be men first, and subjects afterward" (225).

Thoreau's reiterated emphasis on manhood and virtue does more than reflect the common roots of his and Jefferson's political philosophies in Graeco-Roman models. This diction constitutes a train of imagery and a set of tropes that destabilize the grammatical pronouncements he intends to make about liberty. An aporia, as de Man will call it,

separates the registers of Thoreau's text. Thoreau's two examples of
America's lost virtue—the imperialism of the Mexican War and the
tyranny of slavery—both represent continuations of political practices
inherent to the achievements of "democracy" and "republican" government in ancient Greece and Rome. The classically trained Thoreau
knew perfectly well that the democracy of Greece was founded in imperialism and the enslavement of "barbarians" and women, and he knew
as well the like devices of the Romans. Still, these remain the implicit
authorizing figures, along with those of the Revolutionary Fathers,
behind Thoreau's address. Using John Frow's argument about intertextuality, one might say that Thoreau's references to the Greeks, Romans,
and Founding Fathers make up a symbolic discourse whose authoritative character empowers Thoreau's resistance to the civil powers of his
own day. (This subversive way of using the Founding Fathers was
common in Thoreau's time, and we shall witness it again in the case of
Frederick Douglass.)

The scenario becomes even more complicated when one questions
the gender of the rhetoric. Here, as elsewhere in Thoreau, the failure
of virtue is figured as a failure of masculinity. Conjuring the spectacle
of men marching off to war out of an "undue respect for the law,"
"marching in admirable order" against their own consciences, Thoreau
wonders if they are "men at all? or small movable forts and magazines,
at the service of some unscrupulous man in power?" (225–26). Review-
ing how the moral issue of slavery has been lost in the game of politics,
where voting means to cast yourself with a mass of men made "*available
for any purposes of the demagogue*," Thoreau cries out: "Oh for a man
who is a *man*, and, as my neighbor says, has a bone in his back which
you cannot pass your hand through! Our statistics are at fault: the
population has been returned too large. How many *men* are there to a
square thousand miles in this country? Hardly one" (229). Thoreau
criticizes not simply the Mexican War or slavery, but the implicitly
"feminine" position of passivity, obedience, will-lessness, and servitude
they entail. Such behavior violates the classical values of masculinity.
Here we can also detect that analogy between colonialism and enslavement, on the one hand, and femininity on the other hand, which women
abolitionists were openly discussing at the time in their equations of the
conditions of women and slaves.

Thoreau's politics in these matters cannot be separated from a de-
monstrable gender anxiety: he both identifies with the position of emasculation and asserts the ideal figure of a resolute manhood. The figure
of the father is divided between the contemporary patriarchs who castrate and the historical figures who authorize revolution. Why, he asks,

does the government "always crucify Christ, and excommunicate Copernicus and Luther, and pronounce Washington and Franklin rebels? (231). The cure for emasculation lies in disobedience: "When the subject has refused allegiance, and the officer has resigned his office, then the revolution is accomplished. But even suppose blood should flow. Is there not a sort of blood shed when the conscience is wounded? Through this wound a man's real manhood and immortality flow out, and he bleeds to an everlasting death" (233–34). Feminists, and psychoanalysts, might speculate on the anxiety over sexual difference embodied in this image of the bloody wound. The disobedient man who obeys the higher law of conscience attains virtue and manhood, and his refusal to be available or serviceable to the powers that be exposes the femininity of the state: "I saw that the State was half-witted, that it was timid as a lone woman with her silver spoons, and that it did not know its friends from its foes, and I lost all my remaining respect for it, and pitied it" (236).

Thoreau's civil disobedience stands firmly on the grounds of his identification with a historically specific ideal of masculinity, which supplies him with the "higher law" he requires to justify his civil disobedience. His subservience to that ideal empowers the voice that condemns the mass of men for their servitude to the state. His own discourse thus repeats the very structure of patriarchal fidelity he condemns in his neighbors. This style of disobedience conforms to a rhetorical and ideological tradition which the mass of men recurrently invest in, either by deifying their patriarchs or by engaging in an oedipal rivalry with them. The "I" that speaks "Civil Disobedience" obeys the grammar of this conventional enunciation even as it describes the historical effects (imperialism and slavery) of patriarchy. This ambivalence, in which the male speaker identifies both with the position of emasculation (often figured as the feminine) *and* with a renewed power of male virtue, occurs throughout this period in texts by Poe, Emerson, Melville, and especially Hawthorne, who figures this ambivalence by suggesting that Hester, Arthur, and Chillingworth may be read allegorically as the contradictory impulses of a single mind or culture.[21] Thoreau's recourse to the transcendental male constrains the play of his text and gives his address a "phallogocentric" destination.

Michael Rogin reads Melville's "Bartleby, the Scrivener: A Story of

---

21. See Scott Derrick, "Prometheus Ashamed: *The Scarlet Letter* and the Masculinity of Art," in *Nathaniel Hawthorne's "The Scarlet Letter": Modern Critical Interpretations*, ed. Harold Bloom (New York: Chelsea House, 1986), pp. 121–27, and David Leverenz, *Manhood in the American Renaissance* (Ithaca: Cornell University Press, 1989).

Wall Street" as a consciously intended subversion of the program of "Civil Disobedience."[22] Whether or not Melville actually knew Thoreau's text, a comparison of the two does initiate an intertextual dialogue that may enrich our understanding of the subject of authority, and the contests for it, in the literary, political, legal, and economic realms of Jacksonian America. According to Rogin, Melville "undermines the Thoreauvian alternative" of withdrawal by showing that "passive resistance" destroys both parties and exposes the "passive aggression which lies behind nonviolent resistance." But as we have seen, the rhetoric of "Civil Disobedience" also expresses an anxious attempt to appropriate actively the privileged position of masculine authority. There is less a contrast between Thoreau and Bartleby than a different focus, for while Thoreau concentrates on giving voice to the rebel who speaks the Higher Law, Melville mimics the garrulous bad faith of the state's own representative by making a nameless lawyer his narrator.

Rogin's historical and political reading of "Bartleby" sees it as a commentary on the failure of Jacksonian democracy amid the nation's transition from a feudal mode of economic production to a capitalist one.[23] The lawyer's offices are the site where properties are subject to representation and reproduction, and Melville's spatial symbolism is

22. Michael Paul Rogin, *Subversive Genealogy: The Politics and Art of Herman Melville* (Berkeley: University of California Press, 1983), pp. 187–201. Rogin's footnote says that "Egbert S. Oliver, 'A Second Look at Bartleby,' *College English*, VI (May 1945), 431–39, provides evidence that Melville read 'Civil Disobedience' before writing *Bartleby*" (p. 338, n. 24). That's stretching it. Oliver offers only circumstantial indications of the possibility that Melville could have seen a copy of Elizabeth Peabody's *Aesthetic Papers* (1849), which contained the Thoreau essay. Oliver conjectures that the volume would have been in Hawthorne's library, because his "Main Street" was included, and that Melville would have seen it during his visits to Hawthorne in 1850 and 1851. Since Hawthorne and Thoreau were personal acquaintances, the supposition appears plausible, but the only empirical evidence lies in a record showing that Melville borrowed a copy of *A Week on the Concord and Merrimack Rivers* in 1850. There is no hard evidence that he read this book or anything else by Thoreau. They apparently never met, and Melville left no writings that refer to Thoreau directly. Oliver's best "evidence" is the parallels he finds between the incidents, issues, and phrasings of "Civil Disobedience" and "Bartleby." For more on this scholarly chestnut, see Hershel Parker, "Melville's Satire of Emerson and Thoreau: An Evaluation of the Evidence," *American Transcendental Quarterly* 7 (Summer 1970): 61–67; John Seelye, "The Contemporary 'Bartleby,'" *American Transcendental Quarterly* 7 (Summer 1970): 12–18; Christopher W. Sten, "Bartleby the Transcendentalist: Melville's Dead Letter to Emerson," *Modern Language Quarterly* 35 (March 1974): 30–44; and Merton Sealts, *Pursuing Melville, 1940–1980* (Madison: University of Wisconsin Press, 1982), pp. 250–77.

23. Brook Thomas presents what most would recognize as a more orthodox New Historicist reading of "Bartleby" in his *Cross-examinations of Law and Literature: Cooper, Hawthorne, Stowe, and Melville* (Cambridge: Cambridge University Press, 1988), pp. 164–82. Thomas explores the judicial philosophy of Melville's father-in-law, Lemuel Shaw, and attempts to demonstrate the homologies between contemporary problems in legal treatments of economic relations and Melville's treatment of them. He agrees with Rogin when he argues that Melville's story questions the "belief in free agency" that both

structured by the subtitle that gives the story its specific historical address: "Wall Street." Following Marx's thesis that social relations are determined by the mode of production, Rogin interprets the clash between materialism and idealism in the story as an allegory of the transition from familial social bonds to the merciless economy of the cash nexus. Every recourse of the lawyer to the reformist strategies of sentiment, philanthropy, charity, or domesticity fails, and so exposes the hollowness of such ideological resolutions to material and class contradictions. Oddly, Rogin shifts from this reading to a "psychological" one in accepting the oft-heard thesis that Bartleby and the lawyer "are two halves of a single, divided self" (198). Somehow the New Criticism wins when he concludes that Bartleby's "specific, historical origins" explain nothing: "The formal economy and self-sufficiency of this story, by freeing the text from its historical referents, free Bartleby from his textual confines" (201). On the contrary, it is the "formal economy" of the text that activates its play with "historical referents," and this includes the manner in which the text's "psychology" belongs to the economies of the systems of writing Melville inhabited.

In keeping with John Frow's thesis that literary texts figure social authority and textual authority in allegories of power, Bartleby's withdrawal from writing and his refusal to copy may be read as a willed disobedience to every prescription in his culture's "general text." This reading may be reinforced by Rogin's argument that Melville's ambivalence toward his father-in-law, Judge Lemuel Shaw (notorious for his administration of the Fugitive Slave Law), informs Melville's representations of authority figures, thus making the lawyer-Bartleby relation a familial, oedipal one. Unlike Thoreau, Bartleby grows increasingly passive in his refusals, approaching and then attaining the absolute lack of potent or meaningful action—death. Yet his withdrawal does have an emasculating effect on the lawyer, who confesses to "twinges of impotent rebellion against the mild effrontery of this unaccountable scrivener. Indeed, it was his wonderful mildness chiefly, which not only disarmed me, but unmanned me, as it were. For I consider that one, for the time, is a sort of unmanned when he tranquilly permits his hired clerk to dictate to him, and order him away from his own premises."[24]

---

attribute to Thoreau. While Thomas's research fills out the context for Melville's story, it doesn't radically alter our reading of it, and it begs the question of the determination of Melville's text by that context.

24. Herman Melville, "Bartleby, The Scrivener: A Story of Wall-Street," in *The Piazza Tales and Other Prose Pieces, 1839–1860*, vol. 9, *The Writings of Herman Melville: The Northwestern-Newberry Edition* (Evanston and Chicago: Northwestern University Press and The Newberry Library, 1987), p. 27. Subsequent references are to this edition and given parenthetically in the text.

Whereas "Civil Disobedience" challenges the state through the speaker's willingness to copy the manhood of certain precursors, Bartleby pronounces this strategy a dead letter. Instead Bartleby allegorizes a Derridean solicitation of the law, quite literally in the demands Bartleby makes on the lawyer/narrator. Bartleby occupies the very premises of the law, disobediently. He refuses the social contract, disbands the state by withdrawing his signature from its constitution. In this he takes seriously both Jefferson's and Thoreau's thesis that the state originates in the individual's economic choice to trade part of his freedom for the benefits that political association brings. Bartleby would prefer not to. His refusal, however, lacks the transcendental ground Thoreau posits, as Melville's religious allusions indicate. Whereas the disobedience of Thoreau belonged to the culture it criticized, Bartleby's is a pure negation that frustrates every attempt that the law makes to recuperate it. His disregard for the money the lawyer repeatedly offers him signals his estrangement from every conventional economy of representation.

Rogin's alternation between an orthodox Marxist reading that sees "Bartleby" as expressing the truth of its historical moment and an orthodox formalist reading that sees the text as aesthetically transcending history can, I think, be avoided if we examine Melville's representation of the subject of authority. In terms of the literary system, "Bartleby" distinguishes itself through its creation of a narrative structure that initiates modernist experiments in "point of view." As he will also do in "Benito Cereno," Melville places a subject of authority at the center of the narration. The lawyer's address, in every sense, is "Wall Street." Melville puts authority on trial, at play, by forcing it to tell its own story from within a framework of solicitous representation. The lawyer's voice in "Bartleby" constantly solicits the reader's sympathies and responses, loquaciously attempting to explain, justify, exonerate, and otherwise plead his case. This dialogical structure puts the reader in the position of the judge, though it also positions the reader within the premises of the lawyer, challenging the reader to examine how he or she would respond to Bartleby's preferences. Thus the lawyer (like Derrida's deconstructed logos) represents a center that both claims to ground a structure as its origin and yet appears only as an effect of that discursive system. The lawyer, too, is subject to the law, though as the story unfolds it is his subjection to Bartleby's alogical and eccentric mode of being that Melville discloses.

As regards the formal and symbolic systems, then, Melville's text differs from Thoreau's in the way it treats the voice of authority. Whereas "Civil Disobedience" succeeds by empowering an authoritative voice by borrowing the premises of patriarchy, "Bartleby" refuses any

such assumptions (or invoices). Melville's recurrent punning on "preference," "will," "premise," and "assumption" reaches its comic finale when
the lawyer plumes himself on his "masterly" plan for getting rid of
Bartleby. Protecting his authority from the mediations of language, he
devises a scheme of "perfect quietness": no "vulgar bullying, no bravado
of any sort, no choleric hectoring. . . . Without loudly bidding Bartleby
depart—as an inferior genius might have done—I *assumed* the ground
that depart he must; and upon that assumption built all I had to say"
(33–34). Bartleby, however, "was more a man of preferences than assumptions." He is a man without premises, and this groundlessness is
what thwarts the lawyer's various attempts to construct a dialogue with
him. In refusing the lawyer's dictations, Bartleby replays the primal
scene of Western thought Jacques Derrida discovers on a medieval
postcard: it shows Plato dictating to Socrates as he writes.

The various strategies the lawyer adopts—the employer's rights, the
friend's kindness, the businessman's common sense, the philanthropist's
humanity, the logician's accuracy, the theologian's schemas, the coward's evasions, the politician's negotiations—all fail, and together the
series constitutes a kind of history or multidimensional model of authority's various subject positions. Bartleby's refusal to occupy any premises
but those of the law effectively challenges the law to articulate the justice
of its premises and to substantiate its claim to authority. The power of
this negativity and the groundlessness of the law are what combine to
enforce the lawyer's subjection to Bartleby. The history of authority, its
plurality and limits and effects, is solicited by Bartleby's refusal of it. In
this way Melville forces authority to justify itself, and in so doing the
lawyer turns to those methods historically and characteristically available to a subject of his place, class, gender, and occupation.

Another way to conceive of Melville's complexity here is to juxtapose
the historical references of the text and its literary self-referentiality. In
the case of the character of Bartleby himself, the overdeterminations
appear formidable. In terms of history and the cultural archive, he
represents (1) the specific class of alienated wage laborers in nineteenth-
century America; (2) Thoreau or Emerson or the transcendentalist who
posits self-reliant idealism against the materialist reduction of spirit to
the laws of economy; (3) Christ, the mysterious stranger whose innocence is betrayed in a testing of mankind; (4) Melville, the son anxious
about his own authority in the face of the father's; and (5) the fugitive
slave remanded to bondage by such legal minds as Lemuel Shaw. Each
of these references (and others) could be developed into a plausible
partial allegory of the text's historicity.

At the same time, one of the occupants of the position of the subject
of alienated labor is, of course, Melville the writer. Many critics, most

recently Michael T. Gilmore, have read "Bartleby, the Scrivener" as a reflection of Melville's disgruntlement with the demands of the literary marketplace, wherein genius is subservient to the law of the cash nexus.[25] Melville's famous letter to Hawthorne in 1851 exclaims "Dollars damn me. . . . What I feel most moved to write, that is banned,—it will not pay. Yet altogether, write the *other* way I cannot."[26] Obviously the story could serve as an allegory of poststructuralist textuality, from its thematic of copies without originals to its concluding apocalypse in the Dead Letter Office.[27] Even Bartleby's status as an alienated victim is undercut when the grub-man takes him for a "gentleman forger." The identification of Melville with Bartleby, however, ignores the agency of the lawyer as the text's chief image of the writer. The religious and metaphysical issues concerning representation that Bartleby raises by his withdrawal from the legal economy are more than balanced by the political, institutional, and historical concerns raised by having the lawyer also figure as the writer.

We could return, it seems, to Rogin's thesis that Bartleby and the lawyer are "two halves of a single, divided self" and recast its terms. This dialogical encounter stages the indivisibility of two orders of authority, which together disseminate the positions of the subject. One order, itself heterogeneous on inspection, would include the systems of the material world of need and power: the legal system, the economic system, the digestive system, the state, the publishing industry. On the other hand, there are the systems of textuality and of their historical formations: here the subject appears as an effect of modes of representation, such as narrative point of view, grammar, description, psychological portraiture, religious speculation, cultural allusion, and others. What "Bartleby, the Scrivener" constantly dramatizes is this indivisibility

25. Michael T. Gilmore, *American Romanticism and the Marketplace* (Chicago: University of Chicago Press, 1985), pp. 132–45. Gilmore's book awkwardly combines Marxism and New Historicism. He construes the story as expressing an autobiographical pathos as Melville realizes "that the effort to free literature from its alliance with social and economic power is an exercise in futility"; moreover, the construction of a tale "without authorial presence" figures Melville's own alienation from the public (145). I think the text produces knowledge as well as pathos, and that authorial absence may be an advantageous writerly position rather than the subject of lamentation.

26. Merrel R. Davis and William H. Gilman, eds., *The Letters of Herman Melville* (New Haven: Yale University Press, 1960), p. 128. The context is that Melville believes he must "work and slave on my 'Whale' while it is driving through the press."

27. As if he had read Derrida's *The Post Card avant la carte*, Christopher Sten connects this final image to Melville's critique of Emersonian doctrines of the "correspondence" between nature and spirit as it is organically contained in letters: "The 'correspondence' between the ideal and material worlds is at best only an occasional phenomenon and so cannot be trusted as an absolute principle. Like the 'correspondence' which Bartleby puts to the flames in Washington, this kind, too, often ends up in the Dead Letter Office" (Sten, "Bartleby the Transcendentalist," p. 33).

of systems, even as it displays their heterogeneity—including the summoning of the reader's orders into the play by virtue of the dialogical mode of the story's address to the audience.

When, for example, the lawyer discovers the failure of the "doctrine of assumptions," he turns for guidance to "Edwards on the Will" and "Priestley on Necessity." These theological and philosophical arguments in favor of predestination offer a strategy for recuperating Bartleby's eccentric behavior, because they belong to an orthodox literature whose ultimate purpose is to deny the actual existence of errancy or play and to subordinate freedom to a determined destiny. This moment illustrates the desperation of the lawyer as a character, though beyond comedy it seriously links the economy of the law to the traditions Edwards and Priestley represent. The attractiveness of their texts is inseparable from their capacity to function in two ways: to relieve the lawyer's guilt and to provide the law with a transcendent ground for enforcing its determinations. We recall that the hilarious sketches of Turkey, Nippers, and Ginger Nut all turned on the mechanical determination of their temperaments by their bodies, specifically by their diets. Bartleby's withdrawal includes his willful removal from the effects of the digestive system, until eventually he exits the material world by starving himself to death. The contradiction between the spirit of the visionary Bartleby and the finitude of the lawyer's self-interest appears in the linguistic play between I's and eyes in the final dialogue. The prison grub-man asks: "Won't he dine today, either? Or does he live without dining?" The lawyer replies " 'Lives without dining,' said I, and closed the eyes" (45). Bartleby imagines his freedom in terms that Edwards and Priestley would understand and abhor: he conceives liberation solely in the negative, as the lack of determination and as the absolute play of will as whim. Preference knows no predictable laws, and so is itself ultimately unfree, as the cumulative congruence of Bartleby's disobedience and his motionlessness imply. "I like to be stationary," he punningly says near the end, his being now identified with the paper on which others write, or copy, their own wills, properties, premises, assumptions, and laws.

What about the will, freedom, and responsibility of the lawyer?[28] As a legal figure, he belongs to a textual system that has radically historicized the relation between expression and the conditions of its production. By framing the author and speaking subject inside the law of the text, Melville forces us to judge the lawyer's every statement by reference to the mode of its being: by the lawyer's personal and class interests,

28. For a related discussion of the law and ethics from a deconstructive standpoint, see Miller, *Ethics of Reading*, pp. 13–40.

age, gender, cultural matrix, and psychological economy. Voice and truth do not, in such a system, occupy the same position (as Thoreau attempts to do in "Civil Disobedience"). In terms of literary history, this construction of the "unreliable narrator" during the last two centuries is something of a truism; what "Bartleby" (and "Benito Cereno") perform is a play of correspondence between the contextualization of the narrator in the story and the contextualization of the story in the frame of its historical production. What suffices to describe a narrator's point of view? Some metaphysical bias of idea, character, vision, tendency? No. The narrator's point of view is none other than his or her location as a historical subject, which is to say, as a mode of address that is not self-originating but which occurs through the effects of specific determinations whose ultimate consequences and significance, however, belong to no *telos* and remain unpredictable. As an agent of laws, the subject, moreover, is both a subordinate and an essential actor: since the law depends on the agent for its execution, and cannot come into being without the subject's agency, the law is always at the mercy of the agent who is employed to do its errands. In texts like "Bartleby," the subject occupies the position where the historical and the written share certain premises and assumptions, though their preferences may be decisively different.

For the lawyer, the questions of will, freedom, and responsibility present themselves exactly as the effect of Bartleby's undecidability. As Derrida wrote in the passage quoted above, "the principle of indeterminism is what makes the conscious freedom of man fathomable." Any point of view grounded in the assumptions of the law's absolute correspondence to truth and necessity will find Bartleby a blank wall. Only then, by virtue of this interruption of determinism by an equally determined errancy, does the question of responsibility arise at all. The lawyer's dealings with Turkey, Nippers, and Ginger Nut are all automatic, mechanical, and in harmony with Edwards and Priestley. Bartleby's anomalous behavior, however, occasions for the first time in the lawyer's experience the challenge of an ethical decision, in other words, a decision for which no absolute law can provide an a priori judgment. By focusing on the lawyer, Melville situates the dilemma of the modern subject when confronted by an otherness that cannot be accounted for by the traditional economies of religious prophecy or capitalist profit making. There is no address for Bartleby. The lawyer exhausts every conventional strategy available to him as a historical subject, only to find that Bartleby cannot be confined by any of their premises. As a writer, his primary motivation is to build a narrative structure that will both contain Bartleby's errancy and justify his own behavior toward it. Melville makes his failure on each count evident.

The lawyer cannot imagine a responsibility toward the other outside the laws he historically knows, and he implicitly recognizes that in eliciting this responsibility from him, Bartleby summons the lawyer to abandon the mechanical determinism of his own subjectivity. This he will not do.

What we are left with is a historical condition in which the writer and the subject face a common ethical and textual impasse or aporia. The epistemological questions that dominated *Moby-Dick* have given way to pragmatic ones: what actions, in deed or writing, can be justified in the post-age after the collapse of authoritative systems of representation? What is the writer's responsibility toward authority? Toward the indeterminacy of one's own mode of address or that of others? In disobeying the prescriptions of the "general text," does the writer produce a difference that makes a difference, or a silence like that of the tomb? How does the writer manage the economy of self-consciousness? In responding to the power of determining historical conditions, what strategies can the writer adopt both to represent those conditions and to realize something that escapes their laws? What are the modes of the responsibilities of the writer to history? How can a responsibility to history escape the destiny of imitating its script? Is writing inherently a process of civil disobedience, or is this a praxis required by the way we have come to understand our own historical situation? In the chapters that follow, I offer my own limited responses to such questions, realizing that not all my readers share my premises. In the spirit of Melville, I endeavor to respect those who themselves might respond "I would prefer not to."

PART ONE

DISSEMINATING
THE SUBJECT

CHAPTER ONE

Values and Deconstructions

For some time now, our whole European culture has been moving as
toward a catastrophe, with a tortured tension that is growing from
decade to decade: restlessly, violently, headlong, like a river that wants
to reach the end, that no longer reflects, that is afraid to reflect. . . .
For why has the advent of nihilism become *necessary?* Because the
values we have had hitherto thus draw their final consequence; because nihilism represents the ultimate logical conclusion of our great
values and ideals—because we must experience nihilism before we
can find out what value these "values" really had.—We require, sometime, *new values.*

—Nietzsche, *The Will to Power*

Whether it occupies a position on the "left" or the "right" in cultural
criticism, the opposition to deconstructive discourse usually grounds
itself in political, ethical, or moral claims. Deconstruction is portrayed as
a negative theology or absurdist aesthetic that paralyzes any meaningful
action or statement and so threatens to cast both Marxism *and* traditional
Judaeo-Christian humanism into an abyss of sophistical speculations. It
took the specter of deconstruction to make an alliance of the Gramscian
Frank Lentricchia with the Arnoldian Eugene Goodheart, their books
offering the same clarion calls for a return to the decisive necessity of
social criticism, despite the very different views (ostensibly) that each
holds about what ails our culture.[1] The disparity between Marxist and
humanist critics is of less compelling interest than their similarity, since
both camps sense that deconstruction challenges not one particular set
of ideological structures but the very notion of the difference between
truth and ideology, fact and value, that underlies most conventional
cultural commentary.

1. See Frank Lentricchia, *Criticism and Social Change* (Chicago: University of Chicago
Press, 1983), and Eugene Goodheart, *The Skeptic Disposition in Contemporary Criticism*
(Princeton: Princeton University Press, 1984).

On more than one occasion, Derrida has been quizzed about his politics and asked why he doesn't write a book on ethics—as if the ultimate justification of deconstruction hinges on its efficacy for social and moral renovation. Responding in 1986 to criticisms of his writing on apartheid, an irritated Derrida spelled out the *leçons* legible in his arguments from the start:

> Your "response" is typical. It reflects an incomprehension or "misreading" that is widespread, and spread about, moreover, for very determined ends, on the "Left" and the "Right," among those who think they represent militantism and a progressivist commitment as well as among neoconservatives. It is in the interest of one side and the other to represent deconstruction as a turning inward and an enclosure by the limits of language, whereas in fact deconstruction *begins by* deconstructing logocentrism, the linguistics of the word, and this very enclosure itself. On one side and the other, people get impatient when they see that deconstructive practices are also and first of all political and institutional practices.[2]

Although the "political and institutional" dimensions of deconstruction are evident in many brands of postmodernist thought on both sides of the Atlantic, the caricature Derrida here protests against still circulates widely in the United States, despite the efforts of Gayatri Spivak, Michael Ryan, Barbara Johnson, Bill Readings, R. Radhakrishnan, and others.[3] Derrida notes that many wish to believe this version of deconstruction, since it forestalls at the outset any undoing of the simple conceptual or disciplinary boundaries between language and history, textuality and politics, or values and truths.

The resistance to deconstruction, whether in the name of history or politics or feminism or humanism, usually underestimates the value of Derrida's texts for, and their involvement in, cultural criticism. Is this oversight solely the result of sloppy misreadings, or does the recurrence of the charge suggest that, in some way that requires scrupulous investi-

---

2. Jacques Derrida, "But, beyond . . . (Open Letter to Anne McClintock and Rob Nixon)," *Critical Inquiry* 13 (Autumn 1986): 168. On deconstruction, Marxism, and ethics, see the discussion by J. Hillis Miller, Barbara Johnson, Louis Mackey, and others, in *Rhetoric and Form: Deconstruction at Yale*, ed. Robert Con Davis and Ronald Schleifer (Norman: University of Oklahoma Press, 1985), pp. 75–97.

3. See Gayatri Chakravorty Spivak, *In Other Worlds: Essays in Cultural Politics* (New York: Routledge, 1988); Michael Ryan, *Marxism and Deconstruction: A Critical Articulation* (Baltimore: Johns Hopkins University Press, 1982); Barbara Johnson, *A World of Difference* (Baltimore: Johns Hopkins University Press, 1987); R. Radhakrishnan, "Ethnic Identity and Poststructuralist Différance," *Cultural Critique* 6 (Spring 1987): 199–220; Bill Readings, "The Deconstruction of Politics," in *Reading de Man Reading*, ed. Lindsay Waters and Wlad Godzich (Minneapolis: University of Minnesota Press, 1989), pp. 223–43; see also the special issue of *Diacritics*, "Marx after Derrida," 15 (Winter 1985).

gation, deconstructive writing is responsible for provoking this evaluation? As Derrida himself argues in regard to the Nazi appropriation of
Nietzsche, "the law that makes the perverting simplification possible
must lie in the structure of the text 'remaining'."[4] In most instances
the *application* of a deconstructive speculation to a social, political, or
historical problematic requires a *translation* fraught with snares and
difficulties that even Derrida cannot escape. Christopher Norris, who
sets out to rebut the caricature of deconstruction as apolitical, finds
that the tangential and oblique arguments of Derrida regarding the
possibilities of a deconstructive praxis are "unconvincing."[5] It takes
considerable interpretative labor to "see that deconstructive practices
are also first of all political and institutional practices." In the chapters
that follow I intend to test Derrida's claim. The results are mixed. The
conceptual dislocations enabled by the labor of deconstruction make
new positions possible, and so richly enhance any effort to criticize past
forms of intellectual or social organization, or to speculate theoretically
on the terms of a future disposition of knowledge and power. The
infinite deferral, however, of any announcement of what motivates the
labor of deconstructive practice—in the name of what, and for what,
does one deconstruct?—arouses a just frustration, though this should
not be an occasion for simply reverting to the repronouncement of the
old proper names. The question of the value(s) of deconstruction needs,
repeatedly and in specific exemplarly instances, to be addressed.

"Misreadings" of Derrida, then, arise partly because he refuses to
represent history and politics in traditional ways, and so those who seek
these referents in his work come away unsatisfied. The reception of
Derrida has also been muddled by a resistance, sometimes bordering
on ignorance, to the long and complex tradition of European thought
on which deconstruction practices. Although the titulary names of
Marx, Nietzsche, Saussure, and Heidegger are often cited, they are
much less frequently *read* in the United States, especially with an eye
toward how deconstruction emerges in response to their discourse on
the modern history of values.[6] Even when deconstruction is carried over

4. Jacques Derrida, "Otobiographies: The Teaching of Nietzsche and the Politics of
the Proper Name," in *The Ear of the Other: Otobiography, Transference, Translation: Texts and
Discussions with Jacques Derrida*, ed. Christie McDonald, trans. Peggy Kamuf from the
French edition edited by Claude Levesque and Christie McDonald, "Otobiographies,"
trans. Avital Ronell (Lincoln: University of Nebraska Press, 1988), p. 30. A separate
French edition of *Otobiographies* appeared in 1984 (Paris: Galilée) and includes Derrida's
lecture on the Declaration of Independence, not reprinted in the McDonald volume.
    5. Christopher Norris, *Derrida* (New York: Methuen, 1987), p. 144.
    6. One exception is the brief discussion of deconstruction in Barbara Herrnstein
Smith, *Contingencies of Value: Alternative Perpsectives for Critical Theory* (Cambridge: Harvard
University Press, 1988).

(or away) into America, it suffers a double dislocation: it loses the historical context of its cultural production, and it is made to address a culture for which it was not originally destined—though this (as Derrida reminds us) merely reiterates the inherent errancy of the letter. The censure or acclaim in the American response to a Heidegger or a Derrida, a Foucault or a Habermas, depends on the specific historical, institutional, disciplinary, social, and ideological location of the presumptive addressee. Their value "in themselves" cannot be separated from what they may signify "for us" or from what we wish to signify about ourselves by signifying about them. Thus when deconstruction is written in America, a transvaluation occurs, and both deconstruction and America differ from themselves in the process.

The question of nihilism, for example, so often addressed to deconstruction in America, is rarely posed here with much consideration of Nietzsche's writings on the history of European morals and their self-producing annihilations. The American context is rather that of Protestant Manichaeanism—a religious attitude toward the absoluteness of values that pervades even Left critics—or of a native pragmatism that cannot tolerate the speculative language of Continental philosophy.[7] According to the critiques of Nietzsche and Heidegger, Western philosophy obeys the summons to represent transcendental truth, only to find, historically, the reiterated negation of those truths through their own embodiment (a process that Hegelian dialectics attempted to narrate as the evolutionary stages of the teleological progress of the Consciousness of Freedom and Absolute Knowledge). Nietzsche's genealogies argue that the ascetic values of Western metaphysics constantly negate life itself as they seek the supersensory realm of "truth." The oppositional logic underlying the dictate to choose between good and evil, truth and falsehood, or eternity and time prescribes the eternal return of nihilism whenever the eternally good and true turn out, in time, to be other than what was represented. So historically this annihilation becomes the active withdrawal of allegiance to previous values, and an attempt (in modernity) to think not this or that value but the essence of valuation. Heidegger calls modernity a transition "in which the world appears value-less but at the same time demands a new value," an "intermediate state" that can only be overcome through an awareness of the causes of nihilism.[8]

The ludicrous inaccuracy of calling Nietzsche a mere nihilist is

7. See Jacques Derrida, "Deconstruction in America: An Interview," *Critical Exchange* 17 (Winter 1985): 1–33.
8. Martin Heidegger, *Nietzsche*, vol. 4, *Nihilism*, trans. Frank A. Capuzzi, ed. with notes and analysis by David Farrell Krell (San Francisco: Harper and Row, 1982), p. 44.

matched today only by the pinning of the same label on the late Paul de Man. Each rather endeavors to track the genealogy of our "intermediate state," and it is that project which will be the principal focus of the present chapter. From Marx to Nietzsche, from Saussure to Heidegger to Derrida, the question of values is consistently at the forefront of deconstructive discourse, which discloses it in the language, history, politics, and technology of Western culture. Derrida summarizes the lesson of this tradition in speculating that there is a more responsible way to answer the call to reason and values than simply harkening to the summons of obedience. Rather, one questions the call itself, and the value of certain values, in an inquiry into the "fundamental ontology" of values and their intricate positions within the general text that encompasses politics, economics, philosophy, psychology, ethics, and writing.

Heidegger, Habermas, and the Subject of Values

In "Otobiographies," Derrida wryly states that there "can always be a Hegelianism of the left and a Hegelianism of the right," and that goes for Nietzscheanism, Heideggereanism, "and even, let us not overlook it," Marxism. All are subject to this double appropriation or possibility: "The one can always be the other, the double of the other" (32). Can there likewise be a Derrideanism of the left and a Derrideanism of the right? And even if there have been such appropriations of Derrida's signature, can they be justified by the letter of his texts? By his refusal of *a* position and his elaborate adventure into the problem of positionality, Derrida asks that we rethink where the ethical and the political *take place* before we demand their correct pronouncement. Put reductively, this means attending to the signifiers—the economy of representation—as much as or more than to the signified—the so-called facts, referents, and things-in-themselves, since the deconstruction of the values of the signified may be realized through the dissemination of the values produced by the economy of the signifier. Derrida's assertion that the call to values obscures more fundamental assumptions that ought to be questioned is of course an echo of Heidegger's response, in his 1947 "Letter on Humanism," to the followers of Sartre as well as to classical humanists, both camps having pressed him about the value of his "destructive" ontology:

> Because we are speaking against "values" people are horrified at a philosophy that ostensibly dares to despise humanity's best qualities. For what is more "logical" than that a thinking that denies values must necessarily pronounce everything valueless? . . . We are so filled with "logic" that

anything that disturbs the habitual somnolence of prevailing opinion is automatically registered as a despicable contradiction. We pitch everything that does not stay close to the familiar and beloved positive into the previously excavated pit of pure negation which negates everything, ends in nothing, and so consummates nihilism. Following this logical course we let everything expire in a nihilism we invented for ourselves with the aid of logic.[9]

But who philosophized and championed the metaphysical nihilism of Nazism?[10] How does this rhetoric condemning "the habitual somno-

9. Martin Heidegger, "Letter on Humanism," in *Basic Writings*, ed. David Farrell Krell (New York: Harper and Row, 1977), pp. 225–27.

10. On why the question of Heidegger and Nazism has once more garnered international attention, see Luc Ferry and Alain Renaut, *Heidegger and Modernity*, trans. Franklin Philip (Chicago: University of Chicago Press, 1990). See also Thomas Sheehan, "Heidegger and the Nazis," *New York Review of Books*, 16 June 1988, pp. 38–47; Tzvetan Todorov, untitled column, *Times Literary Supplement*, 17 June 1988, pp. 676, 684; and Richard Rorty, "Taking Philosophy Seriously," *New Republic*, 11 April 1988. Sheehan reviews the documentation of Heidegger's enthusiastic collaboration with Nazism, drawing nuanced but tentative conclusions about how his metaphysical dilemmas predisposed him to mistake fascism for a solution. Although Rorty condemns Heidegger's behavior, he also argues vigorously that it is irrelevant to any evaluation of his philosophical writings. "You can be a great, original, and profound artist or thinker, and also a complete bastard. . . . There is no way to correlate moral virtue with philosophical importance or philosophical doctrine" (32). But if we seek an interpretation of Heidegger, and not a quasi-scientific evaluation of his greatness and originality, then Rorty's objections are moot. Between evaluation as condemnation and evaluation as scientific assessment lies the third position, that of Todorov, who insists that while any equation between deconstruction and fascism is "absurd," there remain troubling historical questions that call for understanding. Is it merely a "coincidence that the majority of Heideggereans were engaged in extreme right wing politics between 1933 and 1945"? And if we add to this list of extremists the number of intellectual converts to Marxism in this century, we have "a very thorny problem: whereas over the past two centuries Western countries have embarked on the path of democracy, their intellectuals . . . have systematically opted for violent and tyrannical political systems" (684). (Ferry and Renaut expand this argument in their critique of antihumanism and their call for a return of the subject of democracy.) Todorov's explanation is that the intellectuals took their role as social critics so seriously that they turned against the dominant social movement of their time—democracy. Of course Todorov assumes that this criticism stems purely from envy rather than from any insight into the depredations of capitalism, bureaucracy, rationalization, and the corruption of politics. One can only wonder at the simplicity of Todorov's vision of the "path of democracy" and at the ease with which he dismisses its critics. Part of the complexity of history includes the fact that both fascism and communism were (are?) overdetermined symbolic and material responses to the changes wrought by capitalism and its attendant sociomaterial practices.

Jürgen Habermas makes the best case for a fundamental complicity between Heidegger's philosophical principles and his endorsement of National Socialism. See his chapter on Heidegger in *The Philosophical Discourse of Modernity: Twelve Lectures*, trans. Frederick Lawrence (Cambridge: MIT Press, 1988), and "Work and Weltanschauung: The Heidegger Controversy from a German Perspective," in "Symposium on Heidegger and Nazism," *Critical Inquiry* 15 (Winter 1989): 431–56; other contributors include Arnold Davidson, Hans-Georg Gadamer, Jacques Derrida, Maurice Blanchot, Philippe Lacoue-Labarth, and Emmanuel Levinas. See also the special section on "Martin Heidegger and Politics:

lence of prevailing opinion" sound when we recall Heidegger's active participation in Hitler's revolution? To what extent is Heidegger's "intermediate state" a despairing phrase for his era of disappointment following the failure of National Socialism?[11] When we translate a reading of Heidegger back into the context of his historical moment (even as he is being translated by the exigencies of our own), it appears that his question concerning values entails the subject of politics. For Heidegger's turn against value thinking was worked out from 1936 to 1946 in his massive critique of Nietzsche, who now becomes the last metaphysician rather than the prophet of an authentic transvaluation. A consensus is emerging that this work, and Heidegger's simultaneous essays on technology, must be read, with caution and concern, as an allegory of Heidegger's political unconscious. Since they lay the groundwork for the critique of "metaphysical humanism" so crucial to poststructuralist theory, a reconsideration of them might help clarify the genealogy, thematics, and aporias of deconstructive cultural criticism.

Read from the standpoint of our own historical moment, these texts seem to address their prophetic concerns to the crises of the German people, as had Heidegger's political speeches during his tenure as rector at Freiburg University. Heidegger at once articulates his allegiance to the spirit of National Socialism and, as its self-appointed philosophical counselor, provides a corrective to some of Nazism's misreadings of Nietzsche and of the crisis of modernity. In the years just prior to the Nietzsche lectures, during his brief tenure as rector, Heidegger enthusiastically identified himself with the metaphysical nationalism through which the Nazis imagined themselves as the Subject of History. In "the new Reich that Chancellor Hitler will bring to reality," Heidegger wrote, the "German spirit" will be realized in "the struggle of the entire *Volk* for itself." The *Volk* are "summoned" by the Führer to courageous decisions, such as withdrawal from the League of Nations, which consist "in the most basic demand of all Being (*Sein*), that it preserve and save its own essence." "Our will," he proclaims,

> to national (*völkisch*) self-responsibility desires that each people find and preserve the greatness and truth of its destiny (*Bestimmung*). . . . Their will

A Dossier," in *New German Critique* 45 (Fall 1988); here are reprinted ten chilling examples of Heidegger's pro-Nazi writings from 1933 to 1934, along with a memoir and essay by Karl Löwith and an analysis by Richard Wolin. For a sophisticated philosophical reading of the main texts in this controversy, see Joseph Kronick, "Dr. Heidegger's Experiment" (forthcoming, *boundary 2*, 1990).

11. Habermas puts the case against Heidegger bluntly: "Heidegger's critical judgments on '*das Man*,' on the dictatorship of the public realm and the impotence of the private sphere, on technocracy and mass civilization, are without any originality whatsoever, because they belong to a repertoire of opinions typical of a certain generation of German

to the State will make this people hard towards itself and reverent towards each genuine deed. . . . The nation is winning back the *truth* of its will to existence, for truth is the revelation of that which makes a people confident, lucid, and strong in its actions and knowledge. . . . The National Socialist revolution is not merely the assumption of power as it exists presently in the State by another party. . . . Rather, this revolution is bringing about *the total transformation of our German existence (Dasein)* [emphasis Heidegger's]."[12]

This racist *Dasein* brings the Holocaust. Heidegger amalgamates the *Führerprinzip* with a vulgar Hegelianism as he becomes the institutional agent for "the will to the historical-spiritual mission of the German *Volk* [which] arrives at self-knowledge in the state. . . . The individual by himself counts for nothing. The fate of our *Volk* in its State counts for everything."[13] The Spirit of philosophy identifies with the Fatherland.

Although he resigned from the rectorship, Heidegger continued to teach, and to support National Socialism. In his Nietzsche lectures he rethinks the genealogy of modern nihilism in order to construct a philosophy of Being that will recall the *Volk* to the true spiritual essence betrayed by the vulgarities that had overtaken Nazism. "Being" replaces the state as the origin of the summons or call to decision and responsibility, and thus the individual subject remains subordinated to a transcendental Will. The mystery of this call, which produces the vagueness characteristic of the conclusions to essays such as "The Age of the World Picture" (1938) and "The Question Concerning Technology" (1949–55), appears to allow Heidegger to maintain the value of obedience to the summons while transforming his position into that of a "piety" that dis-closes the world, that "lets Being be" instead of enframing it through technology. The attraction of these essays to thinkers after World War II is understandable: Heidegger gives voice to the general anxiety (romantic and metaphysical though it may sometimes be) over how *techne*—in thought as well as in material formations—threatens life, and he does

---

mandarins." See *The Philosophical Discourse of Modernity*, p. 140. For a contrasting opinion, see Jacques Derrida, *Of Spirit: Heidegger and the Question*, trans. Geoffrey Bennington and Rachel Bowlby (Chicago: University of Chicago Press, 1989), pp. 31–72.

12. Quotations are from Heidegger, "Political Texts: 1933–1934," *New German Critique* 45 (Fall 1988): 101–4, 106–7. For a critique of this kind of rhetoric and its historical context, see the section on "Das Volk" in Klaus Theweleit, *Male Fantasies*, vol. 2, *Male Bodies: Psychoanalyzing the White Terror* (Minneapolis: University of Minnesota Press, 1989), pp. 94–97.

13. Quoted in Richard Wolin, "The French Heidegger Debate," *New German Critique* 45 (Fall 1988): 139, 142. Heidegger's addresses seem indebted to Nietzsche's *On the Future of Our Educational Institutions* (1872); Derrida makes the connection in considering the problem of Nazism's appropriation of Nietzsche. See Derrida, "Otobiographies," esp. pp. 27–36.

so with a pathos that expresses the individual's ambivalent sense of responsibility and helplessness.[14] On the one hand, Heidegger's critique of humanism accurately reflects the loss of autonomy in modernity: this theme of the self's inconsequence before the systems of the state or of ideology will be sounded by philosophers and politicians of various kinds and is the source of the value he has had for many poststructuralist theories of the "end of man." The ruse of the subject's centrality is unmasked. On the other hand, Heidegger rejects any return to the subject, since all possibility for authenticity is now removed from beings and time and reserved for Being. A *descriptive* critique that responded to the grim reality of life in modernity turns into a *prescriptive* celebration of a pastoral utopia beyond alienation.[15]

Heidegger's work on Nietzsche and values is largely summarized in "The Word of Nietzsche: 'God is Dead'" (1936–43). Here Heidegger sketches his metanarrative of the modern forgetting of Being (the authentic remembrance of which he had glimpsed in the spirit of National Socialism). Objecting to simplifications on both the left and the right, he argues against seeing "the dominance of technology or the revolt of the masses as the cause of the historical condition of the age."[16] Instead, following Nietzsche, he analyzes modernity as the rise of the will to power, an epoch in which man, as "subject," kills God (or forgets Being) and brings the world-as-representation into appearance before him as an object of value:

> Objectifying, in representing, in setting before, delivers up the object to the *ego cogito*. . . . Everything that is, is therefore either the object of the subject or the subject of the subject. . . . In this revolutionary objectifying of everything that is, the earth, that which first of all must be put at the disposal of representing and setting forth, moves into the midst of human positing and analyzing. The earth itself can show itself only as the object of assault. . . . With the beginning of the struggle for dominion over the earth, the age of subjectness is driving toward its consummation. (100–101)

14. See Patrice Petro, "Perception, Mass Culture, and Distraction: Martin Heidegger," in her *Joyless Streets: Women and Melodramatic Representation in Weimar Germany* (Princeton: Princeton University Press, 1989), pp. 51–57. Petro's book significantly influenced my rethinking of Heidegger and of the subject of historiography in general.

15. Heidegger's politics might then be analyzed according to Fredric Jameson's "dialectic of ideology and utopia," on which I shall rely in a number of future instances. See Jameson, *The Political Unconscious: Narrative as a Socially Symbolic Act* (Ithaca: Cornell University Press, 1981), pp. 281–99.

16. Martin Heidegger, *The Question Concerning Technology and Other Essays*, trans. William Lovitt (New York: Harper and Row, 1977), p. 65. Subsequent references are given parenthetically in the text.

Once Being is reduced to being an object for a subject's will, it is only measured (argues Heidegger) in relation to the preservation and enhancement of the will to power. Thus "Being has been transformed into a value" insofar as it is seen in terms of its value for the subject's enhancement and preservation; yet once "Being is accorded worth as a value, it is already degraded to a condition posited by the will to power itself" (102–3).

In Chapter 4 I shall have occasion to compare this discourse on the loss of Being with Marxist narratives of alienation and reification. Here it suffices to note that Heidegger does not object to this or that *use* of instrumental reason or value positing, but to the essence of subject-centered thinking and enframing. In so doing, he aims to deconstruct the claims of various disciplinary critiques (political, economic, meta-physical), for these preserve man as the value-positing subject and so perpetuate the cause of modernity's nihilism and inauthenticity. What Adorno calls the "jargon of authenticity" contaminates Heidegger's impassioned jeremiad against his age and causes him to repeat the myth of a lost originality: "When the Being of whatever is, is stamped as a value and its essence is thereby sealed off, then within this metaphysics . . . every way to the experiencing of Being itself is obliterated. Here, in speaking in such a way, we presuppose what we should perhaps not presuppose at all, that such a way to Being has at some time existed and that a thinking on Being has already thought Being as Being" (103–4). Heidegger cautiously notes the metaphysical presuppositions that ground his thought of Being and his use of Being as a touchstone for criticizing the alienated culture of modernity. Is this reservation enough? Clearly not for Derrida. While further developing Heidegger's thesis that a deconstruction of representation must supplement the referential discourses of cultural criticism, Derrida also deconstructs the logocentrism grounding Heidegger's notion of Being.

Derrida's departure from Heideggerean premises shows up too in his use of Freud and in his recurrent speculations on "autobiographical" composition, the proper name, and the signature effect. These projects implicitly challenge Heidegger's polemic against "the subject" and en-hance deconstructive cultural criticism by renewing our ways of thinking the being of subjects. Though it is certainly true that Freud disrupts the self-centered consciousness of the ego's will to power, psychoanalysis retains the analytic category of the subject, and its attention to the play of linguistic values in the patient's symptomatic expressions inspires Derrida to scramble the destiny of the Heideggerean call. Where logo-centrism demands a choice between the subject as center of history and the "death of man," deconstruction analyzes the dissemination of the subject in the margin between these delusory absolutes.

Heidegger takes a wrong turn, then, in arguing that Nietzsche "never recognized the *essence* of nihilism" because his critique remained "within the perspective of value and value-positing," of the subject and the will to power, rather than overcoming these snares through a thinking of the dis-closure of Being (107–10). This move allows Heidegger to translate Nietzsche's critique into one that posits a choice between the subject and value thinking, on the one hand, and an authentic existence on the Way to Being, on the other. Nietzsche's call for new values and for an analysis of the specific historical locations of the metaphysical subject is replaced in Heidegger by a binary opposition which reintroduces metaphysics rather than overcoming it. This turn also positions Heidegger, and philosophy, once more in the place of mastery over history, which cannot be explained (or changed) by a less elevated thought: "Perhaps then," writes Heidegger, "we will recognize that neither the political nor the economic nor the sociological, nor the technological and scientific, nor even the metaphysical and the religious perspectives are adequate to think what is happening in that age" of the consummation of nihilism we call modernity (111). In the abstract this prolegomena suggests a radical opening of critical possibilities, but in context its value for Heidegger may have been the degree of historical *irresponsibility* it accorded to him as a subject.

Heidegger mistakes the necessity to displace a historically specific Subject (Western European Man and His Culture) with the need to overcome subjectivity per se. The end of his project, of course, is the submission of the subject to a system of values or will posited as wholly external to itself or wholly one with itself (Being in any case, but not beings in their contingent locations). This submission represses difference, the other, and hence forgets beings and time. The agency of the subject and the discourse on values can only be forgotten at the cost of other human beings, as the history of Nazism taught most who witnessed it. That Heidegger never learned that lesson is no reason to forget him entirely, but it does caution us to constantly recalculate the value of "the question of Being." That question enabled Heidegger to ask what had been lost when beings were made into objects that had value for a will to power, and so his "destructions" prefigured contemporary efforts to disclose the other which metaphysical discourse or institutional practice represses in the reproduction of its own identity. Heidegger's errancy, however, lay in imagining that such a disclosure of Being could defer the question of the being of its own values or the subject of its historical determination. Heidegger's turn against the subject takes him back to Hegel rather than forward through Nietzschean perspectivism. The atomization of points of view is replaced either by the singular will of the Führer and his *Volk* or by the mystery of the call of Being.

Deconstructive analysis, in contrast, may assist in the *dissemination* of the subject, a process that includes the *affirmation* of those historical subject positions (marked by such categories as race, nationality, class, gender, et al.) previously marginalized by the Subject of History. The subject is not erased from history: on the contrary, a postmetaphysical discourse of subjects is launched so that other positions of agency and value may come into play.

In *The Philosophical Discourse of Modernity*, Jürgen Habermas sees Heidegger's turn against the value-positing subject as merely an episode in a long tradition:

> In the discourse of modernity, the accusers raise an objection that has not substantially changed from Hegel and Marx down to Nietzsche and Heidegger, from Bataille and Lacan to Foucault and Derrida. The accusation is aimed against a reason grounded in the principle of subjectivity. And it states that this reason denounces and undermines all unconcealed forms of suppression and exploitation, of degradation and alienation, only to set up in their place the unassailable domination of rationality. Because this regime of a subjectivity puffed up into a false absolute transforms the means of consciousness-raising and emancipation into just so many instruments of objectification and control, it fashions for itself an uncanny immunity in the form of a thoroughly concealed domination. The opacity of the iron cage of a reason that has become positive disappears as if in the glittering brightness of a completely transparent crystal palace. All parties are united on this point: *These* glassy facades have to shatter.[17]

According to Habermas's metanarrative, modernity is an event of self-reflection that combines self-consciousness, temporality, and rationality. These three operate together to form "subject-centered reason," a mode of knowledge that lives toward the future and seeks normative foundations through its own acts rather than by reference to the past, myth, or tradition. This modern subject generates critique out of a consciousness of the contradictions of the present and is classically expressed in the work of Hegel, who authors both the traditions of reason and of its other through his dialectical speculation. Self-reflection lives in and for history, so that the advent of modernity belongs to the advent of historicism as well. In sociopolitical terms, subject-centered reason

17. Habermas, *The Philosophical Discourse of Modernity*, pp. 55–56. Subsequent references are given parenthetically in the text. For background, see *Habermas and Modernity*, ed. and with an introduction by Richard J. Bernstein (Cambridge: MIT Press, 1985), and *Autonomy and Solidarity: Interviews with Jürgen Habermas*, ed. Peter Dews (London: Verso, 1986). Habermas's reading of modernity's self-destruction owes much to Max Horkheimer and Theodor Adorno, *Dialectic of Enlightenment*, trans. John Cumming (New York: Continuum, 1986).

projects its image on to the political state, whose history and future are narrated as those of a "macrosubject" which can be theorized through the philosophy of self-consciousness.

Philosophical modernity, seeking its self-realization, turns rationality against anything that stands in the way of its enlightenment, which is to say, its freedom. The recurrent paradox of the modernist project of enlightenment, as Horkheimer and Adorno observed, proceeds from its very proper character as self-conscious self-reflexivity. Immanently, it inevitably turns its devices of critique back upon its own validity claims. This self-reflexivity opens up the abyss within the modernist project of enlightenment, so that modernity always already contains, structurally, the agency of its own beyond within it. Addressing this script in Derrida's terms, modernity posts its "post-" to itself in speculation. To Habermas, this means that "postmodernism" has always already been there, in numerous forms, throughout this history of the other of reason. Consistent with his debts to Western Marxism, however, Habermas reads these accounts of reason's other as symbolic discourses that respond to actual social pathologies, no matter the apparent ahistoricism, subjectivism, or metaphysical mysticism he finds in their efforts to imagine the other of reason. Yet in making reason, rather than art, the privileged center for his metanarrative of revolt, Habermas rules out a priori those discourses and performances within modernity that refuse definition within the framework of "reason and its other," practices that embody an/other other. Describing a strategy as one that seeks the other of reason already co-opts that strategy for reason's own story.

Habermas repeats a contention one often hears in America: that in each case the counterdiscourse that solicits the other of reason "can give no account of the normative foundations of its own rhetoric," so that ultimately it can make no claim upon us beyond the aesthetic or the subjective (294). At the level of its own discourse, the other of reason cannot coherently provide the criteria for accepting or rejecting its arguments, since such criteria belong to the regime to be deconstructed. At the level of the social, the other of reason cannot subscribe to any normative view of discourse, since it has cast reason in the role of that which fabricates norms and commonality through a falsification of difference in the interest of power. Counterdiscourse appears to undertake its critiques of various value systems, ideological formations, and disciplinary institutions without setting up another center to govern knowledge. One must ask in the name of what are such projects undertaken, if not in the name of an other whose *value* is being posited? And if the positing of the value of the other is inherent to the deconstruction of reason, an implicit normative claim of some kind haunts each of these texts. Indeed, in rejecting the portrait of the deconstructionist as "skeptic-relativist- nihilist," Derrida asserts that "the value of truth (and all those values associated with it) is never contested or destroyed in my writings, but only reinscribed in more powerful, larger, more stratified contexts."[18]

In attacking the evils of subject-centered reason, the counter- Enlightenment, says Habermas, never succeeds in more than reversing the binary terms of its predicaments, ending finally in distinctive but characteristically similar evocations of an other to whatever regime of thought or discipline of knowledge is under scrutiny. The status of this other— as a repressed truth, an unrepresentable Being, a *différance*—can never be adjudicated precisely because it lies beyond reason, representation, and *techne:* "Thus, it is directly the vital forces of a split-off and repressed subjective nature, it is the sorts of phenomena rediscovered by Romanticism—dreams, fantasies, madness, orgiastic excitement, ecstacy—it is the aesthetic, body-centered experiences of a decentered subjectivity that function as the placeholders for the other of reason" (306). Although the archaeology or disclosure of such an other may in practice yield tremendous critical insight, it cannot per se also offer a metacritical justification of its procedures without lapsing into paradox. Such a metacritical reasoning would, ipso facto, be subject to precisely the same objections as the case under study and thus throw us into the all-too well-known *mise-en-abyme*. Since the theme of the "other of reason" persists in these negative critiques, they never quite, asserts Habermas, escape the confines of subject-centered thought. For Habermas, a resolute, and politically responsible, postmodernism means admitting that "the paradigm of the philosophy of consciousness is exhausted" (296).

Yet while Habermas's erudition enables him to explicate and appreciate the discourses of modernity, his rigid conception of rational communication ultimately thwarts any fusion of horizons with poststructuralism. In his "Excursus on Leveling the Genre Distinction between Philosophy and Literature," Habermas surprisingly repeats the accusation that deconstruction aims to reduce philosophy to a kind of literature, whereas Derrida's effort has always been to render undecidable, in specific cases of considerable import, the traditional value given to this difference.[19] Habermas unabashedly aims to preserve the difference

18. Jacques Derrida, "Afterword: Toward an Ethic of Discussion," *Limited Inc,* trans. Samuel Weber and Jeffrey Mehlman (Evanston: Northwestern University Press, 1988), p. 146.
19. "Just this thesis" of a general literariness, says Habermas with some condescension, "has been the centerpoint of the lively reception Derrida's work has enjoyed in the literature faculties of prominent American universities" (*Philosophical Discourse of Modernity*, p. 191). Norris employs the same view of American deconstruction throughout his *Derrida*, which sets out to save the philosophical seriousness of Derrida from the playfulness of his followers. Habermas and Norris make complementary errors, the one taking

between literature and philosophy along quite conventional aesthetic lines. "The poetic function," he writes, "is not the only function of verbal artistry, merely a *predominant* and *structurally determinative* one, whereas in all other linguistic activities it plays a subordinate and supplementary [!] role" (200; Habermas's emphasis). Habermas merely asserts the position that Derrida has taken such pains to deconstruct. Derrida never claims for rhetoric or verbal artistry any exclusive function; indeed he often shows the hollowness of such claims, for rhetoric and tropes continue to discourse *philosophically*, however they may be set up to exclude such nonaesthetic functions. Habermas's formalistic assertion of the "subordinate and supplementary role" of style does not begin to answer the questions posed by Derrida and others about the undecidability among manner, matter, and meaning, and even seems a bit naive. It took a distinguished hermeneutical and philosophical tradition, reinforced by the powerful inertia of institutions and the subtle force of innumerable cultural practices, to make this difference between philosophy and literature appear so natural.

For Habermas, the most valuable distinction to maintain is between poetry and rationality:

> To the degree that the poetic, world-disclosing function of language gains primacy and structuring force, language escapes the structural constraints and communicative functions of everyday life. The space of fiction that is opened up when linguistic forms of expression become reflexive results from suspending illocutionary binding forces and those idealizations that make possible a use of language oriented toward mutual understanding— and hence make possible a coordination of plans of action that operates via the intersubjective recognition of criticizable validity claims. (204)

Habermas's theory of communicative rationality intends to provide a linguistically sophisticated social theory in harmony with the Enlightenment ideals of democracy, fairness, and justice.[20] Once a discourse gets defined as "poetic" or "reflexive," it ceases, according to Habermas, to make "criticizable validity claims" and so can be of no use (and of real danger, since it foments irrational states of belief) in constructing social

---

Derrida seriously as a literary theorist but not as a philosopher, the other taking Derrida seriously as a philosopher but not as a literary theorist. Both seem to fall victim to that repression of *writing* that Derrida's whole career has sought to undo.

20. See lectures 11 and 12, titled "Communicative versus Subject-Centered Reason" and "The Normative Content of Modernity," in which Habermas articulates the social and political values of his theory. There we learn that while "communicative reason is expressed in a decentered understanding of the world," this mediated and intersubjective process of normative argumentation means that "the theory of communicative action can reconstruct Hegel's concept of the ethical context of life" (315–16).

action. Like Plato, Habermas bans art from the republic. He can only
do so, in classic logocentric fashion, by turning the multiple tensions
and relations of kinds of discourse *within* a text into a binary opposition
between two mutually exclusive entities. Derrida's writings, to take only
one example, constantly employ the rules and conventions of logic and
make criticizable validity claims; they also speculate in "poetic" and
"reflexive" fashion, though these speculations are not separate from the
philosophical argument but (in the Derridean sense) supplementary to
them.

Before the publication of *The Philosophical Discourse of Modernity*,
Christopher Norris suggested that Derrida's recent work "shows distinct
signs of convergence with the project of a critical theorist like Habermas.
That is to say, it seeks new grounds for the exercise of enlightened
critique through an idea of communicative competence which allows
for specific *distortions* in present day discourse, but which also holds out
the possibility of grasping and transcending these irrational blocks."[21]
Habermas has now clearly rejected that "convergence," and we have
seen how fundamentally divergent his position is from Derrida's. Norris
correctly locates the connection between the two in terms of the critique
of instrumental reason articulated both by Heidegger and by the Frankfurt School of Critical Theory. A text like Derrida's "The Principle of
Reason" avowedly carries on, while radically modifying, that critique.
But the dissemination of communications systems pursued in *The Post
Card* utterly short-circuits the ideal of consensual communicative rationality upheld by Habermas. Moreover, as Derrida points out in his
blistering response, Habermas's second chapter on deconstruction ("Excursus on Leveling the Genre Distinction between Philosophy and Literature") violates the basic principles of reasoned, consensual communicative rationality as it pillories Derrida without ever citing a single sentence
of one of his texts. The resistance to writing, Derrida notes, shows
up in the persistent refusal of reading displayed by deconstruction's
critics.[22]

Derrida insists that a deconstruction of representation is a necessary
step in the theorization of a new politics. His texts argue that the
opposition between reason and its other masks the interplay between
truth claims and representational devices; political theory in the postmodern age cannot be a matter of choosing, as Habermas seems to say,

21. Norris, *Derrida*, p. 169. Norris's chapter "Derrida and Kant: The Enlightenment
Tradition" usefully sketches how the legacy of the Enlightenment critique by, and of,
reason impinges on Derrida's texts.
22. Derrida, "Afterword," *Limited Inc*, pp. 156–58. Bill Martin's dissertation, "Matrix
and Line: Derrida and the Possibilities of Social Theory" (University of Kansas, 1990),
provides an excellent coverage of the "non-engagement" of Derrida and Habermas.

between a return to intersubjective rational discourse and a lapse into mystificatory invocations of otherness. The speech-centered notion of communicative consensus in Habermas evokes the social image of the Greek *polis* rather than the postmodern scene of disseminated information networks and reproduced simulcra. One cannot conceive of how these new forms and outworks of representation could be repressed and then replaced by a strictly organized forum of rational argumentation. Social consensus will come through, and is indeed already produced by, the various mediums and institutions of representation, from television and the recording industry to the corporation, the university, the state, and those associations of subjects which arise to address particular social or cultural problems. This disseminated public sphere creates provisional communities of interest and momentary distributions of subject positions; it would be nostalgic, and repressive, to imagine or try to impose a single medium, forum, or place for democratic communication. The politics of difference thrives on the opposition between reason and its other. By dislocating that opposition through a critique of its conceptual, as well as material, production, deconstruction helps cultural criticism avoid some of its most recurrent pitfalls.

Habermas's return to reason not only overlooks the technologies of representation, it revives the very ethnocentric "macrosubject" that postmodernism and postcolonialism reject, and seems once again to cast women, mass culture, and various marginalized groups into the position of a devalued other.[23] Communicative rationality, in Habermas's description of it, has no race, class, gender, national or geographical position. Like Heidegger, Habermas continues to think the subject of values within the confines of the spirit of European thought. Habermas cannot himself escape the autobiographical determination of his own concept of rationality, yet he does not make the contingency and idiosyncracy of "communicative rationality" a theme for self-reflection. Once more we are presented with a true other to subject-centered reason, when what we need is a philosophical critique of modernity that takes the dissemination of subject locations seriously, and which values other forms of discourse.

It would make no sense to offer a set of universal or ideal concepts (such as perspectivism, indeterminacy, play, speculation) as the permanent "values" endorsed by deconstruction, for to do so would only play into the hands of its opponents. It would be better to begin by revising Habermas's genealogy of the deconstruction of values and so suggest

23. See Andreas Huyssen, "Mass Culture as Woman: Modernism's Other," in *After the Great Divide: Modernism, Mass Culture, Postmodernism* (Bloomington: Indiana University Press, 1986), pp. 44–64.

how the contingencies of the modern context help determine the value that play or speculation may now have in addressing philosophical, historical, political, and literary problems. The following pages begin constructing such an alternative account by reading the trope of value in Derrida's "White Mythology: Metaphor in the Text of Philosophy" (1971). Though the importance of this essay for disseminating the differences among rhetoric, literature, and philosophy has been widely remarked, little attention has been paid to how Derrida stages the political and historical dimensions of his argument. He begins by questioning the crucial analogy between linguistic and economic value employed by so many texts, of so many genres, in the Western tradition. Most important, for theorists at least, is the way Derrida pursues the work done by this analogy in the writings of Saussure, Marx, and Nietzsche. His readings demonstrate the value each can have in supplementing, or deconstructing, the models of cultural criticism promulgated by the others. My commentary takes up the value these three have had for Derrida's projects, and I conclude with some final reflections on the value of deconstruction for political criticism.

De-Nominations: From Marx to Derrida

Political economy, linguistics, and deconstruction each analyze the production and distribution of values. The recurrent analogy between language and money, or metaphors and coins, usually implies that some larger, perhaps philosophical or even metaphysical, economy comprehends the two and governs their relation to each other. The analogy between language and money, however (and, as we shall see, analogy per se), rests on ideas of identity and equivalence which themselves result from discursive exchange, and so cannot function as the unmoved movers of value systems. In his readings of Marx, Nietzsche, and Saussure, Derrida discerns that each critic's attempt at a transvaluation of values arrives at an uncanny impasse: each exposes how a historical, material, or psychological system produces values that are then mistakenly taken for transcendent verities, and yet each must do so in the name of values that themselves lay claim to just such a status (historical materialism and the proletariat for Marx, nature and will for Nietzsche, speech and consciousness for Saussure). Thus rather than once more trace the genealogy of the language = money analogy, Derrida hopes to deconstruct the metaphysics of equivalence underlying its concepts and uses, and so both to grasp the values of his predecessors' critiques and to avoid making some of the same mistakes. This, by his own logic, redefines progress as the achievement of different mistakes, arguably ones of sufficient value to offset their errors.

Insofar as deconstruction belongs to a historical moment in which Marxist theory must answer to semiotics (among others), it will share the agenda of poststructuralists such as Jean Baudrillard, who calls for "decoding the birth of the sign form in the same way that Marx was able to uncover the birth of the commodity form in the *Critique of Political Economy.*" Baudrillard would debunk "the alibi of use value," so that "the field of political economy, articulated only through exchange value and use value, explodes and must be entirely reanalyzed as *generalized political economy,* which implies the production of sign exchange value in the same way and in the same movement as the production of material goods and of economic exchange value."[24] In Baudrillard's version of general economy, the difference between political, economic, linguistic, and cultural critique vanishes as all address the "same" system. Derrida's notion of "general economy" resists this reduction to the same, for it holds that systems for exchanging values can never achieve exact equivalence. Little would be gained in replacing the hypothetical totality of logocentrism's economy with a postmodern totality of equally exchangeable signifiers.

Derrida preserves the value of the difference between Saussure and Marx even as he shows how each can supplement the other. Semiotics assists in deconstructing the use value/exchange value opposition and the ontologies of materialism, history, circulation, and production dependent on it. The solidity of the economic base will be dissolved by the dissemination of such fetishized concepts as natural utility, universal needs, property, and the object as a thing-in-itself. These notions belong to a nature/culture hierarchy shared by the signifier/signified split and still informing much of Marx's discourse. Deconstruction reads the history and mode of this vocabulary's production, and Derrida will display the ancient common genealogy of these terms and concepts in the interdependent discourses of economics and metaphysics. The critique of logocentrism, then, is inextricable from the critique *of* ideol-

---

24. Jean Baudrillard, *For a Critique of the Political Economy of the Sign*, trans. Charles Levin (St. Louis: Telos Press, 1981), pp. 112–14. On the limits of Baudrillard, see Joseph Valente, "Hall of Mirrors: Baudrillard on Marx," *Diacritics* 15 (Summer 1985): 54–65. Andrew Parker notes that although "most varieties of contemporary Marxism share a commitment to the linguistic sciences as the preferred manner of mediating between the domains of production and ideology," in fact "this gap cannot be bridged by language since it is itself the *product* of language—of an inversion between cause and effect accomplished through the figure of metalepsis" ("Between Dialectics and Deconstruction: Derrida and the Reading of Marx," in *After Strange Texts: The Role of Theory in the Study of Literature*, ed. Gregory S. Jay and David L. Miller [University, Ala.: University of Alabama Press, 1985], pp. 153–55).

ogy, though "ideology" may not survive the dissemination of its orthodox conceptual apparatus. Semiotics, in turn, loses its discursive provinciality during the unfolding of the undecidability between commodity
and sign transactions. Derrida's deconstructions of classical sign theory
and classical notions of ideology are thus tendered together in a single
negotiation. His critique in *Of Grammatology* (1967) of Saussure's logocentrism can be seen, then, as a demonstration of Derrida's assertion
that his work has long been, in a certain way, focused on political and
institutional concerns.

At least since Marx, ideology has been analyzed as a representational
practice, so that Althusser can summarily write, "ideology is a system
(with its own logic and rigour) of representations (images, myths, ideas,
or concepts, depending on the case) endowed with a historical existence
and role within a given society."[25] Ideology legislates the domain of
truth and reference, adjudicating the value of objects and subjects.
The intervention of Saussurean and poststructuralist language theory,
insofar as they defer the closure of sign and reference that ideological
representation aims toward, participates in the same radical break initiated by *The German Ideology* when it disputes the claims to divine or
natural authorship made by the languages of church, state, and philosophy. Marx promoted a deconstructive inversion that decoded the social
production of supposedly eternal truths: they had been written under
the sign of material, historical, and class struggles. Caught up within
the material conditions evolving under early capitalism, the general text
of German idealism sublated matter into sense, history into spirit, the
production of writing into the mimesis of the transcendental signified.
The historical specificity of this idealism, however, is challenged by
deconstruction, which subverts the difference between ideology and
truthful representation by insisting on the logocentrisms that underwrite discourse in every period. Yet the critique of referential logocentrism does not entail the separation of language from history, or of
writing from politics. On the contrary, it intends to map how such
separations have been managed by various textual strategies. A text's
manifest idealism or pronounced materialism contains the metaphysical
work and political effects of its latent structuralities. "What is produced
in the current trembling," Derrida claims, "is a reevaluation of the
relationship between the general text and what was believed to be, in
the form of reality (history, politics, economics, sexuality, etc.), the

25. Louis Althusser, "Marxism and Humanism" in *For Marx*, trans. Ben Brewster
(London: New Left Books, 1977), p. 231. See also "Ideology and Ideological State Appara-
tuses," in *Lenin and Philosophy*, trans. Ben Brewster (London: New Left Books, 1971), pp.
127–86.

simple, referable, exterior of language or writing, the belief that this exterior could operate from the simple position of cause or accident."[26]

The political implications of Derrida's reading of Saussure have received scant attention in the many accounts of the debt of deconstruction to linguistics. Most handbooks to contemporary theory include quite similar summaries of Saussure, featuring the arbitrariness of the sign, the distinction between synchronic and diachronic analysis, and the relative nature of identities constituted by the play of formal systems. As such summaries indicate, the reactions to Saussure's legacy have fallen into yet another binary opposition. On the one hand, there is Saussure as the father of a new linguistic and philosophic self-consciousness that liberates the play of language, and so aligns structural linguistics with Mallarmé, Blanchot, Joyce, Barthes, and postmodernism. On the other hand, there is Saussure the formalist, father of a new metaphysics of sign-systems divorced from their place in social, political, and historical discourse. Geoffrey Hartman's Saussure inspires epiphanies in echoland, while Fredric Jameson's Saussure stands dour guard before the prison-house of language.

Such readings seriously misrepresent the actual agenda of the *Course in General Linguistics*. They overlook the fundamental role played by "value" in Saussure's theory, the term to which his entire analysis leads and without which the theses on the arbitrariness of the sign and the distinction between synchronic and diachronic levels would indeed remain sterile. The function of value in Saussure's argument, as he explicitly portrays it, cannot be divorced from questions of history and political economy. The *Course* cautions against building a formalist theory on such principles as the "arbitrariness of the sign" and does so through socio-political metaphors:

> The signifier, though to all appearances freely chosen with respect to the idea that it represents, is fixed [*imposé*], not free, with respect to the linguistic community that uses it. The masses have no voice in the matter, and the signifier chosen by language could be replaced by no other. This fact, which seems to embody a contradiction, might be called colloquially "the stacked deck" [*la carte forcée*]. . . . No individual, even if he willed it, could modify in any way at all the choice that has been made; and what is more, the community itself cannot control so much as a single world [*la masse elle-même ne peut exercer sa souveraineté sur un seul mot*]; it is bound to the existing language.
>
> No longer can language be identified with a contract pure and simple

26. Jacques Derrida, *Positions*, trans. Alan Bass (Chicago: University of Chicago Press, 1981), p. 91. For Paul de Man's position on ideology and linguistics, see below, Chap. 2.

. . . language furnishes the best proof that a law accepted by a community
is a thing that is tolerated and not a rule to which all freely consent.[27]

This demystification of a social contract theory of language offers itself
as a course in ideological criticism, which could aim a political semiotics
at those theories of individual freedom, law, and community that figure
themselves as the transparent self-conscious expressions of knowing
subjects. Only in a condition of meaning's pure self-presence to itself
could subjects freely choose any arbitrary sign, since all entangling
connections between the being of the concept and materiality, time, or
the body would be effaced. "A particular language-state," says Saussure,
"is always the product of historical forces, and these forces explain why
the sign is unchangeable, i.e. why it resists any arbitrary substitution"
(72). *Parole* and *langue*, event and system, history and representation,
cannot be forced apart. Language must be thought (1) as an enduring
social institution and (2) as constantly changing in time, even if it operates as "unchangeable" at a given time. Saussure's description of synchronic establishment and diachronic errancy sketches the conditions
in which speakers and writers struggle over the political economy of
values. His account cannot fairly be construed as promoting a hedonistic
liberation of the signifier. Through synchronic analysis Saussure breaks
with the naive historicism of nineteenth-century philology. At the same
time he recognizes in part the link between the discursive and the
political orders, though this takes the deterministic form of describing
the speaking subject's subjection to the grammar of the *langue*.

Saussure's treatment of the social character of language leads directly
into the following chapter, where he discusses the "inner duality of all
sciences concerned with values," the preeminent example of which, he
says, is economics. Here, however, Saussure takes the inextricable fabric
of *parole* and *langue* and tears it in two. The same theoretical "necessity"
that splits economics between political economy (as a synchronic description of the operative rules in a system) and economic history (as a
diachronic account of successive exchange systems) divides linguistics
into the "axis of simultaneities" and the "axis of succession." As "White
Mythology" will argue, the synchronic/diachronic distinction reimposes
a metaphysics of presence ("simultaneity") in order to set meaningful
controls on the historical wanderings of the sign. In an example Derrida

27. Ferdinand de Saussure, *Course in General Linguistics*, ed. Charles Bally and Albert
Sechehaye, in collaboration with Albert Riedlinger, trans. Wade Baskin (New York:
McGraw-Hill, 1966), p. 71. The original of this edition appeared in French in 1916.
Subsequent references are cited parenthetically as *Course*. For a valuable exposition of
Saussure and his importance for modern critical theory, see Jonathan Culler, *Ferdinand
de Saussure*, rev. ed. (Ithaca: Cornell University Press, 1986).

will often disseminate, Saussure asserts the synchronic/diachronic distinction by noting that "historically the French negation *pas* is identical to the substantive *pas* 'step,' whereas the two forms are distinct in modern French. These observations would suffice to show the necessity of not confusing the two viewpoints" (91). This *pas de méthode* is no method, since the ground on which it moves is imperative and tautological: the source of this "necessity" lies purely in the theory's desire to impose identities on the fluctuating values of the sign. The synchronic/diachronic distinction, and that between method and no method, is produced by effacing the different *historical* values of a sign and restricting the possible homophonic economy of exchange between individual utterances (hence Derrida's reliance on the pun). "Etymology and synchronic value," Saussure dictates, "are distinct" (96). Yet he goes on to add that "in practice a language-state is not a point but rather a certain span of time," so that studying it means "disregarding changes of little importance," a procedure that retrospectively excludes certain historical or synchronic differences toward the end of producing the true identity of the sought-for meaning (101–2).

In another rich example, Saussure feels compelled to postulate the independence of each apparently similar sign unit by isolating the correspondence of a "phonic slice" like French *fors* as it operates in variations on the sign "force." Considering the popularity of this term in nineteenth-century physics and politics, in the literary discourse of naturalism, and in philosophy from Hegel to Nietzsche, Saussure's use of it sounds particularly resonant. Saussure holds that each instance of the sound *fors* corresponds with a different concept and so constitutes a different sign: the identity of each sign is thus preserved, and no problematic ambiguity or trace of the sound's other values haunts its present significance. This translates the sign's difference from itself into an absolute difference between identifiable signs and their others. It would be as if the use of the sign "force" could take place without putting into play any of the different connotations and denotations evoked by its phonic signifier (*fors*), as if the history of the sign's employment could be kept from contaminating its present force. The economy between all the sign's (or phoneme's) uses and their histories, and between this "phonic slice" and its other instances, which could lead to an infinite calculus of value, and to the relation of form to force and of necessity to chance, is restricted by Saussure through the enforced construction of each instance as a moment of linguistic self-presence and unitary identity.

The distinct phrases Saussure offers for examples are "la *force* du vent," "à bout de *force*," and of course "il me *force* a parler." The translator of Derrida's essay entitled "Fors" notes that the word is an archaic

preposition meaning "except for, barring, save," and is the plural of
the French word *for*, which "designates the inner heart," so that *fors*
denominates both exteriority and interiority, or a reservation that preserves.[28] Thus Saussure's debarring of the synchronic from the diachronic displays the transgression required by its own enforcement;
Derrida's play with this and other Saussurean examples (*pas, glas, chose,
aigle, legs*) puts back into play the value of the exchanges between
oppositions and substitutes for the restricted economy of proper denomination a general economy of irregular values operating in the
margins debarred by method. "La carte postale" displaces "la carte
forcée."

In "Force and Signification" (1963), an early attack on structuralist
literary criticism, Derrida argues that the totalizing claims of form over
force have distorted the Saussurean legacy: "The structuralist stance,
as well as our own attitudes assumed before or within language, are not
only moments of history. They are an astonishment rather, by language
as the origin of history. By historicity itself."[29] The history of forms and
the forms of history have been colleagues in the institutionalization of
force: recollection of the force of writing, of its capacity to shatter the
technology of representational thought and its ideological allies, brings
about a critical knowledge of the forces of history. This critique of
formalism also holds for "Marxism," "Freudianism," and other brands
of thematic commentary, for these are "only a restraint on the internal
criticism of the work," a way of controlling its difference from itself
(WD 14). Anticipating the program of "Différance" (1968), Derrida
announces that the binary schema of form/force will be countered by
"an *economy* escaping" this metaphysical opposition. Recalling Heidegger's insistence on temporality and his assertion that poetic language
discloses the force of difference, Derrida underscores "the possibility
of concealing meaning through the very act of uncovering it. *To compre-
hend* the structure of a becoming, the form of a force, is to lose meaning
by finding it. . . . Force is the other of language without which language
would not be what it is" (WD 26–27). The liberation of linguistic force
deconstructs the "supreme value" of phenomenology, which rested on
the formal transparency of visualized, objective truths for a "theoretical
subject."

Derrida's compositional style forces open the forms of language by
exploiting the very kinds of phonic and etymological play which Saus-

28. Jacques Derrida, "Fors," trans. Barbara Johnson, *Georgia Review* 31 (Spring 1977):
64n.
29. Jacques Derrida, *Writing and Difference*, trans. Alan Bass (Chicago: University of
Chicago Press, 1978), p. 4. Subsequent references are cited parenthetically as WD.

sure rules out of bounds. His disseminated language aims, in its word play, typography, allusions, and juxtapositions to re-turn the repressed matter or body of the signifier, often through contingent, hazardous, and alogocentric exchanges. In associating *aigle* with Hegel, or *lettre* with *l'être*, or *le poste* (position) with *la poste* (mail), or Freud's *fort/da* with Heidegger's *dasein*, Derrida speculates that such fanciful and unauthor-ized transactions may yield an uncanny dividend, though no "serious" philosopher will count such coinage as proposition or evidence. This de-composition of signs plays out the philosophical deconstruction of the Hegelian *Aufhebung*, essential model for the sublation of sense cer-tainty into absolute sense and knowledge. Once matter is put into signi-fying circulation, not even the necessary laws of linguistics can guarantee a safe return on the investment. As Derrida writes in response to Lacan's reading of Poe: "une lettre peut toujours ne pas arriver à destination" ("a letter can always not arrive at its destination").[30] Which is also to say that Being (*l'être*) can always not arrive at the transcendental position addressed by such metaphysicians of destiny as Hegel and Heidegger, and that when it does appear to come it does so only through such very material agencies of law as linguistics, philosophy, and the postal system.

The work of Derrida's style appears, for example, in the disturbing effects he achieves by mingling the vocabularies of Marx, Nietzsche, Saussure, and Heidegger. In his essay on Bataille and Hegel (1967), Derrida writes that phenomenology

> corresponds to a restricted economy: restricted to commercial values . . . limited to the meaning [*sens*] and the established value of objects, and to their *circulation*. The *circularity* of absolute knowledge could dominate, could comprehend only this circulation, only the *circuit of reproductive consumption*. The absolute production and destruction of value, the exceed-ing energy as such, the energy which 'can only be lost without the slightest aim, consequently without any meaning'—all this escapes phenomenology as restricted economy. (WD 271, Derrida's emphasis)

The diction in this passage suggests that Marx plays an important part in Derrida's departure from phenomenology, even as Heidegger's meditations on matter, history, and technology alter the value of a Marxist vocabulary. In his analyses of Saussure, Derrida explicitly aligns "phonocentrism" and the "psychological" cast of Saussurean semiology with phenomenology's articulations of meaning, self-presence, and the

---

30. Jacques Derrida, *La Carte postale: De Socrate à Freud et au-delà* (Paris: Flammarion, 1980), p. 472; see *The Post Card: From Socrates to Freud and Beyond*, trans. Alan Bass (Chicago: University of Chicago Press, 1987), p. 444.

sign. This Hegelian strain in Saussure may thus be contrasted to Marx's materialist accounts of alienation, which phenomenology answers with a mental solution. The deconstruction of phenomenology and of Husserl's sign theory offered by *Speech and Phenomena* (1967) parallels the critique of Saussure's logocentrism simultaneously spelled out in *Of Grammatology*. Husserl and Saussure are joint proponents of a psychology of consciousness and of intuitive consciousness, of truth as the circuit of self-speaking, self-hearing, and self-understanding.

Modern phenomenology thus repeats Hegel's way, offering to deliver the proper name along with the meaning of sensory experience. This metaphysical tradition—which sublates time, history, and matter into determinate ideas and concepts—is, as Derrida reads it, "in contradiction to other levels of the Saussurean discourse."[31] "Once more," he notes, "we definitely have to oppose Saussure to himself" (OG 52). The doctrine of the arbitrariness of the sign still operates within a mimetic or representational schema and thus is less radical potentially than Saussure's assertion that "in language there are only differences *without positive terms*" (*Course* 120). "We see then," says Saussure, "that in semiological systems like language, where elements hold each other in equilibrium in accordance with fixed rules, the notion of identity blends with that of value and *vice versa.* . . . [T]he notion of value envelopes the notion of unit, concrete entity, and reality," so that "language is only a system of pure values (110–11). No form of signification or system of rules can securely govern the forces of difference at play between these "pure values." If so, then the difference between an "arbitrary" and a nonarbitrary sign disappears, for there is no "thing" for which the sign can be an arbitrary tag, and no basis for a phenomenology transcending linguistics. "Henceforth," Derrida declares in *Of Grammatology*, "it is not to the thesis of the arbitrariness of the sign that I shall appeal directly, but to what Saussure associates with it as an indispensable correlative and which would seem to me rather to lay the foundations for it: the thesis of *difference* as the source of linguistic value" (52). By putting this difference back into play, Derrida uses Saussure's own thesis to bankrupt the phonocentric economics of identity, mimesis, and representation at work elsewhere in the *Course*.

Derrida capitalizes on the undecidability or aporia between force and form in the texts of Saussure and Marx so as to move beyond the restricted economy of proper meanings and property values, beyond dialectical schemes in which "contradiction" always yields to truth's

---

31. Jacques Derrida, *Of Grammatology*, trans. Gayatri Chakravorty Spivak (Baltimore: Johns Hopkins University Press, 1976), p. 40. Subsequent references are cited parenthetically as OG.

master narrative. What lies before or behind or after metaphysics? Derrida answers his Marxist interlocutors in *Positions* (1972) by once again following Heidegger's way, this time back to the pre-Socratics, only to find Marx ahead of him:

> I do not believe that one can speak, even from a Marxist point of view, of a homogeneous Marxist text that would instantaneously liberate the concept of contradiction from its speculative, teleological, and eschatological horizon. If . . . one wishes to relocate what you have called the "repressed" of philosophy, and notably as concerns matter and contradiction, one must not only go back to Marx . . . but much further back, as Marx himself knew, as far as the "Greek materialists," traversing problems of reading and "translation" that are indeed difficult, and whose results are difficult to anticipate in our lexicon. (75)

Marx and Saussure both aid Derrida in demonstrating that the subordination of value to identity, truth, and the proper has been at the center of the history of Western metaphysics, whether in its idealist or materialist cast. From Marx's decipherment of the economic base to Nietzsche's genealogy of morals to Heidegger's destruction of metaphysics, we can now add a linguistics of value, and ask what general text fabricates them together. Economics, philosophy, and language may be theorized as regional sciences within the cultural inscription, reproduction, circulation, and institutionalization of values.

This general text does not function as a totality, however, but rather as a dynamic arrangement of economies and aporias. By disseminating the force of the "contradictions" in "writing," deconstruction enters into the historical movement from restricted to general economy:

> One could submit all the concepts of general writing (those of science, the unconscious, materialism, etc.) to this schematization. The predicates are not there in order to *mean* [*vouloir-dire*] something, to enounce or to signify, but in order to make sense slide, to denounce it or to deviate from it. This writing does not necessarily produce new conceptual unities; and its concepts are not necessarily distinguished from classical concepts by marked characteristics in the form of essential predicates, but rather by qualitative differences of force, height, etc., which themselves are qualified in this way only by metaphor. (WD 272)

The *pas de méthode* of deconstruction dis-invests the surplus value claimed by the sovereign concept and its logocentric system, which profits at the expense of the labor of signifying matter. Derrida continues the effort of Marx to overturn and correct Hegel; but a deconstructive semiotics also turns Marx's critique of "all previous materialisms" back onto Marxism itself. Derrida radicalizes Marx's call for an analysis of "sensuous human activity, practice" ("Theses on Feuerbach") by deconstructing the metaphysics underlying "materialism" and the "sensuous": "Realism or sensualism—'empiricism'—are modifications of logocentrism. . . . It is not only idealism in the narrow sense that falls back upon the transcendental signified. It can always come to reassure a metaphysical materialism. It then becomes an ultimate referent . . . the semantic content of a form of presence which guarantees the movement of a text in general from the outside" (*Positions* 64–65).

"White Mythology" examines how the metaphors that make up materialism work in complicity with a certain empiricism to determine the values of literature, truth, ethics, and politics. Derrida speculates on the value of signs within conceptual structures, particularly signs of the sun and its illuminating correspondents, as he traces the repression or eclipse of the matter of metaphor in philosophy. Solar metaphorics, of course, are not a randomly chosen example: historically the sun has been circulated as the origin, as the metaphor *of* origin, in anthropology, theology, literature, and philosophy. This system's metaphors constitute phenomenology and every discourse of *presence* in its visibility, appearance, and being. Derrida's readings show that this metaphorics begins in an irreducible *catachresis*—in abusive "metaphors" that gesture toward an unnamable play of difference "preceding" ontology, the proper naming of nouns, or the economy of logocentric metaphor. "It is unnamable," writes Rodolphe Gasché, "not because of some Romantic nostalgia for the ineffable, nor because the limited faculties of man as a finite being would be too narrow to express what overpowers them, but because of this irreducible's exorbitant position with regard to the opposition of the proper and the figural, Being and beings, God and men, a position that escapes the logic that ties logos and Being together."[32]

Derrida follows Saussure's method: the value of the sun metaphor is calculated diachronically from Aristotle to Bachelard, and at each juncture the synchronic logic of the lucid sign's value is measured. Here "paleonymic" reinscription sends the sun's sign sliding out of orbit, deviating from its circular pathway of meaning toward the dissemination of helio-tropic flowerings. Derrida's footnotes to *Capital* and the *Contribution to the Critique of Political Economy* suggest that this genealogy

32. Rodolphe Gasché, *The Tain of the Mirror: Derrida and the Philosophy of Reflection* (Cambridge: Harvard University Press, 1986), pp. 294–95. Gasché provides an informative discussion of the philosophical context for Derrida's deconstruction of the "analogy of Being" in "White Mythology." Whereas Gasché focuses only on how Derrida's dissemination of analogy undoes ontology and its dependent discourses, I mean to highlight how that dissemination leads through and to the irreducibility of the problem of values.

of philosophy's most precious coinages deliberately echoes Marx's accounts of money's symbolic evolution out of the exchange of objects and the circulation of gold. "White Mythology" discloses the historic metaphorical value of such founding concepts as "matter" or the "sensual," which traditionally function as origins that precede naming and representation—both in classical mimetic thought and in classical theories of ideology. Derrida implicitly revises the Marxist critique of modern "reification" by questioning the difference between "things" and their always already "ideological" denomination.

Derrida's "Exergue" on coinage, inscription, and usury details the economy whereby the literal and the material are exchanged for the symbolic and the abstract. From either an empiricist or metaphysical viewpoint this transaction produces a surplus of meaning at the cost of the loss, wearing down, or effacement of the "thing itself." Turning first to Anatole France's *Garden of Epicurus*, Derrida recapitulates the etymological argument of Polyphilos that "abstract notions always hide a sensory figure":

> Polyphilos seems anxious to save the integrity of capital, or rather, before the accumulation of capital, to save the natural wealth and original virtue of the sensory image, which is deflowered and deteriorated by the history of the concept. Thereby he supposes . . . that a purity of sensory language could have been in circulation at the origin of language, and that the *etymon* of a primitive sense always remains determinable, however hidden it may be.[33]

Of course "this etymologism interprets degradation as the passage from the physical to the metaphysical" and thus depends on a "completely philosophical opposition" rather than on an original sense certainty (MP 211). This myth of a fall into abstraction would reverse history by recovering the primitive sensory figures hidden in philosophy's generalities. But the result, as often in Heidegger, is even more allegorical, and metaphysical, than the discourse of rationality. When Polyphilos sets out to reawaken all the sleeping figures in the sentence "The spirit possesses God in proportion as it participates in the absolute," what ensues is an interminable and ludicrous translation, accompanied by satirical asides (MP 212–13).

The problem of translation, in fact, haunts any attempt to think the economy of notions like the proper, the true, the literal, or the material, and frustrates theories that wish to position an ethical subject who could

---

33. Jacques Derrida, "White Mythology: Metaphor in the Text of Philosophy," in *Margins of Philosophy*, trans. Alan Bass (Chicago: University of Chicago Press, 1982), pp. 210–11. Subsequent references to this collection are cited parenthetically as MP.

act on the basis of such concepts. Polyphilos's comic renderings recall Heidegger's discussion of the difficulties in translating Heraclitus's saying, *ethos anthropoi daimon* (usually rendered as "A man's character is his fate"). Heidegger translates it as "The (familiar) abode is for man the open region for the presencing of god (the unfamiliar one)" ("Letter on Humanism" 234). *Ethos* becomes an abode, a haunted *oikos*, though in the end the gods come home as Heidegger translates "daimon" back into divinity. (Later in his essay Heidegger claims that "the reference in *Being and Time* [p. 54] to 'being-in' as 'dwelling' is no etymological game" [236].) Freud's article "Das Unheimliche" ("The 'Uncanny' ") similarly begins with quotes from the dictionary, exploiting the etymological and conceptual networks haunting the opposition between *heimlich* and *unheimlich*, before reiterating Hoffman's tale of the Sandman as an example of castration anxiety (loss of the thing-in-itself).[34] Heidegger's translation appears all the more obscure in context, since it is summoned to answer a letter from Jean Beaufret, itself a response to Sartre's *Existentialism Is a Humanism*. In answering Beaufret and Sartre, Heidegger recalls a young friend's question: "When are you going to write an ethics?"

The correspondence between Heidegger and Derrida on this question appears to be marked "Return to Sender, Address Unknown," for both assert the priority of fundamental ontology over any question of ethics. One cannot, they contend, take up ethical questions without "first" rethinking the being of the "human" and of "objects," since ethics is the discourse on the behavior of humans toward humanity and the world. Ethics presumes experience, whereas fundamental ontology questions the very conditions and possibility of experience. Ethics and translation, then, intersect in the question of the thing and its proper representation. If the system of representation constituting subjects and objects is disclosed as groundless, then perception, experience, and ethics are at best difficult to conceive. And the ethical translation is one that preserves the proper sense of an object in a communication for a subject. The language of ethics is a discourse of characters. The being of the human takes place in repetition and translation, that is, as the signifying subject. But this character is truly odd, since what he remarks on is the impossibility of his own position, his own "ethos," his own property and propriety. Hence cognition, representation, translation, and ethics are stations within the topographics of positionality; an economy of exchange between them cannot help but mark the production

34. Sigmund Freud, "The 'Uncanny'," in *The Standard Edition of the Complete Psychological Works of Sigmund Freud*, ed. James Strachey, 24 vols. (London: Hogarth Press, 1953–74), 17: 217–56.

of values and delineate the obscure passages where politics unexpectedly takes place.

By granting ontology the first hearing, Derrida and Heidegger master the anxiety of *ethos anthropoi daimon*—the riddle of the historical destiny of human being. Their speculations attempt to get "beyond" ethics by returning to a place "before" it, thus constantly traversing ethical territory in a *pas de (deux) méthode*. Banished by ontology, ethics nevertheless comes again, since the thing's disclosure awakens the sleeping figures that dwell within it *and* the character of the subject who occupies various positions toward it. Just as translation dictates a ceaseless exchange between proper and metaphorical sense, so any attempt to translate philosophy into *either* ontology *or* ethics must fall into the margin between them. Thus insofar as the "Letter on Humanism" privileges ontology over ethics, it makes the same political error that Heidegger made in turning completely against the value-positing subject, and it does so in a context that short-circuits, at a convenient historical moment, the lessons of experience. Deconstructive ontology, in other words, inherits the legacy of ethics despite its desire to relinquish it.

As Polyphilos follows the ethic of translation to its proper etymological end, he concludes by mocking the philosophers: "the very metaphysicians who think to escape the world of appearances are constrained to live perpetually in allegory. A sorry lot of poets, they dim the colours of the ancient fables, and are themselves but gatherers of fables. They produce white mythology" (MP 213). Polyphilos's scorn, however, still rests on the distinction between abstract and figurative language; Derrida's intent is "rather to deconstruct the metaphysical and rhetorical schema at work in his critique, not in order to reject and discard them but to reinscribe them otherwise" (MP 215). How? By rereading the fundamental figurative transactions of conceptualization itself, in which an economy of analogical equation produces the signified effect of the literal and the material. Economics, philosophy, and writing are all matters that hinge on ethics of transaction, transcendence, or translation.

Derrida's deconstruction of the language of philosophy continues explicitly the critiques of Marx and Nietzsche. As in *The German Ideology*, here metaphysics is "the white mythology which reassembles and reflects the culture of the West: the white man takes his own mythology, Indo-European mythology, his own *logos*, that is, the *mythos* of his idiom, for the universal form of that he must still wish to call Reason." As in Nietzsche's "On Truth and Lies in an Extra-Moral Sense," for Derrida "metaphysics has erased within itself the fabulous scene that has produced it, the scene that nevertheless remains active and stirring, inscribed in white ink, an invisible design covered over in the palimpsest"

(MP 213). Nietzsche and Marx stand behind Derrida, but on shifting grounds, their eyes turned upward to the sun, to the origin *of* language. Gasché notes that the positions "that philosophy is a white mythology on the one hand and on the other that philosophy is free of all metaphors—are not positions on which to capitalize, but whose implicit logic is, rather, to be exhibited." (Gasché, like other commentators, doesn't stop to exhibit the racial pun at work in "White Mythology"). Derrida's essay posts itself to a position beyond those stations of traditional oppositional logic transmitting the exchange between sides over the priority of literal and figurative language. What has truly been invested here, and what Derrida takes a chance in gambling with, is not the value of one term or the other (literal versus figurative, philosophy versus literature, etc.) but the meaning of the difference between them, a difference which must always be the same, be capitalized as the orbit of the proper name, for the concept of metaphor to do its work. In this sense the materialisms of Marx and Nietzsche will be found on the same side of the coin, on the side of the metaphysics of the Same, already crowded with the figures of the Greeks, whose impressive tropes have left their stamp on philosophy from Socrates to Heidegger and beyond.

A second irony in Polyphilos's argument, alongside the dissemination that a return to origins brings, occurs in the extreme cases of those negative terms so popular among metaphysicians: ab-solute, in-finite, in-tangible, non-Being. With these the "*absolute usure* of a sign," writes Derrida, produces an "unlimited surplus-value." The more degradation, the more meaning. The relation "between metaphorization . . . and negative concepts remains to be examined" (MP 212). The value of these philosophical metaphors rests in the depth of being's encryptment, in the death of the thing's presence—in what remains (*la restance*). "The provisory loss of meaning," explains Gasché, "that metaphor implies is subordinated to the teleology of meaning as one moment in the process of the self-manifestation of meaning in all its propriety" (293). Like the circulations of golden coins and returning suns, the movement of metaphor takes the risk of a negative way to meaning. Thus posted, it too may never come, or may end up in the Dead Letter Office. This version of *usure* as profitable loss recalls the history of coinage and numismatics, in which money takes the place of the thing, and the inscription on the coin revalues the golden material on which it is stamped. The analogy of *usure* to the economy of the Hegelian sublation, or *Aufhebung*, and thus to the metaphysical determination of Being as a return that eclipses time, distance, and difference, is all too apparent.

"White Mythology" must then show that the economy of analogy, per se, is likewise predicated on the possibility of never arriving. Gasché notes that "what Derrida's analyses consistently show is that the attempt to name analogy properly, and consequently to ground it in that name, take place only through analogies of analogy" (305). But which analogies? Derrida observes that when Marx, Nietzsche, Saussure, and others try to explain or signify the metaphorical process, "the paradigms of coin, of metal, silver and gold, have imposed themselves with remarkable insistence" as the exemplars of analogy (MP 216). Theorists of metaphor borrow from the bank of economic tropes to demonstrate the systematic relationship of terms *within* a metaphor or figurative expression (such as "commodity fetishism," which predicates analogies among the economies of religion, sexuality, and the marketplace). Perhaps this is because coins appear to show so neatly the difference between brute matter and imprinted meaning, and thus to provide a natural ground for theories demarcating the literal and the figurative. In metaphor, the exchange of properties between words is supposedly governed by a discursive economy that regulates the difference between proper and figural meaning—or that knows the difference between a fanciful association and a true analogy. Yet the attempt to illustrate the metaphorical process of analogy by recourse to monetary metaphors repeats, in the very structure of the comparison, the problem the illustration set out to clarify. A metaphor can only be grounded through another metaphor, and so we are cast once more into the *mise-en-abyme:* "Before metaphor—an effect of language—could find its metaphor in an economic effect, a more general analogy had to organize the exchanges between the 'two regions.' The analogy within language finds itself represented by an analogy between language and something other than itself" (MP 216). This "more general analogy," as we discover in the following sections on Aristotle and metaphor, is the economy of logocentrism, in which the being of meaning is thought as a translation that begins with a self-same and self-present object as the proper thing of comparison, thus providing the grounds for all future empiricisms, materialisms, and idealisms. "Inscription on coinage," continues Derrida, "is most often the intersection, the scene of the exchange, between the linguistic and the economic. The two types of signifier supplement each other in the problematic of fetishism, as much in Nietzsche as in Marx" (MP 216). As critical tools, notions of ideology and fetishism at once attack the claims of concepts to natural or divine authority and yet persist in grounding their critiques in the difference between natural objects (or use value) and cultural signs (or exchange values). The translation of the critique of ideology into the deconstruction of logocentrism may be located exactly here, where the economy of analogy labors to produce the fetish of the thing itself. Insofar as the fetishism of Marxism remained caught within an empiricist opposition between real and fantasized objects, the discourse on reification only repeated, albeit on the verso, what Plato had already dictated.

Now itself a commonly used coinage, the Nietzschean token is once more paid out, though Derrida's use of it alters its value: truths, writes Nietzsche, "are worn out metaphors which have lost their sensory force, coins which have their inscription [*Bild*] effaced and now are no longer of account as coins but merely as metal."[35] The contrast of coin to metal, however, indicates the remains of an empiricist ontology within the Nietzschean critique. The famous example of the leaf illustrates the problem:

> Every notion [*Begriff*] originates through positing the equation [*Gleichset-zen*] of unequal things. Just as it is certain that one leaf is never totally the same as another, so it is certain that the idea "leaf" has been formed arbitrarily by letting these individual differences fall out [*Fallenlassen*], and by forgetting their distinguishing qualities [*des Unterscheidenden gebildet*]. This awakens the idea [*Vorstellung*] that, in addition to the leaves, there exists in nature the "leaf": the primal form according to which all the leaves were woven, sketched, measured, colored, curled, and painted—but by unskilled [*ungeschickten*] hands, so that no specimen [*Exemplar*] had turned out to be [*ausgefallen wäre*] a correct, trustworthy, and faithful likeness [*Abbild*] of the original model. (83)

A rigorous destruction of the Platonic Idea, this demystifying of the sign "leaf" rests on the ground with the leaves themselves, in their different and distinguishable natures; while reversing the mimetic narrative—historical and philosophical [*Geschichte*]—of a fall from Idea to object, Nietzsche returns us to the garden where original material things are truly themselves, even if differently, as they are recollected by the logos of nature. Yet in German, *Falle* may signify a snare or trap, an artifice designed by clever hands [*geschickt*] rather than by fate or destiny [*Geschick*]. Turning over these leaves, we wonder at the address of the letters, the direction of their destination, and suspect that Nietzsche's writing has set us up for more than one fall. So framed, the choice of "leaf" as an example for a discourse on metaphor is not an innocent one: Nietzsche exploits the fallen state of language in his play on words for idea, representation, image, inscription, copy, model, likeness, and

35. Friedrich Nietzsche, "On Truth and Lies in a Nonmoral Sense," in *Philosophy and Truth: Selections from Nietzsche's Notebooks of the 1870s*, trans. Donald Breazeale (Atlantic City: Humanities Press, 1979), p. 84. I have modified the translation and interpolated key words from the German original, "Über Wahrheit und Lüge im Aussermoralischen Sinn," *Sämtliche Werke Kritische Studienausgabe*, vol. 1 (Berlin: De ä Gruyter, 1980).

so forth. The effect defers the presence of unmetaphorical materiality, as the matter of metaphor turns and tropes in ways that render the difference between representation and object of questionable value. Here, too, there is exhibited a disseminative level of the discourse that conflicts with the grammatical enunciation.

Although many who have borrowed this citation circulate it in order to illustrate the illusory nature of the truths of language, Derrida's reading is quite different. At one level, Nietzsche's materialism here is strictly metaphysical, his leaves empirical; in turning a cold shoulder to Plato, Nietzsche may simply receive his message backward, verso for recto. Reversed, the deck remains stacked, the position forced. Gasché notes that Nietzsche's enterprise "is grounded in etymological empiricism," and he quotes a lengthy passage from Derrida's essay on Levinas (1964) in which we read that "etymological empiricism" is "the hidden root of all empiricism. . . . As Hegel says somewhere, empiricism always forgets, at the very least, that it employs the words *to be*. Empiricism is thinking *by* metaphor without thinking the metaphor *as such*" (WD 138–39). If we turn to the Levinas essay, we find, not by chance, that the etymology at stake is that "concerning 'Being' and 'respiration,' " spirit as breath, an example central to the speech of Polyphilos. Derrida quotes a letter of Descartes's arguing that " 'I breathe, therefore I am' concludes nothing, if it has not been proven previously that one exists, or if one does not imply: *I think that* I breathe." Derrida notes that "the *signification* of respiration is always but a dependent and particular determination of my thought and my existence, and a fortiori of thought and of Being [*l'être*] in general" (translation modified). Even if "the word 'Being' is derived from a word meaning 'respiration' (or any other determined thing), no etymology or philology . . . will be able to account for the thought for which 'respiration' (or any other determined thing) becomes a determination of Being among others." Like philosophy, etymology and philology cannot account for the thought that requires that there be a metaphor, and this metaphor, in place of Being. Derrida concludes: "One must travel other roads—or an other reading of Nietzsche—in order to trace the genealogy of the unheard-of meaning of Being [*généalogie inouïe du sens de l'être*]," and that road leads to "White Mythology" (WD 139).

This suspension of the power of etymology to determine the ground of the concept in an original act of metaphor replays the critique of Saussure, though here in reverse, since now Derrida resists the suggestion that the signifier is the cause of the signified. Etymology, like history (with which it is essentially involved), will be granted its effects, but not at the cost of foreclosing the systemic or synchronic labor of regulation and *différance* at work "before" or "beyond" any particular determina-

tion. Since ethical values have traditionally been thought either as transcendental ideas *or* as deductions from experience, the passage beyond
this opposition marks the way toward the transvaluation of value. Both
in the Levinas essay and in the logic of "White Mythology," however,
Derrida persists in pursuing, repetitively, Heidegger's step "back" to
ontology "before" the meaning of value and ethics can be determined.
The compulsion to such speculation, as in Derrida's reading of Freud,
creates a strategic defense and deferral of determination. One may note
that it is this emphasis on the value of undecidability which troubles
political and humanistic critics of deconstruction, and it must be admitted that deconstruction has had more to say, overtly, about the dissemination of ontology than about the rewriting of ethics. If it is indeed not
a matter of taking sides between metaphoricity or literality, idealism or
materialism, play and judgment, then deconstruction must still address
the value of soliciting undecidability in the course of analyzing a particular work or cultural event. More recently Derrida put it this way: "A
decision can only come into being in a space that exceeds the calculable
program that would destroy all responsibility by transforming it into a
programmable effect of determinate causes. There can be no moral or
political responsibility without this trial and this passage by way of the
undecidable. . . . 'deconstruction' should never lead either to relativism
or to any sort of indeterminism."[36]

In "White Mythology," Nietzsche's words on coinage appear at the
end of Derrida's paragraph, which begins by recalling Marx's treatment,
in *Contribution to the Critique of Political Economy*, of *usure*, "coinage speaking different languages," and the fetishistic symbolism of gold. In
Marx's analogies, observes Derrida, the "reference seems to be economic
and the metaphor linguistic," reversing the common pattern (money as
a metaphor for language) without necessarily questioning its natural
ground (MP 216–17). Yet in a provocative footnote whose marginality
characteristically encrypts a radical break in the argument, Derrida cites
passages from *The German Ideology* where Marx's "target is the reduction
of economic science to the play of language, and the reduction of the
stratified specificity of concepts to the imaginary unity of an *etymon*"
(MP 217 n. 13). Read carefully, Marx's lines point toward a deconstruction that may be aimed directly at the remains of a naturalist ideology
lurking in the overt materialism of "Marxism." "His critique of etymologism," notes Derrida, "chose the *proper* as its example," including
Destutt de Tracy's "plays on the words *property* and *proper*" and Stirner's

---

36. Derrida, "Afterword," *Limited Inc*, pp. 116, 148. See also J. Hillis Miller, *The Ethics of Reading* (New York: Columbia University Press, 1987), pp. 1–12.

on *Eigentum* and *Eigenheit* (property and individuality). Stirner attempts to refute the abolition of private property by a wordplay demonstrating that, even after the revolution, he could still *have,* i.e., own as proper to himself, a stomachache. The exploitation of etymology that allows Stirner to analogize property and the proper or individual worries Marx less than its repetition of the exchanges that produced the bourgeois concept of "property" in the first place: "All this theoretical nonsense," Marx writes, "which seeks refuge in bad etymology, would be impossible if the actual private property which the communists want to abolish had not been transformed into the abstract notion of 'property'." Marx himself recognizes that "*after* the abolition of (*actual*) property it is, of course, easy to discover still all sorts of things which can be included in the term 'property'" (MP 216–17 n. 13). And Marx gives a further set of wordplay examples linking property and the proper with such economic terms as value, worth, and exchange. This discovery, of the general economy constituting the proper as the economy of self-present objectivity, is what interests Derrida, who finds that this critique "opens, or leaves open, the questions of the 'reality' of the proper, of the 'abstraction' and the concept (not the general reality) of the proper" (MP 217 n. 13). The value of Marx's critique of the proper—seen now as the sublation into eternal truth of the property relations of capitalism—will be reinvested by Derrida in his argument that logocentrism always already funds the capitalization of the Proper (and the Proper Name) in every concept's mode of production, from Plato to Rousseau to Freud and beyond. Marx's text, as in the cases of Saussure and Nietzsche, will be read against itself to mobilize the force of its "contradictions": the deconstruction of the concept of "property," which Marx uses here to mock Stirner's empiricism, will elsewhere be forgotten when Marx must utilize a distinction between the inherent properties of gold and the arbitrariness of paper script in his analysis of monetary evolution.

The *Contribution to the Critique of Political Economy* appears to offer a genealogy or diachronic account of the evolution of paper money out of commodity barter and coinage. Each synchronic state seems to move us one more step toward an abstraction from the material base of use, nature, and objectivity, until paper currency becomes a signifying script whose relation to what it signifies is only arbitrary and conventional. The use of inscribed coinage marks the decisive step in this decline of values, since the "abrasion sustained in the course of its worldly career" means that the coin will quickly *be* less of a thing than the value inscribed on its face: "The longer a coin circulates," observes Marx, "the greater becomes the divergence between its existence as a coin and its existence as a piece of gold or silver. . . . the coin becomes increasingly ideal as a result of practice, its golden or silver substance being reduced to a mere pseudo existence."[37] But Marx quickly describes this "disparity between its nominal content and its real content" as provoking a "*second* idealisation of metal currency." The first idealization occurred in the "first" act of exchange, in which incommensurable items (linen, gold) circulated on the basis of the *idea* of their equality or analogy. The degradation of the coinage requires a second, legal, supplement, a second (and in practice infinitely repeated) codification of the exchange value of money: "The amount of silver or copper these tokens themselves contain is, therefore, not determined by the value of silver or copper in relation to that of gold, but is arbitrarily established by law," the state administering the *Aufhebung* of loss and profit (*Critique* 112). As Saussure said of the imposition of the arbitrary sign, value cannot be separated from historical practice and its social regulation. Thus at the end of the history of money, "relatively worthless things, such as *paper*, can function as symbols of gold coins" (*Critique* 113). History and diachrony teach that the synchronic economy of values is a form of "writing" authorized by the state, reproducing its identity and effects of positionality through a process of negation, circulation, and subl(im)ation.

"In the circulation of tokens of value," writes Marx, "all the laws governing the circulation of real money seem to be reversed and turned upside down. Gold circulates because it has value, whereas paper has value because it circulates" (*Critique* 121). But does gold "have value" as a proper essence, any more than Stirner has his stomachache? Marx's rhetorical insistence here on the distinction between gold coinage and paper money, and the subsequent methodological strictures it allows, function analogously to Saussure's imposition of the distinctions between synchrony and diachrony and signifier and signified. Marx's text resists its own logic and analogies, since it has elsewhere mobilized the equivalence of coinage and writing in order to think the general history and system of value circulations and their representations. The analytic identification of money, gold, and metaphor here, however, would disclose the "written"—or differential—character of the value we give to gold itself, revealing the work of an arbitrary "paper currency" of ideas and desires constituting the realm of material things and our relations to them. In fact, this other narrative deconstructing the origin of material values runs alongside the commonly read demystification of paper currency, creating a kind of aporia that classical Marxism has busily bridged over.

37. Karl Marx, *A Contribution to the Critique of Political Economy*, ed. Maurice Dobb, trans. S. W. Ryazanskay (New York: International Publishers, 1970), p. 109. Subsequent references are cited parenthetically as *Critique*.

From the start the opposition between use value and exchange value is not a simple one based on a discernible difference between objective worth and cultural evaluation: "The commodity is a use-value for its owner only so far as it is an exchange-value," argues Marx, and a "commodity can only therefore become a use-value if it is realised as an exchange-value, while it can only be realised as an exchange-value if it is alienated and functions as a use-value" (*Critique* 42–43). A general economy of undecidable exchange labors "before" the construction of objects, commodities, uses, and values; the legal-linguistic regulations delimit a restricted economy and a narrative of its successive cultural systems out of this excess of relation. To take the analogy of linguistics and economics seriously here, one would have to read this genealogy of paper currency and its values as a metaphor for the history of writing, and thus as a deconstruction of the history of such philosophical coinages as the "objective," the "proper," and the "thing itself." One would, indeed, have to write "White Mythology." The stability of the analogy between linguistics and economics loses its grounds, then, first by a double reversal of the genealogy of the transference between them (linguistics cannot be established through an analogy to money, and money cannot be coined through an analogy to language), and then by a displacement in which the economics of analogy itself is disseminated through the deconstruction of its capital concepts of matter, substance, and the ontology of the Being of the Same.

Marx submits the basic concepts of classical economics to a (perhaps) analogous critique in the Introduction to the *Grundrisse,* where he reverses and displaces the simple opposition between production and consumption. Much of the recent psychoanalytic and political commentary on the fantasmal quality of consumer capitalism is anticipated in these pages:

> If it is clear that production offers consumption its external object, it is therefore equally clear that consumption *ideally posits* the object of production as an internal image, as a need, as drive and as purpose. . . . Production not only supplies a material for the need, but it also supplies a need for the material. As soon as consumption emerges from its initial state of natural crudity and immediacy . . . it becomes itself mediated as a drive by the object. The need which consumption feels for the object is created by the perception of it. The object of art—like every other product—creates a public which is sensitive to art and enjoys beauty. Production thus not only creates an object for the subject, but also a subject for the object.[38]

38. Karl Marx, *Grundrisse: Foundations of the Critique of Political Economy,* trans. Martin Nicholaus (New York: Vintage, 1973), pp. 91–92. Marx's argument here would severely complicate any easy acceptance of Baudrillard's attack in his chapter titled "Beyond Use Value" (*Political Economy of the Sign,* pp. 130–42).

No simple logocentric notion of use or need or subjectivity can survive this speculation, nor can the phenomenology of Hegel or his followers stand up to its scrutiny. The analysis threatens to render the concepts and systems of political economy undecidable, and to take with them much of the classical discourse on epistemology, ontology, and subject-object relations. The argumentative and political value of soliciting this undecidability lies in its power to shake the formal institutions of capitalist philosophy.

Marx then focuses his discussion on the relative value of concrete and abstract terms in the analytic vocabularies shared by capitalism and its opponents. "The conclusion we reach," he decides, "is not that production, distribution, exchange and consumption are identical, but that they all form the members of a totality, distinctions within a unity" (99). One need not belabor the well-known implications of this recourse to totality and unity. It continues in the following, very rich, section on "The Method of Political Economy," where Hegel's speculative dialectic of consciousness is detailed and rejected in favor of a dialectical materialism grounded in the incessant methodological and historical interplay of realization and negation between the concrete and the abstract.

Marx acknowledges that abstraction—defined as the forgetting of real historical differences—is a necessary feature of any politico-economic discourse (*Grundrisse* 104–5). He argues that "the most general abstractions arise only in the midst of the richest possible concrete development," so that debunking the abstractions of bourgeois capitalism means recalling the historical differences obscured by the universalizing ideology of its individualist and humanist lexicon (104). Marxism thus offers a deconstructive reading of such abstract metaphors as "identity," "resemblance," "production," "circulation," "exchange," and "consumption." To be consistent, this reading must scrutinize its own abstractions in light of its own concrete context in history. As a result, an interminable self-reflexiveness goes hand in hand with a real critical historicism, considerably complicating claims for unity and totality.

Derrida feels uneasy in the presence of Marxist abstractions, which explains in part his use of Saussurean linguistics as a corrective to the rhetorical strategies of Marx's texts. Derrida's "Exergue" turns from Marx and Nietzsche to a deconstruction of "the Saussurean distinction" between "signification" and "value." Like the distinction between "use value" and "exchange value," this difference tries to maintain a border that will not stay closed. Indeed, Derrida positions "value" as a metaphor for that which is both agent and product of the economic interchange between abstract and concrete, synchronic and diachronic, system and history. Derrida quotes the passage where Saussure "elaborates the analogy" between economics and linguistics: "Here [in linguistics] as in political economy we are confronted with the notion of *value;* both sciences are concerned with *a system for equating things of different orders*— labor and wages in one and a signified and a signifier in the other" (*Course* 79). But can one delimit linguistics and political economy as the only discourses that obey the "inner necessity" of a "radical duality" that constitutes "two clearly separated disciplines within a single science"? To display the general economy of "duality" underwriting Saussure's delimitation, Derrida tracks how "in order to define the notion of value, even before it is specified as economic or linguistic value, Saussure describes the general characteristics which will ensure the metaphoric or analogic transition, by similarity or proportionality, from one order to another" (MP 218). A theory of value as the equation of unequal things grounds itself on the value of the analogic equation between language and money—so that a *philosophical* or metaphysical rationality of similarity, proportion, and truth as the sameness of Being already operates as the general conceptual economy encompassing the restricted systems of linguistics, economics, and their resemblance.

The problem with the synchronic view of the signifier-signified model of signification is that "language is a system of interdependent terms in which the value of each term results solely from the simultaneous presence of the others" (*Course* 115). Saussure observes that "even outside language all values are apparently governed by the same paradoxical principle. They are always composed: (1) of a *dissimilar* thing that can be *exchanged* for the thing of which the value is to be determined; and (2) of *similar* things that can be *compared* with the thing of which the value is to be determined" (*Course* 115). How, then, can Saussure stabilize the significations produced by these operations of analogy performed by language? As Derrida remarks, "the five-franc piece once more pays the expense of the demonstration" as Saussure uses the duality of the coin's value (exchanged for dissimilar things [commodities] and compared to similar things [other monetary forms]) as his analogy: "In the same way a word can be exchanged for something dissimilar, an idea; besides, it can be compared with something of the same nature, another word" (*Course* 115). In order to ground the terms of language, Saussure must define language by analogy to its other, and so once more the analyst's illustrative metaphor repeats the very problem that he had hoped to solve.

At the same time, however, Saussure's text opens the way to dissemination as he argues that the *signification* of the sign is only a variation on its values:

Instead of pre-existing ideas then, we find in all the foregoing examples *values* emanating from the system. When they are said to correspond to concepts, it is understood that the concepts are purely differential and defined not by their positive content but negatively by their relations with the other terms of the system. Their most precise characteristic is in being what the other are not. . . . But it is quite clear that initially the concept is nothing, that is only a value determined by its relations with other similar values, and that without them the signification would not exist. . . . The foregoing principle is so basic that it applies to all the material elements of language, including phonemes. (*Course* 117–19)

Yet in studying the ways language "limits arbitrariness" in order to create concepts (*Course* 133), Saussure arbitrarily limits the relations of the sign along the synchronic and diachronic axes, and so erases the traces of history that haunt the presence of the sign's value. As a "system" of values, language, like money, cannot be defined in terms of a present; rather it is a practice, a set of instituted conventions. Value, unlike linguistic signification, cannot be limited to the present meaning articulated by the system, for the axis of differential relation runs diachronically as well as synchronically. The value of the sign consists also in the way it differs historically, or in the way it makes history by making a difference. While such difference, and its value, can never be systematized absolutely, it can be read according to its structures and effects. At this point *rhetoric*, rather than linguistics, offers the necessary theoretical supplement since it is the discipline that focuses on the *parole*, on the historical address of the letter (see below, Chapter 7).

"White Mythology" does more than deconstruct the binary oppositions of concept and metaphor, philosophy and literature, linguistics and politics, and system and history. It argues that the general economy taking place between such polar terms always comes down to a question(ing) of values, so that deconstruction puts the subject in a position of responsibility rather than one of logocentric obedience or nihilistic free play. The argument leads Derrida to a statement of principles which owes much to Saussure:

While acknowledging the specific function of a term within its system, we must not, however, take the signifier as perfectly conventional. Doubtless, Hegel's Idea, for example, is not Plato's Idea; doubtless the effects of the system are irreducible and must be read as such. But the word *Idea* is not an arbitrary *X*, and it bears a traditional burden that continues Plato's system in Hegel's system. It must also be examined as such, by means of a stratified reading: neither pure etymology nor a pure origin, neither a homogeneous continuum nor an absolute synchronism or a simple interiority of a system to itself. Which implies a *simultaneous* critique of the model of a transcendental history of philosophy and of the model of systematic structures perfectly closed over their technical and synchronic manipula-

tion (which until now has been recognized only in bodies of work identified
according to the "proper name" of a signature). (MP 254–55)

One cannot write a history of ideas by tracking the diachronic development of concepts, as if "idea" were an arbitrary sign or an essence,
and one cannot write descriptions of synchronic systems (periods, disciplines, authorial careers) as if their terms and concepts did not already
carry a traditional burden whose value is at stake. Does this reduce
"history" to an "idea"? Or vice versa? I think instead that it proposes a
way of conceptual self-criticism for historical analysis, and a way of
historical self-reflexivity for conceptual speculation. Surely Derrida's
choice of "Idea" as his example here is not innocent. But his statement
does not directly speak to the political terms in which the differences
between "history" and "idea" are necessarily cast. If "history" and "idea"
are both metaphors that forget or foreclose the "other"—including the
play of force, desire, event, and institution as well as those subjects
written out of the traditional Western history of ideas—then it is a
responsibility of criticism to address the politics of their utterances.

Toward an Other Politics

The deconstructive approach to the question of values offers ways of
rethinking the technological powers of knowledge and of reevaluating
the specific effects of certain systems, institutions, and their metaphors.
This demands, as we have seen, transforming how we undertake ethical,
political, and historical questions, which remain imperative. To use a
phrase Derrida elaborates elsewhere, the inquiry is ultimately into "the
end(s) of man" (MP 109–36), for the displacement of truth by value
disseminates effects across the entire range of cultural criticism. (The
specific effect here, among others, could concern the gendered and
geo-national teleology that has characterized Western discourses of
"man" since their inception.) The notion of truth as classically established prescribes a mimetic technology of thought and practice, dictating the history of the responsibilities of representational man. Deconstruction, on the other hand, investigates how truth operates as the
foreclosure of values, as the expropriation of wills and desires. Whereas
truth establishes a proper position for the subject—as knower and
master of himself and other objects—the questioning of values opens
up possibilities of positionality while evaluating their force and effect. A
critique of values makes historical criticism possible, because it unbinds
thought from the abstract universalism—the white mythology—of humanist logocentrism, though such a liberation must proceed along a

hermeneutical way that begins within the legacy of the tradition. Like truths, values are terms for which we are responsible.

Value analysis, like that of semiotics, focuses on systems and structures in both their genealogical and practical forms, and its method must also challenge its *own* values and *their* effects. Joining two traditions, it combines a historical materialism of values with a critique of the fundamental ontology of how things get their names and properties. Truths are theological; values are political. This crude formula should suggest the specificity of asking about where politics *takes place*, for politics now appears as a name for the economy that denominates, distributes, and reproduces values and properties. Technology and science, for example, are perhaps the most politically charged and ideologically repressed discourses of our epoch, since they may most alter the way we value things, and each other. No account of colonial imperialism, the rise of the multinational corporation, the fall of communist totalitarianism or the current upheaval of traditional cultures in the Third World would be sufficiently political unless it contained a thorough assessment of the function technology has played, especially as it alters a culture's representations, epistemologies, relations of production, and structures of desire from the social and class contradictions of global industrial manufacture to the dissemination of copiers, telephones, fax machines, video cameras, and televisual reception.

In correspondence, the modern devaluation of philosophy and of the human sciences plays a crucial role in the hegemony of technical cognition and its practical imperialism, a development aided whenever cultural analysis separates method, fact, or form from value. The debate of late over the crisis of the university will not carry us far unless it recognizes the inherent nihilism of that vocationalism which today threatens to transform education into a personnel training-center for specific intellectual, corporate, economic, and social groups. The human sciences will complete their suicide should they pursue the goal of learning how better to service the desires of such interests. The claims to value-neutrality on the part of scientific and business technocrats are curiously but profoundly analogous to the value-neutral aestheticism that has long served as a self-defeating justification for the study of the humanities.[39] Undoing the difference here, as well as reversing the value judgment of our culture vis-à-vis techo-scientific and value-oriented discourses, is a fundamentally political and ethical matter. Likewise the current banality of explicitly political discourse, stalled between the delusions of liberal capitalism and the hypocrisy of communist practice, should itself be enough to send us looking for where politics is actually

39. See Ryan, *Marxism and Deconstruction*, pp. 138–58.

taking place. Granted that the contribution of deconstruction to an other politics remains oblique and nascent, it should be clear by now that deconstruction belongs to a historical moment of cultural reevaluation of which it is both symptom and critique.

But doesn't the emphasis of deconstruction on undecidability, its refusal of mastery and totality, and its reluctance to posit an actual alternative to the dominant sociopolitical practices of Western logocentrism make any talk of a deconstructive politics futile? So argues Barbara Foley in an avowedly "Marxist-Leninist" attack on "the political bankruptcy of deconstruction." "We are quite willing these days," she writes, "to admit that all discursive activity is in some sense political, but we are ordinarily quite imprecise, even naive, when actual political questions arise."[40] The confidence expressed here in knowing the difference between "actual political questions" and discursive ones is, I suggest, the real naïveté, and evinces an a priori refusal to entertain the most basic of deconstructive hypotheses. Her essay proceeds by measuring deconstruction against an unapologetically dogmatic and traditional interpretation of Marx and Marxism. She concludes, for example, "that Marx's defetishization of political economy sets forth a model for other procedures of defetishization—philosophical, literary, and historical—and does not need any supplementation by deconstructive undecidability" (131). Of course I have argued the opposite—that deconstruction enacts its responsibility toward Marx by extending "defetishization" to the very terms of Marxism, extending the reach of both philosophical and political criticism. The legacy of political fetishism and of oppressive techno-empiricism has lived long into this century on both sides of the Iron Curtain (that veil of difference deserving a deconstruction equal to that so lately visited on the Berlin Wall).

If the terms of Marx's analyses were so exact and enduring, his texts so clear, then neither capitalists nor the "communists" of today would have survived to practice their respective duplicities. To "argue that the political implication of Derrida's project is fundamentally anti-progressive" requires either an unreflective notion of progress or a failure to investigate how previous concepts of progress have led to so much contemporary regression and repression.

Surely we cannot ask ourselves to accept without question the old terms of Marxism (the material base, class struggle, the proletariat, et al.) unless we wish to abandon that *rereading* of history and texts which produces political criticism. Can we, for example, so quickly juxtapose "real relations of class and power" to "formalistic argument," without

40. Barbara Foley, "The Politics of Deconstruction," in Davis and Schleifer, *Rhetoric and Form*, p. 115.

asking about the forms that underly and assist the reproduction of such
entities? Is a politics that traffics in such worn-out metaphors a valuable
alternative to deconstruction? Do we really know what "power" now is,
or how and where it operates, beyond the crude reality of its recurrent
manifestation in the law and the military, or in torture and expropriation? Can anyone deny that in our time the powers of representation
often exceed the gross and clumsy mechanisms of immediate material
coercion? When the racist government of South Africa sought to stem
the tide of world condemnation, it killed the messenger: a blackout was
imposed on any representation of events deemed contrary to the state's
interests, a totalitarian erasure that sought to forestall change by forbidding its signification. When student protesters were beaten by the communist secret police in Czechoslovakia, videotapes of the event were
shown constantly in shop windows and taken into the small towns and
countrysides, where they played a key part in mobilizing the populace.
If the material control of the means and modes of representation is so
vital to political history, then the theoretical analysis of representation
and its reception are no less important for those who hope to understand, much less change, the world.

Certainly "Marx's project is very different indeed from that of Derrida," as Derrida has shown. Yet this doesn't change the fact that Derrida's project includes a response to Marx and orients itself within that
horizon. Derrida does not share Foley's confidence that Marx was a
Marxist, or that Marx's project was as univocal as she portrays it. Her
Marx is the recognizable nineteenth-century figure of dialectics and the
proletarian revolution. Derrida and others find Marx's texts far more
riven and locate *his* Marxism in the rhetoric, as well as the grammar, of
his work, and perhaps especially in the economy between the two.
Dogmatic Marxism is only one reading, and *its* "political bankruptcy"
as the twentieth-century wanes is hardly undecidable. As Albert and
Hahnel stress, the "most important question about orthodox Marxism
is not who held what thoughts, but rather, what is the value of the
thoughts themselves in the context of our current needs and possibilities? What can we retain from the orthodoxy? What can we learn through
analyzing its weaknesses?"[41] One notes with irony that at the very time
that communism around the globe is rapidly losing its attraction as a
mode of political organization, Marxism as a mode of theory is quickly
gaining new adherents, especially in the United States. Ihab Hassan
observes that "Marxist theoretical chic" is of course part of our bourgeois
"self-criticism, our genuine malaise, mid lingering poverty, racism, sex-

---

41. Michael Albert and Robin Hahnel, *UnOrthodox Marxism: An Essay on Capitalism, Socialism, and Revolution* (Boston: South End Press, 1978), p. 13.

ism, in an affluent and pluralist society." "Marxist theory without Marxist praxis," Hassan argues, "is no Marxism at all; 'theory' becomes a
high-minded illusion meant to save Marxism from its history, save ideas
from their consequences," and so becomes an "intellectual exercise" in
obtaining "moral superiority" without any risk.[42] It remains to be seen
whether deconstructive discourse, after "saving the text," will take on
the greater challenge of saving Marxism as a resource for cultural
criticism and social action.

The various appropriations of Marx now found among feminists,
film theorists, philosophers, literary critics, and a myriad of postmodern
or poststructuralist thinkers suggest that efforts toward a viable use of
Marxist perspectives may be well under way, though they will leave the
terms of Marxist analysis transformed (perhaps unrecognizably) in the
process.[43] This development still leaves open the vexed issue of praxis,
which has haunted Marxist cultural criticism from Lukács to the Frankfurt School and beyond, and appears decisively important in light of
recent events in Eastern Europe, China, Latin America, and the U.S.S.R.
Does cultural criticism as a praxis constitute an extension or evasion of
the traditional imperatives of praxis conceived as an action that actually
revolutionizes the modes and relations of production? Although it is
not an ultimately sufficient response, the use of critical theory to alter
the discourse and institutions of "higher learning" represents a real
aspect of praxis, since it addresses the actual productive machinery
housing the intelligentsia and determining their social functions.
Granted one should always beware of mistaking academic revolution
for total cultural upheaval, and given that academic politics cannot
substitute entirely for interventions at other sites of socioeconomic reproduction, nonetheless it remains vital that we recurrently consider
how and where politics takes place in pedagogy, scholarship, and their
institutions.

While charges of "ahistoricism" are flung at deconstruction, then,
Marxism's Marx has often stood above history (and criticism), his work
removed from the temporality that produced it. History lives on, however, and the attempt to isolate Marxism from history, so as to govern
history, inevitably falls victim to the transvaluation generated by any
transcendental idea. Deconstructive analysis might set out, then, to
recover Marx and Marxism *for* history and against the reification of its
own practitioners. Rejection of a Leninist position does not entail a

42. Ihab Hassan, *The Postmodern Turn: Essays in Postmodern Theory and Culture* (Colum-
bus: Ohio State University Press, 1987), p. 219.
43. Work by many of the best contemporary Marxist critics appears in *Marxism and the
Interpretation of Culture*, ed. Cary Nelson and Lawrence Grossberg (Urbana: University of
Illinois Press, 1988).

relapse into anarchism or liberal pluralism. It does signal the postmo-
dernity of our political situation, for we have entered another "intermediate state," one between capitalism and Marxism and, *simultaneously,*
between the era of their rivalry and that of their mutual decline. The
difference between the two systems has long since been busy deconstructing itself, which does not mean that both have not had their
specific achievements and evils. It does mean that the requirements of
an other politics have begun, if only intermediately, to take shape and
demand our response.

That politics pushes critical theory toward projects of cultural criticism, rather than toward the aesthetic or technical specialization of
knowledge. The role of the intellectual is challenged, and revitalized,
in an insistence on a value-oriented self-reflexivity in the conduct of
criticism. By including the university in the discourse on marginality,
theory takes up the issue of the specialization and rationalization of
intellectual labor and the critique of its role in institutional and ideological reproduction. More specifically, deconstruction has set off a necessary struggle over the meaning of the political itself. Traditional political
positions, categories, and the choices they offer appear to require the
same severe displacement once practiced by Marx on the lexicon and
system of bourgeois capitalism. One does not need deconstruction, as
many have pointed out, to take a position on nuclear war or apartheid;
and taking such a position would not in turn validate the values of
deconstructive critics. The apparatus for making such decisions is in
place; the continuing failure of such oppositional positions to produce
any real change suggests a fundamental problem in the way the question
is being posed.

The political value of deconstruction, then, begins in its paradoxical
deferral of the "political" as it may be conventionally defined in some
specific context. Deconstruction reinscribes politics and its vocabulary
in the general text of the modern crisis of representational thought and
its mechanisms. Bill Readings correctly maintains that deconstructing
the opposition between the rhetorical and the literal, or the literary and
the real, takes us *closer* to the political. Politics is that social practice
which claims the real as its grounds, so that domination can take place
through enforcing as literal or natural what exists historically as institutions and ideologies. Adapting Paul de Man's analysis of *prosopopeia,* or
tropes of address which give face or voice to figurative deities, Readings
writes: "To appeal to the 'real' is always to lend a voice to the state of
things—what we do when we appeal to a 'political reality' is to *personify*
literality. . . . The voice of pure literality, which might speak the law as
such, always performs the operation of terror, in that to assert the
law as literally representable is to silence its victims by relegating the

operation of resistance to the condition of transgression."[44] Political struggle passes through the deconstruction of hegemonic representations, not as a way to establish the dominance of a correct position toward the real but as a way to solicit an/other hearing. Nevertheless, no deconstruction can proceed except through the strategic occupation of numerous local stations of decision and position (what Derrida calls the phase of reversal). Derrida *does* take up positions toward Plato and Rousseau, Blanchot and Mallarmé, Marx and Freud, writing and technology, apartheid and fascism, and these do constitute moments of knowledge in his texts. The provisional quality of these positions makes them more, not less, effective, since it underscores the historicity of deconstruction's own readings. In the university, praxis will involve decisions at the local levels of curriculum, pedagogical style, disciplinary formation, funding, range of texts analyzed, development of interdepartmental working groups, application of criticism to mass culture, and the self-reflexive politicization of critical writing.

Recognizing the dangers of such a reduction, we can say that the value orientations of deconstructive criticism are toward the *different* and the *other*, or, in Spivak's punning title, toward a discourse "in other worlds." When forced to schematize deconstruction as a method, Derrida sketches a procedure in which one first isolates the binary oppositions enabling a discourse and its truths, then reverses this hierarchy in a strategic revaluation of the formerly subordinated term, and then turns toward the process of disseminating the opposition itself. The political application of this procedure includes taking up easily identified oppositions of an apparently empirical nature and overturning their hierarchical relation.[45] These would include man/woman, white/black, high class/low class, First World/Third World, art/mass culture, and so on. In *Positions*, Derrida emphasizes that to "overlook this phase of overturning is to forget the conflictual and subordinating structure of opposition. Therefore one might proceed too quickly to a *neutralization* that *in practice* would leave the previous field untouched, leaving one no hold on the previous opposition, thereby preventing any means of *intervening* in the field effectively" (41). In this phase of reversal, deconstructive criticism is a strategy of affirmative action: it affirms the other and solicits its value. This first and by no means simple stage of critical struggle is perceptible in the fashionable but no less necessary invocation of terms like "race," "class," and "gender" in so much contem-

44. Readings, "Deconstruction of Politics," p. 232.
45. Fredric Jameson holds that Derrida's procedure still blindly pursues metaphysical (or superstructural) issues instead of locating their causes in industrial and consumer capitalism (the base). See *The Political Unconscious*, p. 114.

porary theory. The empowerment of these terms cannot be abandoned
in a rush to deconstruct the conceptual identities and abstractions informing them. Their affirmation, on the contrary, is required by a
politico-discursive situation that everywhere exhibits the cost of their
previous denigration or erasure. Here the return of a certain will to
believe can be justified. Nonetheless, at another level, one recognizes
the ongoing necessity to rethink such empirical categories, themselves
fabricated by disciplines deconstruction subverts. "Woman" and the
"colored man" are, in an important sense, rhetorical inventions with a
history and system that require decoding, rather than material referents
that need celebration. The effort to submit terms of racial and sexual
identity to poststructuralist scrutiny is now widespread among African-
American, Third World, and feminist thinkers.

The tradition of cultural critique behind deconstruction urges that
we abandon the philosophy of the truth of the Same for the activity of
the knowledge of differences—this is what is at stake, theoretically, in
Marx's meditations on abstraction, Nietzsche's on metaphor, Saussure's
on language, Heidegger's on Being, or Derrida's on writing. A political
criticism formed by this tradition will be doubly written, questioning
the ontology of reigning ideological formations *and* questioning the
historical technology conditioning this very questioning. One asks what
difference has been forgotten in producing those truths and positions
that reign in a particular political circumstance, and how this repression
of difference has been accomplished at the levels of linguistic and
institutional reproduction. An allegiance to the different conforms to
a respect for alterity and the other (even as it must vigilantly avoid
recolonizing them). Obviously this allegiance and respect must orient
discourse in the regions of feminism, racism, and international politics,
and guide the ethics of reading cultural texts in light of the others
they exploit or exclude. Concrete historical situations will demand the
recognition, and the taking, of positions of difference and alterity.
This critical politics of resistance must include a resistance to its own
recuperation as the law of the truth of the Same. The pursuit of an other
criticism will discover an other politics as an inseparable consequence of
its principles. The "intermediate stage" of our postmodernism, in theory
and politics, may never end. This openness to events in time may turn
out to be its crucial value, for it signals the interruption of logocentrism
by a resilient historicity that will generate, rather than foreclose, the
production of new values.

CHAPTER TWO

Paul de Man:
Being in Question

> The need to revise the foundations of literary history may seem
> like a desperately vast undertaking; the task appears even more
> disquieting if we contend that literary history could in fact be para-
> digmatic for history in general, since man himself, like literature, can
> be defined as an entity capable of putting his own mode of being into
> question.
>
> —de Man, "Literary History and Literary Modernity"

This chapter was substantially composed before the debate arose over
the character of Paul de Man's writings prior to his emigration to the
United States. Fortunately, it is neither necessary nor appropriate for
me to add to that debate here, though I have made some changes as a
result of it.[1] More than ever, Paul de Man must be closely read, yet now
with a difference we can scarcely predict. My original purpose was to
contribute to such an expository reading of deconstruction in America,

---

1. See Jacques Derrida, "Like the Sound of the Sea Deep within a Shell: Paul de Man's
War," *Critical Inquiry* 14 (Spring 1988): 590–652, and the various responses, together with
Derrida's lengthy rejoinder, in *Critical Inquiry* 15 (Summer 1989), which also includes
Shoshana Felman's provocative contribution, "Paul de Man's Silence" (704–44); Derrida's
essay, with a few changes, is reprinted at the end of his *Mémoires—for Paul de Man*, rev.
ed., trans. Cecile Lindsay, Jonathan Culler, Eduardo Cadava, and Peggy Kamuf (New
York: Columbia University Press, 1989). Other readings of de Man I have found instructive (in addition to those mentioned in notes below) include Suzanne Gearhart, "Philosophy *before* Literature: Deconstruction, Historicity, and the Work of Paul de Man," *Diacritics*
13 (Winter 1983): 63–81; "The Lesson of Paul de Man," special issue of *Yale French
Studies* 69 (1985); Stephen Melville, *Philosophy beside Itself: Deconstruction and Modernism*
(Minneapolis: University of Minnesota Press, 1986), pp. 115–38; Michael Sprinker, *Imaginary Relations: Aesthetics and Ideology in the Theory of Historical Materialism* (London: Verso,
1987), pp. 237–66; Jonathan Culler, "Paul de Man," in *Modern American Critics since 1955*,
vol. 67 of the *Dictionary of Literary Biography*, ed. Gregory S. Jay (Detroit: Gale Research
Co., 1988), pp. 74–89.

though from the start I intended to explore the gap between statement and trope in de Man's own work, particularly as regards the figure of the subject and its mode of textual appearance. Thus obliquely my reading crosses recent efforts to trace how "Paul de Man" takes place in the texts that bear his signature. In addressing the question of the subject's (and the critic's) relation to literary history, I inadvertently but perhaps fatefully stepped toward what Derrida's reading of de Man suggests: that de Man's skeptical attitudes toward history and politics, like those of many European modernists, were conditioned by the epoch of totalitarianism, in whose wake the various "post-" discourses still seek their destinations.

Christopher Norris and Geoffrey Hartman argue persuasively that de Man's essential task was to deconstruct any and all versions of the mistaken identification of nature or sensuous experience with cognition or linguistic structures.[2] "Aesthetics" for de Man is that discourse which wrongly conflates perception with expression. The "ideological" character of this mistake turns on its recourse to tropes of the organic and the natural, which join world and mind in a single vision. Hence the assertion of "natural" grounds for positions in fields such as economics, ethics, and politics rests on an erroneous application of aesthetic principles. Though de Man directs his deconstructions at certain aesthetic interpretations of romanticism, his target is also the totalitarian aestheticism of fascism, which the younger de Man himself endorsed. Like his early hero Heidegger, de Man (and other modernists) hoped to avert the crisis of Europe "through the reconciling power of an authentic meditation on the destiny of national cultures" (Norris 172). After the horror of the failure of this dream, de Man schooled himself in New Criticism's "paradoxes" so as to save Heidegger, and himself, from the blindness of a reactionary, totalizing organicism. For almost twenty years, roughly until the ascension of Derrida, de Man wrestled with the ghost of Heidegger, showing that the romanticism of Heidegger coexists with a textual thinking that deconstructs it: Heidegger is thus both condemned and excused. Without going further into the complexities of this story, I suggest that the mistaken turn against "the subject" in the work of Heidegger gets rewritten by de Man in a highly personal way. Norris is right, I think, to insist on the "existential pathos" of de Man's work, even if this means, as Hartman notes, risking the aesthetic fallacy by reading de Man's existence together with his written works.

2. Christopher Norris, *Paul de Man: Deconstruction and the Critique of Aesthetic Ideology* (New York: Routledge, 1988); Geoffrey Hartman, "Looking Back on Paul de Man," in *Reading de Man Reading*, ed. Lindsay Waters and Wlad Godzich (Minneapolis: University of Minnesota Press, 1988), pp. 3–24.

Just as Heidegger's destruction of metaphysics contains an allegory of his politics, so de Man's deconstruction of the subject of literary history contains an allegory of how he puts his own mode of being into question.

Literature/Aporia/History

What direction can the writing of literary history take in the aftermath of deconstruction? In 1949, Wellek and Warren asked a similar question in the wake of the New Criticism: "Is it *possible* to write literary history, that is, to write that which will be both literary and a history?[3] Their emphasis on the study of literature as an intrinsic, formalist enterprise led Wellek and Warren to call for a literary history written in accordance with such principles: "Why has there been no attempt, on a large scale, to trace the evolution of literature as art?" rather than "as mere document for the illustration of national or social history" (252–53). Critical theory today, with its emphasis on textuality, discourse, and rhetoric, has once more forced us to ask what relation—if any—links literature to the referents of history, politics, psychoanalysis, and the other human sciences. How we name that relation will largely dictate how we construct our versions of literary history, if indeed we do not abandon the project altogether. "One feels at times envious," writes Paul de Man, "of those who can continue to do literary history as if nothing has happened in the sphere of theory, but one cannot help but feel somewhat suspicious of their optimism."[4] Derrida argues that de Man was also suspicious of the political narratives informing and exploiting literary commentary, so that what has happened in the modern sphere of history also makes us approach any theory of literary history with some wariness. De Man will dispute attempts to ground literary history in terms of its referents, but he will also reject the aesthetic formalism embodied in Wellek and Warren's tautological formula that "our starting point must be the development of literature as literature" (264). His critiques of ideological literary histories and of aesthetic totalities will both involve the displacement of the humanistic subject—"de Man."

Paul de Man's approach to the question of literary history, like that of Wellek and Warren, turns on the question: What is literature? Throughout his career, however, from "Form and Intent in the Ameri-

3. René Wellek and Austin Warren, *Theory of Literature*, 3d ed. (New York: Harcourt Brace, 1956), p. 252. On this question, see Jonathan Culler, "Literary History, Allegory, and Semiology," *New Literary History* 7 (Winter 1976): 259–69.
4. Paul de Man, *The Rhetoric of Romanticism* (New York: Columbia University Press, 1984), p. ix. Subsequent references are cited parenthetically as RR.

can New Criticism" to "Resistance to Theory," de Man rejected any
literary theory based on aesthetics (this lesson seems to have escaped
many of those who have blindly accused de Man of aestheticism).[5] For
the New Critics, literary ontology centered itself in those "ambiguities"
or "paradoxes" that Cleanth Brooks named as constituting literary language as such.[6] De Man tropes "paradox" with "aporia," a term for
textual impasses that resist the unifying hermeneutics of formalism,
aestheticism, ideology, and onto-theology. In "The Dead-End of Formalist Criticism," de Man argues that the delusory ontological unity
ascribed to the poetic artifact is an effect of reading as it defends against
aporia. In a formulation he will never veer from, de Man declares: "The
text does not resolve the conflict, it *names* it."[7] Relying unabashedly on
his reading of Heidegger, de Man reinscribes the Marxist and Sartrean
explanations for contradiction, alienation, and difference: "The problem of separation inheres in Being, which means that social forms of
separation derive from ontological and metasocial attitudes. For poetry,
the divide exists forever" (BI 240). Obviously this cautions against economic determinism in the interpretation of culture, though at the same
time it also rejects the idea of ideological or cultural unity by stressing
the difference inherent to representation. After the spectacle of modern
political theater and totalitarian political discourse, this is understandable.

The consequences of this poetic ontology for the writing of literary
history are spelled out at the end of "Literary History and Literary
Modernity," as de Man wonders "whether a history of an entity as self-
contradictory as literature is conceivable. . . . It is generally admitted
that a positivistic history of literature, treating it as if it were a collection
of empirical data, can only be a history of what literature is not. . . . On

5. See de Man's essay on Jauss, for example, where psychoanalysis and deconstruction
combine to undo the subject of the aesthetics of reception, in *The Resistance to Theory*
(Minneapolis: University of Minnesota Press, 1986), pp. 54–72. Subsequent references
are cited parenthically as RT.

6. Cleanth Brooks, "The Language of Paradox," in *The Well-Wrought Urn* (1947)
(New York: Harcourt Brace Jovanovich, 1975), pp. 3–21.

7. Paul de Man, "Form and Intent in the American New Criticism," *Blindness and
Insight: Essays in the Rhetoric of Contemporary Criticism*, 2d ed. rev. (Minneapolis: University
of Minnesota Press, 1983), p. 237. Subsequent references are cited parenthetically as
BI. Allen Stoekl documents how "de Man reads Heidegger against himself, valorizing
division—what he calls dialectic [and later aporia]—against the common ground as unity,
which comes to be identified in Heidegger with dwelling . . . poetically man dwells, yet
the poetic, unlike complacent dwelling, is defiance and combat. . . . Poetic activity is not
a bridge but is opposition or difference *in* language and time. . . . We should note here
that 'history' for de Man, and 'the dialectic,' refer to the incessant process of the upheaval
and destruction of permanence" ("De Man and the Dialectic of Being," *Diacritics* 15 [Fall
1985]: 40–41).

the other hand, the intrinsic interpretation of literature claims to be anti- or a-historical, but often presupposes a notion of history of which the critic is not himself aware" (BI 162–63). (Here are some of the words that come back to haunt our reading of de Man.) De Man's allusion to Wellek and Warren echoes the division of *Theory of Literature* into sections on "Extrinsic" and "Intrinsic" approaches and recalls the dilemma of their book's concluding chapter on "Literary History": its placement at the end of the book implies the achievement of a totalization that the argument of the chapter fails to establish, except in its circular insistence on studying "literature as literature."

Wellek and Warren's final paragraph collapses into a series of qualifications, self-doubts, apologies, and prophesies that betray the cost of their paradigmatic opposition between referential and artistic discourses. The mere reversal of the binary opposition between extrinsic and intrinsic approaches is offered as an "antidote" to the disease of discursive speculations that threaten the "integrity" of literature as it has been traditionally conceived. The ontological, aesthetic, and even political character of this antidote is, in retrospect, fairly clear, and constitutes part of the legacy of a reactionary critical modernism writing after fascism and a second global war and within the confines of Cold War liberalism. The omnipotence of political ideologies in appropriating cultural artifacts and discourses to their own purposes is countered here by the insistence on the autonomy of art. Yet the blindness of this insight lies in the retention of aesthetic criteria which ultimately coincide with those of ideology.

De Man unleashes the radical potential of New Criticism by replacing paradox with aporia, for no notion of "integrity" will survive the hypothesis that "separation inheres in Being." De Man pursues another way of reading that would resist the parallel temptations to the mimetic and aesthetic fallacies: "Could we conceive of a literary history that would not truncate literature by putting us misleadingly *into* or *outside* it, that would be able to maintain the literary aporia throughout, account at the same time for the truth and the falsehood of the knowledge literature conveys about itself, distinguish rigorously between metaphorical and historical language, and account for literary modernity as well as for its historicity?" (BI 165). As we shall see, this forecasts de Man's reading of romanticism as a case study in the blindness and insight of attempts to write a literary history for modernity.

De Man's antipathy to formalism pervades "The Resistance to Theory," where he assaults the error made in assimilating "literariness" to "aesthetic response" and warns against the "strong illusion of aesthetic seduction" (RT 10). But he similarly mocks how, as he puts it in "Semiol-

ogy and Rhetoric," "critics cry out for the fresh air of referential meaning."[8] De Man muses upon the anxiety of reference that haunts so many
of his humanist or Marxist antagonists, and he resolutely maintains his
position that the study of texts cannot be reduced to the referents which
are one of their effects: "In a genuine semiology as well as in other
linguistically oriented theories, the referential function of language is
not being denied—far from it; what is in question is its authority as a
model for natural or phenomenal cognition." Reinscribing Marx, de
Man cunningly argues that what "we call ideology is precisely the confusion of linguistic with natural reality," so that "more than any other
mode of inquiry, including economics, the linguistics of literariness is a
powerful and indispensable tool in the unmasking of ideological aberrations, as well as a determining factor in accounting for their occurrence"
(RT 11). In pointed contrast to Fredric Jameson, for instance, who
writes a kind of literary history that subordinates textuality and deconstruction to dialectical materialism through a theory of the "political
unconscious" and its symbolic *resolutions* of social contradictions, de Man
appears implacable in his subordination of all other interests to the
study of the irreconcilability distinguishing textual economies. Those
seeking utopian schemas for literature or culture will find no champion
in de Man, who turns rather to the subject of what totalities overlook,
forget, or repress on their way to the new order.

We cannot, then, canonize de Man as the heir apparent in the genealogy of formalist criticism. This would be, first, to completely ignore his
repeated injunctions against formalism, which are based on his career-
long concern with rhetorical figuration, a process of temporality which
formalism submits to closure and reification. If one has not understood
the displacement of formalism in de Man's work, one has not read de
Man. Second, we cannot overlook de Man's insistent and ironic troping
of terms from the human sciences and their referential discourses.
Stylistically, de Man's irony includes a mode of repetition, wherein the
conceptual terms of aesthetics or psychoanalysis or phenomenology or
speech act theory or classical rhetoric are reinscribed, and often mixed
together, as in the following excerpt from *Allegories of Reading:*

> The very pathos of the desire (regardless of whether it is valorized posi-
> tively or negatively) indicates that the presence of desire replaces the
> absence of identity and that, the more the text denies the actual existence
> of a referent, real or ideal, and the more fantastically fictional it becomes,

8. Paul de Man, *Allegories of Reading: Figural Language in Rousseau, Nietzsche, Rilke,
and Proust* (New Haven: Yale University Press, 1979), p. 4. Subsequent references are
cited parenthetically as AR.

the more it becomes the representation of its own pathos. Pathos is hyposta-
tized as a blind power or mere "puissance de vouloir," but it stabilizes the
semantics of the figure by making it "mean" the pathos of its undoing. (AR
198–99)

The pathos of *our* undoing lies in calculating the effect of this Babylonish
dialect. We may even read it self-reflexively: "the more fantastically
fictional it becomes, the more it becomes the representation of its own
pathos." In any case the effect is not to destroy reference or annihilate
form; it is rather to disseminate them. "Contrary to received opinion,"
writes de Man, "deconstructive discourses are suspiciously text-produc-
tive" (AR 200).

Perhaps the most frequently reinscribed concept in the texts of de
Man is that of the "self," which suffers an extreme identity crisis under
the pressures of a post-Freudian, post-phenomenological, and post-
Saussurean critique. In de Man's rhetorical injunctions against literary
conceptions of selfhood, however, one reads the traces of an authorial
desire, and the continued return of phenomenological and psychoanalytic tropologies. This ironic revoicing will, in turn, bear quite crucially
on the narration of literary history. As de Man inherits it, the self stands
as the conjunction between synchrony and diachrony, or consciousness
and history: a purely "literary" history would entail the erasure of the
author, whose self does not belong to the history of literature; and a
history of literature as the history of consciousness would once more
repress writing.

If literature is to have a history, it will consist of heterogeneous moments, of temporal differences and delays, of punctuations and articulations which by definition are not identical and do not occur at the "same
time." The "self" appears as one name and instance grounding such
events of difference. Of the referent-effects that function as such articulations and identities, the self has occupied a valorized position, especially
insofar as it offers its voice as the origin of meaning. An allegory of de
Man's readings, then, detects him opening up the otherwise closed systems of criticism through a synchronic account of the ever "present" aporia inhabiting all signification; yet the aporia is not a form in any conventional sense but a name for the temporality and difference energizing any
production of meaning. A re-turn of diachrony, history, genealogy, and
even subjectivity occurs, methodologically and thematically, whenever de
Man sets out upon their deconstruction, since it is not their absence, but
their ironic ontology, that fascinates him.

De Man's deconstruction of the literary self appears highlighted in
the rhetorical figure of *prosopopeia,* which he calls "the master trope of
poetic discourse" (RT 48). The "figure of prosopopeia," says de Man in

"Autobiography as De-Facement," is "the fiction of an apostrophe to an absent, deceased, or voiceless entity, which posits the possibility of the latter's reply and confers upon it the power of speech." Prosopopeia confers "a mask or a face" along with a voice, and is thus the "trope of autobiography" as well (RR 75–76). The rhetorical double play of de Manian prosopopeia parallels that of Derrida's supplement: "*prosopon-poiein* means to *give* a face and therefore implies that the original face can be missing or nonexistent" (RT 44). Thus de Man nominates proso-popeia as his master trope (or as the trope of mastery) because its supplementary work disfigures or de-faces the masks of meaning pro-duced by authorship, grammar, and reference. "As soon as we under-stand the rhetorical function of prosopopeia as positing voice or face by means of language," says de Man, "we also understand that what we are deprived of is not life but the shape and the sense of a world accessible only in the privative way of understanding," that is, of a consciousness apprehending itself and its world as the integrity of a singular presence (RR 80–81). The "self" itself is one of prosopopeia's masks, so that a deconstructive rhetoric makes a babel of the univocal subject. Consciousness *is* prosopopeia, and the philosophy of the subject a matter of listening in on slips of the tongue.

De Man would save us from the privation of understanding so that we may better experience what *Allegories of Reading* calls our "state of suspended ignorance" (AR 19). This latter phrase is exemplary, since it enacts the de Manian irony between statement and figure: is our "state" one in which our "ignorance" endures without resolution, or is our literary "state" one in which our ontological "ignorance" is recur-rently "suspended"—deferred, abrogated, left undecided, held in abey-ance, kept buoyant, even bridged over—by the work of language, which would thus cross over the aporia in the act of knowing it? (Later de Man will punningly use "suspended" as a translation of Hegel's *aufgehoben;* his repeated use of "suspend" (or its cognates) marks his own tropologi-cal undoing of dialectical sublations, including that of the State.) Is the temporality of language the narrative of just such an undecidable and seductive suspension? In such doubly written passages, the de Manian style double-crosses the declarations of epistemology, suspending them over the aporia of rhetoric and grammar. The sublimity of perspective afforded by such a suspension bridge may be ecstatic, even sublime, for the subject, though this abysmal speculation can be as fatal as it is constitutional for the knowing eye.[9] This tropology is difficult to untan-

9. Compare the metaphorics of bridging, sublimity, and the abyss in Jacques Derrida, "The Principle of Reason: The University in the Eyes of Its Pupils," *Diacritics* 13 (Fall 1983): 3–20.

gle, since it interweaves metaphors of vision with metaphors of voice—
as if language, as in phenomenology or a certain kind of romanticism—
gave voice to visions. The word "reading" might be construed as a
catachrestic metaphor naming this abusive tropology, for the reading
eye/I sees voices when it articulates a text. A deconstruction of aesthetics
goes by way of a dissemination of the difference between perception
and reading.

De Man's interest in prosopopeia, I suspect, stems in part from this
tropological mixture of vocal and visionary phenomena: prosopopeia
gives voice to invisible, often apparently dead, subjects—like consciousness or literary history. We should not be surprised, then, to find de
Man declaring that prosopopeia, "as the trope of address, is the very
figure of the reader and of reading" (RT 45). Reading de Man's gram-
matically explicit statements or rhetorically inflected doubts about the
relation of language to other domains, one thus must give voice to the
figures his rhetoric contains: those of history, politics, phenomenology,
semiotics, psychoanalysis, and the author. Barbara Johnson quite clev-
erly discovers that, in a crucial passage on the "eclipse of the subject"
in language, de Man's own sentence contains a "grammatical anacoluthon," for he has left out the grammatical subject itself, so that his
text "*enacts* the eclipse of the interpreting subject that it describes."[10]
Ironically, this example necessarily lapses into formalism, since now
form and meaning unite in the art of de Man's grammatical lapse.[11]
Elsewhere de Man's prosopopeia turns literary history into a kind of
overdetermined ventriloquism or deconstructive vaudeville. De Man
gives voice and face to what a previous grammar would call nonexistent
or unheard-of figures. This is precisely the case when his figure inter-
poses itself in the debate over literary history: the deconstruction of
literary history by de Man intervenes historically, we shall see, to correct
the genealogy of criticism and point toward a future of properly rhetorical analysis, while its own mode of intervention marks the ironic return
of the subject it seemed to banish.

What could critical prosopoeia give voice to in an analysis of de

10. Barbara Johnson, "Rigorous Unreliability," *Critical Inquiry* 11 (December 1984):
284.

11. De Man frequently cautions against mistaking deconstruction for the fallacy of
imitative form—self-reflexive or not. For example, commenting on the fragmentary style
of Auerbach and others, de Man counters that "I feel myself compelled to repeated
frustration in a persistent attempt to write as if a dialectical summation were possible
beyond the breaks and interruptions that the readings disclose. The apparent resignation
to aphorism and parataxis is often an attempt to recuperate on the level of style what is
lost on the level of history. By stating the inevitability of fragmentation in a mode that is
itself fragmented, one restores the aesthetic unity of manner and substance that may well
be what is in question in the historical study of romanticism" (RR ix).

Man's *Allegories of Reading?* One may overhear how his own rhetoric
supplements not an absence but prior figures of reading and of literary
history (including his own earlier work). The Preface imposes a retrospective coherence on this collection of essays when it states that "*Allegories of Reading* started out as a historical study and ended up as a theory
of reading." Figured here is a critic whose intended "historical reflection
on Romanticism" is thwarted by "local difficulties of interpretation." De
Man finds this shift "typical of my generation." "It could, in principle,"
he writes, "lead to a rhetoric of reading reaching beyond the canonical
principles of literary history which still serve, in this book, as the starting
point of their own displacement" (AR ix). These "canonical principles"
will include theme, authorial origin, chronology, reference, and historical context. The displacement of each of these devices for constructing
literary history is the most salient feature of de Man's chapters. Yet we
note that the canonical principle of the aporia between history and
literature, inherited from Wellek and Warren as well as from the debate
between E. R. Curtius's historical topology and Erich Auerbach's figural
historicism, reappears as the very fate of de Man's own readings. The
attempt to write literary history has once more ended in a meditation
on the impossibility of the task.[12]

The breakdown of canonical literary historiography, however, is itself
narrated as a historical event, "typical" of a specific "generation" and
thus represented by de Man in terms that seem to contradict his explanation that "local difficulties of interpretation" were the ahistorical determinants of his readings. Within the history of de Man's own career, the
itinerary stated here follows the program outlined at the end of "Literary History and Literary Modernity." There de Man argued that though
the "need to revise the foundations of literary history may seem like a
desperately vast undertaking," especially "if we contend that literary
history could in fact be paradigmatic for history in general," solace is
found in the recognition that "all the directives we have formulated as
guidelines for a literary history are more or less taken for granted
when we are engaged in the much more humble task of reading and
understanding a literary text" (BI 165). Literary history takes place in
the figural dynamics of the text, particularly in the tropes and allegories
of its aporias, so that attention to the aporias becomes the most authentic
approach to how suspension, bridging, meaning, and narration come
into being, bringing history and the subject along with them. This

---

12. The paradox between generational imperatives and the lessons of close reading,
as well as most of the generalizations on the problems of writing a history of romanticism,
appears summarized in de Man's Introduction to a special issue of *Studies in Romanticism*
18 (1979): 495–99.

process will in fact be the chief concern of *Allegories of Reading*, as it is of de Man's reading of romanticism. One must then take quite ironically, if still seriously, the announcement in the preface to *The Rhetoric of Romanticism* that "except for some passing allusions, *Allegories of Reading* is in no way a book about romanticism or its heritage" (RR vii). At least one chapter, "Genesis and Genealogy (Nietzsche)," explicitly addresses the problem of literary history in the case of romanticism.

De Man's admission of a genealogical imperative in the history of his own book comes as a surprise in light of his recurrent critique of the genetic fallacy. De Man takes indirect aim at Harold Bloom in attacking critics who see romanticism as a Hegelian narrative of "the emergence of a true Subject" (AR 80). In contrast, de Man undertakes to read Nietzsche's *Birth of Tragedy* in "the clarity of a new ironic light" that will expose the "hollow" at the core of geneticism and undo the biological and familial models used by Bloom and others to conceive literary history. This chapter bears close scrutiny, for its investigation of Nietzsche's historiography and Nietzsche's voice often serves to mirror de Man's own problems. The displacement of articulate authorial consciousness by a figure of rhetorical prosopopeia in Nietzsche's (and de Man's) text will cause great difficulties for the subject of literary history.

"Genesis and Genealogy" begins with a four-page theoretical preface challenging "the genetic pattern of literary history and of literary texts" used in most descriptions of romanticism. Repeating his now familiar criticism of the "detour or flight from language" by scholars who "feel more at home with problems of psychology or of historiography," de Man charges that the recourse to the "nonlinguistic referential models used in literary history" is motivated by the analysts' anxiety before the "very semiological properties" of the text—especially its aporias. These are suspended or bridged by metaphors of representation and narratives of dialectical progress. "Romanticism," de Man notes, "is itself generally understood as the passage from a mimetic to a genetic concept of art and literature, from a Platonic to a Hegelian model of the universe" (AR 79). Theorists of romanticism or postromanticism, in other words, project their own genetic methodology onto the textual structures and literary history of romanticism, resolving its aporias into certain reassuring narratives. For de Man, the genetic model recalls and totalizes temporality into a presence of meaning, and is inseparable from the paradigms of memory, perception, imagination, and consciousness so frequently thematized in romantic texts and criticism. Consciousness is the agency (and agon) of genealogy. The traditional portrayal of romanticism as an onto-theology of recollected presence united in a genetic whole "is caught in a non-dialectical notion of a subject-object dichotomy, revealing a more or less deliberate avoidance of the moment of negation that coincides, for Hegel, with the emergence of a true Subject." Ironically, the pursuit of Hegelian negation may end up "with an altogether un-Hegelian concept of the subject as an irrational, unmediated experience of particular selfhood (or loss of selfhood)." The "true Subject" returns, however negatively, in the narrative of this loss—this alienation and end of Man—which (even in the work of Foucault) invokes the metaphorics of genealogy: "The allegorization and ironization of the organic model," concludes de Man, "leaves the genetic pattern unaffected" (AR 80).[13]

This structure of mere reversal holds true for literary histories that try to situate romanticism within "an organically determined view of literary history." In this view romanticism appears either as a "high point" and "splendor" followed by a "decay" of "apocalyptic proportions" or as "a moment of extreme delusion" outgrown in the "assertion of a new modernity." The "deconstruction" of the "organic model" creates "radical discontinuities and disrupts the linearity of the temporal process to such extent that no sequence of actual events or no particular subject could ever acquire, by itself, full historical meaning" (AR 80–81). Here de Man repeats the argument of "Literary History and Literary Modernity," which (again using Nietzsche) has disputed the narrative granting "modernity" its teleological finality: modernity is instead the eternal recurrence of difference. Any narrative, however "deconstructive," which simply reverses the traditional poles but still arranges them as a sequence from absence to presence or vice versa is not truly historical, or literary, since it forecloses textual and temporal aporias through the imposition of an a priori paradigm of self-identical essences.

De Man's close reading of romantic texts discloses the extent to which they themselves resist such foreclosure and geneticism. Consequently, if "the so-called Romantics came closer than we do to undermining the absolute authority of this system . . . one may well wonder what kind of historiography could do justice to the phenomenon of Romanticism." De Man's antipathy to modernity does not lie so much in a perception of its unorginality as in his resistance to the systems of "absolute authority" that underwrite its ideological formations. Romanticism "would then be the movement that challenges the genetic principle which necessarily underlies all historical narrative. The ultimate test or 'proof' of the fact that Romanticism puts the genetic pattern of history in question would then be the impossibility of writing a history of Romanticism"

13. De Man thus continues the critique of his 1960 essay, "The Intentional Structure of the Romantic Image," which attacked the organic and naturalist readings of romantic metaphor and suggested an alternative, Heideggerean account of division within poetic language (RR 1–17).

(AR 82). This climactic "impossibility," de Man wryly observes, is confirmed by the "abundant bibliography that exists on the subject," presumably including Wellek and Warren's futile discussion of romanticism and the problems it raises for the concept of literary periods. Current enthusiasms for the differences made by "modernism" or "postmodernism" in transcending the legacy of romanticism, de Man implies, display their blindness in reading their own insights as successful supplements to the supposed grandeur or naïveté of their precursors. Moreover, this "impossibility" would also short-circuit any attempt to use romanticism as the authorizing source of modernity's totalitarian discourses.

De Man pursues these theses through an intricate dissection of Nietzsche's *The Birth of Tragedy,* a text whose very title suggests its involvement in genealogy even as its author voices "the radical rejection of the genetic teleology associated with Romantic idealism" (AR 82). Readers will recall Nietzsche's argument that Greek tragedy descends from Dionysian ritual, that Apollo and Socrates are reductive aesthetic declensions from Dionysian power, and that Wagner and modernity promise a rebirth of Dionysian plenitude. De Man finds, however, that "the diachronic, successive structure of *The Birth of Tragedy* is in fact an illusion," for he shows that "whenever an art form is being discussed, the three modes represented by Dionysos, Apollo, and Socrates are always simultaneously present and that it is impossible to mention one of them without at least implying the others" (AR 85). This synchronicity is rewritten by geneticism, which recasts the protagonists in parental or other genealogical metaphors. Ultimately the teleology is from the decadence of Socratic epistemology to the modern rebirth of art, which Nietzsche advocates in pronouncements of a thoroughly epistemological kind.

Nietzsche's double writing does not bother de Man, and in his commentary we hear a rebuttal to his own critics: "One cannot hold against him the apparent contradiction of using a rational mode of discourse—which he, in fact, never abandoned—in order to prove the inadequacy of this discourse." "Nietzsche is entirely in control of this problem," says de Man, which he takes over from Kant and Schopenauer, whom Nietzsche calls those "great men . . . able to use the devices of science itself in order to reveal the limits and relativity of all knowledge" (AR 86). This internal division of epistemology, however, forms only a paradox and "logical complication" that as yet remains within genealogy: "the ambivalence of the epistemological movement, as the critical undoer of its own claim at universal veracity, is represented as a genetic development from the Alexandrian to the truly modern man, and undoubtedly owes some of its persuasiveness to the narrative, sequential mode of presentation. It does not however, in this text, put this mode explicitly or implicitly into question" (AR 86). Critics have often pin-pointed exactly this "ambivalence of the epistemological moment" in de Man's own writing and wondered naïvely how logic could logically question itself, though nothing is more logical, or historically deter-mined, than such questioning.

Ambivalence does not yield a radical critique. Something more must be considered if geneticism is to be thwarted, whether in Nietzsche's or de Man's analysis. If we seek "an underlying, deeper pattern of valorization that confers genetic coherence and continuity upon the text and that transcends the thematics of the Apollo/Dionysos or the Socrates/Dionysos dialectic," we discover that "Nietzsche [and de Man?] might be in the grip of a powerful assumption about the nature of language, bound to control his conceptual and rhetorical discourse regardless of whether the author is aware of it or not" (AR 87). De Man will use the question of literariness as a wedge to reopen the closures imposed by the machinery of thematics and historiography. In Nietz-sche's text "little is explicitly being said about the nature of literary language," and the "importance of language is consistently undercut" by a move "towards the suppression of text in favor of mime and symphonic music," or, in other words, from representation to presence (AR 87). This "dispossession of the word in favor of music" accords, notes de Man, with Derrida's description of logocentrism in *Of Gramma-tology*. Nietzsche's "melocentrism" refines "the claim that truth can be made present to man" and thus ironically "recovers the possibility of language to reach full and substantial meaning" (AR 88). Contemporary readings of Nietzsche's book, in fact, agree on its "logocentric ontology," but de Man's commentary hopes to displace even these decipherments by demonstrating *their* complicity in the genetic model and the greater rigorousness of Nietzsche's text. The "new Nietzsche" of poststructural-ism seems to be only a renovation of the modernist Nietzsche, still conceived genealogically, this time as the father and/or rebellious son of logocentrism (AR 90).

Nietzsche's chief theme is the Dionysian origin, and end, of art: "the priority of the musical, nonrepresentational language of Dionysos over the representational, graphic language of Apollo is beyond dispute" (AR 92). Yet this raises a question central to Heidegger and pursued by the deconstructors of phenomenology: why must the plenitude of Being eclipse itself in the limiting, delayed, and deferred forms of representa-tion? "Why then," asks de Man, "if all truth is on Dionysos's side, is Apollonian art not only possible but even necessary? Why the need for metaphorical appearance since the proper meaning is all that counts?" (AR 92). Nietzsche's answer is that Dionysian insight is "*tragic* insight," from which we are sheltered by "the protective nature of the Apollonian moment" (AR 93).

Nietzsche's own voice here does not speak the unmediated truth of Dionysos, however, but adopts an Apollonian mask: "It is time," notes de Man, "to start questioning the explicit, declarative statement of the text in terms of its own theatricality. The system of valorization that privileges Dionysos as the truth of the Apollonian appearance . . . reaches us through the medium of a strongly dramatized and individualized voice," a "harangue that combines the seductive power of a genetic narrative with the rhetorical complicity of a sermon" (AR 93).[14] As orator, Nietzsche manipulates the "I" and "we" to convince us that he "has our best interests at heart and we are guaranteed intellectual safety as long as we remain within the sheltering reach of his voice" (AR 94). This voice is the suspension bridge that transports the reader over the text's many digressive breaks and discontinuities. *The Birth of Tragedy* is also a drama, a spectacle of the undecidability between Dionysos and Apollo. Thus the book "is curiously ambivalent with regard to the main figures of its own discourse: the category of representation that underlies the narrative mode and the category of the subject that supports the all pervading hortatory voice" (AR 94). As a text, it cannot serve as the end, or origin, of a literary history grounded in Dionysian art or epistemological representation, since the difference between the two cannot be articulated without irony.

Nietzsche's aporia recurs structurally, as when he criticizes the use of the *deus ex machina* in Euripides to ground the origin and end of the drama. This recourse to a deity who guarantees "the credibility of the story" and the "reality of the mythological plot" is repeated in Nietzsche's own recourse to Dionysos and the plot of his return. *The Birth of Tragedy* is "a text based on the authority of a human voice that receives this authority from its allegiance to a quasi-divine figure" (AR 95). It should be clear by now that de Man's attunement to Nietzsche's voice continues his concern with the trope of prosopopeia, now overheard as Nietzsche's articulation of Dionysos. And in giving voice to this prosopopeia, de Man himself repeats the structure ironically, as the authority of his own voice stems from its rigorous allegiance to the return of Nietzsche, except that in place of a quasi-divinity we have a figure riven by aporia.

For Nietzsche betrays himself on the subject of music. Music had been

14. For an extraordinary and extended meditation along these lines, see Peter Sloterdijk, *Thinker on Stage: Nietzsche's Materialism*, trans. Jamie Owen Daniel (Minneapolis: University of Minnesota Press, 1989).

distinguished, and valorized, precisely on the basis of the difference between imitative realism and a pure art liberated from representation. But a "representational moment" reappears when we learn that the "tragic Dionysian insight is not, as for Rousseau, an absence of all meaning, but a meaning that we are unable to face for psychological or moral reasons" (AR 96). Subjective discourses (psychology and ethics) inform the knowledge motivating Dionysos's pure art. Only a will that represents the world to itself could feel such pathos or arrive at such a knowledge, such a will to music, and so representation and the subject remain intrinsic to the spectacle of their deconstruction, which operates through the seductions of rhetoric: "The authority of his voice has to legitimize an act by means of which the aporia of an unmediated representation, by itself a logical absurdity, would be suspended [aufgeh-oben]" (AR 96). Nietzsche's voice remains in the register of Hegel, though we overhear the dissonance of its sublation. Heidegger's criticism of the residual subjectivity in Nietzsche's philosophy seems to underlie de Man's discovery of Nietzsche's voice, except that de Man makes this return of the will a necessary feature of language rather than a matter of subjective or even historical choice. That is, whatever he thought he was doing, Nietzsche did not will to will; the ethical or psychological voices or registers are (like referentiality) unavoidable if aberrant features of language, not reflections or misrepresentations of Being.[15] De Man's voice speaks, in prosopopeia, of Rousseau, subject of his final chapters as he attempts to move his own deconstructions past the psychological and moral thematics of Nietzsche and toward the linguistics of the aporias these thematics suspend.

The Voice of Criticism

The construction of Allegories of Reading makes a mockery of the premises of literary history. The subtitle, Figural Language in Rousseau, Nietzsche, Rilke, and Proust, seems to promise a conventional chronological investigation of these literary figures in a narrative of tropology's increasing sophistication, perhaps reinforcing the view that sees (post)-modernism as an undoing of romantic theories of language. The table of contents, however, shows that we move backward in time, from Proust to Rousseau, ironically upsetting the genetic model. More dizzyingly, de Man has arranged his chapters into a series of increasingly fecund

15. See the chapter on de Man in J. Hillis Miller, The Ethics of Reading (New York: Columbia University Press, 1987), and the commentary on it by Norris (Paul de Man, chap. 4).

deconstructions, each generated by aporias of grammar and rhetoric and each emptying out yet another critical illusion, until the final chapter on Rousseau gives us the language machine as the genesis of all that we read. Historiographically, this recourse to Rousseau will parody again the return to Dionysos, since Rousseau will function as a deconstructive *deus ex machina* whose text discloses "*l'effet machinal*" of textuality (AR 294). Thus at the beginning of "Romanticism" we find the end of its subjective and narrative thematics, "as soon as the text is said not to be a figural body but a machine" (AR 299). *Allegories of Reading* is indeed not a history of romanticism but the demonstration of the impossibility of that history, especially when de Man tells us how much more radically Rousseau's text surpasses, in deconstructive rigor, the ambivalence of Nietzsche's: "Far from seeing language as an instrument in the service of a psychic energy, the possibility now arises that the entire construction of drives, substitutions, repressions, and representations is the aberrant, metaphorical correlative of the absolute randomness of language, prior to any figuration of meaning" (AR 299). It is this very passage in which Johnson discovers the dangling clause and anacoluthon of the grammatical subject. Who does this "seeing," and for whom does this possibility arise, when the subject and the narrative of progressive cognition have been suspended?

For "de Man," of course, who here constructs a prosopopeia of deconstructive authority—not as the absence of the subject but as the difference between Nietzsche and Rousseau, Nietzsche and de Man, Heidegger and de Man, Freud and Lacan and de Man. The asceticism of linguistic deconstruction before the "seduction" of psychologisms, historicisms, fictionalisms, and ontologisms is remarkable here, as elsewhere, in the severity and irony of de Man's resistance to grammatical or conceptual copulations. How allegorical, then, is the deconstruction of Nietzsche's celebration of Dionysos, god of the erotic, of union and desire? The strange cognitive and rhetorical status of de Man's prescriptions follows the methodological paradigm evolved in "Genesis and Genealogy": "the deconstruction does not occur between statements, as in a logical refutation or in a dialectic, but happens instead between, on the one hand, metalinguistic statements about the rhetorical nature of language and, on the other hand, a rhetorical praxis that puts these statements into a question" (AR 98). De Man's own "metalinguistic statements" about the priority of the language machine form an aporia with his rhetorical praxis of willfully denouncing the weakness of those who succumb to the temptations of reference, history, psychology, theme, and meaning. As in Nietzsche, this latter cognition, which is also represented as a moment of progress in the history of literary criticism, may be "translated into a statement," but "the authority of this second

statement can no longer be like that of the voice in the text when it is
read naïvely" (AR 99). After reading de Man's analysis of Nietzsche's
rhetoric, one should no longer underestimate the necessary theatrical-
ization of de Man's own voice in his cognitive moments. De Man's careful
placement of "naïvely" here (as elsewhere) mimics exactly, "ironically,"
the rhetorical recourse in Nietzsche to terms of ethical rigor and personal evaluation—to a rhetoric of subjects and their development
(strength, health, will, values, and so on). To borrow de Man's question,
who would dare admit, after such a passage, to not being one of the
happy few among the sophisticated critics? (AR 97).

   De Man continues by concluding that the "nonauthoritative secondary statement that results from the reading will have to be a statement
about the limitations of textual authority" (AR 99). It is this residual
statement that resists the totalitarianism of the genetic model, for it
cannot ground either a subject or a history of cognition. The myth of
Dionysos, on the other hand, is erotic genealogy *par excellence* and provides the allegory of the linguistic aporia of essence and appearance:
"what we have called the genetic pattern is precisely the possibility
of this bridge, of this translation . . . performed in the metaphorical
narrative by means of which Dionysos can enter into a world of appearances and still somehow remain Dionysos" (AR 101). The problematic
of de Man's own "textual authority" occurs self-reflexively here, for we
cannot defer infinitely the sexual allegory of this textual myth.

   Dionysos is a phallic fertility god whose ritual dismemberment and
resurrection offers yet another instance of suspension and *Aufhebung*.
Almost comically, de Man implies that Dionysos should have been more
of an ascetic, should have resisted the desire to "enter into a world of
appearances." Mistaking an aporia for a hymen, Dionysos puts his
character into the reproductive organs of time and appearance, and so
risks losing his fetishized identity. (The play on asceticism here and
elsewhere in de Man tropes the analysis of the ascetic priests in Nietzsche's *Genealogy of Morals*.) On closer inspection, the Dionysisan economy of essence and appearance, presence and representation, coincides
with the *fort/da* speculation of Freud's *Beyond the Pleasure Principle*, whose
castration metaphysics Derrida has playfully explicated in *The Post Card*.
In fact, de Man is "entirely in control of this problem" and can state it
with full thematic clarity in his climactic chapter on Rousseau: "Writing
always includes the moment of dispossession in favor of the arbitrary
power play of the signifier and from the point of view of the subject,
this can only be experienced as a dismemberment, a beheading or a
castration" (AR 296). The gender remarked in the signature "de Man"
appears at play. Only by withholding himself from representation could
Dionysos keep his head, but only by risking his essence in the play of

appearance could he become the truth of art and the origin of its organic genealogy. The difference between Dionysos and the priests of asceticism may not be a binary opposition, and thus one must wonder whether the asceticism of de Man's rigor is not implicated in its own rhetorical erotics. Should one listen naïvely to the seduction of Paul de Man?

"Contrary to common belief," writes de Man elsewhere, "literature is not the place where the unstable epistemology of metaphor is suspended by aesthetic pleasure, although the attempt is a constitutive moment of its system. It is rather the place where the possible convergence of rigor and pleasure is shown to be a delusion.[16] The "rigor" of literature lies in its incessant aporetics, which thwarts our desire to bridge or identify differences. Meaning, presence, and the self would each be the delusory products of such suspensions, and their deconstruction would interrupt the structure of historical narrative that depends on them for its motivation and articulation. "Whether one wishes it or not," wrote Bachelard, "metaphors seduce reason."[17] De Man's prophylactic rhetoric repeatedly cautions against succumbing to such seductions. For example, his resistance to a phenomenological criticism centered on a communion with authorial consciousness emerges in the choice of Proust and Rilke for deconstruction: "since the ostensible pathos of their tone and depth of their statement make them particularly resistant" to linguistic determinism, "one could argue that if *their* work yields to such a rhetorical scheme, the same would necessarily be true for writers whose rhetorical strategies are less hidden behind the seductive powers of identification" (AR ix). The seduction of Paul de Man, however, entails just such an identification for, as with Nietzsche, we are constantly invited to identify with de Man's voice, with the knowing prosopopeia of deconstructive authority. The narrative of *Allegories of Reading* depends on this seductive identification, even as the grammar of its reading and the rhetoric of its injunctions forbid such copulation.

The "relapse into the seductions of metaphor is inevitable" anytime "needs" are spoken of, including the need for rigor: "Needs reenter the literary discourse as the aberrant proper meaning of metaphors *against* which the allegory constitutes itself," a formula that informs de Man's book (AR 210). In resistance to the pleasure principle of rhetoric, we

16. "The Epistemology of Metaphor," in *On Metaphor,* ed. Sheldon Sacks (Chicago: University of Chicago Press, 1979), p. 28. This essay also treats the figure of prosopopeia quite suggestively.

17. Gaston Bachelard, *La Formation de l'esprit scientifique* (Paris: Vrin, 1938), p. 78. Derrida quotes this passage in his discussion of Bachelard's metaphorology, in "White Mythology: Metaphor in the Text of Philosophy," *Margins of Philosophy* (Chicago: University of Chicago Press, 1982), p. 259.

adhere to an ironic reality principle that defends against the "seductive"
"fantasies about the adequation of sign to meaning" (AR 262). Here the
Derridean critique of Saussure becomes a parody of our attempt to
preserve critical identity in a chaste deconstructive epistemology of
differences, as if no desire excited such rigor. De Man's book opens
with a question that figures, in its tropes rather than its grammar, the
work of eros (or errors) that his readings disengage: "Does the metaphor
of reading really unite outer meaning with inner understanding, action
with reflection, into one single totality?" (AR 13). Or should the resistance to seductive identifications compel a method of *hermeneuticus interruptus,* reading and literary history as the rigorous frustration of desire?
(De Man may be seriously rewriting Freud's *Civilization and Its Discontents.*)

   "To the extent that metaphor can be thought of as a language of
desire and as a means to recover what is absent," de Mans warns, "it is
essentially anti-poetic," for it suspends or provides an intercourse that
momentarily crosses the division inherent in language and Being (AR
47). Yet de Man's master trope of prosopopeia would seem inseparable
from the dialectics of desire, since it performs the imaginative function
of ascribing subjectivity to the other and thereby makes poetry—and
perhaps criticism—out of identification with another. One might, in the
last instance, also consider the politico-historical determination of this
defense against the seduction of metaphor in light of de Man's previously quoted assertion that what "we call ideology is precisely the
confusion of linguistic with natural reality." Ideology becomes the siren
song of the politics of totality, and prosopopeia a term for the interpella-
tion of the subject.

   According to de Man, even self-reflexive texts that engage in free-
(or endlessly fore-) play endanger our composure: "when literature
seduces us with the freedom of its figural combinations, so much airier
and lighter than the labored constructs of concepts, it is not the less
deceitful because it asserts its own deceitful purposes" (AR 115). De
Man's calculated rhetoric figures language as a seductress whose undecidable provocations increase her authority and heighten the impotence
of man's ambivalence. To make explicit what Derrida has called the
"woman *is* truth" economy of epistemology and castration, we might
say that de Man reminds us not to trust even the self-confessions of that
whore who is language (or, in other versions, who is politics or mass
culture). "Woman, in the text of phallogocentrism," Derrida observes,
"is but one name for that untruth of truth."[18] The masculine tropology

   18. Jacques Derrida, *Spurs: Nietzsche's Styles/Eperons: Les styles de Nietzsche,* trans. Barbara
Harlow (Chicago: University of Chicago Press, 1979), p. 51.

of de Man's literary theory shows up again in the following formulation: "A concatenation of the aesthetic with the meaning-producing powers of language is a strong temptation to the mind but, precisely for that reason, it also opens up a Pandora's box. The aesthetic is, by definition, a seductive notion that appeals to the pleasure principle, a eudaemonic judgment that can displace and conceal values of truth and falsehood likely to be more resilient to desire than values of pleasure and pain" (RT 64). The metaphors of "Pandora's box," "temptation," and seduction belong to the recognizable narratives of male sexuality, which are here projected on to the story of the fall into figurative language. Are sexual tropes determinant of linguistic theories, or, as de Man would have it, are sexual themes the aberrant effects of linguistics problems? The double writing of de Man's rhetoric contains an ironic identification, since in giving voice to language's wiles he himself becomes a figure for her: is de Man any the less deceitful because he asserts the deceitful purpose of language? What can we make of de Man when he writes like a woman?

An answer perhaps appears in de Man's chapter on Rousseau's *Julie*, which concerns, thematically and analytically, the relation of letters to seduction. As the title indicates, this section presents a theory of allegory, and offers self-reflexively the most detailed, point-by-point correspondence to the construction of *Allegories of Reading*. The two-part structure of *Julie* will parallel the narrative mode of de Manian deconstruction, which moves from the undoing of figural identifications to the allegory of reading, wherein the mistakes of the first part are repeated, however ironically, in the knowledge of the second. "Naïvely reductive readers" as well as "critics most astutely responsive to the seduction of Rousseau's reflective inwardness" have failed to detect that love does not act as the dialectical agent of failed or achieved unity in *Julie*, whether of an erotic or theological kind (AR 190, 192). All the thematics in the novel, including love, obscure its radical message about "the problematics of reading." "The letters are no invitation to a shared erotic or passionate experience," argues de Man (AR 194). As in Rousseau's *Essay on the Origins of Language* they depict "human passions (fear, pity, love, freedom) but these passions all have, by definition, the self-deceiving structure . . . that forces the narrative of their deconstruction to unfold" (AR 197). Rather than operating as the origin of language, desire functions retrospectively as a *reading* of aporias: "Like 'man' [de Man?], 'love' is a figure that disfigures, a metaphor that confers the illusion of a proper meaning to a suspended, open semantic structure" (AR 198).

De Man makes Julie herself into the allegory of the deconstructive author/reader. According to de Man, letters are never "an effective act of seduction" for Julie (AR 193, n. 20). Julie delivers the ascetic's

"antihedonistic sermon" against the substitution of "pleasure for love";
as with Nietzsche (and de Man), "her own plea is nevertheless dependent
on the seductive vocabulary of pleasure," though this "does not permit
us to discard the statement" of error (AR 210, n. 31). In a manner de
Man ascribed to numerous literary critics in his previous book, "at the
moment when Julie acquires a maximum of insight, the control over
the rhetoric of her own discourse is lost, for us as well as for her" (AR
216). Having authored a deconstruction of the figural language of eros,
Julie "at once repeats the notions she has just denounced as errors,"
her theological morality and eroticism drawing on all the discredited
language of her affair with Saint-Preux (AR 217). De Man applauds the
"rigor of Julie's insight into the aberrations of 'romantic' love" and
then delivers this self-reflexive dictum: "The problem is not that Julie
remains mystified, but that a totally enlightened language, regardless
of whether it conceives of itself as a consciousness or not, is unable to
control the recurrence, in its readers as well as in itself, of the errors it
exposes. Julie, the best conceivable critical reader, is apparently unable
to read her own critical text critically" (AR 219, n. 36). Reading and
writing like Julie, de Man repeats her errors as an allegory of the eros/
errors that tempt deconstruction to a seductive romance with "a totally
enlightened language." De Man's reading of Rousseau turns out to be
a critique of the Enlightenment and its legacy. (De Man, by the way,
seems to be having great fun with Lacan's assertion that the unconscious
is structured like a language.)

De Man's identification with Julie is troped by his prosopopeia of
Rousseau himself, specifically in the chapter's long introductory analysis
of the indeterminacy of authorship discussed in *Julie's* second Preface.
Is *Julie* pure fiction, Rousseau is asked, or a found document with actual
historical referents? De Man delights to discover that Rousseau himself
doesn't know: "Who could decide whether or not I am caught in the
same doubt in which you find yourself: Whether all this mystery and
evasion is not a feint in order to hide my own ignorance of what you
are trying to discover?" (quoted in AR 200). (How uncannily this now
addresses de Man's own readers.) The "referential" mode of the text is
suspended by this undecidability, and so the elusive author "is not
initially a subject but the metaphor for readability in general" (AR 202).
The undoing of the figure of the author prepares the way for the
transition from a deconstruction of metaphor to an allegory of reading
(or of its impossibility). Rousseau's statement "undoes both the intelligi-
bility and the seductiveness that the fiction owed to its negative rigor"
(AR 205). In moving from knowledge to "rigor," we have moved from
epistemology to rhetoric, from the constative to the performative, from
cognition to ethics: "The ethical category is imperative . . . to the extent

that it is linguistic and not subjective." This new morality, however, "does not result from a transcendental imperative but is the referential (and therefore unreliable) version of a linguistic confusion" (AR 206).

Here one reads the allegory of the "ethics" of deconstructive "rigor," which operates in the suspension of transcendental imperatives. The ensuing generalizations make it impossible to distinguish de Man from Rousseau: they are everywhere conditioned by the rhetorical and sub-jective value-terms of conscious awareness and enlightened self-re-straint, so that the genealogical "progression" from the innocence of romanticism to the skepticism of deconstruction is rendered untenable:

> From the first, one has to expect a mental attitude that is highly self-reflective, persistently aware of the discrepancies between the formal and the semantic properties of language, fully responsive to the seductive plays of the signifier yet wary of their powers of semantic aberration. It supposes an austere analytical rigor that pursues its labors regardless of the conse-quences, the most rigorous gesture of all being that by which the writer severs himself from the intelligibility of his own text. (AR 207)

Just as de Man's ascetic reading of *Julie* depended on his identification with its figures and his response to "the seductive plays of the signifier," so Rousseau's subversion of authorial ontology also entails a "persistence of the referential moment." Rousseau's

> radical critique of referential meaning never implied that the referential function of language could in any way be avoided, bracketed, or reduced to being just one contingent linguistic property among others, as is postu-lated, for example, in contemporary semiology which, like all post-Kantian formalisms, could not exist without this postulate. Rousseau never allows for a "purely" aesthetic reading in which the referential determination would remain suspended or be nonexistent.
>
>   . . . Suspended meaning is not, for him, disinterested play, but always a threat or a challenge. The loss of faith in the reliability of referential meaning does not free the language from referential and tropological coercion, since the assertion of the loss is itself governed by considerations of truth and falsehood that, as such, are necessarily referential. (AR 207–08)

One need only read such passages carefully to see how resolutely op-posed de Man's position is to any naïvely Kantian aestheticism, and how little his argument conforms to the accusations of formalism and ahistoricity made against him. The real aesthetes are those "historicists" who somehow can conceive a realm of pure art or trope radically hetero-geneous from any function of reference, or vice versa. Readers seeking protocols by which to decipher the reference of de Man's texts to their historical conditions of production could find no better passage for guidance. The suspension of mimetic and aesthetic modes of reference constitutes "a threat or a challenge" to specific versions of history, politics, and language, and as such is never reducible to "disinterested play." The end(s) of man never cease to concern de Man.

The deconstructive allegories of authorship and reference again intersect with the illusions of temporality: "A recurrent theme exalting or denouncing the seductions of the moment runs through the book" (Rousseau's, that is) (AR 214). Here the seduction would be of a moment in which duration, presence, inwardness, unity, and fulfillment would coalesce and thus make history (at least of a certain kind) possible. Since "desire is organized around the moment that separates possession from its opposite," passion and presence will always depend on and undo each other: "The ambiguity fully appears when consciousness, as duration, has to realize that it can come into being only at the expense of the passion that produced the experience of inwardness in the first place" (AR 215). Already in Rousseau we have the unhappy consciousness, which appears to be the eternal recurrence of Dionysos's tragedy. Passionate presence *is* prosopopeia. The aporetic structure of the relation between temporality and signification suggests why history is always literary, and vice versa. It is this thesis that justifies de Man's somewhat puzzling claim at the opening of the chapter on *Julie*. There he announces his challenge to the "historical investment" critics have made in Rousseau as the father of romanticism, symbolism, and modernism. The rereading he offers of *Julie* may prompt a "parallel rereading of texts assumed to belong to the genealogical line" of Rousseau—a rereading that will bankrupt our confidence in the "existence of historical 'lines' " themselves. It is our investment in a specific ideology of the "historical," suggests de Man, that explains our resistance to such a rereading (AR 190).

For de Man, literary history is a supplementary series of prosopoeial acts whose grammars of pronouncement always carry with them the traces of their rhetorical seductions. As prosopopeia, the telling of literary history becomes a narrative of what desire and cognition give voice to in their suspensions of conflict. The referentiality of these voices and narratives is no less essential than is their unreliability. History, then, *takes place* as a response, or responsibility, to the demanding calls of those aporias that must be addressed even as they escape determination. The subject is the instance or agency of address and response, and as such cannot govern the system or be erased from it. Thus history is always already, in de Man's sense, rhetorical, which is another way of describing the subject's condition as cast or thrown into a condition it hasn't authored but must rewrite. Whether in subject or text or history, one overhears a voice of reading supplementing what it took to be the aporia it inherits from time, and in deconstructing previous metaphors of understanding, the discourse generates other abysses that are in turn crossed by other epistemological romances. History—literary, political, or otherwise—would be unthinkable without the inevitable and willful seduction of the writer and the reader, speaker and addressee, by the illusions of figurative language and their social correspondences. As prosopoeial genealogy, literary history unfolds a network of textual voices that are always read for their eros as well as their errors, until the difference between these strategies itself becomes undecidable.

The voice of the author returns: "Ego recuperation," says de Man, may be an effect "accomplished by the rigor with which the discourse deconstructs the very notion of the self. The originator of this discourse . . . remains . . . a center of authority to the extent that the very destructiveness of his ascetic reading testifies to the validity of his interpretation" (AR 173–74). Unless we intend to take this final allusion as confirmation of de Man's identification with E. D. Hirsch, we must overhear de Man's own willingness to be seduced, as well as seducer. Or, in looking for de Man, we might seek the figure who feels some guilt for his seduction and who, like Rousseau, cannot make excuses without also inscribing the story of the rhetoric which can never be forgiven.

It is often claimed that Paul de Man was the most influential practitioner of deconstruction in America. By now the oddity of his being so described should be striking. Paul de Man was a late emigrant to America, and to deconstruction. Under circumstances that still remain obscure, de Man permanently left behind his home and family to start a new life in the United States after World War II; clearly he had personal, political, and intellectual reasons for doing so. Sorting out the exact substance of these motives and the balance among them can only be a speculative endeavor. Though de Man did translate *Moby-Dick* into Flemish during the last years of the war, he appears never to have written an essay on an American writer or text, other than his commentaries on the New Criticism. Christopher Norris reads de Man's "passage to America" as "a turning point" in his intellectual history, a transition from the "Eurocentric standpoint" of his youth to an open, pragmatic skepticism that took readily to the concern of the New Criticism with close reading (174). The Eurocentric bias of de Man's interests, however, shows up in the basically small and unchanged list of texts that concerned him throughout his career: German, French, and English romantics, their modernist successors, and related theorists.

De Man himself spoke of the contrast between academic life in Europe, which "is of course much closer to ideological and political questions" and in the States, where "one is much closer to professional questions" (RT 115). Although his itinerary might be seen as one from politics to linguistics and back again, he claims that questions of ideology and politics were "always uppermost" in his mind: "I have always maintained that one could approach the problems of ideology and by extension the problems of politics only on the basis of critical-linguistic analysis, which had to be done in its own terms, in the medium of language, and I felt I could approach those problems only after having achieved a certain control over those questions" (RT 121). De Man's life in America, his tutelage to New Criticism, his adaptation of Derrida's deconstruction, these comprise a kind of life in exile from ideology and politics, though these latter realms remain, like the exile's native land, "always uppermost" in mind. The discourse on literary theory produced by de Man then turns out to be an allegory of a cultural criticism that never left its home in the European catastrophe of ideology and politics from 1930 to 1945. Shoshana Felman even reads *Moby-Dick* as an allegory of de Man's torn consciousness: "De Man's future is foreshadowed, enigmatically and paradoxically, by *both* the destinies of Ahab and of Ishmael. He at the same time dies as Ahab and survives as Ishmael . . . what survives is not the memory of Ahab [who had chased the totalitarian whale, which he both loved and despised] but the witnessing by Ishmael," who only lives to tell the tragic tale in allegory. No *literal* account, speculates Felman, could excuse or express the holocaust of Nazism; Paul de Man's "silence" stood allegorical witness to a division in historical being which language could never adequately represent.[19] One cannot overlook, however, that even as some things could never be given words, some things should have been said, and were never uttered. Like Heidegger, Paul de Man condemned himself with his own silence.

What made for de Man's popularity and leading role in deconstruction in America? There are many answers, but one in particular follows from the above story of exile and allegory. De Man and deconstruction gained notoriety in the United States at the end of the 1960s, precisely during a time of ideological and political upheaval. With Nixon and Watergate, and later with the ascent of Reaganism, the collapse and failure of the Left in the United States brought to dismal conclusion the hopes of the 1960s. The generation of young academic literary intellectuals attracted to de Man's work may have found in it their own therapeutic exile from America, though like him they may always have had ideology and politics uppermost in mind. Reversing de Man's Atlantic crossing to New Criticism, they abandoned Wellek and Warren for

19. Felman, "Paul de Man's Silence," pp. 718–19.

the news from the front in Paris. Unlike some commentators, and probably out of my own autobiographical involvement in this genealogy, I do not see the deconstructive exile of American criticism as escapist and irresponsible. Instead I am convinced of the relative justness of de Man's claim that a sojourn in "linguistic-critical analysis" is necessary in order to rethink the very terms, ontology, and performance of ideology and politics, especially if the naïveté of the 1960s is to be avoided in the future. The passage of American criticism during the 1980s and 1990s "back" to questions of history and power should not, does not, signal the abandonment of de Man and deconstruction, though their texts will now be translated to quite different locales of struggle. Even as this movement (*pas de méthode*) repeats and reverses de Man's, it marks the places in his work, and our own, where an unreadable silence about the "other" nonetheless commands our response.

CHAPTER THREE

Freud and the Death
of Autobiography

But the *goal* is . . . the point where knowledge no longer needs to go beyond itself, where knowledge finds itself, where Notion corresponds to object and object to Notion. Hence the progress towards this goal is also unhalting, and short of it no satisfaction is to be found at any of the stations on the way. Whatever is confined within the limits of a natural life cannot by its own efforts go beyond its immediate existence; but it is driven beyond it by something else, and this uprooting entails its death. Consciousness, however, is explicitly the *Notion* of itself. Hence it is something that goes beyond limits, and since these limits are its own, it is something that goes beyond itself.
—Hegel, *Phenomenology of Spirit*

Death alone allows me to grasp what I want to attain; it exists in words as the only way they can have meaning. Without death, everything would sink into absurdity, and nothingness.
—Maurice Blanchot, "Literature and the Right to Death"

We can assume that any theory of the subject has always been appropriated by the "masculine."
—Luce Irigaray, *Speculum of the Other Woman*

Paul de Man's claim, in *Allegories of Reading,* that the psychological elements of Rousseau's *Confessions* are the aberrant products of the machinery of language seems to distance him from Derrida and American deconstructionists who keep returning to Freud. One might conflate de Man's analysis with the linguistic turn in deconstructive or Lacanian readings of Freud, but this would paper over a substantial difference of emphasis. Though de Man borrows ironically from Freud's lexicon, he never writes extensively about him; literary theory precedes any theory of the subject. For de Man, the unconscious is not structured *like* a language, it *is* language, or one could say that the unconscious is one of language's more seductive effects. In the work of Derrida and others the referents of psychoanalysis (desire, sexuality, the unconscious) maintain a more persistent, if disseminated, profile. What does join de Man and Derrida is a common interest in exploring what I shall call *disciplinary self-reflexivity*. This notion should not immediately be reduced to the thesis that texts deconstruct themselves, or that texts tell the allegories of the subjects who write them, or that the power politics of disciplines is the true story behind the text. Though all three play a part in the economy of textual production and commentary, no one of them holds a privileged place as final determinant. Indeed it may be the irreducible gap between these narratives which motivates the construction of a text's bridges toward meaning. De Man's work can be cited as example since he ironically turns literary theory into a reflection on its own impossibility, mediates his personal history through textual structures, and challenges the forms of ideology and disciplinary authority (disciplining his own authority in the process). Our ability to interpret de Man in these ways is enabled by the kind of speculation Derrida performs on Freud in *The Post Card*. Derrida simultaneously unravels each of these three threads of determination (and more) in his close reading of the narrative self-reflexivity, personal anxiety, and disciplinary desire of *Beyond the Pleasure Principle*. His attempt to follow the steps of the psychoanalytic movement leads into a maze of speculations on the institutional agency of the "auto-bio-graphical."

Psychoanalysis and the Address of Speculation

Psychoanalysis is the only discipline in the human sciences whose movement began, and in some sense continues, as a sustained act of autobiographical reflection. No understanding of its principles or history can be separated from a consideration of Freud's own project of self-analysis, which began in earnest in the summer and fall of 1897 and supplied vital materials for so many of Freud's texts. "From the *Letters to Fliess* to *The Interpretation of Dreams*," notes Shoshana Felman, "what Freud is instituting is a radically new way of writing one's autobiography, by transforming personal narration into a path-breaking theoretical discovery."[1] In the second Preface (1908) to his dream book, Freud wrote: "It was, I found, a portion of my own

1. Shoshana Felman, "Beyond Oedipus: The Specimen Story of Psychoanalysis," in *Lacan and Narration: The Psychoanalytic Difference in Narrative Theory*, ed. Robert Con Davis (Baltimore: Johns Hopkins University Press, 1983), p. 1022.

self-analysis, my reaction to my father's death—that is to say, to the most important event, the most poignant loss, of a man's life."[2] "In Freud's later work," observes Steven Marcus, "autobiographical examples are rarer."[3] This is true of autobiographical reflections of the literal kind, though even these are more frequent than Marcus implies. What his observation overlooks is that psychoanalysis changes where and how the "autobiographical" *takes place,* since it changes fundamentally how we conceive of the self, of writing, and of the movements of institutional discourse.

Psychoanalysis encourages us to seek the traces of self-analysis where they seem least immediately evident, where they take place in movements of displacement. Since recurrent self-analysis was stipulated by Freud as a necessary condition of the practicing analyst's career, one might look to where and how that self-analysis informs Freud's technical or philosophic writings. In fact, the mature Freud's movement back and forth between "scientific" and "metapsychological" writings has its roots in the youthful Freud's "strong attraction towards speculation," a tendency he later felt compelled to "ruthlessly" check in favor of rational and scientific inquiry.[4] In his *Autobiographical Study* (1925), Freud declares that "neither at that time [his youth], nor indeed in my later life, did I feel any particular predilection for the career of a doctor. I was moved, rather, by a sort of curiosity, which was, however, directed more towards human concerns than towards natural objects" (SE 20: 8). Two years later he declared that "the triumph of my life lies in my having, after a long and roundabout journey, found my way back to my earliest path. . . . In my youth I felt an overpowering need to understand something of the riddles of the world in which we live and perhaps even to contribute something to their solutions" (SE 20: 253).[5] The ambivalence Freud feels when faced with the choice between the path-

2. Sigmund Freud, *The Interpretation of Dreams,* in *The Standard Edition of the Complete Psychological Works of Sigmund Freud,* ed. James Strachey, 24 vols. (London: Hogarth Press, 1953–74), 4: xxvi. Subsequent references to Freud's works are to this edition, abbreviated and cited parenthetically by volume and page.

3. Sigmund Freud, *The Origins of Psychoanalysis: Letters to Wilhelm Fliess,* ed. Marie Bonaparte et al., introductory essay by Steven Marcus (New York: Basic, 1954), p. 30.

4. Ernest Jones, *The Life and Work of Sigmund Freud,* 3 vols. (New York: Basic, 1957), 1: 29.

5. In *Beyond the Pleasure Principle,* Freud writes: "The repressed instinct never ceases to strive for complete satisfaction, which would consist in the repetition of a primary experience of satisfaction. No substitutive or reactive formations and no sublimations will suffice to remove the repressed instinct's persisting tension; and it is the difference in amount between the pleasure of satisfaction which is *demanded* and that which is actually achieved that provides the driving factor which will permit of no halting at any position attained. . . . [T]he backward path that leads to complete satisfaction is as a rule obstructed by the resistances which maintain the repressions" (SE 18: 42).

For relevant accounts and commentary, see Jones, *Sigmund Freud,* 1: 27–35; Philip Rieff, *Freud: The Mind of the Moralist* (Chicago: University of Chicago Press, 1979), pp.

ways of science and speculation informs the development of psychoanalysis as a discipline, structures its movement and the subsequent debate over whether it is an empirical, philosophical, or even imaginative or fictional endeavor. Uncertainty over the *genre* of psychoanalysis is inseparable from the story of its founder's identity formations.

The radical contribution of psychoanalysis to the theory of autobiography lies in the way its approach to human identity can move us beyond the dichotomy between scientific empiricism and imaginative speculation that so haunted Freud. Psychoanalysis argues that we are not what we are—that our empirical selves are actors in a script whose authorship is essentially unconscious, on both a personal and a cultural level. Human identity turns out to be speculation *par excellence*, an image formed as a reflective compromise between wishes and defenses that engage in a ceaseless struggle for ascendancy. That struggle, so evident in Freud's own self-assessments, lies at the heart of the theory of the libido and its "economy" that psychoanalysis elaborates. Likewise the theories of dream work and of symptom formation argue that the body and its actions become the self's lexicon for expression, a set of metaphors utilized in self-discourse (as in the gestures of the hysteric or in everyday slips of the tongue). The split between body and soul, or empiric and speculative, returns in the postulate of the unconscious and its fantasies. Contrary to popular impression, psychoanalysis does not portray humanity as determined by its physical drives; the theory of neurosis is founded on the opposite assertion—that unreal events, fantasies and desires, are what make us ill, and that our actions are determined by metapsychological conflicts.[6]

After Freud, autobiography is the tale not of things done but of meanings made and unmade; every action is a symptom, every statement a symbol, every narrative a dream of desire. In the analytic treatment, the subject's autobiography is elicited by the analyst, who participates dialogically in the construction of past events and present significances. This *mise-en-scène,* as Freud discovered through the phenomenon of transference, may constitute a "writing" about the subject's character more significant than the "actual" incidents, referents, or narrated primal scenes evoked in the process of the analysis. For psycho-

---

3–27; Ronald Clark, *Freud: The Man and the Cause* (New York: Random House, 1980), pp. 3–77; and Peter Gay, *Freud: A Life for Our Time* (New York: Norton, 1988), pp. 3–54.

6. See Jean Laplanche, *Life and Death in Psychoanalysis,* trans. Jeffrey Mehlman (Baltimore: Johns Hopkins University Press, 1976), pp. 16–30. A fundamental indeterminacy originates when sexuality detaches itself from the purely self-preservative instincts (e.g., the need for the mother's breast) and seeks satisfaction in other body areas or images that *symbolize* the object of desire. See the entries on "Anaclisis," "Sexual Instinct," and "Sexuality" in Jean Laplanche and J. B. Pontalis, *The Language of Psycho-Analysis,* trans. Donald Nicholson-Smith (New York: Norton, 1973).

analysis, then, the autobiographical subject takes place repetitively, inscribing itself in the history of desires and their representational management. Character formation, in turn, takes shape as a speculative
"investment" (cathexis) of desire. This economy cannot be circumscribed and limited to the analytic scene in the literal sense; the drama
of patient, analyst, transference, representation, and deferred interpretation is equally applicable to self-analysis, whether it appears in explicitly autobiographical texts or in the "impersonal" analyses of scientific,
technical, or metapsychological treatises, since these latter contain an
important spectacle of disciplinary self-reflexivity as well. In Freud's
case, the investment in the superego of rational science entailed an
incessant return of repressed speculations, repeated steps back to an
earlier path. The identification of the self with the process of symbolic
construction means that a text's way of composition, rather than its
narrative events or referents, may contain the "truer" autobiography,
since its ambivalent signifying movements enact the defenses and displacements that constitute the itinerary of identity and concept formation. Thus Freud's autobiography is not conventionally represented in
An Autobiographical Study, which slights the details of his life in favor of
a history and exposition of the psychoanalytic movement itself. To find
the latent text of Freud's "autobiography," one must turn to the early
letters to Fliess, to the massive effort at self-analysis in *The Interpretation
of Dreams,* to the metapsychological papers on narcissism and repression,
to the strange philosophizing of *Beyond the Pleasure Principle* and *The
Future of an Illusion,* and to such pieces of reminiscence as "Screen
Memories" and "A Disturbance of Memory on the Acropolis."

In the chapter of *The Post Card* titled "To Speculate—on 'Freud,' "
Jacques Derrida pursues just such a reading of the autobiographical
traces in *Beyond the Pleasure Principle,* where Freud's observations on his
grandson's game of *fort/da* (gone/there) are read as a self-reflexive text
about the movements of psychoanalytic speculation. The "description
of Ernst's serious game, of the eldest grandson of the grandfather of
psychoanalysis, *can no longer be read solely* as a theoretical argument"
but can also be read "as an autobiography of Freud. Not simply an
autobiography confiding his life to his own more or less testamentary
writing, but a more or less living description of his own writing, of his
way of writing what he writes, most notably *Beyond.* . . . The autobiography *of the writing* posits and deposits simultaneously, in the same movement, the psychoanalytic movement" (LCP 323—24/PC 303).[7] The play

7. Because Derrida's linguistic work in this text is so rich and untranslatable, I cite
page references for the French as well as the English editions, and shall be quoting from
each as follows: Jacques Derrida, *La Carte postale: De Socrate à Freud et au-delà* (Paris:

of presence and absence in writing, of theses continually advanced and withdrawn, is repeated in the grandson's dispatch and recall of a toy, a wooden reel; the "real life" recalled in writing must first be gone, past, dead, without meaning, for it to be made meaningful in the composition that restores it, immortalizes it, as something other than what it was, or something that wasn't itself until it returned. This is the resurrectional movement of the "bios" in autobiography, which will be repeated in the metapsychological speculation on the originality of the "death drive." The speculative investment in writing and death yields, ideally, a return, an immortality, since in the end the male autobiographer receives his letters back—his life and character back—as his own. This self-engenderment out of one's own death, this self-fathering through the death of a father, and of one's offspring, constitutes the mail/male system.

"How can an autobiographical writing," asks Derrida, "in the abyss of unterminated self-analysis [*auto-analyse*], give to a world-wide institution [psychoanalysis and its movement] *its* birth?" (LCP 325/PC 305). This movement, as followers of Oedipus's analysis might guess, involves paternal priority: "every autobiographical speculation, to the extent that it constitutes a legacy [*legs*] and the institution of a movement without limit, must take into account, in its very performance, the mortality of the legatees. As soon as there is mortality, death can in principle overtake one at every instant. The speculator then can survive the legatee, and this possibility is inscribed in the structure of the legacy, and even within this limit of self-analysis whose system supports the writing somewhat like a grid" (LCP 326/PC 305). Psychoanalysis lives on, in Freud's name, surviving his analytic progeny and marking his recurrent originality. While psychoanalytic speculation, especially on the death drive, may appear to be the most unempirical, the most errant of movements, it is in fact the most philosophical in the ideal sense, since it narrates an uncanny account of self-recovery and self-originality: "One then gives oneself one's own movement, one inherits from oneself for all time, the provisions are sufficient so that the ghost at least can always step up to the cashier. He will only have to pronounce a name guaranteeing a signature" (LCP 326/PC 305). From Augustine to Proust to Freud and beyond, the recollected man depends on the mortality of previous figures.

Flammarion, 1980), abbreviated LCP, and *The Post Card: From Socrates to Freud and Beyond*, trans. Alan Bass (Chicago: University of Chicago Press, 1987), abbreviated PC. See also Samuel Weber, *The Legend of Freud* (Minneapolis: University of Minnesota Press, 1982), pp. 8–31 and 146–64, on speculation, observation, and figurative language in Freud. On the deconstruction of the autobiographical genre elsewhere in Derrida's work, see Jane Marie Todd, "Autobiography and the Case of Signature: Reading Derrida's *Glas*," *Comparative Literature* 38 (Winter 1986): 1–19.

Derrida's reading of the movement of speculation in Freud plays seriously with Hegel's description of the movement of speculative philosophy in the *Phenomenology*.[8] Throughout Derrida's career, Hegel's dialectic has inspired numerous critiques and parodies aimed at tracing the derailment of the philosophical subject in its movement through negation back into the Absolute Notion of itself. Derrida's essay "Différance," for example, while owing much to the radical thinking about difference in Nietzsche and Heidegger, introduces us to a kind of self-negation or internal difference which cannot be sublated and cannot be the subject of knowledge.[9] Abstractly, this "differal" of the dialectical movement (comparable to de Man's "suspension") provides the paradigm for much of Derrida's work. In his reading of Freud, Derrida discerns a way of thinking that produces such a differal of the Hegelian project, so that psychoanalysis constitutes a privileged moment in the undoing of any history or notion of consciousness as the subject of knowledge. Derrida's reading posits psychoanalysis as a deconstruction of phenomenology and indicates the real extent to which Freud's project tropes Hegel's. For Hegel, the "royal road to Science" lies not through common sense but "exists solely in the self-movement of the Notion."[10] For Freud, "The interpretation of dreams is the royal road to a knowledge of the unconscious activities of the mind" (*Interpretation of Dreams*, SE 5: 608). For Derrida, Freud's "legs" stumble along the way through language, risking errancy as the condition of cognition, so that the movement of knowledge never quite arrives at its destination. The allusion here is to Heidegger's *Weg* with words, as in *Unterwegs zur Sprache*. Writes Derrida: "No *Weg* without *Unweg*: the detour does not overtake the road, but constitutes it, breaks open the path" (LCP 304/ PC 284). The royal road of the fathers, of PR (*principe de réalité/père*) and PP (*principe de plaisir/pépé* [grandfather]), leads to a dead end, a negative or other way that is the death of the subject of speculation: *en voie de mort*. As Derrida discloses it elsewhere, the crypt of Absolute Knowledge (*savoir absolu*, SA) unknowingly contains nonconsciousness itself (*Ça*, French translation of *Id*).[11] The self-negating movement of the dialectic is traduced by Derrida as the desire of the psychoanalytic movement, as the rhythm of the *fort/da*, of *mort/sa*, of *la mort propre* as

8. On the tradition of speculation, see Rodolphe Gasché, *The Tain of the Mirror: Derrida and the Philosophy of Reflection* (Cambridge: Harvard University Press, 1986).

9. Jacques Derrida, "Différance," in *Margins of Philosophy*, trans. Alan Bass (Chicago: University of Chicago Press, 1982), pp. 1–28.

10. G. W. F. Hegel, *Phenomenology of Spirit*, trans. A. V. Miller (New York: Oxford University Press, 1977), pp. 43–44.

11. On the Sa/Ça pun and other Derridean witticisms, see Geoffrey Hartman, *Saving the Text: Literature/Derrida/Philosophy* (Baltimore: Johns Hopkins University Press, 1981).

the desire of address: "et quand je t'appelle mon amour, mon amour, est-ce toi que j'appelle ou mon amour? Toi, mon amour, est-ce toi que je nomme ainsi, a toi que je m'adresse?" (LCP 12; "and when I call you my love, my love, is it you I am calling or my love? You, my love, is it you I thereby name, is it to you that I address myself?" [PC 8]).

In Hegel's Preface, the dialectic is represented as an alternative to the equally dissatisfying roads to Truth taken by advocates of immediate intuition and proponents of abstract or objective fact. The "labour of the negative" must be accounted essential in the becoming of knowledge, so that difference, time, and subjectivity realize their sublation rather than suffering from evasion, suppression, or reduction into dead thingness. Hegel insists on the dialectical relation of self-identity, negativity, and thought: "But this self-identity is no less negativity; therefore its fixed existence passes over into its dissolution. The determinateness seems at first to be due entirely to the fact that it is related to an *other*, and its movement seems imposed on it by an alien power; but having its other-ness within itself, and being self-moving, is just what is involved in the *simplicity* of thinking itself; for this simple thinking is the self-moving and self-differentiating thought, it is its own inwardness, it is the pure Notion" (34). From Marx to Levinas, post-Hegelian speculation will be concerned with this *other* and its possible involvement in the economy of identities and values—with what Derrida calls "speculation sans terme."

Hegel calls his philosophical alternative to romanticism and empiri-cism by various terms: *der Ernst des Begriffs* ("serious speculative effort"), *das spekulative* ("speculative philosophy"), and *begreifende Denken* ("specu-lative thinking").[12] Hegel follows the "rhythm of its movement," whose dialectic cannot be contained in "narrative exposition" or in the "habit of picture thinking [*Vorstellung*]" (35). Rather, borrowing from grammar, Hegel represents speculative thinking in terms of the dialectic between Subject and Predicate. In merely ratiocinative thinking,

the self is a *Subject* to which the content is related as Accident and Predicate. This Subject constitutes the basis to which the content is attached, and upon which the movement [*Bewegung*] runs back and forth. Speculative thinking behaves in a different way. Since the Notion [*Begriff*] is the object's own self, which presents itself as the *coming-to-be of the object*, it is not a passive Subject inertly supporting the Accidents; it is, on the contrary, the self-moving Notion which takes its determinations back into itself. . . . The solid ground which argumentation has in the passive Subject is therefore shaken, and only this movement itself becomes the object. . . . Usually, the

12. Hegel, *Phenomenology*, pp. 3, 34, 36. See G. W. F. Hegel, *Phänomenologie des Geistes* (Frankfurt am Main: Suhrkamp Verlag, 1973), pp. 14, 55, 56. In numbered editions these are paragraphs 4, 56, and 59 of the Preface.

Subject is first made the basis, as the *objective*, fixed self. . . . Here, that
Subject is replaced by the knowing "I" itself, which links the Predicates
with the Subject holding them. But, since that first Subject enters into the
determinations themselves and is their soul, the second Subject, viz. the
knowing "I," still finds in the Predicate what it thought it had finished with
and got away from . . . it is really still occupied with the self of the content,
having to remain associated with it, instead of being for itself. (37–38)

Derrida espies this movement's ruses: "the predicate speculates in
order to send itself the subject" (LCP 35/PC 30). Derrida exposes the
Hegelian narrative underlying Freud's philosophizing—the return of
the Subject into a being for itself—and at the same time indicates the
traces of the unconscious in Hegel—the Subject's inability to cease
differing from itself—the *Ça* (or Id) in the *SA* (conscious self-possession,
savoir absolu). Psychoanalytic speculation also "runs back and forth,"
fort/da, en train, in a narrative of self-recovery. In Derrida's reading of
Freud, however, there is a differal of the moment when the Subject
arrives at the station or destination of the "for itself," the properly
owned, the SA. Derrida also demonstrates the essential function of the
"accidental" in the "labour of the negative," in the labor of signification,
so that what befalls language by chance—or through the unpredictable
movements of invention—interrupts the totalizing dream of sublation.
Speculation is always already *au-delà,* interminably beside itself.

Derrida's "method" is to offer a *mimicry* of Hegel's diction and argument through an invention process worked up through Freud's text,
articulating Hegel and Freud together in a relationship that displaces
the dialectic. In Freud "speculation, *this* speculation thus would be
foreign to philosophy or metaphysics. More precisely, speculation
would represent the very thing which philosophy or metaphysics guard
themselves from, which philosophy or metaphysics consist in guarding
themselves from, maintaining with it a relation without relation, a relation of exclusion which signifies simultaneously the necessity and aporia
of translation [*l'aporie de la traduction*]" (LCP 296/PC 277). Freud tra-
duces Hegel's concept of "speculation" by translating it into psychoanalytic terms, carrying it beyond itself and beyond recuperation by any
concept, any *Begriff,* no matter how *Ernst.* "The speculation which is in
question in this text [*Beyond the Pleasure Principle*] cannot purely and
simply refer to the speculative of the Hegel type, at least in its dominant
determination" (LCP 296/PC 277). Freud goes beyond Hegel, and Derrida surpasses him: *la mort de père.*

Derrida plays *fort/da* with Hegel and Freud, repeating their texts in a
rhythm that transforms Hegel's commentary on the dialectics of reading
into a psychoanalytic movement. Hegel notes that many complain

against philosophical writing because it must be "read over and over and over before it can be understood. . . . The philosophical proposition, since it *is* a proposition, leads one to believe that the usual subject-predicate [S and P, Socrates and Plato] relation obtains, as well as the usual attitude towards knowing. But the philosophical content destroys this attitude and this opinion. We learn by experience that we meant something other than we meant to mean; and this correction of our meaning compels our knowing to go back to the proposition, and understanding it in some other way" (39). There is always an "other way," but this path leads as well to Freud's road, Heidegger's *Weg*, and Derrida's train of thought about textuality. For Hegel pictures the movement of the Notion as the movement of Reading Itself, of a "going forth from, and returning to, itself" (40). Reading/writing compose the primary process (PP) of the labor of the negative, so that the Hegelian dialectic may be read as "meaning" that one can recover from reading or writing, get back to one's home by some "other way" of address. Philosophical speculation turns out to be an antidote to the *pharmakon* of textuality, a way of controlling, sublimating, and profiting from the difference it introduces. The back-and-forth movement within philosophy appears to belong not to itself but to reading/writing; the identity of philosophy, indeed, becomes its difference from textuality, insofar as philosophy arrives at itself by positing an end to textuality. This difference between philosophy and writing, of course, is a distinction that the movement of deconstruction subjects to differal in following how the "other way" back always branches out again, uncannily, until one has no notion that can represent knowledge. Such is the destination of the *l'être* of speculation.

Derrida locates the particular anxiety of originality in *Beyond the Pleasure Principle* in Freud's reiterated denials of intellectual debt to the paternal ghosts of Nietzsche, Schopenhauer, and philosophy in general. "Priority and originality are not among the aims that psycho-analytic work sets itself" declares Freud (SE 18: 7), but this denial is all too transparent a ploy, as are the denials of debt to Nietzsche in the *Autobiographical Study*. Yet Freud acknowledges this in speaking of his "way back" to philosophical concerns, a movement beyond philosophy that returns eternally to it, but so as to occupy a position either before the fathers (priority) or in supersession of them (originality). Not coincidentally, the topics of *Beyond the Pleasure Principle*—once the anecdote of grandfather and grandson is played out—concern identity and immortality, and the threats to them from powerful forces within and without the self.

In *Beyond the Pleasure Principle*, Freud attributes our "belief in the internal necessity of dying" to the "illusions" of "poets," who convince

us of death's inevitability rather than burden us with the renewal of our
desire for immortality (SE 18: 44–45). The passage is curious, since the
wish for immortality seems more "poetic" than the sober recognition of
death's necessity—of the goddess *Ananke.* "We must therefore turn to
biology," says Freud, "in order to test the validity of the belief" in mortal
doom, but "we may be astonished to find how little agreement there is
among biologists on the subject of natural death" (SE 18: 45). What
ensues are Freud's wildest speculations on the potential immortality of
protozoa. Biology apparently provides a physiological substantiation of
metapsychological hypotheses. But one may read this rhetoric, with the
aid of psychoanalysis itself, as the expression of an unconscious defense
against the forces of death and the body—one may see the treatise as a
whole as a fantasy of immortality. The grandson's game of *fort/da* would
then be of the gravest interest to the grandfather, representing as it
does the anxiety toward absence as a sign of death, the desire to control
it, the return to the Source as antidote to death, and the return of
absence as the return of the repressed. The attempt to base speculation
in biology signifies the wish to relate body to soul systematically and so
to defeat death through the sublime perception of the ideal in the
material—another version of that *Aufhebung* or dialectical overcoming
of time, sensory life, and negation immortalized by Hegel's *Phenomenology* and noted as a common topos in literature and philosophy since
romanticism. Such a graphic speculation would reinvest the "bios" with
the eternal life of the auto-analytic soul.

But Freud's "bios" is no more certain or empirical an entity than
his "auto" or self. The ontological deconstruction of subjectivity in
psychoanalysis is accompanied by an absolutely correlative suspension
of phenomenological sense certainty, for the being of the body has
become that of a sign. Psychoanalysis thus participates in the deconstruction of materialism and empiricism and of any restricted economy of
the value of objects "in themselves." What psychoanalysis speaks of is a
realm accessible only through symptoms—or metaphors. As Freud put
it at the beginning of the *Introductory Lectures on Psychoanalysis:*

Neither speculative philosophy, nor descriptive psychology, nor what is
called experimental psychology (which is closely allied to the physiology of
the sense-organs), as they are taught in the Universities, are in a position
to tell you anything serviceable of the relation between body and mind or
to provide you with the key to an understanding of possible disturbances
of the mental functions. . . . This is the gap which psycho-analysis seeks to
fill. It tries to give psychiatry its missing psychological foundation. It hopes
to discover the common ground on the basis of which the convergence of
physical and mental disorder will become intelligible. With this aim in view,

psycho-analysis must keep itself free from any hypothesis that is alien to it, whether of an anatomical, chemical, or physiological kind, and must operate entirely with purely psychological auxiliary ideas; and for that reason, I fear, it will seem strange to you to begin with. (SE 15: 20–21)

The "gap" addressed by psychoanalysis lies between body and mind, between the sensible and the intelligible, in the "graphic" economy between the "auto" and the "bio." With its tropes and metaphors, psychoanalysis bridges this distance with a strange language whose powers of reference are paradoxically measured by resistance to any literal determination. The discourse of psychoanalysis—its "purely psychological auxiliary ideas"—insists on its autonomy and rejects any simple cause-effect paradigm for the relation of physiology to mentality. The "convergence of physical and mental disorder" is sought, strangely, through a supplementary set of ideas whose consistent postulate is that symptomatic representations operate according to laws independent of physiological substructures. Metapsychology outlives the body.

The hypotheses of the unconscious and of the censorship give this inevitable discontinuity an explanatory structure, their analytic function being to account for the deceptive relation between signifiers and signifieds or representations and their origins. Yet the interpretation of dreams, parapraxes, symptoms, artworks, or cultural phenomena never leads conclusively back to an organic origin. The problem of causality in psychoanalysis is extraordinarily complex; suffice it to note that Freud repeatedly insisted on the capacity of psychic fantasies to operate as the cause of neurotic symptoms, whether alongside or in the complete absence of actual experiential or physical trauma. The indeterminacy of the reality of the "primal scene"—discussed at length in the case of the "Wolf Man" and in chapter 23 of the *Introductory Lectures*—is only the most famous of many examples (as Ned Lukacher recently reminded us).[13]

When Freud does attempt to describe a convergence of mind and body, he proceeds through the use of biological metaphors rather than through the observation of physical events, thus further complicating any conception of a cause-effect relation between somatic and psychic experience, since the possibility arises that the former is a fantasy of the latter. In other words, psychic experience (and its interpretation) borrows the materials of biology and the body to express its own metaphysical formulations. A metaleptic and catachretic rhetoric operates the reverses and double-crosses of the body-mind relation: the biological

13. Ned Lukacher, *Primal Scenes: Literature/Philosophy/Psychoanalysis* (Ithaca: Cornell University Press, 1986).

metaphor assumes the body as literal and the psychic as a trope of the sensory base; yet the significance of the trope is that psychic life has its own heterogeneous wishes, and that these wishes employ the body metaphorically to express their own independent ends. Thus the body would always be originally figurative. The language of the unconscious plays with and upsets the categorical distinctions of standard discourse, and this disturbance in turn becomes the topic and method of psychoanalytic writing. When Freud treats the value of empirical science or the psychology of the death drive, this "gap" structure intervenes once more to short-circuit the recuperation of sensory experience in immortal significance. Consequently the project of an auto-bio-graphical writing will display the same errant characteristics as the language of psychoanalysis.

Freud's biological metaphors provide a material basis for immaterial concepts; the structure of metaphor, however, works in the opposite direction, departing from the sensible toward the intelligible in the hopes of sublating/sublimating the bodily in the spiritual. Hence we are not surprised to find that Freud's argument that neither speculative philosophy nor physiological psychology could "tell you anything serviceable of the relation between body and mind," so that psychoanalysis must remain free "from any hypothesis . . . of an anatomical, chemical, or physiological kind," is contradicted by the strange postulations of *Beyond the Pleasure Principle*. There the "repetition compulsion" and the "death drive" are described as traces of an instinct "inherent in organic life to restore an earlier state of things" when physiological equilibrium reigned without disturbance from inner or outer influences (SE 18: 36, 55–56).[14] Freud's recourse to "proofs" from "the phenomena of heredity and the facts of embryology" indicates a fundamental ambivalence toward the project of making bodily and mental phenomena converge. Psychoanalytic speculation cannot give up its autonomy to any physiological determination—cannot surrender its own claim to immortality—but finds itself drawn back to the language of the body in a divided effort both to cancel and preserve the biological reality it signifies. The retreat from speculation had been from the start an anxious denial of spiritual longings and a transference of divine authority to the material sciences. A repressed wish for immortality returns in the physiological metaphors Freud adopts, for they once more enable the transcendence of the sensory in the spirit of metapsychology.

14. On the relationship between the "repetition compulsion" and the structure of narrative desire in Freudian psychoanalysis, see Neil Hertz, "Freud and the Sandman," in *Textual Strategies*, ed. Josué V. Harari (Ithaca: Cornell University Press, 1970), pp. 296–321.

Cultural History as Family Romance

The theory of cultures set forth in *The Future of an Illusion* (1927) (and later made famous in *Civilization and Its Discontents* [1930]) translates metapsychology into metahistory in asserting that every "civilization must be built up on coercion and renunciation of instinct" (SE 21: 7).[15] The acceptance and introjection of the father's prohibition against desire for the mother (the installation of what Lacan calls the "nom-du-père," the Name and No of the Father) begins the process of civilization and lays the foundation for the superego, embodied by those cultural father figures for whom we work in exchange for psychological and monetary rewards. Civilization is speculation *en masse*, and since every son desires the father's death, "every individual is virtually an enemy of civilization" (6), which in turn builds and defends itself through the economics of defense, through internal and external institutions of coercion, reconciliation, and recompense (conscience, the family, the law, and other establishments of patriarchal ideology). But "what is perhaps the most important item in the psychical inventory of a civilization" consists of "its religious ideas in the widest sense—in other words (which will be justified later) in its illusions" (14). The anthropology of religion reveals that the protective economy of renunciation and reward informing religion is modeled on the son's relation to "the father who had all along been hidden behind every divine figure as its nucleus" (19). What seems remarkable in retrospect is not this insight—available from any number of anthropologists—but Freud's feelings toward the *parental* figures behind his portrait of *nature* and *fate* as "majestic, cruel, and inexorable" (16). Once more we have here an identity or organism threatened by an overpowering influence or force. The history of idealistic illusions also turns out to be that of the anxiety of influence, and Freud's place in it will be evident before his treatise is done.

As his debunking of religious illusions proceeds, Freud increasingly casts it in the nineteenth-century terms of a debate between science and theology. His emotional investment in rational empiricism and stated antipathy toward philosophy are a displacement of his own anxiety for protection against the meaninglessness of biological experience. Rational, scientific, and psychoanalytic truth will take the place

15. It may be pointed out that Freud repudiated *The Future of an Illusion* in a letter to Sandor Ferenczi dated October 23, 1927: "Now it already seems to me childish; fundamentally I think otherwise; I regard it as weak analytically and inadequate as self-confession" (Jones, *Freud*, 3: 138). These are intriguing sentiments, but they did not stop Freud from repeating his argument at length when, in 1933, he concluded his *New Introductory Lectures* with a chapter on the scientific *Weltanschauung* in contrast to the illusions of art, philosophy, religion, and Marxism (SE 22: 158–82).

of the antique fathers, continuing the lineage of primal struggles in
which the son usurps the place of authority. Yet, as Freud himself
realizes, these new ideals may themselves be mere illusions: "And
once our suspicion has been aroused, we shall not shrink from asking
too whether our conviction that we can learn something about external
reality through the use of observation and reasoning in scientific
work—whether this conviction has any better foundation" (34). Such
a radical and endlessly speculative brand of metacriticism is avoided,
however, since "observation" is constantly directed away from "our
own selves" and toward "external reality." But that reality itself turns
out to be inextricable from the structure generated by wishes and
fantasies, since here the authority of reality is constituted by the
economy of an Oedipal metaphorics that wishes to invest the empirical
with original governing power. The realm of the empirical, in other
words, is under the reign of the fetish.

Freud's identification with the superego of empirical science murders
the speculative philosopher and theologian within him. The repression
confirms, however, his place in the genealogy of Jewish Oedipal agons
from Abraham, Moses, and Job through the Kabbalah to Marx, Bloom,
and Derrida.[16] The Hebraic God always was a terrifying, stern patriarch,
and one who forbade the representation of this truth or power in the
false images of human icons or signs. Jehovah's iconoclasm passes on
to his prophets, who turn it against the idols of many tribes. Freud uses
it against religion itself and in doing so, ironically repeats the very
tradition he opposes. He is the rebellious son who will become the father
of the new science of truth—psychoanalysis. But the basic parental
narrative of authority, conflict, usurpation, and guilt remains intact,
with reason now enthroned where an inexplicable and harsh Yahweh
once reigned. "For it cannot be denied," declares Freud, like the deity
of Genesis, "that psychoanalysis is my creation" (36).

The analogy between individual and cultural history holds for the
historical development of mature psychoanalytic reason as it rejects its
religious upbringing. Freud assumes the identity of reason's patriarchal
spokesman. "Our behavior should therefore be modeled on that of a
sensible teacher" who eases the transition from childish illusions to
reality principles, because "the time has probably come . . . for replacing
the effects of repression by the results of the rational operation of the

16. For a discussion of this genealogy, see Susan Handelman, *The Slayers of Moses: The
Emergence of Rabbinic Interpretation in Modern Literary Theory* (Albany: SUNY Press, 1982),
and Harold Bloom, *Agon: Towards a Theory of Revisionism* (New York: Oxford University
Press, 1982), pp. 91–144.

intellect" (43–44). The parental analogy, at once the truth and the illusion of religion's symbolic disguisings of our primal wishes, governs the representation of science's image of truth as well: "We have become convinced that it is better to avoid such symbolic disguisings of the truth in what we tell children and not to withhold from them a knowledge of the true state of affairs commensurate with their intellectual level" (44–45). The same prohibition against nonliteral language had earlier been directed at philosophers who "stretch the meaning of words until they retain scarcely anything of their original sense. They give the name of 'God' to some vague abstraction which they have created for themselves" (32). Such preferences for "original sense" come as a surprise from the author of *Jokes and Their Relation to the Unconscious* and the literary artist who received the Goethe prize. This desire to restrict words to a single, literal proper meaning—to a *Logos*—is the theological wish in essence. The science of psychoanalysis is, like religion, an art of desire and illusion.

This art and Freud's ambivalence are evident in the narrative structure of *The Future of an Illusion,* which is set up as a dialogue between Freud and an imagined opponent (a tactic that recalls the traditional debate between flesh and spirit). The dispute culminates in chapter 10, when Freud's antagonist points out that whatever replaces religion—including reason—will require the "same sanctity, rigidity and intolerance, the same prohibition of thought—for its own defense" (51). The voice of Freud's spiritual unconscious, which paradoxically also speaks for the truth of desire, expresses the subversive irony pervading the book: "I think I have now shown that your endeavors come down to an attempt to replace a proved and emotionally valuable illusion by another one, which is unproved and without emotional value" (52). Freud is not "inaccessible" to such criticism: "I know how difficult it is to avoid illusions; perhaps the hopes I have confessed to are of an illusory nature, too." He holds fast, however, to a distinction: "my illusions are not, like religious ones, incapable of correction" by observation and experience (53). Whereas religious wishes answer the dictates of instinctual life, science heeds "the voice of the intellect," which instructs us in how to defend ourselves against not only the external threats of nature but those internal ruptures instigated by instinct and its illusions as well: "The primacy of the intellect lies, it is true, in a distant, distant future, but probably not in an *infinitely* distant one. It will presumably set itself the same aims as those whose realization you expect from your God (of course within human limits—so far as external reality, *Ananke*, allows it), namely the love of man and the decrease of suffering" (52). The passage evidences a strange and characteristic ambivalence toward *An-*

anke—goddess of fate, destiny, and necessity—for she is imaged, through condensation, as both the Law of the Father and Death *and* as Mother Nature, agent of Eros.

The identification of *Ananke* with "external reality," nature, death, and the parents was spelled out in Freud's 1924 essay titled "The Economic Problem of Masochism." After recounting the historical development of the superego out of the Oedipus complex and itemizing the succession of authority figures linked to it, Freud follows his speculation into metapsychological pathways:

> The last figure in the series that began with the parents is the dark power of Destiny which only the fewest of us are able to look upon as impersonal. There is little to be said against the Dutch writer Multatuli when he replaces the *Moira* [Destiny] of the Greeks by the divine pair *Logos kai Ananke;* but all who transfer the guidance of the world to Providence, to God, or to God and Nature, arouse a suspicion that they still look upon these ultimate and remotest powers as a parental couple, in a mythological sense, and believe themselves linked to them by libidinal ties. In *The Ego and the Id* I made an attempt to derive mankind's realistic fear of death, too, from the same parental view of fate. It seems very hard to free oneself from it. (SE 19: 168)

Indeed. *The Future of an Illusion*, like *Beyond the Pleasure Principle*, suggests that Freud could not free himself from the wish to conceive nature and fate through parental metaphors. While it appears that the relations of family life would serve as the literal base for the superstructure of illusions in religion and philosophy, we simultaneously recall that the family romance is itself a fantastical construction, and the figures of mother and father themselves are more metaphysical metaphors than objective referents.

As the essay on masochism clearly shows, Freud attributes the "fear of death" and the subservience to *Ananke* to an illusory transference generated by castration anxieties and Oedipal conflicts. To weaken or destroy the spell cast by such parental figurations—to read death and nature as other than familiar and familial figures—would thus be to resolve the neurotic fear of mortality (and, one might add, masculinity). Psychoanalysis forestalls our doom by disclosing that it is only our parents who scare us to death. The function of this parental nightmare, Freud implies, is to translate the senseless changes of material life/death into the comprehensible and ultimately satisfying terms of the family romance, whose metaphors give nature a pattern and time a meaning. Freud's own reading of the "fear of death" cannot, of course, escape this significant imperative or help but betray the instinctual wish motivating it. Paul Roazen explains the book's severity toward religious illusion by reference to Freud's own "stoic" and "sagelike endurance of his cancer" (167). This is only one of numerous attempts to find the autobiographical origin of Freud's metapsychology of death in his biological illnesses or in the actual passing of family or friends. Ernest Jones is surely right, however, to argue that Freud's interest in death was lifelong, and that we ought to look to the theories of psychoanalysis itself to explain the recurrence of this uncanny topic (Jones 2: 40–41). As early as the *Project for a Scientific Psychology* (1895), Freud described psychic life as an economy of equilibrium, the job of the "ego" being to regulate the impact and discharge of energic quantities so as to maintain the proper structure of its own formal character: "The aim and end of all thought-processes is thus to bring about a *state of identity*" (SE 1: 332). "Death" becomes a metaphor for any quantity of excitation— from outside or inside—that shatters this economy and so prevents the establishment of a state of identity. The economy of the Oedipus complex will follow this formula, as the child's developing identifications will regulate the impact of the father's influence and the discharge of affection for the mother. It may then be that it is Freud's philosophy that determines the role of death in his life, and not his body that determines the role of death in his life's work.

Freud's demystification of the parental metaphor and its way of making sense of death decidedly emphasizes the figure of the castrating and lethal Father; Freud's unmasking of this figure constitutes an attempt to rob it of its power and thus to free him of the constraints it imposes on his desires. The wish to be rid of Him coincides with the wish to be rid of death, and so as a defense indicates the primal wish to restore the economy of identity and life. By retracing the patriarchal genealogy of philosophy, religion, and morals, Freud dethrones the paternal aspect of *Ananke* and nominates a scientific Logos to replace it. This Logos takes on the authority of the Father but supplements it with the infusion of the Mother's love, allowing the aspirant to realize in fantasy his desire to take the Father's place and undo the death threat whose metaphors are "castration," "fate," and "external reality." The critique of religion and of paternal figures does not escape the structure of wish fulfillment but repeats it in a dispatch and reversal of figures: the ego fantasizes its defeat of tyrannical *Ananke* and its return to the breast of a rational Eros, to "the love of man and the decrease of suffering," that "earlier state of things" in Freud's youth to which the path of psychoanalysis had finally returned him in the *fort/da* movement of his career.

Three years before his death, Freud expresses these anxieties again in "A Disturbance of Memory on the Acropolis" (1936), in which he

tries to explain his strange conviction that he had never before believed
in the real existence of the Acropolis before seeing it, with his younger
brother Alexander, in 1904. We might recall, as Freud does not, that
when *Civilization and Its Discontents* seeks a metaphor for the unconscious
itself, it chooses another set of historical layers and ruins, the "Eternal
City" of Rome, only to dismiss the metaphor because "the fact remains
that only in the mind is such a preservation of all the earlier stages
alongside of the final form possible, and that we are not in a position
to represent this phenomenon in pictorial terms" (SE 21: 71). Nonetheless, the metaphor serves to illustrate the argument that the psyche
preserves archaic desires, most pointedly "the longing for the father,"
whose priority displaces the mother in the somewhat weird assertion
that "I cannot think of any need in childhood as strong as the need for
a father's protection" (72). The text on the Acropolis (which takes the
form of a letter to Romain Rolland) begins by recounting the origins
of psychoanalysis in Freud's self-analysis, thus justifying theoretically,
more "attention to some events in my private life than they would
otherwise deserve" (SE 22: 239). Freud's feeling on the Acropolis is
one of "derealization," of denial or disbelief in the present scene, the
theoretics of which he bequeaths to "my daughter [Anna], the child
analyst, [who] is writing a book [*The Ego and the Mechanisms of Defence*]
upon them" (245). Like grandson Ernst, Anna receives the legacy of
psychoanalysis, only to return it to Freud in the form of a disturbance
and recollection of his own identity. Freud's extraordinary, and on the
surface implausible, account of his disbelief in the Acropolis's reality is
explained, he says, by Oedipal guilt. In an association whose connotations are not to be underestimated, he recalls Napolean's words to his
brother Joseph during the coronation at Notre Dame: "What would
Monsieur notre Père have said to this, if he could have been here to-day?"
(247). Freud concludes that to deny the reality of the Acropolis is to
deny his own *position* atop this ancient symbol of the source of Western
Civilization: "It must be that a sense of guilt was attached to the satisfaction in having gone such a long way" (247), especially since his own
businessman father "had no secondary education," and thus neither the
means nor desire to achieve the place the son now occupies, beyond
him. Past the father, the son stands at the origin: "there was something
about it that was wrong, that from earliest times had been forbidden.
It was something to do with a child's criticism of his father, with the
undervaluation which took the place of the overvaluation of earlier
childhood. It seems as though the essence of success were to have got
further than one's father, and as though to excel one's father was still
something forbidden" (247).

Who speaks here, the son of Freud's father, the father of psychoanaly-

sis, or the father of Freud's daughter, Anna, who is busy going beyond
her father in a book on mechanisms of defense? The identification with
the position of the surpassed and impotent father is underscored by
Freud: "I myself," he ends, "have grown old and stand in need of
forbearance and can travel no more." Incapable of taking another step
(*pas de méthode?*), Freud nonetheless goes beyond his progeny by going
back to Athens, back to the position of the son who surpasses the
father and precedes the daughter: his own stillness, the "death" of an
immobility strangely resembling the equilibrium and absence of tension
discussed in *Beyond the Pleasure Principle* as a return to the origin, is
here both accomplished and reversed as he sends a message to himself
confirming his own place of priority. Forever wed to Athena, Freud is
stationed to outlive the movement he begins.

Yet another step, however, seems to shadow this self-fathering path,
for the writing of the daughter threatens to usurp the father's control
of the mechanisms of defense. The position of Anna Freud here, at the
end (or beginning) of Freud's psycho-analysis, uncannily repeats the
origin of the psychoanalytic movement in Breuer and Freud's analysis
of the case of Anna O.—in the enigma of *her* desire. In Freud's final
figuration it is Anna who, like Athena, seems to spring from her father's
forehead in a step yet to be accounted for except in the figures of repression and its representational vicissitudes. The father's cryptic reference
to Anna leaves a remainder here, and a reminder of she who comes before
and after the father in the figure of woman and mother. It is her motions
of creation and analysis that are here folded back into the primal scene of
the father's priority. Anna Freud never married and had no children. She
was her father's devoted aide, and took his place, reading his words at
conferences once he was too old to travel beyond Vienna.[17] *PR* also means
poste restante (PC 287n.).

Feminist critics today, anxious to resist the father's seduction even
while carrying on in his name, rightly insist that we remember that
psychoanalysis began as an effort to read the text of female psychoneu-
roses—to answer the question "What do women want?" As Irigaray asks
in *Speculum of the Other Woman*:

> What is the relationship of that "envy" to man's "desire"? In other words,
> is it possible that the phobia aroused in man, and notably in Freud, by the
> uncanny strangeness of the "nothing to be seen" cannot tolerate *her* not
> having this "envy"? *Her* having other desires, of a different nature from
> *his* representation of the sexual and from *his* representations of sexual
> desire. From his projected, reflected *auto-representations* shall we say? If

17. See Gay, *Freud*, pp. 428–46.

woman had desires other than "penis-envy," this would call into question
the unity, the uniqueness, the simplicity of the mirror charged with sending
man's image back to him—albeit inverted. . . . This doesn't mean that the
question of castration isn't raised for woman but rather that it refers back
in reality to the father's castration, including the father of psychoanalysis—
to his fear, his refusal, his rejection, of an *other* sex. For if to castrate woman
is to inscribe her in the law of the *same* desire, of the *desire for the same*,
what exactly is "castration"? And what is the relationship of the agent of
castration to the concept and its practice?[18]

Women in psychoanalysis figure as nothing other than male desire,
the desire for the sign of the male and for the letter of the Law. In such
a correspondence, the male always comes, though perhaps not on or
in, time, and arrives at its ancient destination. It would be naive to
accept the defensive narrative of this subject's autobiography—at least
in the way Freud has traced it, without considering the degree to which
auto-analysis locates and defends against the woman as other, recuperating the self in a recurrent tale of its death and rebirth within a
masculine legacy. With the coming of women's writing and its analyses,
the autobiography of this masterful discipline may survive, and live on,
the death that Freud could, or can, not forever defer. The immortal,
erect structures he saw upon the Acropolis may be the necropolis of the
Father's desire. If Freud lives on, cryptically, in the work of his daughters, it is not in any form we could assimilate to the classical project of
autobiography and the Father's sublation, or even to Freud's, since
the genealogy they delineate, from Athena to Antigone to Anna and
beyond, will never reassure man that his identity is his own.

Lost in the Funhouse

"A Disturbance of Memory on the Acropolis" appears to function as
a kind of self-inscribed epitaph for Freud. Here time, absence, death,
and representation function reassuringly for the autobiographer who
recollects himself, and thus indicate that those texts which seem to resist
"death" may also desire to incite and profit from it. This latter, perverse
speculation is the one stressed by both Derrida and Paul de Man. Psycho-

18. Luce Irigaray, *Speculum of the Other Woman*, trans. Gillian C. Gill (Ithaca: Cornell
University Press, 1985), pp. 51, 55. Irigaray's witty, powerful, and persuasive deconstruction of Freud's phallogocentrism inserts the "speculum" of *l'écriture féminine* into the
body of male speculation, and so provides startling new perspectives on the tradition of
masculine philosophy and its major metaphors. See Jane Gallop, *The Daughter's Seduction:
Feminism and Psychoanalysis* (Ithaca: Cornell University Press, 1982), and Gay, *Freud*, pp.
501–22.

analysis, deconstruction, and the theory of autobiography come together as they narrate or mimic the displacement *of* death, where the
double genitive again articulates the faulty steps of the journey through
language to self-restoration. If we ask, "What do men want and lack?"
the answer seems to be the displacement of the desiring subject, and by
this movement the end of a speculation that always entails its own
mortality. The irony of such a desire is decipherable in de Man's prophylactic rhetoric, which so repetitively cautions against succumbing to
the "seduction" of metaphor. The speculation this suggests is that the
displacement of death in Freud and the displacement of desire in de
Man follow a common path within the general textual structures of
autobiography and disciplinary self-reflexivity.

As we saw in the previous chapter, de Man's "Autobiography as
De-Facement" argues that the "dominant figure of the epitaphic or
autobiographical discourse is . . . the prosopopeia, the voice-from-be-
yond-the-grave," so we may expect that his theorizing on autobiography
will perform that *fort/da* of the subject of literary history we tracked
in his other essays.[19] Analyzing Wordsworth's *Essays upon Epitaphs*, de
Man attacks "the larger question of autobiographical discourse as a
discourse of self-restoration," of a "restoration in the face of death"
accomplished by uncanny metaphors of voice (74). *Fort/da:* the repetition of death in elegy and epitaph appears as an instance beyond the
pleasure principle. De Man begins, however, with a definitive discussion of why "autobiography lends itself poorly to generic definition,"
whether through distinctions of aesthetics, history, fictionality, or
reference, concluding that:

> Autobiography, then, is not a genre or a mode, but a figure of reading or
> of understanding that occurs, to some degree, in all texts. The autobio-
> graphical moment happens as an alignment between two subjects involved
> in the process of reading in which they determine each other by mutual
> reflexive substitution. The structure implies differentiation as well as simi-
> larity, since both depend on a substitutive exchange that constitutes the
> subject. This specular structure is interiorized in a text in which the author
> declares himself the subject of his own understanding, but this merely
> makes explicit the wider claim to authorship that takes place whenever a
> text is stated to be *by* someone and assumed to be understandable to the
> extent that this is the case. Which amounts to saying that any book with a
> readable title page is, to some extent, autobiographical. (70)

As is so often the case, de Man's arguments roughly coincide with
Derrida's, each working out the problematics of self-reflection, specula-

19. Paul de Man, "Autobiography as De-Facement," *The Rhetoric of Romanticism* (New
York: Columbia University Press, 1984), p. 77.

tion, and the signature, though in terms of their own choosing. Irony is the presiding trope of de Man's theoretics, so we are not surprised when he immediately adds: "But just as we seem to assert that all texts are autobiographical, we should say that, by the same token, none of them is or can be" (70). Whereas the generic extension of autobiography threatens to reduce every text to a uniform aesthetic and history, as perhaps seemed the danger in our search for Freud's autobiographical moments, the linguistic explanation threatens to be the death of autobiography. The "specular moment" we identify as autobiography is but "the manifestation, on the level of referent, of a linguistic structure," in other words, of that substitutive arrangement of tropes that constitutes the effect of any reference. Thus autobiography does not reveal "reliable self-knowledge" but "demonstrates in a striking way the impossibility of closure and of totalization . . . of all textual systems made up of tropological substitutions" (70–71). Many readers will recognize the by-now familiar moves of de Manian deconstruction. The determination of the subject of autobiography is rendered undecidable through a reading of the aporia within the tropology of its constitution—here in the ambivalence of Wordsworth's use and abuse of prosopopeia as a defense against death—as what Derrida, after Blanchot, calls *l'arrêt de mort*.[20] "Death," ends de Man, "is a displaced named for a linguistic predicament" (81). One wishes it were so.

De Man's ironic voice is itself the prosopopeia of the aporia of the autobiographical subject, both restoring and entombing critical identity and authority. As much as his analysis privileges this metaphorics of the voice, we need remember the link of Wordsworth's essay to the topoi of the *genius loci,* of the spirit of place, and recall the inseparability of the constitution of voices and positions in writing.[21] De Man's position is established by the linguistic displacement of the subject, which he carefully designates as its "de-facement." Freud's position is achieved by a prosopopeia of the father, a defacing of the monuments that enables the desired replacement, through language, of the position of authority. Derrida's positions are undecidable, for his genre is that of

20. Signifying, among other things, both the triumph of life and the death sentence, *l'arrêt de mort* and its untranslatability are the subject of Derrida's "Living On: Border Lines," *Deconstruction and Criticism,* ed. Harold Bloom et al. (New York: Seabury, 1979), pp. 75–176; the phrase is also at play in *La Carte postale,* pp. 303ff., where it participates in the errancy of the homophonic liaison of *la mort/l'amour.*

21. On the relation of poetic voice to the position of the *genius loci,* see "Wordsworth, Inscriptions, and Romantic Nature Poetry" and "Romantic Poetry and the Genius Loci" in Geoffrey Hartman, *Beyond Formalism: Literary Essays, 1958–1970* (New Haven: Yale University Press, 1970). Hartman's analyses of poetic voice and priority ought to be compared to Harold Bloom's writings on the "anxiety of influence," developed at about the same time.

parapraxis—slips of the tongue that disseminate the voices of prosopopeia and multiply the signatures of auto-bio-graphy in the work. In each case, we must read the question of *genre* both as a regional incident within the general text of identity formation in philosophy and culture, and as a rhetorically exemplary moment of the disclosure of the generic structure of self-reflection.

In his reading of *Essays on Epitaphs,* de Man notes that Wordsworth omits six lines from his terminal citation of Milton's sonnet "On Shakespeare":

> For whilst to th'shame of slow endeavoring art,
> Thy easy numbers flow, and that each heart
> hath from the leaves of thy unvalu'd Book
> Those Delphic lines with deep impression took,
> Then thou our fancy of itself bereaving,
> Dost make us Marble with too much conceiving.

These lines, comments de Man, "cannot fail to evoke the latent threat that inhabits prosopopeia, namely that by making the death speak, the symmetrical structure of the trope [i.e., the author of the sonnet is also, like Shakespeare, speaking from a position beyond the grave] implies, by the same token, that the living are struck dumb, frozen in their death," uttering perhaps a funeral *glas* before their transformation into marble tombstones inscribed with their own epitaphs (*Rhetoric* 78). The erection of such a memorial column of writing is, however, as Freud's essay on "Medusa's Head" argues, compensatory, for it is also the achievement of an image of potency through a defensive *frisson:* "The sight of Medusa's head makes the spectator stiff with terror," and so he is resurrected as the very thing he has lost. De Man resists the seductive ease with which one could read this encounter in terms of Bloom's "anxiety of influence," "our fancy" bereaved "with too much conceiving." Shakespeare occupies the position of the father/precursor whose lamented death both expresses the son's belatedness and compensates for it by an act that buries the father and erects the son's words in his place. Here the poet's autobiography adopts the self-reflexive genre of the elegy to a dead poet, so that Milton dies only to come again—as uncanny prosopopeia, death's *genius loci,* and as the marble testimonial to his own displacement in time.[22] The Oedipal and castration narratives, then, produce the differences of gender and genre, forming the

22. Here I depend on Herman Rapaport's provocative use of Derrida's *Glas* in *Milton and the Postmodern* (Lincoln: University of Nebraska Press, 1983).

narration of self-recuperation through imaginative speculation and an identification with the phallic imago of identity.

The problems of sex and gender at work in such theorizings on the writing subject are explicitly made the comic topic of John Barth's metafictional story *Lost in the Funhouse*. Barth's text provides a contemporary American analogue to European speculations on textuality even as he laughs at the predicaments so soberly written of elsewhere. The homology between the structures of narration and of male desire in Barth's story mirrors the work of another Barthes, in *S/Z*, who similarly mocks and parodies the characters of literary theory. Barth's description of Ambrose, his autobiographical protagonist, might be applied to Freud, de Man, or Derrida:

> He envisions a truly astonishing funhouse, incredibly complex yet utterly controlled from a great central switchboard like the console of a pipe organ. . . . He would be its operator: panel lights would show what was up in every cranny of its cunning of its multifarious vastness; a switch-flick would ease this fellow's way, complicate that's, to balance things out; if anyone seemed lost or frightened, all the operator has to do was. He wishes he had never entered the funhouse. But he has. Then he wishes he were dead. But he's not. Therefore he will construct funhouses for others and be their secret operator—though he would rather be among the lovers for whom funhouses are designed.[23]

Ambrose's autobiography is always already lost in the funhouse, which offers an image of the aporia shadowing its interminable self-reflexiveness:

> *The day wore on.* You think you're yourself, but there are other persons in you. Ambrose gets hard when Ambrose doesn't want to, *and obversely.* Ambrose watches them disagree; Ambrose watches him watch. In the funhouse mirror room you can't see yourself go on forever, because no matter how you stand, your head gets in the way. Even if you had a glass periscope, the image of your eye would cover up the thing you really wanted to see. (81–82)

One's own head is always the necessary blindspot in acts of self-reflection, a joke seriously belabored from Kant and Hegel to Freud and the theorists of the hermeneutic circle. The eye/I gets in the way. In response, the replication of self-images forms a chain of supplements, a series of additional and/or substitutive identities that take the place of the "original," itself now a phantom and unremarkable save for the

23. John Barth, *Lost in the Funhouse* (New York: Bantam, 1969), pp. 93–94.

shadow of the trace that it leaves. Self-reflection disseminates one's "own" figure in a multiplicity reminiscent of that depicted by Freud in "Medusa's Head": "To decapitate = to castrate. The terror of Medusa is thus a terror of castration that is linked to the sight of something. . . . The hair upon Medusa's head is frequently represented in works of art in the form of snakes. . . . This is a confirmation of the technical rule according to which a multiplication of penis symbols signifies castration" (SE 18: 273). This "technical rule" of the psychoanalytic funhouse operator makes Medusa's head an instance of the mirror-room's *mise-en-abyme*. The movement of psychoanalysis, as the narrative of loss and return, belongs to the Oedipal genre of castration. In self-reflection men lose their heads, or their eyes/I's. The phallogocentric logic of identity, as Hélène Cixous mockingly notes, comes down to a choice between castration or decapitation, though the difference is again delusory.[24]

One recent study of the theory of autobiography considers Freud's importance for that genre in terms of narrative strategy:

> The whole idea of a cure in psychoanalysis, of course, depends on the subject's ability to fashion a narrative, a discursive formulation of the meaning of past events identified *in* the process of analysis as significant. It is both the linguistic ground and the creative potential of such a retrospective process of introspection that connects the narrativizing in an autobiographical text like Augustine's with the narrativizing at the very heart of the psychoanalytic process.[25]

The referentiality of such construed texts—literary or psychoanalytic, if this difference any longer makes sense—is considerably clouded by their productive symbolic function, that is, by the manner in which "past" events or images are recollected in the speaking subject's acts of reflective prosopopeia or self-composition. Lacan's contribution, in part, has been to trope the tradition of speculative philosophy through the theses of the Mirror Stage and the Imaginary and to underscore the genealogy and function of the Symbolic register in the ontology of that genre we call the subject (see below, Chapter 9). A result of Lacan's influence may be a chastening of the very notion of the "talking cure," or at least a questioning of the adequacy of the phase in accounting for the narrative strategies of analysis. The appearance of the subject as

24. Hélène Cixous, "Castration or Decapitation?" *Signs* 7 (Autumn 1981): 41–55.

25. Paul Jay, *Being in the Text: Self-Representation from Wordsworth to Roland Barthes* (Ithaca: Cornell University Press, 1984), pp. 24–25. For a detailed discussion of narrative strategies in psychoanalysis, see Roy Schafer, "Narration in the Psychoanalytic Dialogue," *Critical Inquiry* 7 (Autumn 1980): 29–54.

representation entails the repetition of displacement at the very moment of its utterance. Lacan discusses this paradox in terms of *aphanisis*, the "fading of the subject" in a fatal movement of desire and defense, themselves tropes within the problematic of the self's representability: "There is no subject without, somewhere," says Lacan, "*aphanisis* of the subject, and it is in this alienation, in this fundamental division, that the dialectic of the subject is established."[26] Narrative constitutes, displaces, names, represents, and represses this lack *of* the subject. Régis Durand discusses the relation of this *aphanisis* to the disappearance of the "old-fashioned subject" in modernist and postmodernist fiction, concluding that "Lacan's lesson (in the field of narrative analysis at any rate) is that not resolution but punctuation is what is required, and that a step toward it may be taken if texts are seen as existing 'around the living moment of the *aphanisis* of the subject.' "[27] It would, for example, be difficult to classify the autobiographical moments of Freud's texts as "therapeutic," since this would involve activating a teleological theory of interpretation and narrative that postmodern psychoanalysis belies. There is no cure for death, or for writing, for the cure is *of* desire and identical with the instance of loss in representation.

Yet we witness, repeatedly, precisely such narratives in Freud's work: the stories of identity threatened, a defense erected, a displacement of the threat, an internalization of the displacement, a sublimation of desire as defense, an achievement of authority, a return to origins. The pattern seems to be autobiography per se: it outlines the journey or quest from initial selfhood through crisis and obstruction to resolution and recaptured identity. The interminability of self-analysis may be a matter of its circularity, and so evidence of its place in a tradition from Augustine to Wordsworth, Hegel, and Proust.[28] On the other hand, the detour of the symbolic may itself dictate this interminability, since the

26. Jacques Lacan, *The Four Fundamental Concepts of Psycho-Analysis*, trans. Alan Sheridan (New York: Norton, 1978), p. 221. Chapters 16 and 17, on alienation and *aphanisis*, are quite suggestive for theories of autobiographical representation. In the Introduction to *Lacan and Narration*, Robert Con Davis observes that Lacan's "narrative model poses a serious threat to the empirically-based tradition of interpretation as a transparent and focusable lens, an open subjectivity, through which a detached investigator peers into a stable . . . narrative structure. Positioned in a different paradigm, Lacan's concept of narration *and* of narrative interpretation rests squarely on an ontological fault line, the radical split of a subject irretrievably unwhole—the subject of what Lacan calls *aphanisis*" (857). The connection of this split subject to prosopopeia, and to the rift of Being's ontology in Heidegger, is explored by Lukacher.

27. Régis Durand, "On *Aphanisis*: A Note on the Dramaturgy of the Subject in Narrative Analysis," in Davis, *Lacan and Narration*, p. 868.

28. Such an itinerary of self-recuperation through self-representation is perhaps best seen in M. H. Abrams, *Natural Supernaturalism: Tradition and Revolution in Romantic Literature* (New York: Norton, 1971), especially in the chapters on "crisis-autobiography."

autobiographical character (letter/*l'être*), or the disciplinary movement, is constituted by the possibility that it may never arrive at its destination—that its fate be from the start and repeatedly displaced/deferred. The recollected self of the specular moment requires an accession to representation, viewing, distance, and difference that repeats—even as it bridges—the gap between the self that lacks and the image it misses.

The thesis of the Mirror Stage goes beyond even these speculations, in that it posits a radical unoriginality of the subject. A sojourn in this funhouse is no laughing matter. "It is an experience," says Lacan, "that leads us to oppose any philosophy directly issuing from the *Cogito*":

> We have only to understand the mirror stage *as an identification,* in the full sense that analysis gives to the term: namely, the transformation that takes place in the subject when he assumes an image. . . . But the important point is that this form situates the agency [*Instanz*] of the ego, before its social determination, in a fictional direction, which will always remain irreducible for the individual alone, or rather, which will only rejoin the coming-into being [*le devinir*] of the subject asymptotically, whatever the success of the dialectical syntheses by which he must resolve as I his discordance with his own reality.[29]

The Mirror Stage persists, diffracted through the discourse of the Other, into the Symbolic register. There the operator/autobiographer/analyst designs a speculation on the displacement of death, one in which absence and desire reflect one another, so that the story of our love life and our love for life are superimposed: *la vie l'amour/la vie la mort.*[30] In this homophonic condensation, Derrida suggests the economy of representation encompassing the pleasure principle, the death drive, and the autobiographical signature. The self invests in speculative representations in the hopes that the letters will arrive (back) at their destination, returning the origin to itself. In the necessity of this detour, Derrida marks the trace of the self's unoriginality, and of the value death has for it, since this passage beyond the self becomes the only hope of its return-to-sender. Heidegger had sought Being on the way (*Weg*) to language, but for Derrida the way (*voie*) of representation,

29. Jacques Lacan, *Ecrits,* trans. Alan Sheridan (New York: Norton, 1977), pp. 1–2.
30. The rapport or domestic economy of the "pleasure principle" and the "death instinct" prompts Derrida's speculations on *la vie la mort,* and catches up the threads of the love letters constituting *La Carte postale's* "Envois." The homophony of *la mort/l'amour,* when overheard, renders numerous passages unreadable, at least within the economy of proper meaning. See, for example, the paragraphs on *arrêt de mort* (305) ("La thèse serait l'arrêt de mort de la différance"), and the chapter "Courriers de la mort," which begins: "Silence de mort sur la mort" (376).

following the traces of Freud's Unconscious (*Ça*), marks the death of absolute self-knowledge (*savoir absolu, SA*). *Envois de vie.*

It appears destined, then, that Derrida comes upon the autobiographical drive of *Beyond the Pleasure Principle,* displayed symptomatically in Freud's discussion of the death instinct. Here Derrida's analysis focuses on the paradox of this drive: why would the inorganic thing leave its state of equilibrium only to return, after a long detour, to this earliest state of things? Why this passage of identity into the system of representations, this delegation of property to messengers, couriers, way stations, relays, deferrals, and delays? Why this Postal Principle that dictates that pleasure comes in *différance?* "What we are left with," writes Freud, "is the fact that the organism wishes to die only in its own fashion [*eigenen Todesweg des Organismus*]" (SE 18: 39). Identity and originality are not present at the earliest state of things but are the achieved effects of a "return" or "repetition" that both requires and sublates death in the economy of the "proper [*eigen*]" (LCP 381/PC 355).[31] Derrida suggestively associates the "authenticity" achieved by this "being-for-death" with Heidegger's *Daseinanalyse* and the *fort/da* of grandson Ernst. In each case the economy of representing absence or one's "own" death yields the profit of the autobiographical speculation, as *la mort propre* becomes *l'amour-propre.* The errant way of this economy, moreover, is extended by Derrida from autobiography to the problematic of the "signature," the mark of auto-affection and auto-appropriation. What has been said of Freud and Heidegger holds too for Rilke, Husserl, and Blanchot: "The proper name does not come to erase itself, it comes by erasing itself, to erase itself, it comes only in its erasure, or according to the other syntax, it *amounts to, comes back to erasing itself. It arrives only to erase itself*" (LCP 382/PC 360).[32] Such is the *jouissance* of the mail/male

---

31. Derrida writes that Freud speaks of "la loi de la-vie-la-mort comme loi du propre. La vie *et* la mort ne s'opposent que pour la servir. Par-delà toutes les oppositions, sans identification ou synthèse possible, il s'agit bien d'une *économie* de la mort, d'une loi du propre (*oikos, oikonomia*) qui gouverne le détour et cherche inlassablement l'événement propre, sa propre propriation (*Ereignis*) plutôt que la vie *et* la mort, la vie *ou* la mort. L'allongement ou l'abrégement du détour seraient au service de cette loi proprement économique ou écologique du soi-même comme propre, de l'auto-affection auto-mobile du *fort:da*" (LCP 381–82/PC 359).

32. In "Literature and the Right to Death," *The Gaze of Orpheus and Other Essays,* trans. Lydia Davis (Barryton, N.Y.: Station Hill Press, 1981), Maurice Blanchot writes: "The writer who writes a work eliminates himself as he writes that work and at the same time affirms himself in it. If he has written it to get rid of himself, it turns out that the work engages him and recalls himself to himself, and if he writes it to reveal himself and live in it, he sees that what he has done is nothing. . . . Or again he has written because in the depth of language he heard the work of death as it prepared living beings for the truth of their name: he worked for this nothingness and he himself was a nothingness at work.

system. The theory of autobiography as displacement without origin, then, is assimilated finally to the general patriarchal economy of the signature effect, positioned as an exemplary instance of what occurs when characters of "proper" identity are put into circulation.

The death *of* autobiography. DOA. Derrida. "*Ça envoie.*" *Envois SA.* Mort/Da. Dada. Papa. Da-sign d'amour.

But as one realizes the void, one creates a work, and the work, born of fidelity to death, is in the end no longer capable of dying; and all it brings to the person who was trying to prepare an unstoried death for himself is the mockery of immortality" (58).

PART TWO

AMERICAN
LETTERS

CHAPTER FOUR

Economy and Literary History,
or Marx and Freud in Concord

This conception of history thus relies on expounding the real process of production—starting from the material production of life itself—and comprehending the form of intercourse connected with and created by this mode of production, i.e., civil society in its various stages, as the basis of all history; describing it in its action as the state, and also explaining how all the different theoretical products and forms of consciousness, religion, philosophy, morality, etc., etc., arise from it, and tracing the process of their formation from that basis. . . . It has not, like the idealist view of history, to look for a category in every period, but remains constantly on the real ground of history; it does not explain practice from the idea but explains the formation of ideas from material practice.

—Marx and Engels, *The German Ideology*

And this history, if it has any meaning, is governed in its entirety by the value of truth and by a certain relation, inscribed in the hymen in question, *between* literature and truth. In saying "this history, if it has any meaning," one seems to be admitting that it might not. But if we were to go to the end of this analysis, we would see it confirmed not only that this history [of the relation of literature and truth] has a meaning, but that the very concept of history has lived only upon the possibility of meaning, upon the past, present, or promised presence of meaning and of truth. Outside this system, it is impossible to resort to the concept of history without reinscribing it elsewhere, according to some specific systematic strategy.

—Derrida, *Dissemination*

In this and the following chapters, American literature provides the material for assessing that return of the subject of history so evident in recent criticism. I shall be examining a variety of theoretical models for mediating between writing, subjectivity, and history, including Marxism, psychoanalysis, old and new historicism, African-American criticism, and poststructuralism. At times the investigation will take the form of metacommentary, deconstructing previous theoretical work on American literary history. At other times I shall be offering readings of specific authors and texts in order to explore alternative directions for historical interpretation. In any case I shall be arguing throughout that efforts to write historically in the United States have always to some degree foundered on the problem of the subject's location and agency in history; moreover, the history of the United States has promoted a tradition in which writers and theorists have sought to identify—and identify with—a totalizing Subject of History. One thinks of the notions of the American Dream, the Errand into the Wilderness, the Virgin Land, the Representative Man, or the American Adam. To borrow Fredric Jameson's terms, these figures have an ideological function in the service of oppressive powers that has at least matched their utopian desire to imagine a better world elsewhere.[1] Their partiality in determining which people may actually become the subject of history has traditionally been obscured by that most American of ideologemes—"democracy." Even as the deconstruction of traditional literary and sociopolitical structures helps advance the cause of cultural democracy (and so crosses paths with democracy's rejuventated popularity around the globe), one should not forget what Marxist analysis can teach about the limitations of meaning, and life, under capitalism.

Reification and Logocentrism

Marxism offers a philosophy of history that coincides with a critical praxis aimed at debunking the histories of politics, economics, literature, society, and philosophy itself. The revolutionary position of authority it offers to the critic who discovers its truth and thus becomes one with the subject of history is doubtless a tempting one (as Georg Lukács discovered). The feeling of urgency and legitimacy infusing the current American return to Marx also stems (somewhat ironically) from the stature granted him by the very Continental speculators who brought us poststructuralist textuality. Histories of contemporary criti-

---

1. See Fredric Jameson, *The Political Unconscious: Narrative as a Socially Symbolic Act* (Ithaca: Cornell University Press, 1981), pp. 281–99. In Jameson's dialectical model "even hegemonic or ruling-class culture and ideology are Utopian, not in spite of their instrumental function to secure and perpetuate class privilege and power, but rather precisely because that function is also in and of itself the affirmation of collective solidarity" (291).

cism now widely repeat the story of how the initial infatuation with French theory remained within formalism, and how the way beyond aestheticism requires the remedy of dialectical materialism. Some critics seek an alliance between deconstruction and Marxism, arguing that Marx's critique of idealism and his exposure of the modes of production underwriting society's truth-claims parallel Derrida's short-circuiting of Hegelian dialectics and his deconstruction of the West's logocentrism.[2] Yet, as Andrew Parker has argued, such an accommodation avoids the imperative to *read* the concepts and tropes in Marx's texts, especially those of "materialism" and "history."[3] These notions are shaken systematically by Derrida's adaptation of Heidegger's fundamental ontology, now reaimed through Nietzsche and Saussure, so that the being of things and the structures of time are inseparable from interpretation and "writing." As I tried to show in the first chapter of this book, Derrida has been busy *reading* Marx since the outset of his career. That reading takes place in no single essay but in the displacement and dissemination of traditional concepts; it occurs in the insistent, calculated, almost monotonous *reinscription* of Marx's major terms: idealism, materialism, dialectics, contradiction, history, value, production, property, authority, circulation, gold, and above all *economy*. Derrida deploys Freud and Heidegger with Nietzsche and Saussure to decipher the "metaphysical materialism" still shadowing the figures of Marx. At the same time, Marx's genealogy of commodity fetishism plays an influential role in Derrida's tracing of the metaphysical economy at the center of psychoanalysis, linguistics, and philosophy.

Endeavors to correct literary theory with the aid of Marxism or to extend textuality into the domain of history can partly be measured by the degree to which they recognize the problems raised by Derrida's reinscription of Marx. Carolyn Porter's *Seeing and Being: The Plight of the Participant Observer in Emerson, James, Adams, and Faulkner*, for example, offers itself as a Marxist rejoinder to the "ahistoricism" of much American literary criticism and ends by sketching a fusion of semiotic and ideological analysis to bridge the gap between writing and history.[4] While never directly confronting deconstruction, Porter's critique implicitly stands as an alternative to those methods perceived as privileging

2. See Michael Ryan, *Marxism and Deconstruction: A Critical Articulation* (Baltimore: Johns Hopkins University Press, 1982).

3. Andrew Parker, " 'Taking Sides' (On History): Derrida Re-Marx," *Diacritics* 11 (Fall 1981): 57–73, and "Between Dialectics and Deconstruction: Derrida and the Reading of Marx," in *After Strange Texts: The Role of Theory in the Study of Literature*, ed. Gregory S. Jay and David L. Miller (University: University of Alabama Press, 1985), pp. 146–68.

4. Carolyn Porter, *Seeing and Being: The Plight of the Participant Observer in Emerson, James, Adams, and Faulkner* (Middletown, Conn.: Wesleyan University Press, 1981).

the forms of language over the forms of society. Her considerable achievements, however, bring us to the limitations of her version of Marx, which relies on questionable definitions of the historical and the material. At the same time, the success of her commentaries on self-contradictory texts suggests the return of literary problematics at the expense of historical determination.

Porter's study also conveniently allows Americanists an indirect debate with Marxism's best current literary theorist, Fredric Jameson, since her chief source is Georg Lukács, the thinker to whom Jameson is most indebted. *Seeing and Being* and *The Political Unconscious* both appeared in 1981. Revising and renewing Lukács's writings on modernism, Jameson does extraordinary work on how the forms of nineteenth-century European fiction reflect the lived conditions of capitalism; it makes sense to try the Lukácsean model on American literary and political history in the same era, recognizing that this dislocation will entail many modifications.[5] Porter's Preface explains that she had found a recurrent pattern in American literary history—the "crisis in which the observer discovers his participation within the world he has thought to stand outside" (xviii)—and yet lacked a thesis for it. The answer came when she "happened upon Lukács' essay 'Reification and the Consciousness of the Proletariat.' This discovery was followed by my first serious reading of Marx and led to the conclusions adumbrated in this essay" (xvii).[6] Unfortunately, Lukács's theory of reification may be precisely what prevents a serious reading of Marx. Such a reading would detail how the genealogy of commodity fetishism goes beyond economy in the literal sense, how the concepts of the thing, the subject, materiality, ideality, and history are themselves conceptual fetishes.

Lukács's theory of reification should be understood against the larger backdrop of his place at the advent of "Western Marxism." Lukács returns to Hegel and to dialectics in order to insist that Marxism is a

---

5. While Porter could not have read *The Political Unconscious*, she does cite Jameson's earlier books. More crucially, her first chapter quotes at length from Jameson's essay "Criticism in History," where he rehearses his model for a Marxist stylistic criticism of European fiction (see Jameson, *The Ideologies of Theory: Essays 1971–1986*, 2 vols. [Minneapolis: University of Minnesota Press, 1988], 1: 119–36). Porter writes that Jameson's "model suggests how we might pursue the issue of hegemony in the American literary tradition as a means of constructing a literary history bearing some relation to its European counterparts other than that of a binary opposition which merely serves to privilege one tradition over the other, depending on whether one favors the romantic or the realistic" (21).

6. Compare John Flores's excellent assessment of Lukács's career in "Proletarian Meditations: Georg Lukács' Politics of Knowledge," *Diacritics* 2 (Fall 1972): 10–21. Flores too hopes that an elucidation of the "Hegelian rationalist backbone of Marxism . . . could stimulate that much needed undertaking of philosophically amplifying and substantiating the intellectual tenets of American criticism" (21).

method, not a dogmatic *content;* that method achieves real historical understanding by analyzing contradictions as indicative of objective relations in a concrete social totality (which is impossible to represent *as such,* though it can be reconstructed from its effects).[7] Consciousness is both the effect and the agency of ideology, and ultimately reflects the subject's class position.[8] Epistemology turns out to be a branch of political science, and only the proletariat are historically destined to know themselves as the subject-object of history. The theory of reification is aimed both at scientific empiricism *and* "vulgar" materialism (Marxist or otherwise), so that Lucien Goldmann can argue that a profound common project links Lukács to Heidegger, since both challenge the instrumental rationality and objective cognition essential to modernity.[9] "Reification and the Consciousness of the Proletariat" explicitly theorizes the socially constructed character of perception, and so belongs to that tradition from Hegel to Derrida that analyzes the ruses of sense-certainty.[10] Thus we should not be surprised that Derrida's critique of logocentrism, derived from Heidegger's work on technology and language, should offer suggestive resemblances to the critique of reification, though we should be prepared to find Derrida objecting to Marxist theory for the same reasons that Heidegger objected to Lukács.

Building on the work of Max Weber and George Simmel, Lukács tries to account for the cognitive, scientific, and aesthetic structures of modernity (the binaries of idealism/materialism and subject/object, the experiences of rationalization and alienation, the contemplative aesthetic, etc.) by placing the consciousness of reification at the center of the history described by dialectical materialism. His originality lay not only in articulating dialectical criticism as a method for cultural analysis, but in his extrapolations from Marx's few scattered passages on commodity fetishism. Within a context of rapid international industrial development, the ongoing transition to a consumer economy, a move among German intellectuals back to Hegel and away from the ruling positivism of the late nineteenth century, and the growing influence of psychoanalysis and other discourses of desire, the theory of commodity

7. See Georg Lukács, "What Is Orthodox Marxism?" in *History and Class Consciousness,* trans. Rodney Livingstone (Cambridge: MIT Press, 1971), pp. 1–26; for Jameson's extension of Lukács's position, see "Towards Dialectical Criticism" in his *Marxism and Form: Twentieth-Century Dialectical Theories of Literature* (Princeton: Princeton University Press, 1971), pp. 306–416.

8. In Louis Althusser's formula (often cited by Jameson), "Ideology represents the imaginary relationship of individuals to their real conditions of existence." See Althusser, *Lenin and Philosophy,* trans. Ben Brewster (London: New Left Books, 1971), p. 162.

9. Lucien Goldmann, *Lukács and Heidegger: Towards a New Philosophy,* trans. William Q. Boelhower (London: Routledge and Kegan Paul, 1977).

10. See *History and Class Consciousness,* pp. 110–49.

fetishism now appeared to be Marx's key insight. But a look back into Marx's texts discloses serious obstacles to the way in which Lukács and his heirs narrated reification.

"Only the conventions of our everyday life," writes Marx in *A Contribution to the Critique of Political Economy*, "make it appear commonplace and ordinary that social relations of production should assume the shape of things, so that the relations into which people enter in the course of their work appear as the relations of things to one another and of things to people. . . . All the illusions of the Monetary System arise from the failure to perceive that money, though a physical object with distinct properties, represents a social relation of production."[11] Objects, facts and values are the ideological result of historical processes and mystified representations. Lukács brilliantly capitalizes on Marx's thesis to elaborate its subversive consequences for our trust in science, the subject-object dualism, and the philosopher's "thing-in-itself." Nevertheless, his essay is betrayed by a residual idealism that represses the more radical implications of Marx's text.

Heidegger's passing remarks in *Being and Time* on reification already suggest how a deconstruction of Marxist terms would proceed. The question of "fundamental ontology" upsets the materialist ground of the theory reification and, as I showed in my first chapter, this questioning becomes Derrida's way of connecting the histories of philosophy, economics, and figurative language.[12] From a deconstructive perspective, the "Monetary System" may be only a species of a larger metaphysical economy of *denomination* which includes classical ontology and the theory of metaphor. For Marx, "gold becomes the measure of value only because all commodities are measured in terms of gold; it is consequently merely an illusion created by the circulation process to suppose that money makes commodities commensurable" (*Critique* 67–68). Marx's footnote to this passage discusses the theory of "commensurability" in Aristotle, where, as Derrida demonstrated, it illustrates a metaphysics of truth as rational equivalence and self-identical presence. Following Heidegger's lead, Derrida links the Marxist critique of the false commensurability produced by money (and reproduced in the phenomena of technology and rationalization) with a critique of the delusory identities produced by the circulation process of language.

Thus the relation of economics to language, and of modes of produc-

11. Karl Marx, *A Contribution to the Critique of Political Economy*, ed. Maurice Dobb, trans. S. W. Ryazanskay (New York: International Publishers, 1970), pp. 34–35.

12. See Martin Heidegger, *Being and Time*, trans. John Macquarrie and Edward Robinson (New York: Harper, 1962), pp. 72, 472, 487, and Goldmann, *Lukács and Heidegger*, pp. 12–13, 40–51. One must be skeptical, however, about Goldmann's alliance of Lukács

tion to literary forms, cannot be fitted to a base/superstructure model. If the relation between the histories of monetary and linguistic denomination is *supplementary* (in Derrida's sense), then history cannot be pictured as running from a purely authentic origin to an essentially debased end. While Marxism often depends on certain logocentric tropes and strategies to mount its critiques, its own analyses unfold in ways that betray such assumptions. So it is that any thought of an original economy that was untainted by reification proves as untenable as the thesis that language originated in a natural nomenclature without metaphor. As *Capital* puts it, the difference between facts and values is inscribed in a "social hieroglyphic . . . for the characteristic which objects of utility have of being values is as much men's social product as is their language."[13] And the same may be said of their characteristic of being perceptible objects. "Pure immediacy and fetishism are equally untrue" writes Adorno, who rejected the nostalgia in reification theory and urged that a "negative dialectics" replace the binary thinking that sets up a false choice between subjective immediacy and objective alienation.[14] Marx's texts describe the economy of a "circulation process" at work well before the advent of modern "capitalism," and suggest that the rigorous distinction between matter and signification underwriting the theory of reification may be "merely an illusion." Such a reading of Marx will stymie even the most sophisticated efforts to localize reification as the determined effect of a particular historical or socioeconomic condition. The phenomena of reification belong to an overdetermined history of "object relations" which would include the contributions of ontology as well as of psychoanalysis.

In Porter's *Seeing and Being*, the concrete history of American capitalism as a mode of production receives foregrounded attention in accounting for the forms of literary consciousness. As she summarizes it, "reification refers to a process in the course of which man becomes alienated from himself. This process is generated by the developing autonomy of a commodified world of objects" which presents men and their works in the alien guise of things. Mystified as to the sociohistorical genesis of things, reified man views his world "as a given, an external and objective reality operating according to its own immutable laws." This delusion will "infiltrate the consciousness of everyone living in a

---

with Heidegger; see, for example, Lukács's criticisms of Heidegger in his essay on existentialism, collected in Lukács, *Marxism and Human Liberation*, ed. E. San Juan, Jr. (New York: Dell, 1973), pp. 243–66.

13. Karl Marx, *Capital*, vol. 1, trans. Ben Fowkes (New York: Vintage, 1977), p. 167.

14. Theodor Adorno, *Negative Dialectics*, trans. E. B. Ashton (New York: Continuum, 1973), p. 374.

society driven by capitalist growth." Man assumes a " 'contemplative' stance in the face of that objectivized and rationalized reality" hallucinated by reification (xi–xii). Reification, in Lukács's hands, combines a Marxist emphasis on material conditions of determination with a phenomenological schema of mental structures. This bridge between the forms of production and consciousness provides Porter with her passage from an essay on literary psychology to a reading of how economics shapes writing. From Emerson's "transparent eyeball" through the observant minds in the works of James, Adams, and Faulkner, the "plight of the participant observer" turns out to be a function of contradictions inherent to American capitalism.

However modified or extenuated, Marxist literary histories depending on Lukács and reification invariably locate a Fall from authenticity at the decisive juncture of capitalism's appearance as a new mode of production. Many continue to place this event in the period from 1750 to 1848, despite abundant historical evidence, offered by Marxists and others, of the long and discontinuous history of economic organization in the West. The persistence of this postlapsarian narrative reflects the traditionally literal interpretation of Marx and Engels's writings; at another level it testifies to the metaphysical economy informing most Marxist accounts of history. As Rosalind Coward and John Ellis have shown, for many Marxists "the subject is presupposed as having some essential nature, which is alienated and distorted by ruling ideology. It is a presupposition which is very far from the materialist process proposed by Marx."[15] Lacanian psychoanalysis likewise traces this process to an economy of the signifier that splits the subject even as it constitutes it; this production of the subject in turn involves the assumption of a position in social discourse, or ideology. "Reality" and "objectivity" come about through the economy of desire's investments in images, so that the fantasy of reification in fact describes the accession to perception and language. Marx, Lacan, Althusser, and Derrida all contribute to the argument that the subject has no "nature," that the "material" always takes the form of a desire, and that there is no unalienated origin before, outside, or beyond the technologies of inscriptive production. Porter's opening definition—"reification refers to a process in the course of which man becomes alienated from himself"—participates in a mythic historiography of truth's self-estrangement and recovery in time. Is the "plight of the participant observer" original to capitalism, or is there always already "reification" when we employ matter and meanings to do our work?

15. Rosalind Coward and John Ellis, *Language and Materialism: Developments in Semiology and the Theory of the Subject*, (London: Routledge and Kegan Paul, 1977), p. 90.

Lukács's strictures regarding the historical uniqueness of reification are the moments in his book when Marx's speculations on the circuitous economy of denomination are foreclosed by the critic's design for a meaningful history. "Before tackling the problem itself," Lukács warns, "we must be quite clear in our minds that commodity fetishism is a *specific* problem of our age, the age of modern capitalism" (84). Any "divorce of the phenomena of reification from their economic bases" would simply reaffirm the delusions upon which capitalist ideology prospers (95). Lukács's reading of Kant likewise begins with a categorical constriction of focus: "Modern critical philosophy springs from the reified structure of consciousness. The specific problems of this philosophy are distinguishable from the problematics of previous philosophies by the fact that they are rooted in this structure" (111). This historicism does not resemble the genealogy of economy in Marx, where we find instead the story of a "circulation process" as old as recorded history, in which the dialectics of quantity/quality or base/superstructure are undone by a supplementary economy between matter and signification.

In the *Critique* Marx narrates how paper money emerges as the logos of economic denomination. The emergence of this abstract script parodically repeats the history of metaphysical philosophy, replicating both the eternally recurrent structure of philosophy's various truths and the teleological fable of knowledge coming to itself in time. This seeming homology and unified history, however, is subverted by Marx's own analysis of the problematics of denomination and perception: at the "origin" the primal scenes of unmediated perception, of barter, of use value, of communal production are always already imbued by metaphysics, insofar as the script of language begins with illusory feats of "commensurability," with metaphorical equations which allow us to name, know, and use objects in the world. Abstract denomination is not unique to the *end* of the monetary economy as it arrives at paper money; rather such metaphysics are requisite to the production of economy per se, to the coinages that enable an appropriation, exchange, or distribution of values.

Alongside the developmental or diachronic history of the monetary system, then, runs the allegory of another history, of a "capitalism" coincident with the synchronic structure of metaphysical conceptualization itself. Hegelianism stood on its feet is capitalism, a restricted economy of translations, exchanges, and metaphors that enables the ascription of properties and the capitalization of proper nouns. It is in order to trace this other history that Derrida substitutes "logocentrism" for "reification." All the classical tropes of metaphysics—lucidity, conscious intention, self-knowledge, the unity of historical periods, the existence of true grounds, the unproblematic naming of specific and distinguish-

able identities, the root of things in their original and proper structure—
necessarily come into play when Lukács imposes a history of meaning
on capitalism. Capitalism might instead be read as the economy of the
history of meaning, including what has historically been relegated to
the margin between political, philosophical, natural, and literary economies.

In retrospect, Lukács himself saw problems in claiming an absolute
historical specificity or uniqueness for the phenomenon of reification.
His 1967 Preface concedes that

> objectification is indeed a phenomenon that cannot be eliminated from
> human life in society. If we bear in mind that every externalisation of an
> object in practice (and hence, too, in work) is an objectification, that every
> human expression including speech objectifies human thoughts and feel-
> ings, then it is clear that we are dealing with a universal mode of commerce
> between men. And in so far as this is the case, objectification is a neutral
> phenomenon; the true is as much an objectification as the false, liberation
> as much as enslavement. Only when the objectified forms in society acquire
> functions that bring the essence of man into conflict with his existence,
> only when man's nature is subjugated, deformed and crippled can we
> speak of an objective societal condition of alienation and, as an inexorable
> consequence, of all the subjective marks of an internal alienation. (xxiv)[16]

Thus, though "reification is closely related" to "alienation," the two
are not socially or conceptually identical, however *History and Class
Consciousness* had confused them (xxv).

Three terms are actually at work in the passage: objectification, alienation, and reification. The first is a "neutral" phenomenon of sociomaterial existence per se; the second is a permutation of that phenomenon when objectification works to oppress man; the third is the unique
form that oppressive objectification takes under capitalism. All three
get mixed in various formulas by the many critiques of reason, whether
by the Frankfurt School, the Heidegger of the technology essays, Derrida, or Foucault. For Derrida, Lukács's admission that "every human
expression including speech objectifies human thoughts and feelings"
would have to be recast in terms of the history of logocentrism, and this
via Derrida's Heideggerean account of how representation conceals
what it reveals. The idea of a representation that could objectify *neutrally*

16. One might note, though, that the 1947 essay on existentialism reaffirms the theses
on commodity fetishism and reification in charging that the "nothingness" produced by
life under capitalism is reified into an ontological datum by the existentialists, preeminently Heidegger. Heidegger "lodges the entire problem in the fetishized structure of
the bourgeois mind, in the dreary hopeless nihilism and pessimism of the intellectuals of
the interval between the two world wars" (*Marxism and Human Liberation*, p. 254).

makes no sense from an ontological standpoint (in the wake of deconstruction): since the being of Being and the being of representation
are never coincident, objectification in representation always involves a
reduction of quality to quantity, a loss of value in the attachment of a
price. The priority of language's world-disclosing power—its prece-
dence to any particular identity—means that "thoughts and feelings"
cannot be the origins for whom representatives transparently stand. In
this view the difference between objectification and alienation loses its
force. And insofar as it can be demonstrated that language and the
commodity form operate according to strictly analogous and interwoven
economies, the differences between objectification, alienation, and reification cease to appear decisive.

   The question of language's role in reification is one of two principal
problems to pose. The second concerns the centrality of the subjective
in Lukács's diagnosis (though strictly speaking this can be seen as precisely the emphasis that allows for the repression of the question of
language). Lukács had originally developed his theory of reification by
adapting Max Weber's notion of "rationalization" to a reading of Marx's
chapter on "commodity fetishism." The result was a specification of the
particular form that oppressive rationality takes in market capitalism—
a form marked by its subjective, psychological constitution. Lukács's
Hegelian turn allowed him to theorize reification as a subjective state;
Marx's chapter seemed to provide an exact locus where the structure
of capitalism as an economic system and the structure of consciousness
under capitalism converged. This conjunction was crucial to Lukács's
metanarrative, in which the proletariat realized their alienation and so
became the subject-object of history, accomplishing their achievement
of self-identity through a revolution that would destroy the conditions
of their alienation. Weber's pessimism would be cured by the Hegelian
figure of the proletariat as subject of history. When Lukács looked back,
he concluded that his "account of the contradictions of capitalism as
well as of the revolutionisation of the proletariat is unintentionally
coloured by an overriding subjectivism" (xviii). Considering the zeal
with which the young Lukács supplemented Marx with Hegel, this
professed lack of intentionality rings false. Only the figures of subjectivity could allow Lukács to humanize the phenomena for which "reification" became the metaphor. Unfortunately, reification theory usually
ends up back in the subject/object dualism Lukács hoped to escape, and
its subjective emphasis gets appropriated by thinkers who are quite at
odds with a Marxist materialism: "The cause of human suffering,"
observes Adorno, "will be glossed over rather than denounced in the
lament about reification. The trouble is with the conditions that condemn mankind to impotence and apathy and would yet be changeable

by human action; it is not primarily with people and with the way conditions appear to people."[17] Adorno gets beyond Lukács, but his formula still leaves us with the challenge of describing, and deconstructing, the representational economy between "conditions" and their "appearance."

Lukács's subjectification of rationalization could be read as another instance of logocentrism—not simply in the sense of the repression of writing, mediation, and alienation—but as an attempt to impose a metaphysical regime on the phenomena of cultural history. As Habermas has stressed, at its origins Western Marxism, by virtue of its recourse to Hegel, must construct its metanarrative by figuring cultural history under the metaphor of the self-reflecting, self-knowing, self-totalizing subject. This will make it a rich source for the reading of texts from the cultural history it is attempting to interpret, but these readings will pay for their insight with the blindness stipulated by the philosophy of consciousness and its attendant closures of the play of representation. Its readings of texts will appear correct exactly in proportion to the degree that these texts serve its self-reflection: it will produce its own analyses, never its own cures. At the same time, this subjectivism will allow revisionists like Althusser and Jameson to update Lukácsean Marxism by way of psychoanalysis, thus both perpetuating the errors of subjectivism *and* providing analyses that point to theories of the subject beyond those of bourgeois individualism and aesthetic formalism. The subject might then return as an agency for change.

When Jameson recasts the ideas of *Marxism and Form* in *The Political Unconscious,* he does so through poststructuralism, particularly through Lacan's theory of the subject and its adaptation by Althusser.[18] (The rich complexity resulting from this new way of adapting psychoanalysis is, as we shall see, missing from Porter's book.) "From a Marxist point of view," Jameson writes, "this experience of the decentering of the subject and the theories, essentially psychoanalytic, which have been devised to map it are to be seen as the signs of the dissolution of an essentially bourgeois ideology of the subject" (125). Following Lukács's argument that the increased *quantity* of reification under capitalism dialectically produces a distinctive *quality* of (alienated) life, Jameson theorizes that the mode of production is, in the last instance, determi-

17. Adorno, *Negative Dialectics,* p. 190. Adorno acknowledges the importance of *History and Class Consciousness,* and is more concerned to attack the way reification theory has been taken up by humanists, theologians, and romantic antimodernists. For his critique of Heidegger in this regard, see pp. 61–131.

18. Jameson prepared for this move by writing his influential 1977 essay "Imaginary and Symbolic in Lacan: Marxism, Psychoanalysis, and the Problem of the Subject," reprinted in *Ideologies of Theory,* 1: 75–118.

nant of the inflection given to a culture's structure of denomination. To amalgamate heterogeneous terms, one might say that while logocentrism is always already at work in culture, reification is the dialect of its utterance under capitalism.

Yet because reification depends on a *narrative* that casts differences in value as points on a spectrum from original authenticity to estrangement and loss, Jameson is constantly in danger of resurrecting the ghost of a metaphysical *telos* for literary and cultural history. On occasion Jameson is unabashedly totalizing, as when he describes human history as "the unity of a single great collective story" (19). In this story the episode of reification in modernity "conveys the historical situation in which the emergence of the ego or centered subject can be understood: the dissolution of the older organic or hierarchical social groups, the universal commodification of the labor-power of individuals and their confrontation as equivalent units within the framework of the market, the *anomie* of these now 'free' and isolated individual subjects to which the protective development of a monadic armature alone comes as something of a compensation" (153–54). By the end of his book Jameson admits the "Althusserian and post-structuralist critique" of "the notion of a 'subject of history,' " yet insists that "it seems possible to continue to use a Durkheimian or Lukácsean vocabulary of collective consciousness or of the subject of history 'under erasure' " (294). This maneuver may be respected, along with the achievements it enables, even as one questions the manner in which Lukácsean Marxism theorizes "the subject of history," especially in the way it privileges logocentric notions of class and economic mode of production at the expense of other more marginalized subject positions and histories. The modern history of critical Marxism, in fact, includes attempts to think the consequences of admitting such subjects as women, persons of color, gays, and lesbians and Third World people to the category of the subject (as Jameson himself does in other contexts). Deconstruction points out how the historical exclusion of these subjects coincides with the exclusion of the subject of writing, since the economy of representation was always already essential to the reproduction of the economy of the empowered subject of history.

From Emerson's Nature to Gatsby's Shirts

Employing the theories of Lukács, Jameson, and Raymond Williams, Porter's *Seeing and Being* respectfully contests the ahistoricism characterizing much of the best writing about American literary history; that ahistoricism repeats—rather than analyzes—the mystifications afflicting

America's authors. Critics such as D. H. Lawrence, Leslie Fiedler, Richard Poirier, R. W. B. Lewis, Richard Chase, F. O. Matthiessen, and Charles Feidelson all tend to tell a tale of the American desire to "get away" from society, but to tell it in a fashion that turns our attention away from history and toward the fetishized forms of mythic, personal, or aesthetic criticism. Porter would have us (contra Nietzsche) remember history, and so she will have to write that history, again, herself and provide it as the origin for her readings. Surrounding her textual commentaries with chapters of historical material, she shows that American literary history, when its reifications are decoded, "harbors a set of texts in which is inscribed, in its own terms, as deep and as penetrating a response to history and social reality as any to be found in the work of a Balzac or a George Eliot" (xvii). Porter's opening chapter shrewdly shows that the tendency to see American literature as a flight from social experience into utopias or purgatories of style and psychology—a tendency common to both left- and right-wing critics—stems from a false opposition between industry (or business or technology or the city) and nature (or agriculture or art or the country). Following Williams, she accurately insists that such dualisms mask the reality of *capitalism,* the term deceptively avoided by such ahistorical nomenclatures.

The effects of capitalism on American literature may be explained through Williams's chapter on Gramsci's theory of "hegemony." Hegemony, Porter recounts, goes beyond "the rigid category of class rule as the direct determinant of all social and political formations" and thus is "a useful tool for integrating cultural formations within one's vision of society understood as a total, dynamic process, and for avoiding the pitfalls of 'abstract models' such as base/superstructure, ideology, and the like, which tend to reduce our vision of society to a tableau depicting the domination of one class by another" (15). (Porter's turn from class ideology to hegemony seems to abandon the pivotal thesis Lukács puts forward in the book that contains the essay on reification: *History and Class Consciousness.*) The rehistoricization of American literature means reading the effects produced by the hegemony of American capitalism in its special historical circumstances. In the absence of a monarchical state or feudal society, American capitalism and middle-class society grew phenomenally in the nineteenth century. The peculiar form of asocial, "atomistic freedom" imposed on Americans shows that alienation arrives more quickly and forcefully than in Europe, along with its literary forms and expressions, including the turn from public rhetoric to private style and from social concern to psychological, epistemological, natural, or aesthetic epiphanies and catastrophes: "Why should anomie, atomization, subjectivism, a concern with language—all features of modernism as Jameson defines it—appear in the literature of pre-Civil War northeastern America? The question for Marxist criticism is how this early evidence of modernism is related to the accelerated pace of capitalist expansion during the pre-Civil War years" (21). Certainly this is an important and neglected question, but its premises obscure as much as they reveal. The citation of Jameson is telling, since his version of modernism everywhere displays Lukács's imprint. Unlike Paul de Man and others who have recently proposed we deconstruct the historical periodization of modernism—who read modernism as an effect of contradictions in language that always occur wherever literature tries to have a history—Porter and Jameson endorse a narrowly "historical" view of the advent of alienation, reification, and a "concern with language."

Porter's chapter "Reification and American Literature" presents a cogent and careful explication of Lukács's theses, but it does not anticipate or answer the kinds of deconstructive objections I have sketched above. She does conclude that what has been reified is "neither man per se nor a primary nature out there beyond the objectivized world of immediacy, but rather that 'sensuous human activity' encompassing both which we shall hereafter take as the referent for 'history' " (30). This rightly resists the subject/object and nature/culture dualisms; the causal link, however, between literal capitalism and this mystification of production remains intact, along with the "sensuous" as the "referent for history.' " The reference of reification to capitalism is what will not stay grounded; indeed, the more Porter piles up her overwhelming evidence of the self-undermining character of these texts, the more their uncanniness appears to exceed any conventionally historical explanation. De Man rather than Lukács would be the appropriate mentor here, where history seems to be one of the effects of trying to put a stop to the indeterminacy of any rhetorical epistemology.

The absorption of historical determinism by a vaster contradictory economy happens again when Porter invokes the uncertainty principle of Heisenberg, which recognizes the participatory "interference of our instruments of observation in the behavior being observed" (30–31). This paradox (also explained by Heidegger's meditations on technology) cannot be restricted to the age of capitalism; for Heisenberg, it is a scientific universal. If we translate Heisenberg's insight into contemporary terms and say "there is no metalanguage," the historical and conceptual antiquity of the observer/participant dilemma (or aporia) shows through. Nor can one argue that capitalism now makes possible (or forces upon us) a knowledge of this paradox; that would require reverting again to a teleological narrative of truth's accomplishment in time and entail ignoring the evidence of this aporia in texts from Plato to Shakespeare. Significantly, Porter's summary accounts of Emerson,

Adams, James, and Faulkner that complete the chapter rely more on
Heisenberg than Lukács or Marx. She nonetheless finds that the "formal, stylistic, and thematic extremities to which American literature has
resorted reflect not a flight from the constraints of civilized life, but a
radical understanding of the mediated nature of the given social world"
(53). This is probably so, but what "social world," pre- or mid- or
late-capitalist, is not "mediated" by technologies of representation that
inherently prescribe the undecidable economy between observation and
participation?

In "Emerson's America," describing the concrete socioeconomic context shaping the chasm between seeing and being in transcendentalism,
Porter begins with the thesis that Emerson's "Oedipal revolt" against
the culture of the fathers should be historicized by a look at the class
structure of early nineteenth-century Boston. What follows, however,
is a much broader sketch of American economic life from 1820 to 1840
that provides keen commentaries on agrarian capitalism, the specialization of labor, the transition from craftsmen to factory workers, and the
rationalization of everyday life. The rhetorical gambit that translated
capitalism into technological innovation and productive industrialism
was the age's preeminent piece of hegemonic social mythmaking: "The
result was a dominant cultural vision—formed in the discourse of both
Whig and Democrat, both industrialist and reformer—of America in
transition from a rural to an industrial society, a transition given the
general name Progress, and the general result Prosperity" (88–89). Her
stunning grammar of this rhetorical hegemony convinces us, unintentionally, of the inadequacy of Lukács and reification as a sufficient
explanatory model. It suggests rather that the double bind of observa-
tion/participation always occurs in the expressive domain of any hegemony, not just those of capitalism, and in any place where a discourse
imposes its truth and power. If so, "commodification, rationalization,
and specialization" are not constitutive of this double bind as such, but
are the topoi it inhabits in a particular historical moment. They are the
inflections of logocentrism, as reification is a genre of metaphysical
denomination. These qualifications can be made by way of Foucault as
well as Derrida, or by reference to such analysts of cultural discourse
as Stephen Greenblatt, whose pioneering work in "new historicism"
describes "the process whereby subversive insights are generated in
the midst of apparently orthodox texts" during the Renaissance.[19] Or,

19. Stephen Greenblatt, "Invisible Bullets: Renaissance Authority and Its Subversion,"
Glyph 8 (Baltimore: Johns Hopkins University Press, 1981), pp. 40–61. Porter's book
often appears closer in practice to "new historicism" than to the poststructuralist
Marxism of Jameson; for more on the difficulty of distinguishing these movements,
see below, Chap. 7.

following the later Jameson, one might seek in the "problem of the subject" a place where the mediation between writing and history, or logocentrism and reification, takes both specific and unpredictable forms. (In my chapter below on Douglass I sketch how rhetorical theory might provide an account of this process.) A theory of the work of desire in language would have to supplement any deterministic account of the economy's prescriptions for literature, and this would open the door to the errancy or "relative autonomy" of the signifier.

"Emerson's America" is one of only two chapters in *Seeing and Being* (the other is "Faulkner's America") composed solely of historical materials to the exclusion of interpretive commentaries. The Preface justifies this as an avoidance of naive reductionism: "We do not need to examine in detail what was happening in society at the time these writers were active, because we can see the reifying process acting within the texts they produced" (xix). While disclaiming mimetic or homological fallacies, this thesis (which seems to explain the disjunction between her theoretical, historical, and exegetical chapters) relies on a visual metaphor Porter's own book challenges. As an observer of reification, she finds herself participating in the very divorce of writing from history her text criticizes. In this she follows the attempts of Lukács and Jameson to supersede the vulgar determinism of the base/superstructure model. Porter's American texts "constitute and record a series of 'social projects' in and of themselves, projects in whose rhetorical and narrative complexities lie sedimented the social contradictions generated by the reifying process" (xix). The metaphor of sedimentation eludes defining the mechanism of this geneticism and allows for the recovery of formalism ("in and of themselves"). The historicist rapprochement with form and textuality founders unless it more radically deconstructs the concepts of the material, the formal, the meaningful, and the historical.

This may be illustrated by Porter's treatment of Emerson's theory of language. She does not tie Emerson's essays to specific political, economic, or social events; nor does she examine his writings on history, politics, or wealth. Her subject is Emerson's rhetoric, her evidence the usual canon of *Nature*, "The American Scholar," "Self-Reliance," "Circles," and "Fate." Her unusual conclusion is that Emerson's attribution of spiritual symbolism to natural objects repeats the very alienation of man it had been designed to heal. But can any attempt to represent the truth of nature or the substance of the material escape leaving the traces of its artificial construction? Doubtless *Nature* was written in revolt against the transformations being wrought by capitalism. Its second section is entitled "Commodity," and like Thoreau's opening chapter on "Economy" in *Walden*, it strikingly resembles Marx's 1844 manuscripts in questioning the costs involved in recent systems for producing values. In response to the ideological imposition of commodity values, Emerson insists that the forms of perception and society are man-made, hence susceptible to change. This change and the end of alienation depend on our ability to use nature as a sign-system. Porter expertly reminds us that the "process of signification . . . constitutes the real content of the essay" (105). Moreover, she shows that Emerson's idea of spirit is conjured to check the endless proliferation of signification and to install a text the poet reads (observation) rather than writes (participation). Emerson's legacy to James and Adams, then, is the return of idealism and reification.

But is this return a function of language? Of capitalism? Of both? Emerson laments that the alienation of language from nature in his time means that "a paper currency is employed, when there is no bullion in the vaults".[20] His metaphor borrows from the bank crises of the Jacksonian period and suggests the confluence of monetary and linguistic speculation, points made by Michael Gilmore in a reading that parallels Porter's except in its sociological concreteness. For Gilmore, "Emerson as well as Marx is concerned to make sense of, and ultimately to redeem, a world converted into articles of exchange."[21] To "make sense of" the world, however, entails converting it into "articles of exchange"; as Marx clearly argues in the *Critique,* use value and exchange value derive from a supplemental economy in which neither is the true original. The discourses of Marx and Emerson displace "nature" and "use value" during speculative readings that attempt their redemption. They display the operation of metaphor—exchange value—in the production of concepts like "nature" and "use." Emerson's etymologism in *Nature* ("Words are signs of natural facts") proposes a material genealogy to restore worthless linguistic currency to its primal sensual values, yet loses nature once more in defining it as an economy of metaphysical substitution ("Nature is the symbol of spirit"). The problematic of use value and exchange value repeats that of literal and metaphorical language (or of materiality and ideality), as Derrida outlines with specific reference to Marx in "White Mythology." What Emerson confronts as Ananke—fate, necessity, compensation, and death—is the ineluctable play of exchange value in a world in which there are differences but no positive terms. The accumulation of surplus value in literature, philosophy, and capitalist society sparks Emerson's divided attempt to regulate metaphorically the economy of signs through the production

20. Ralph Waldo Emerson, *Nature,* in *Works,* 14 vols. (Boston: Houghton Mifflin, 1883), 1: 35.
21. Michael T. Gilmore, "Emerson and the Persistence of Commodity," in *Emerson: Prospect and Retrospect,* ed. Joel Porte (Cambridge: Harvard University Press, 1982), p. 74.

of a transcendental referent; Marx's recourse to a historical rather than eternal referent reiterates this strategy as if in a mirror, though he too writes another history that subverts the concepts of natural use and uninterpreted matter.

The strange economy between use value and exchange value plays a crucial role in Porter's chapter on Henry James, though Lukács's influence prevents her from following the often-discussed connections between commodity fetishism and its correlates in epistemology and psychoanalysis—that train of substitutions in which penis, feces, money, gold, and truth constantly replace one another. For example, in discussing the problem of inaction in James's contemplative protagonists, Porter stops briefly over the case of Lambert Strether in *The Ambassadors*. In one long paragraph, she uses the word "impotence" or its cognates seven times to describe the powerlessness of his imagination. "James's long struggle with the seer's impotence" is "an issue which arises" early in the career and lasts through its climax in *The Golden Bowl* (126–27). Her diction can hardly be unwitting, for the issues of impotence and castration are familiar in James criticism. Strether is only one in a series of bachelor visionaries who have traded their sex for knowledge in a dubious epistemological transaction. The comedy of the novel turns on the innocence of the fifty-five-year-old seer who cannot see the carnal nature of Chad's relation to Madame de Vionnet, until that jarring moment when the vacationing lovers drift downstream into Strether's vision and shatter his aesthetic contemplation of a landscape he seems to possess in Edenic wonder. Of course Strether's impotence and psychic castration were the blindness that made his insights possible. The return of the repressed primal scene overthrows the dream of an artistic European order distinct from the chaos of America's vulgar mercantile materialism. The truth of Europe has been castration-truth, a fetish, a fantasy object predicated on the substitution of a presence/absence economy (culture versus nature, Europe versus America, et al.) for an intercourse of differences. Truth did not reside in the presence or absence of sexuality, Strether belatedly discovers, but in an exchange of personal properties that exceeded the business of morality.

The point is brought home by James's comic refusal to name the mysterious and trivial object manufactured in Woollett, Massachusetts in the factory owned by Mrs. Newsome, Strether's intended and Chad's mother. Like Strether's phallus, it goes unspoken yet serves as the center for the novel's various processes of circulation. Strether's decision to return to Woollett marks perhaps his recognition of the inevitability of exchange value (he is, after all, an editor by profession) and his insight into how innocent it was to seek beyond America for a domain of transcendental values, natural or cultural. The phallus and the word are each ambassadors, purveyors of truth, forever in circulation, valued and useful only in their displacement and exchange.[22] Reification may not be the consciousness of capitalism but a gender-specific anxiety peculiar to the object-relations of the mail/male system.

Can women be subjects of reification, even in male texts? In James's *The Golden Bowl*, American tycoon and connoisseur Adam Verver and his daughter Maggie "purchase" Prince Amerigo in a marital agreement that commodifies Europe and its truths. When the Prince resumes his liaison with Charlotte—now Mr. Verver's wife—Maggie becomes an artist of silence and misrepresentation to recoup her investment. Maggie gets Amerigo back, but Porter objects that "the novel's resolution is accomplished on grounds which presuppose a commodified world" (148). Should we see here a spectacle of natural relations and art perverted by money? Or, like Maggie, replace the speculations of the father with a gamble in which the return will never be the Same? For Maggie imagination, knowledge, figural language, and sexuality entail "economic" transactions, all those pervasive *calculations* at work in the novel's characters, scenes, and language. At least we should examine whether the play of Maggie's desire and her excess of consciousness subvert, as they mimic, the patriarchal system of reification and its needs.

If Maggie's location in the novel de-centers the *genre* of reification, this accords with James's disseminated speculation in the economy of metaphors without organic origins. *The Golden Bowl* abounds with an incongruous and extravagant number of sea and ship metaphors. They have no referent in the plot of the novel but do recall the commonplace textbook illustrations used to explain figurative tropes as a carrying away of meaning. Gold, too, turns up everywhere, underscoring the undecidable exchange between figurative and literal, or metaphor and money (as I explained it in Chapter 1).[23] The unrestricted economy of Jamesian metaphor again shows the instability of the use value/exchange value opposition, and so creates an aporia with any claim for the historical specificity of the "commodification" of life and art in *The Golden Bowl*. Porter, in a note summarizing *Capital's* argument, states: "The point is that commodities are never merely objects" (316 n. 21). The point as well is that objects are always commodities, as proper nouns are always metaphors. Porter knows that "only the act of exchange can prove whether a commodity has a use-value," but the extended

22. While his use of Lacan produces a better commentary on James, Jameson ultimately recasts and reendorses the conventional Left argument that James's work is in the service of bourgeois ideology. See *The Political Unconscious*, pp. 221–22.

23. See Jacques Derrida, *Dissemination*, trans. Barbara Johnson (Chicago: University of Chicago Press, 1981), pp. 262–65.

implications of this crack in Marx's golden bowl go unappreciated. She describes the Prince's movement from a commodity transaction to an exchange-value economy this way: "The Prince's straightforward honesty as seller of one commodity (his public identity), and buyer of another (his scientific future), would be all very well if he were dealing with another such innocent trader in a relatively primitive marketplace where most people trade in order to meet their needs and satisfy, as well as possible, their desires. But the Prince's desires are by no means so limited as to be met in such a market" (144). The errancy of the Prince's desires, however, traces a flaw in this formulation. Whether we learn it from James, Freud, Derrida, or the advertisements of a consumer society, we know by now that there are no innocent traders. Even in a "relatively primitive marketplace," exchange value contaminates use value. Moreover, the difference between needs and desires, so crucial to this oppositional economics, can never itself be anything but an original and risky investment. Need and desire also circulate in a supplemental process or, in Freud's term, connect through an *anaclisis* or dependency of the literal and the figural that frustrates a decisive hierarchy or chronological narrative. Need strictly conceived is the end or foreclosure of desire, the absolute mechanization of differential motion (translation) into a restricted economy of stimulus and response (incorporation of the proper). Need, in this sense, is *true,* while desire admits of delusion and miscarriage. The flaw in the logocentrism defining need as opposed to desire shows even in contemporary political discourse, wherein the lexicological tautology "truly needy" serves to mystify the interests of a vicious class ideology ("O reason not the need," exclaimed King Lear). Need works as a logos for the economics of use and exchange, yet need is the product of an economy between need and desire. Do we need "need" or desire it?

The major figure who stands alongside James in the critique of nineteenth-century American bourgeois culture is Henry Adams, who as history professor, novelist, political journalist, and autobiographer chronicled the breakdown of Western metanarratives from the subject's shattered point of view (see below, Chapter 6). Adam's ironic dismantling of the alternatives offered by religion, science, capitalism, and communism does not satisfy Porter. She sees his double writing as the "logical suicide to which his posture as impotent spectator and complicit participant led him" (203). Her reading finds fault with Adams despite her sensitivity to the symbolic construction of *The Education of Henry Adams,* which makes any ethical objections to the narrator's statements and predicaments quite difficult to sustain. As with Lukács, evaluative judgment short-circuits close reading. Porter prefers William Faulkner on the basis of the "purity" of his "ambivalence," his "stoic and open-faced acceptance of despair," his "recognition, registered in his greatest work, that the very project he himself pursues in his fiction, the drive to go beyond one's situation, is both irresistible and doomed" (48). After Adams (or after Freud and many others), can we accept authorial consciousness as the center of reliable interpretive judgment? Can we read at face value Faulkner's representation of his awareness of the duplicities in representation?

Seeing and Being arrives at the evolved truth of American socioliterary history in finding that Faulkner simultaneously exposes the mystifications of American ahistoricism and thwarts the reader's own reified interpretive habits. "Faulkner's America" asserts convincingly that the main failure of previous accounts of Thomas Sutpen in *Absalom, Absalom!* stems from blindness to the historical complicity of capitalism and slaveholding. Sutpen's career is "a register of American history" and his design a "mirror of the contradictions inherent in capitalist society" (238). This strictly Lukácsean construal of the forms of writing as reflections of forms of social relation gives way, in "The Reified Reader," to the somewhat asymmetrical contention that the novel is in essence unreadable. Abandoning Lukács's infamous objections to modernism and sounding more like Brecht or Adorno or de Man, Porter shows that the complexities of Faulkner's text shatter the hermeneutic complacencies of the reified reader. Faulkner's work merits a formal privilege by its disruption of the reader's mystified ideological conceptions.

These provocative claims elicit at least two modifications. First, the idea that a text "resists" the reader assumes a certain formal structure objectively prior to the interpretive act; in practice the perception or ignorance of obstacles to reading is as much a function of the reader's theoretical paradigm as of the text's forms, which arguably appear only upon the application of a critical technology. Second, Porter ends by stating that the indeterminacy of Faulkner's conclusion "leaves us as readers in an impossible position, for our endeavor to assemble events into an ordered and completed whole has drawn us into the role of participants in the same activity which constitutes the novel's major line of action—narrative construction" (275–76). This will not come as news to students of Faulkner, of modernism, or of recent critical theory. "We have," writes Faulkner, "a few old mouth-to-mouth tales; we exhume from old trunks and boxes and drawers letters without salutation or signature, in which men and women who once lived and breathed are now merely initials or nicknames out of some incomprehensible affection which sound to us like Sanskrit or Chocktaw."[24] All the fasci-

24. William Faulkner, *Absalom, Absalom!* (New York: Vintage, 1972), pp. 100–101.

nating and important historical material marshaled by the critic won't change the fact that the "reified reader" is not peculiar to the age of capitalism and that textual indeterminacy is synonymous with "writing."

On the other hand, Faulkner's construction of history as a rhetoric does point toward a complicity between the economies of language and slavery. In *Absalom, Absalom!* the frustration of historical designs (Sutpen's, the South's, those of the various narrators) begins with the exclusion or nonrecognition of black people—the others whose work nonetheless allows the system to function. Each effort to make sense of the blacks' role in Southern or American history (or in this novel) risks repeating this original enslavement, this translation into matter, commodity, property, and value. The truth about history turns out to be miscegenation, but this is no fall from purity, since the logic and institution of slavery hinges on articulating a racial difference that is not essential or original. The discourse of slavery must produce and establish that difference interminably. Thus genealogical dissemination and historical crisis proceed from the very attempts of rhetoric and political economy to denominate proper identities and their authorized transmission through time.

A text Porter does not discuss, but which seems ideally suited for examining the "general economy" between capitalism and literary forms, or between Marxism and deconstruction, or between historicism and psychoanalysis, is Fitzgerald's *The Great Gatsby*. Ross Posnock's Lukácsean interpretation of the economic and sexual themes in that novel provides a useful corrective to those traditional readings of *Gatsby* that explicate its formal aesthetic achievements at the expense of any sophisticated analysis of its critique of capitalism.[25] Of course critics have not been ignorant of *Gatsby's* achievement in social criticism—indeed, it has become a canonical source for representations of American life in the 1920s. But Posnock's strong insistence on a Marxist framework for his reading of Gatsby stands out, for it offers a more complex theoretical understanding of the economic themes in the novel and presents Fitzgerald more as the critic rather than the exponent of "the American dream."

The models Posnock draws on—Marx's account of commodity fetishism and Lukács's theory of reification—appear distinctly appropriate to the world of Gatsby and his shirts, and one can only agree that at a certain level these models explain much about the universe of desire, fashion, alienation, expropriation, and mutual assured destruction that

25. Ross Posnock, " 'A New World, Material without Being Real': Fitzgerald's Critique of Capitalism in *The Great Gatsby*," in *Critical Essays on F. Scott Fitzgerald's "The Great Gatsby*," ed. Scott Donaldson (Boston: Hall, 1984), pp. 201–13.

the novel depicts. Yet the limitations of Posnock's reading follow from the models he adopts, which like Porter he utilizes with no substantial qualifications (despite a belated reference to Adorno). The difficulties of this model are particularly evident in the case of reading *Gatsby*, since the novel itself is busy theorizing the relations between aesthetics, economics, sexuality, and even metaphysics in ways that considerably qualify the models of orthodox Marxism. Posnock follows his thematics to the point where his commentary relies on the very romanticism that, I would argue, Fitzgerald's text deconstructs (and in so doing Posnock testifies to the core of romanticism at the heart of orthodox Marxism, a contradiction that accounts for many of its strengths as well as its weaknesses). And despite his footnote to Judith Fetterley's interpretation of *Gatsby*, Posnock overlooks the modifications of our understanding of the novel that feminist and gender studies demand.

"The individual's suppression of spontaneous desire," writes Posnock, "reflects the condition of capitalist culture, which reduces the immediate in favor of the tyranny of fashion" (207). The binary oppositions at work here—individual/society, spontaneous/conditioned, immediate/mediate, fashion/natural expression—belong to a rhetoric of metaphysics and romanticism that it is precisely Fitzgerald's (ambivalent) effort to disclose. This rhetoric, moreover, as I tried to show above, inheres in any reading based on a simple application of the theses of commodity fetishism and reification. Posnock unwittingly promotes this rhetoric, and so joins Nick and Gatsby in their ideological lament for the loss of a mythical world of natural innocence and joyful immediacy. Posnock speaks of their "artificial, denatured world," of how the "transformation of reality into symbol defines the condition of commodity fetishism—the passionate chase after symbolic representations of other men's desires," of how nothing is valued "in and for itself" (207). This naturalist, logocentric rhetoric contradicts Posnock's earlier thesis statement that "the novel's account of man's relation to society, we shall see, profoundly agrees with Marx's great discovery that it is social reality rather than individual consciousness that determines man's existence" (202). The burden of deconstruction has been to insist that "Marx's great discovery" needs to be qualified by the demonstration of its own reliance, at strategic moments, on a rhetoric of metaphysical organicism, spontaneous desire, and natural truth. The real "American dream" of the novel consists in this nationalization of logocentrism and reification, so that the metanarratives of innocence and experience, originality and belatedness, nature and culture can be projected into a fabulously (or tragically) unique "American" history which is at once the essence and the end of history. What goes on in *The Great Gatsby* is a work of cultural criticism that enacts both the metaphysical nostalgia for a nature uncor-

rupted by capitalism *and* the intellectual analysis of how the social subject
can never be conceived, even *ab ovo*, as the inhabitant of a world outside
commodification, exchange, spectacle, and speculation. The interplay
between Marxism and romanticism (literary as well as philosophical) in
the novel, moreover, includes a psychoanalytic component that constantly challenges the claims of any single determinative interpretive
model.

In *The Resisting Reader: A Feminist Approach to American Fiction*, Judith
Fetterley maintains that "*The Great Gatsby* is a book about power, and
the romantic investment and indignant divestment of women is an
aspect of and mask for the struggle for power between men which is its
subject."[26] Fetterley indicts the economy of sexism, not that of capitalism. She says that "the pattern which best defines the central action of
The Great Gatsby is that of investment/divestment, through which the
golden girl is revealed to be a common weed and the fresh green breast
of the new world turns pander to men's dreams, feeding them not on
the milk of wonder but on the foul dust of bootleg liquor" (73). While
Gatsby invests Daisy with transcendence, Nick is busy divesting her of
her glory, effectively directing his own (and the reader's) disillusionment against women. This economy transforms Daisy into a scapegoat,
elevates Myrtle to a specious divinity that costs her her life, and prepares
the way for Nick's ultimate investment of glory in Gatsby. Nick's identification with Gatsby comes not from their geographical or class com-
monalities only, but from their position as men. Nick, who is appropri-
ately a seller of bonds, attaches himself to Gatsby in a kind of
"homosocial" identification which, as Eve Sedgwick has theorized it,
entails a misogynistic traffic in women, whether at the literal level of
sexual practice or the specular level of the sexual imaginary.[27] "When
men invest women with the significance of ultimate possessions," observes Fetterley, "they make them the prime counters in their power
games with each other" (83). So the struggle for power between Tom
and Gatsby focuses on the possession of Daisy. Whether this power
struggle belongs to the history of sexuality or the history of capitalism,
or both, is a question Fetterley doesn't pursue. Whereas Posnock locates
commodification, via Lukács, in the specificity of modern capitalism,
Fetterley charts the economy of investment/disinvestment as an apparently timeless transaction of the patriarchal mind.

26. Judith Fetterley, *The Resisting Reader: A Feminist Approach to American Fiction*
(Bloomington: Indiana University Press, 1978), p. 79.

27. Eve Kosofsky Sedgwick, *Between Men: English Literature and Male Homosocial Desire*
(New York: Columbia University Press, 1985). Fetterley's discussion of economics and
the exchange of women between men foreshadows Sedgwick's theory about homosocial
bondings and their essential misogyny.

Fetterley's indictment of this masculine mentality explicitly includes the author himself: "in the male mind, which is at once Gatsby, Carraway, and Fitzgerald, the impulse to wonder is instinctively associated with the image of women, and the ensuing gambits of the romantic imagination are played out in female metaphors" (73). The trope of instinct used by Fetterley, however, appears to obscure or beg the question of the male subject's construction through culture. The "romantic imagination," after all, belongs to the modern history of the West, and it is the peculiar interrelationship between this imagination and capitalism that the novel explores. The "male mind," thus, needs to be historicized here, and the further point made that as an ideological construct, this patriarchal mentality may be assumed by subjects of both biological genders (the Thatcher syndrome). *The Great Gatsby* is certainly a masculinist novel and does equate masculinity with various metanarratives, from those of individual psychological development to those of cultural history (the American Dream as fantasy of the return to the mother's breast). But does the novel represent this patriarchal mentality as a value to be reproduced, as Nick evidently reproduces it, or is his reproduction of it what we must read critically? Does the text represent this mentality in such a way as to analyze, situate, historicize, or even deconstruct it? When Daisy weeps for Gatsby's shirts, those fashionable commodities of value that take the place of the phallus and capture her feminine gaze, can we say that the novel endorses her position? Whose lack do they display?

Thus one is a bit uncomfortable when Fetterley appears to close down her reading by judging the author and his novel "sexist" and "dishonest" (94). Fetterley makes the charge, powerfully, by demonstrating the "cultural double standard" at work in the text as it consistently condemns women and exonerates men. Nick's "dishonesty," she argues, is not a mistake on Fitzgerald's part or a sign of his carelessness, rather it is the reflection of an ideological bad faith and blindness inherent to the author's own vision. She allows that "certainly there is in the Carraway/ Fitzgerald mind an element that is genuinely and meaningfully critical of the Gatsby imagination and that exposes rather than imitates it" (99). Setting aside the questionable conflation of author and narrator, I would argue that the "element" that is "critical" of "the Gatsby imagination" *belongs* to the structure of that imagination, that romanticism and idealism and realism and sexism and commodification are "elements" of a general economy encompassing capitalism, sexuality, and representation: that economy, in the world of *Gatsby,* is one of plagiarism.

The basic paradox in the novel goes something like this, and seems well to fit Jameson's notion of the dialectic of ideology and utopia. The quest for an innocence uncorrupted by time and society—a quest which structures Gatsby's itinerary back to the mother's breast—is also the very vehicle exploited by consumer and commodity capitalism. Capitalism structures symbolic exchange so as to elicit desire, manipulate its character, and teach it to find sublimity in prescribed objects. When one compares the socioeconomic and psychoanalytic registers in the novel, it appears that they align along the culture/nature binary opposition. The book's romanticism (and that of its characters) consists of imaginatively seeking the transcendence of nature over culture. This is most apparent in the regressive movement of Gatsby's fantasy and in Nick's paeans to innocence.

Yet one can also read the novel as deconstructing this binary, revealing à la Lacan that desire is always already symbolic, that the mother's breast is always already a sign in the economy of a cultural system, and as such no more or less artificial in its satisfactions than the pleasures bought by money. The function of the color green in the text, from the green light to the American dollar to the fresh green breast of the New World, does not function finally to prove the radical discrepancy between breasts and coins, nature and culture, love and money; rather it indicates their coincidence and undecidability. A romantic reading of the text, and this includes Marxist accounts like Posnock's as well as feminist accounts like Fetterley's, privileges nature over culture and offers *The Great Gatsby* as a treatise on our decline and alienation from nature and love. The novel's explicit equation of this romantic attitude with regression to the infantile, melancholia, and imperialist conquest ought to prevent such interpretations. One could say, instead, that the binary myth of the natural is exactly what commodity capitalism depends on for its success. Only if purchased objects are consumed as symbolic part objects, that is, as inadequate representations of original natural satisfactions, will the economic system of exchange continue to thrive. The anxiety to return to and possess a state of preoedipal pleasure, then, is essential to the cultural system of manufactured, imaginary, fetishistic coinage.

At the level of the literary, these paradoxes reappear as the question of style: in Gatsby's world the achievement of style belongs to commodity reification. Style is an object of pleasurable consumption and a sign of the social position of producer and consumer in a larger symbolic system. Fitzgerald's novel displays, through allusion and symbol and plot, its debt to literary romanticism and thus its anxiety about its own originality. The green light at the end of Daisy's dock, supposedly the sign of original innocence and hope, is lifted from Coleridge's "Dejection: An Ode," suggesting the complex of desire that entangles the lures of stylistic and monetary success. Everywhere the text theorizes this anxiety through the coincidental problematics of plagiarism and gossip. The economy of capitalist style in *The Great Gatsby* is one of imitation or plagiarism, from Gatsby's name, life story, and mansion to Myrtle's romance, her tabloid reading, and her apartment. As the two lower-class questers, Gatsby and Myrtle are the most victimized by the economy of capitalist plagiarism. They struggle to fill up their lack of identity by inserting themselves into prescribed cultural plots and then manipulating the commodities and social signs available there to construct themselves as upwardly mobile subjects of desire. The tragedy of the novel, if one still cares to use that language, is that the desires of Gatsby and Myrtle are themselves unoriginal, plagiarized, and subject to the (Lacanian) symbolic. They invest their considerable drives into cultural systems that degrade and destroy them. Most ironically, they invest in a system whose symbolic and socioeconomic structure dictated, *ab ovo*, the lack they now try to fill by recourse to the signifying objects (whether bodies or consumer items) offered by that very system.

The above analyses suggest that the strict application of reification theory to American literary history may simply reproduce the canonical topoi and metanarratives of that history: the edenic new world, the fall from nature, alienated man's flight from the social, style as a world elsewhere, the artist as representative consciousness, history as the telos of democratic freedom, etc. (For more on the deconstruction of the metaphysics of American literary historiography, see below, Chapter 8.) The Marxist analysis might only be a shift of mode—from the affirmation of utopia to the critique of ideology—that doesn't displace the fundamental scheme. Reification theory cannot but repeat the base/ superstructure hypothesis in its most general form, that of the binary oppositions material/ideal, object/fetish, or natural/rationalized.

The structure of perception, cognition, social expression, and representation described by reification theory may also be described by the psychoanalytic account of desire in the subject and the deconstructive account of logocentrism in language. Poststructuralist Marxism (such as Jameson's) often supplements Lukács by taking seriously the psychoanalytic dimension of commodity fetishism, but it rarely pursues the more radical implications of the poststructuralist reading of Freud since that would considerably complicate the notions of materiality, causality, and history still pervasive in Western Marxism. This is why the dialogue between the theory of reification and the theory of logocentrism is necessary, since the latter provides the critique of representation that solicits the residual metaphysical presuppositions in reification theory. These three approaches to the circulation of valued coinages—Marxist, psychoanalytic, deconstructive—cannot be conflated, for they are relatively autonomous in their historic development and operations. Interpretive cultural criticism, however, ought to actively trace and speculate on the interplay between their respective economies. That interplay, we have seen, drives the formation of many American texts, and in the chapters that follow we shall trace how that interplay positions a variety of American subjects.

CHAPTER FIVE

Poe: Delivering the Male

But human megalomania will have suffered its third and most wound-
ing blow from the psychological research of the present time which
seeks to prove to the ego that it is not even master of its own house,
but must content itself with scanty information of what is going on
unconsciously in its mind. We psychoanalysts were not the first and
not the only ones to utter this call to introspection.
—Freud, *Introductory Lectures on Psychoanalysis*

Can the dispossession of consciousness to the profit of another home
of meaning be understood as an act of reflection, as the first gesture
of reappropriation?
—Ricoeur, *Freud and Philosophy*

But evil things, in robes of sorrow,
Assailed the monarch's high estate
. . .
And, round about his home, the glory
That blushed and bloomed
Is but a dim-remembered story
Of the old time entombed.
—Poe, "The Haunted Palace"

Contemporary critical theory has insistently haunted two related
structures: romantic literature since Blake, and philosophy after Locke.
Some have argued that all "modern" writing should be defined by
its response to the romantics; in philosophy, most particularly on the
Continent, it is Kant and Hegel who serve as the commanding centers
from which others try to depart. Thus we should not be surprised that
poststructuralist criticism finds Edgar Allan Poe so amiable a subject,
for Poe's chief struggle was his attempt to emerge, as a writer and a
thinker, from the influential shadow cast by romantic poetry and idealist

philosophy (German and American).[1] With the aid of recent theorists, we may better understand what Edward H. Davidson asserted in his pioneering study: "that Poe was a 'crisis' in the Romantic symbolic imagination. He came near the end (if such directions have 'beginning' and 'end') of the Idealist or Romantic expression and mind."[2] But Davidson's formula sounds too passive, however fated Poe's inherited dilemmas may be. Although from "Tamerlane" to *Eureka* Poe's work shows a desire to recover the Ideal, the True, and the Beautiful, his stories and poems and essays constantly repeat a pattern of aggression against the transcendental. The increasing number of confessional tales, in fact, suggests a compulsive need to confess a kind of "guilt" for the "murder" of what is elsewhere lamented as lost. This violence in Poe's texts, moreover, is mainly directed against the bodies of women. The literary and metaphysical crises allegorized by Poe cannot be separated from a crisis of the subject's gender. Metaphysics and sexuality linger in a fatal embrace throughout Poe's involvement with romantic idealism.

The mental flights, reflections, and ratiocinations of Poe's protagonists yield not only a confession of guilt but a related dissolution of self and identity. The horrible results of Poe's ecstatic states upset the romantic commonplace that proposes an access to the divine through abnormal states of consciousness. Often his narrators seem condemned by genealogy to extraordinary speculations. "I am," writes William Wilson (but which one?), "the descendent of a race whose imaginative and easily excitable temperament has at all times rendered them remarkable" (CW 2: 427).[3] In Wilson's case, introspective speculation produces a Doppelgänger who becomes a mortal antagonist. Murder or revenge is regularly carried out against doubles of the self in Poe ("Loss of Breath," "Metzengerstein," "The Tell-Tale Heart," "The Purloined Letter," "The Imp of the Perverse," "The Cask of Amontillado"), as well as

1. For a compendium of recent theoretical work on Poe, see *The Purloined Poe: Lacan, Derrida, and Psychoanalytic Reading*, ed. John P. Muller and William J. Richardson (Baltimore: Johns Hopkins University Press, 1988). R. C. DeProspo reviews the scene in "Deconstructive Poe(tics)," *Diacritics* 18 (Fall 1988): 43–64. DeProspo finds much redundancy in Americanist and deconstructionist readings that emphasize Poe's critiques of romanticism and transcendentalism and/or his anticipation of (post)modernism. DeProspo believes we ought to establish Poe's discourse as "other-than-modern," but his brief attempt to do so is vague and unpersuasive. I would suggest that the two novel directions for Poe criticism lie in historicizing his textual production and in analyzing his sexual thematics in other than orthodox Freudian or Lacanian terms (i.e., in challenging, as I suggest further on, the address of the male system).

2. Edward H. Davidson, *Poe: A Critical Study* (Cambridge: Harvard University Press, 1957), p. ix.

3. All quotations from Poe's fiction and poetry are taken from *The Collected Works of Edgar Allan Poe*, ed. Thomas Olive Mabbot, 3 vols. (Cambridge: Harvard University Press, 1978), and are cited parenthetically as CW.

against the bodies of those women conventionally symbolizing sublime knowledge. "The essential Poe fable," observes Michael Davitt Bell, "however elaborately the impulse may be displaced onto a double or a lover, is a tale of compulsive self-murder."[4] Bell's interpretation of this murder as primarily a symbolic destruction of the sexual or sensual self, however, misses the important conjunction of sexuality, philosophy, and textuality in Poe's works. The unproblematic assimilation of the lover's (or mother's) gender in such doublings requires some skeptical analysis. As Eve Sedgwick's theory of the "homosocial" bonding between men suggests, Poe's plots of premature burial and murder enact a kind of "traffic in women": the entombment or cryptic destruction of the woman puts her in circulation between men—even as a letter (or *l'être*) sent by Man to Himself to confirm his correspondence to the image of his own desired identity.[5]

The dethronement of the self's monarchy by the irruptions of buried passions does signify at the sexual level, to be sure; yet this upheaval belongs to the general crisis of self and identity as philosophical concepts, or as viable notions for the writer. The Hegelian romantic/transcendental placement of the subjective self at the center of philosophy's union with beauty, spirit, or the over-soul makes of coherent personal identity a prerequisite to truth itself. Since the writer's character or identity, be he philosopher or poet, proceeds from that of the text, the truth of writing becomes susceptible to a double assault. First, there are elements in the text that repeat those of other texts, thus threatening the dream of original identity (Poe's purloinings from other writers are notorious). This fear comes out in Poe's obsessions with the burdens of family inheritance and the problems of discerning plagiarism, both of which raise questions about the relationships between creativity and repetition. Second, there are parts of the self that seem not its own, residing in an unconscious which, like Poe's many ancestral mansions, houses the decaying but persistent recollections of an influential past. To bemoan inheritance, rail against plagiarism, or entomb one's double is to seek an exclusion of the other who shadows identity, especially when this figure challenges the decidability of sexual difference and the cultural narratives predicated upon it. In so often exposing truth as a deceptive effect of violence or revisionary experience, Poe discovers (often in horror) that fissure which ultimately destroys the romantic

---

4. Michael Davitt Bell, *The Development of American Romance* (Chicago: University of Chicago Press, 1980), p. 99.

5. Eve Kosofsky Sedgwick, *Between Men: English Literature and Male Homosocial Desire* (New York: Columbia University Press, 1985). See especially chap. 5, "Toward the Gothic: Terrorism and Homosexual Panic," pp. 83–96.

and idealist structures of patriarchal reflection he so perversely inhabits and haunts.

Whether seriously or parodically, in "Ligeia" or "How to Write a Blackwood's Article," Poe reiterates the language, plots, symbols, and ideas that are his legacy from Gothic fiction, British poetry, and German metaphysics. To read Poe is to interpret the significance of his re-arrangements of these family estates. They are ruined from within, either by the return of the repressed other or by a hyperbolic mockery of the visionary's pretensions. In both his "arabesques" and "grotesques," Poe's method may aptly be compared to Derrida's definition of "deconstruction" as "inhabiting" structures *"in a certain way . . .* borrowing all the strategic and economic resources of subversion from the old structure."[6] The subsequent reappropriation results, not in a new mastery of truth (which is what Dupin would like us to believe), but in an edifying collapse of both terms in the dualism (true/false, construction/deconstruction, self/other, male/female, etc.). Like the "House of Usher" and its narrator, deconstructive reflection, writes Derrida, "always in a certain way falls prey to its own work" (24).

A deconstruction of truth cannot itself be "true" in the old sense. It becomes rather, as in Poe's deployment of his literary borrowings, a rhetoric of signifying effects. Here we recall Poe's aesthetic principle that poetry "has no concern with Duty or with Truth" (SW 506).[7] Without that concern, however, and the desires it engenders, Poe's work is inexplicable. He ceaselessly explores the imagination's power to know the "Supernal Loveliness." Poe's critique of truth's place in the imagination's work displaces the center of romantic and philosophical discourse, but that displacement (or "murder") serves as prelude to the appearance of an idea of beauty that functions in much the same structuring way as truth once had. Yet truth is not beautiful in Poe, or vice versa. Contradicting the lingering transcendentalism of Poe's optative moods, the "death" of truth which keeps reappearing is the prerequisite of ideal beauty and cannot be dialectically resolved. As Joseph N. Riddel has argued, the presence of beauty "is inextricable from language in Poe" and so beauty is "marked by time and change" and "the Death implicit in every repetition."[8] The same holds true for the identity of a self produced by the murder of the other. In either case, we end up in a

6. Jacques Derrida, *Of Grammatology,* trans. Gayatri Chakravorty Spivak (Baltimore: Johns Hopkins University Press, 1976), p. 24.

7. "The Poetic Principle," in *Selected Writings,* ed. David Galloway (New York: Penguin Books, 1967). Unless otherwise noted, references to Poe's literary criticism are from this volume and are cited parenthetically as SW.

8. Joseph N. Riddel, "A Somewhat Polemical Introduction: The Elliptical Poem," *Genre* 11 (Winter 1978): 464–65.

world where both truth and self are rhetorical effects and, as such, vulnerable to the temporal and textual unsettlings of identity that language and interpretation always fall prey to.

As "The Purloined Letter" demonstrates, the orientation of subjective action by desire, which is to say by the desire of and for identity, means that subjects are the agents of the truth, or what Derrida punningly calls the *facteurs*—the purveyors and mailmen—of the letter of the law. The struggles for the letter, for the truth, and for identity belong also, then, to the history of the agencies of power. The crisis of the truth of the subject in romanticism may then be connected to the radically altered conditions of subjectivity experienced during the transition to industrial capitalism. Romanticism offers various utopias—nature, the soul, the body, art, sexuality—as alternatives. The appropriation of the body of woman as the site for man's symbolic struggle against his alienation under capitalism may help explain the relation between the sexual and politico-economic dimensions of romanticism, even as it suggests we must historicize and en-gender the subjects of romanticism.

Sublimated Differences: Us/Her

The romantic or idealist visionary moment of the soul's knowing union with the world becomes in Poe the nightmare of the self's inhabitation by conflicting scripts. This is not to question the strength of Poe's imaginative lamps, but rather to question the identity or location of authorship. When the text negotiates a rhetorical conflict of repression and expression, who writes? Who authors our nightmares? Poe's work shows a morbid sensitivity to this issue, in its narrators (who scarcely know what they say), in its plots (whose characters seem condemned to repeat old stories), and most literally in his "modernist" deployment of quotes, phrases, ideas, characters, names, and fabricated citations taken (consciously or not) from other writers. These traces form the archive of Poe's rhetoric of borrowing, his cryptic writing or his *écriture*. Commenting on the latter term, Richard Poirier argues that "the performing self is never free of its environment, never a so-called 'imperial' or unconditioned self. No such thing exists in the history of literature, no self ever has been successfully imperial, because nature (and not just the repressiveness of our selves) dictates that the only materials a 'free' self can be constructed from are those by which it is imprisoned."[9] Poirier goes on to defend Emerson against the charge

9. "A Conversation with Richard Poirier," *Salmagundi* 52–53 (1981): 112.

that he was happily oblivious to the traces of the *écriture* against which self-reliance struggles. Poe often used that portrait of Emerson as naive idealist for his straw imperial man. In Emerson, Poe could see the combination of romantic and German themes also united in this pronouncement of Hegel's: "The tendency of all man's endeavors is to understand the world, to appropriate and subdue it to himself; and to this end the positive reality of the world must be as it were crushed and pounded, in other words, idealized."[10] Emerson's self-reliance hoped to put the self back into mastery of its own house. Freud's "call to introspection" was Concord's historical dilemma, as Emerson himself described it: "The young men were born with knives in their brain, a tendency to introversion, self-dissection, anatomizing of motives."[11] "The American Scholar," "Self-Reliance," and "The Over-Soul" try to purge introversion of historicity, to free self-consciousness from personal or cultural determination of *écriture*.

Ever since the Pilgrims, myths of American literary history have depicted the American experiment as an attempt to write a revised script on the new land, to constitute and declare an independent identity to resist and redirect the legacy of the Old World. The central text for interpretation was first the Bible, then the political documents of the Revolution, and then what Emerson called "Nature," a "not-me" including culture as a component. Mingling Cotton Mather and Jonathan Edwards with Kant, Coleridge, Goethe, and Hegel, Emerson formulates philosophy, poetry, and self as grounded in the reading of this Nature: "A life in harmony with Nature, the love of truth and of virtue, will purge the eyes to understand her text. By degrees we may come to know the primitive sense of the permanent objects of nature, so that the world shall be to us an open book, and every form significant of its hidden life and final cause" (*Works* 1: 40). Emerson tries to imagine the purgation of otherness, time, and mediation from consciousness in his audacious introduction to *Nature*, which cries out for a liberation from the "dry bones of the past." In the place of the repressed influences of the past, Emerson elsewhere posits the inspiration of nature's "oversoul" as the center of the introspective self: "Our being is descending

10. G. W. F. Hegel, *Logic*, trans. William Wallace (Oxford: Oxford University Press, (1975), p. 69.
11. Ralph Waldo Emerson, "Historic Notes of Life and Letters in New England," in *The Works of Ralph Waldo Emerson*, 14 vols. (Boston: Houghton Mifflin, 1883), 10: 311. (Subsequent references to Emerson are from this edition and are cited parenthetically.) "In literature," he observes, "the effect appeared in the decided tendency of criticism. The most remarkable literary work of the age has for its hero and subject precisely this introversion: I mean the poem of Faust. In philosophy, Immanuel Kant has made the best catalogue of the human faculties and the best analysis of the mind. Hegel also, especially" (10: 310).

into us from we know not whence. . . . I desire, and look up, and put
myself in the attitude of reception, but from some alien energy the
visions come" (*Works* 2: 252). This "Revelation" is "always attended by
the emotion of the sublime. For this communication is an influx of the
Divine mind into our mind." An "ecstasy," "trance," "ravishment," and
"certain tendency to insanity" afflict such visionaries, but the light is the
Word, and "Revelation is the disclosure of the soul" (*Works* 2: 263–65).[12]
Significantly, the eye of the transcendentalist Emerson negates the body
of (mother) nature through a sublim(e)ating vision of its essence as
ideally male; Emerson spells out a fantasy of masculine parthenogenesis
in *Nature's* section on "Language": "That which, intellectually considered, we call Reason, considered in relation to nature, we call Spirit.
Spirit is the Creator. Spirit hath life in itself. And man in all ages and
countries embodies it in his language, as the FATHER" (*Works* 1: 33).
Reason and Spirit deliver the male, "hath life in itself," without detour
through the female body of the other.

Emerson's "influx of the Divine" appears in Poe as the (usually female)
corpse of the sublime. Where Emerson's self-reliant introspection discovers eternal identity, Poe's horrified introverts disclose the anomaly
of the living dead, the mortality of beauty and truth, the puzzle of
inscriptions, and the collapse of identities into their speculative doubles.
Harold Bloom, anxious to make Emerson his precursor prophet of
earliness, claims "that a poetic repression brings about the Sublime
wildness of freedom."[13] Once more Bloom tries to make repetition a
master's game, a boy's initiation into manhood, but he can only do so
by ruling out his antagonist from the start. Bloom must "deny the
usefulness of the Unconscious, as opposed to repression, as a literary
term."[14] With the discourses of the other excluded, the "wildness of
freedom" follows as an ineluctable wish-fulfillment of a patriarchal
poetics. Poe's texts insistently put the unconscious in the same structural
position (culturally, psychologically, even cosmically) as the over-soul,
or, more accurately, his writing suggests that the over-soul is a strategically adopted persona of the unconscious. The sublimation of sexual
difference will fail in its task of underwriting the meta-physical identity
of the subject.

12. The sexual metaphors often used to describe religious experience pervade Emer-
son's account, as they do the writings of his precursor Jonathan Edwards. See also Eric
Cheyfitz, *The Trans-Parent: Sexual Politics in the Language of Emerson* (Baltimore: Johns
Hopkins University Press, 1981).

13. Harold Bloom, "Emerson and Whitman: The American Sublime," *Poetry and
Repression* (New Haven: Yale University Press, 1976), p. 237. See also Bloom, "Emerson:
The Self-Reliance of American Romanticism," *Figures of Capable Imagination* (New York:
Seabury Press, 1976).

14. Bloom, *Poetry and Repression*, p. 24.

Hegel's method was to make the negations and divisions of the self dialectical. The spirit, he wrote, "sunders itself to self-realization. But this position of severed life has in its turn to be suppressed, and the spirit has by its own act to win its way to concord again. The final concord then is spiritual; that is, the principal restoration is found in thought, and thought only. The hand that inflicts the wound is also the hand which heals it."[15] Emerson would have delighted in the felicity of a translation that made the "final concord" spiritual, just as Derrida takes pleasure in noting the common psychoanalytical movement (*fort/ da*) of castration and dialectics. Poe, however, fears the metempsychosis or immortal spirit of written thoughts, their ghostly persistence. In "The Power of Words," two spirits talk of the infinity of influence, taking as their model the original immortality of the Word:

> It is indeed demonstrable that every such impulse *given the air,* must, *in the end,* impress every individual thing that exists *within the universe;*—and the being of infinite understanding—the being whom we have imagined— might trace the remote undulations of the impulse—trace them upward and onward in their influences upon all particles of all matter—upward and onward for ever in their modifications of old forms—or, in other words, *in their creation of new*—until he found them reflected—unimpressive *at last*—back from the throne of the Godhead. . . . And while I thus spoke, did there not cross your mind some thought of the *physical power of words?* Is not every word an impulse on the air? (CW 3: 1214–15)

The hopeful turn of influence into the creation of new forms again expresses the dilemma of tradition and the individual talent. That is also the theoretical theme of "The Fall of the House of Usher," in which the "final concord" does not restore the mansion of the self but instead replays the power of other impulses.[16]

A letter from Usher summons the narrator to this gloomy address. That letter at once suggests a recourse to the *fort/da* of representation in its self-restorative capacity—that is, as an agency of presence—and an "original" splitting of the subject *of* language *by* language. As Derrida contends, the letter or character of the subject may not always arrive at its destination, most uncannily, perhaps, when he thinks it has already arrived. Usher's letter bears the stamp of regression as it takes this double subject back to a childhood primal scene to replay the trauma that subsequent sublimations have only exacerbated. The return to the

15. Hegel, *Logic,* p. 43.
16. Here I should note my debt to Richard Wilbur's "The House of Poe," in *Poe: A Collection of Critical Essays,* ed. Robert Regan (Englewood Cliffs: Prentice-Hall, 1967), pp. 98–120.

father's house begins as an analysis of the diseased and degenerate structure of patriarchy and discovers there, or therapeutically fantasizes, the lost body of the mother.

The narrator, at the start of his quest to restore the foundations of sanity, experiences a "depression of soul" in his inability to translate the sight of the Usher building into "aught of the sublime." This may be explained by his separation from Usher: "Although, as boys, we had been even intimate associates, yet I really knew little of my friend" (CW 2: 398). (Compare "William Wilson.") Up until now, the narrator's rationality has relied on keeping his distance from something with which he was once intimately associated, and whose return will undo him. The House of Usher is Poe's most hyperbolic image for the transmission of influences within the structures we inhabit. As if its "excessive antiquity" and arabesque furnishings were not enough, Poe dwells on the repetition compulsion of this "ancient family." Its "direct line of descent," with "very trifling and very temporary variation," turns the narrator's thoughts to "the perfect keeping of the character of the premises with the accredited character of the people" (note the pun on "premises"), prompting him to "speculating on the possible influence which the one, in the long lapse of centuries, might have exercised upon the other." Finally, it is the "undeviating transmission, from sire to son, of the patrimony with the name, which had, at length, so identified the two as to merge the original title of the estate in the quaint and equivocal appellation of 'The House of Usher' " (CW 2: 399). Like the power of words, this heritage forms a strange "sentience" in the "home of his forefathers," "above all in the long undisturbed endurance of this arrangement, and in its reduplication in the still waters of the tarn." This "arrangement" is a perverse celestial music, an "atmosphere" of the "importunate and terrible influence which for centuries had moulded the destinies" of the Usher family (CW 2: 408).

Hoping to "annihilate" the "sorrowful impression" the building makes upon him (correlative to the unhappy irruption of the other back into his consciousness, also taking the form of Usher's letter to him), the narrator seeks relief in representations: "I reflected, that a mere different arrangement of the particulars of the scene, of the details of the picture" would suffice. Thus he stops at "the precipitous brink of a black and lurid tarn," where glimmer "the remodelled and inverted images" of the house (CW 2: 398). Once again the abyss is identified with reflection and our impish perversity in sinking into representations. The remainder of the tale unfolds in the space of the narrator's reflection, in his re-cognition of the dazzling depths out of which character emerges.

The narrator begins with the delusion that such reflection can restore him to himself. He too is remodeled and inverted as he enters this abysmal mansion, where he replaces the doctor and the lady Madeline as Usher's physician and twin. Within this frame Poe once more gives us the story (Usher's) of a belated imagination, his soul a ruin, his idealism the product of a sensual repression culminating in his sister's premature entombment. Yet the involvement of the narrator changes the familiar pattern. Usher and Madeline live in the narrator's rhetorical house of therapeutic writing. His project is to revise the Poe script so as to save the imagination from the return of the repressed. He will finally resort to the agency of letters in his last attempt to save Usher's identity (and thus his own) and to keep Madeline in her place. The ghastly comic staging of this effort comes when the narrator tries to soothe Roderick by reading to him! The "antique volume" is the "Mad Trist" by "Sir Launcelot Canning" (a quaint appellation Poe later used as his own pseudonym). The joke is on everyone, for this text is a copy of a nonexistent original, the only "truly" fictitious work in Usher's library. Poe's invented volume parodies our desire to be canny readers, to pierce the mystery of uncanny stories. The narrator hopes to treat Usher with writing: "I indulged a vague hope that the excitement which now agitated the hypochondriac, might find relief (for the history of mental disorder is full of similar anomalies) even in the extremeness of the folly which I should read" (CW 2: 413). A good pre-Freudian doctor, the narrator wants to take Usher's diseased libidinal energy ("excitement") and sublimate it, cathect or attach it to a safe object. What he doesn't see is that reading may be precisely the cause of such "excitement," and that the redirection of libidinal energy will only repeat, albeit in distortion or displacement, the original structure of impulses the narrator hopes to quiet.

The ensuing spectacle in which reality and literature double or haunt one another is indeed a "Mad Trist" and illustrates Freud's hypothesis that "the uncanny is nothing else than a hidden, familiar thing that has undergone repression and then emerged from it."[17] The narrator reads on blindly, ignoring how the text awakens the unconscious, while Roderick hears mesmerically the echoing of surface and depth as each incident

---

17. See Freud's "The 'Uncanny' " (1919) in *The Standard Edition of the Complete Psychological Works,* ed. James Strachey, 24 vols. (London: Hogarth, 1953–74), 17: 217–56. Freud's great essay turns on a pertinent linguistic play between *heimlich* (pertaining to the home) and its opposite, *unheimlich* (the uncanny). *Heimlich* also means secret or hidden, a "*heimlich* meaning, *mysticus, divinus,*" so that "*heimlich* is a word the meaning of which develops towards an ambivalence, until it finally coincides with its opposite, unheimlich." (Yes, *heimlich is* used to refer to private bodily parts.) Freud surveys virtually all the uncanny phenomena used in Poe's fiction (e.g., haunted houses, premature burial, evil eyes, symbolic castration, the Doppelgängers) to conclude that it is the element of repetition, of an "involuntary" return of an unheimlich thing from its absence, that defines the uncanny.

in the tale is matched by a movement of Madeline as she works her way
from crypt to bedroom. The narrator evidently agrees with those critics
who find literature a means of entertainment, or (and it amounts to the
same thing) a salvation from chaos, as it seems to offer the divided self
a safe transportation to already privileged truths. This literary episode
deconstructs the narrator's rationale of reading, exposes with lunatic
hilarity his dominant concern with holding the house of his own sanity
together.

The psychoanalytical movement of the "Mad Trist" invites multiple
interpretations. Marie Bonaparte finds it an allegory of the Oedipal
struggle, with Ethelred slaying the father to gain the mother; this, to
her, would be the content of the repressed.[18] Yet Ethelred's entrance
by force into the dwelling of the hermit also repeats the motion of
Usher's letter to the narrator, as well as that of the narrator's arrival at
Usher's mansion. Ethelred is "drunken," in an arabesque state that
empowers him to shatter the door, slay the dragon of fire who has
replaced the hermit, and gain the protective shield of authority, "breaking up . . . the enchantment which was upon it." Usher (and others)
turn the "Trist" into an allegory of Madeline's return, and thus of the
return of Usher's own unconscious desires. Usher, however, also seems
to accusingly scream "MADMAN" at the *narrator*. The madness of the
narrator lies in his rationality as a reader, his refusal to recognize the
other inhabiting the text. Ethelred could be read as the figure of the
narrator's quest to break the enchantment of the unconscious that keeps
us from truth. Reading would then be an arabesque liberation of formal
powers enabling the slaying of the monstrous other. Ethelred's shield
would be his phallogocentric emblem, or so antique romance would
have it. Madeline's reappearance for her final mad tryst with Roderick
is equally unreadable. She is a representation whose "original" identity
(as truth or as the narrator's unconscious or as Roderick's sensual self)
is multiple, a hall of mirrors, and always enchanting. Her return will
destroy both Roderick and the narrator, her other double. The failure
of the narrator's talking cure reflects upon himself as the identity of the
text he reads is haunted by spectral visitations. The stories-within-stories
and interpretations-within-interpretations build into an intensity of
overdetermination that exceeds the capacity of any single deciphering
consciousness or reading strategy. It may also be that this scene of two
men analyzing each other through reading an Oedipal text allegorizes
a homosocial mise-en-scène of psychoanalytic theory, a spectacle un-

18. Marie Bonaparte, *The Life and Works of Edgar Allan Poe: A Psycho-Analytic Interpretation*, trans. John Rodker, Foreword by Sigmund Freud (London: Imago, 1949), pp. 237–
50.

done by the uncontrollable female figure that their textual exchange had hoped to repress. It is "us" against "her" as they read for their lives.

The narrator "fled aghast" from the scene of all this attraction and repulsion of correspondences. His own writing effort, and the containment of speculation it desired, shatters along with the house which was its chief representative. It had seemed to the narrator as if "the superhuman agency of" Roderick's "utterance" had "found the potency of a spell" to open the door for Madeline's enshrouded body (CW 2:417, 416). The "potency" of the narrator's own rationalized ejaculations has, in like manner, inadvertently brought forward the figures of the Ushers from within himself. Their collapse into each other's arms is that "fatal embrace" that is Poe's typical negative union. This would seem to purge the narrator cathartically of the conflicts the Ushers embodied, and so cure him, but the treatment is not entirely successful. When the narrator flees the collapsing House of Usher, the crack that splits the structure captures his fascinated gaze: "The radiance was that of the full, setting, and blood-red moon, which now shone vividly through that once barely discernible fissure, of which I have before spoken as extending from the roof of the building, in a zigzag direction, to the base" (CW 2: 417). This image suggests the sight of the bleeding wound of the undecidability of sexual difference, and so places Poe's texts in the tradition of male anxiety whose theoretical *summa* is Freud's "Some Psychical Consequences of the Anatomical Distinction between the Sexes."[19] One of the consequences of Lacan and Derrida's debate over Poe is to underscore the irreducible network wherein the truth of philosophy, the truth of letters, and the truth of gender correspond with one another through the mail/male system. Thus while my reading of Poe is stamped by the literary psychology of Harold Bloom, I also intend to deconstruct the male box into which he sends every poetic text.

The climactic fall of the mansion into its own images serves as an apt

19. The following famous passage from Freud's notorious essay might be read self-reflexively, as an unconscious allegory of the psychoanalyst's philosophy of composition, or as a description of the narrative strategies of writers in the male system: "when a little boy first catches sight of a girl's genital region, he begins by showing irresolution and lack of interest; he sees nothing or disavows what he has seen, he softens it down or looks about for expedients for bringing it into line with his expectations. It is not until later, when some threat of castration has obtained a hold upon him, that the observation becomes important to him: if he then recollects or repeats it, it arouses a terrible storm of emotion in him and forces him to believe in the reality of the threat which he has hitherto laughed at. This combination of circumstances leads to two reactions, which may become fixed and will in that case, whether separately or together or in conjunction with other factors, permanently determine the boy's relations to women: horror of the mutilated creature or triumphant contempt for her." Freud, "Some Psychical Consequences of the Anatomical Distinction between the Sexes" (1925), *Standard Edition*, 19: 252.

commentary on the workings of self-reflection in Poe and on the effect this can have on the identity of a literary text: "While I gazed, this fissure rapidly widened—there came a fierce breath of the whirlwind—the entire orb of the satellite burst at once upon my sight—my brain reeled as I saw the mighty walls rushing asunder—there was a long tumultuous shouting like the voice of a thousand waters—and the deep and dank tarn at my feet closed sullenly and silently over the fragments of the '*House of Usher*'" (CW 2: 417). Poe sets the "*House of Usher*" apart with quotation marks, in italicized script, as if it were the title of a tale. Riddel correctly reads this scene as a textual deconstruction, the story falling into itself, the proper name in fragments.[20] I would argue, however, that textuality should not be a privileged analytical metaphor. These closing lines, like so much of Poe, won't allow us to abstract textuality from sexuality. Inspiration has become demonized and passionate, "a fierce breath of the whirlwind." The anatomy of the red fissure and "mighty walls rushing asunder" combines a vision of abysmal vaginal horrors with echoes of apocalypse, as if this were a creation catastrophe. The "long tumultuous shouting sound like the voice of a thousand waters" reminds us that the house of generation is both echoic and spermatic: Bloom is right to insist that writing is a family romance, a history of relations. This climax consummates the affair of sex and writing, makes that coupling the final terror, and images its reburial in reflection. The "silence" of the text's "fragments" is not complete, since writing cannot silence the traces left by those shouting voices of the past, for they are also voices of desire.

Desire inspires both lover and writer. The dialectic of Eros and Thanatos some critics find in Poe ought to be replaced by an analytics of eros and *écriture*, and then supplemented by speculations on gender. One may prematurely bury the corpus of this dilemma, this peculiar intimacy of sexuality and textuality, "sullenly" put it in its place, but the very act of interment leaves its epitaph in script and capital letters: "US" and "HER," male identity versus the female as other. Luce Irigaray provides this commentary on psychoanalytic theories of sexual difference:

> The "differentiation" into two sexes derives from the a priori assumption of the same, since the little man that the little girl is, must become a man minus certain attributes whose paradigm is morphological—attributes capable of determining, of assuring, the reproduction-specularization of the same. A man minus the possibility of (re)presenting oneself as a man = a normal woman. In this proliferating desire of the same, death will be the only representative of an outside, of a heterogeneity, of an other:

20. Joseph Riddel, "The 'Crypt' of Edgar Poe," *boundary* 2 7 (Spring 1979): 117–44.

woman will assume the function of representing death (of sex/organ), castration, and man will be sure as far as possible of achieving mastery, subjugation, by triumphing over the anguish (of death) through intercourse, by sustaining sexual pleasure despite, or thanks to, the horror of closeness to that absence of sex/penis, that mortification of sex that is evoked by woman; the trial of intercourse will have, moreover, as teleological parameter the challenge of an indefinite regeneration, of a reproduction of the *same* that defies death, in the procreation of the *son*, this same of the procreating father. As testimony, for self and others, of his imperishable character, and warranty of a new generation of self-identity for the male seed.[21]

The house of Poe's writing both traffics in and violates the economy of sex. These fragments and fissures picture another castration, a textual/ sexual *sparagmos* of the proper that follows from the primal scene of Roderick and Madeline's "Mad Trist." This fissure also images the catastrophic birth scene of the narrator, his deliverance. Yet the dissemination of these "thousand waters" generates the recapitation of the "HOUSE OF USHER." Tomb, phallus, vagina, text, the "HOUSE OF USHER" rises up at the end in writing, a typographic inverse double of the house and story now disappearing into the tarn. Its recapitation delivers the male back to himself, though one can scarcely imagine what future address could make him feel at home. Bonaparte sees the house as the "Mother-Mansion" rather than the embodiment of patriarchy's genealogy; the nightmare is that it is both, though only in the sense that the horror of the woman's body appears as its undecidable difference from the man's.

Visionary Negations of the I

Poe's journeys into the disestablishment of inherited constructs are subversive versions of standard romantic themes. For his own purposes he took up the romantic reaction against empiricism and "common sense" philosophy. In "How to Write a Blackwood's Article," Blackwood advises the Signora Psyche Zenobia: "Be sure and abuse a man called Locke" (CW 2: 341). Northrop Frye made "The Case against Locke" his opening explanation of Blake's romanticism, and Robert Langbaum begins with Wordsworth's reaction to Locke in his own fine account of

21. Luce Irigaray, *Speculum of the Other Woman*, trans. Gillian C. Gill (Ithaca: Cornell University Press, 1985), p. 27.

literature and identity.[22] The romantic critique of rational reflection included a general, but variously imagined, substitution of perception for reasoning. Higher, even divine, truths might be approached by a visionary experience requiring the initial dissolution or making-absent of mundane sensory realities. The list of such enabling experiences of the other of reason is lengthy, and most appear in Poe (e.g., childhood, drugs, dreams, liquor, artwork, books, moonlight, remembrance, sleep-lessness, orgasm, mesmerism, sea voyages, madness). In Wordsworth the distinct necessity of overthrowing the "absolute dominion" of the "bodily eye" and of replacing it with creative "recollection" is especially clear. When "the light of sense/Goes out," the "invisible world" stands revealed, though in an aspect more heartening than the terror-inspiring apparitions of the recalled Ligeia or Madeline Usher.[23] Emerson gives the American version in *Nature's* chapter titled "Idealism," a text Poe could hardly not have read: "If the Reason be stimulated to more earnest vision, outlines and surfaces become transparent, and are no longer seen; causes and spirits are seen through them. The best mo-ments of life are these delicious awakenings of the higher powers, and the reverential withdrawing of nature before its God" (*Works* 1: 54). "As a matter of fact," wrote Hegel, "thinking is always the negation of what we have immediately before us."[24]

The recurrent narrative pattern in Poe takes us along with a protago-nist on just such an extraordinary voyage of visionary negation, borrow-ing this structure in a way usually both sympathetic to its aspirations and critical of its results. Example after example could be adduced to demonstrate how such arabesque *rites de passage* work in Poe, not simply as "excuses" for the "supernatural," but as critical variations wrought on the tradition. Even Dupin's ratiocination, which in the trajectory of Poe's career is entertained as a possible substitute for and improvement on the visionary, becomes a double of hypnosis: "I cannot better explain my meaning," says Vankirk in "Mesmeric Revelation," speaking of his insights into God and immortality, "than by the hypothesis that the mesmeric exaltation enables me to perceive a train of ratiocination" (CW 3: 1031). In "The Imp of the Perverse," Poe drops such devices of artificial exaltation, positing our impulse to throw ourselves into the "abyss" as a fatal law of character admitting of "no intelligible principle."

22. Northrop Frye, *Fearful Symmetry* (Princeton: Princeton University Press, 1947); Robert Langbaum, *The Mysteries of Identity* (New York: Oxford University Press, 1977).
23. William Wordsworth, *The Prelude*, in *Poetical Works*, ed. Thomas Hutchinson, revised by Ernest de Selincourt (London: Oxford University Press, 1969), Book 13: 127–31 and Book 6: 592–608.
24. Hegel, *Logic*, p. 17.

But such a defensive abstraction of motive comes late in the career, after countless passages like the following from "Berenice":

> My baptismal name is Egaeus; that of my family I will not mention. Yet there are no towers in the land more time-honored than my gloomy, gray, hereditary halls. Our line has been called a race of visionaries; and in many striking particulars—in the character of the family mansion—in the frescoes of the chief saloon—in the tapestries of the dormitories—in the chiselling of some buttresses in the armory—but more especially in the gallery of antique paintings—in the fashion of the library chamber—and, lastly, in the very peculiar nature of the library's contents, there is more than sufficient evidence to warrant the belief.
>
> The recollections of my earliest years are connected with that chamber, and with its volumes—of which latter I will say no more. Here died my mother. Herein was I born. . . . Thus awakening from the long night of what seemed, but was not, nonentity, at once into the very regions of fairy land—into a palace of imagination—into the wild dominions of monastic thought and erudition—it is not singular that I gazed around me with a startled and ardent eye—that I loitered away my boyhood in books, and dissipated my youth in revery; but it *is* singular, that as years rolled away, and the noon of manhood found me still in the mansion of my fathers— it *is* wonderful what stagnation there fell upon the springs of my life— wonderful how total an inversion took place in the character of my com- monest thought. The realities of the world affected me as visions, and as visions only, while the wild ideas of the land of dreams became, in turn, not the material of my every-day existence, but in very deed that existence utterly and solely in itself. (CW 2: 209–10)

Like Usher and Dupin, Egaeus is most at home in the library. He is a place where other writings meet, less a soul than an intertextual confluence. His identity and that of Poe's work appear to be that of a shadow cast by others. Egaeus's "anxiety of influence" so holds him that the "noon of manhood" finds him still in the mansion of his forefathers, an edifice of historicism as well as textuality. The predicament afflicts many of Poe's narrators, for the intertextuality of his creations necessar- ily involves the danger of unoriginality. The significant twist here is in the result of Egaeus's "inversion" of "everyday existence." This making- absent of the mundane world and its replacement with the "wild ideas of the land of dreams" takes him backward into repeating the character- istics of the past, and of his fathers. Poe draws a structural parallel between a personal and a literary or cultural unconscious. Egaeus's "wild dreams" will represent, in good Freudian fashion, the conflicts and desires of his individual unconscious, thus disrupting his coherent identity with impulses from elsewhere that he (the idea of the unified self) does not author. At the level of writing or culture, we are likewise born into a context of influences; when we come to consciousness of ourselves as individuals, we do so always already through the categories and axioms we have inherited as the subjects of history.

The poetic "anxiety of influence," so evident in Poe's romantic protagonists and in his own responses to Coleridge, Byron, Wordsworth, and Shelley, is only a local manifestation of that general tension between traditions and individual talents that shapes cultural history as a whole. The "ancestral mansions" and genealogical systems in Poe's work represent the machinery of inheritance in the largest sense and inform Poe's dark criticism of the contemporary American rage for the idealism of literary and national self-reliance. Genealogy becomes the aptest structural metaphor because of its theoretical and historical strengths as a system for denominating and regulating the passage of identity, authority, and property through the mutability of time (recall Paul de Man's critique of genealogy as a model of history). It is no accident that so many of Poe's transcendental seekers of truth are aristocrats. Poe's attraction to the hierarchies of aristocracy is one with his temptation toward the transcendental, but both fall victim to the discovery of the work of the unconscious and the other, those bastards and outcasts and women whose exclusion enables the system, and who cannot forever be denied the recognition of their kinship.[25]

Egaeus begins as a version of the "belated" romantic mind. His cousin Berenice's disease (which like those afflicting his other heroines appears to result from no intelligible principle) coincides with a drastic change in his own imagination, with ghoulish results. When Egaeus explains how he came to rip the teeth from the prematurely buried Berenice, he focuses on the difference between the "attentive" and the "speculative" imaginations. The speculative he inherits presumably from German philosophy; the attentive is the "disease" he falls into when Berenice grows ill. The attentive imagination, like the deconstructive reader, fixes on "frivolous" objects of contemplation, such as the "device on the margin or in the typography of a book." His reveries sometimes involve

25. It may also be that the theme of the dark other in Poe belongs to the discourse on race and slavery in antebellum America. The romanticism of the South's feudal representation of slavery's paternalism masked the capitalist reality, in which white identity and culture were produced through the subjection and exploitation of black bodies. Miscegenation was an economic and philosophical problem as well as the result of the rape of black slave women. Poe's anxious, impotent aristocrats belong to the political unconscious of American slavery, just as romanticism's flirtation with the other of reason acted in correspondence with Europe's imperialist subjugations of colonialized lands and peoples. These connections could of course be drawn out in readings of texts such as Poe's "The Narrative of Arthur Gordon Pym" as well as in most of Melville's work.

the "frequent repetition" of a word until it ceases to convey any idea whatever (CW 2: 211–12) ("Quoth the Raven, 'Nevermore' "?). He hopes to banish the words of the fathers and to transcend their influence. Berenice's fatal illness seems to cause Egaeus's mental derangement and his efforts to dissolve everyday reality. In fact, his disease comes immediately after her spells of epilepsy, trancelike states resembling "positive dissolution" and ending in an abrupt return to life. The same pattern holds for the workings of the "attentive" faculty. Unlike the "speculative," it cannot transcend objects, but "pertinaciously returning in upon the original object as a centre" (CW 2: 212), remain fixated to the world, the body of the other.

His previous attitude toward Berenice—"not as a being of the earth, earthy, but as the abstraction of such a being"—was a "speculation" now diseased by an interior malady, an irruption of the other within the self. For Egaeus, her illness is the insistent return of what had been repressed, her "earthy" self, and his own mortality. What drives him mad as he watches her die "are the less important but more startling changes wrought in the *physical* frame of Berenice—in the singular and most appalling distortion of her personal identity" (CW 2: 213). The "death" of his betrothed inspires his ghastly attempt to assert her immortality by wresting her symbolically pure white teeth from the grave. The horrible paradox governing him is this: the desire for immortal identity runs into a fatal conflict with the immortal identities of others; to murder or repress those others in the service of one's own identity involves an intense attention to them as objects, and a repetition of them in reflection that subsequently leaves a resistant trace of the other in the dream of originality. Berenice's premature burial makes Egaeus's perverse attempt to transcend mutability possible, but her teeth remain traces both of the body and of Egaeus's own repressed fears. Her mouth signifies to him (as others have noted) a displaced *vagina dentata*.[26] It resembles other "abysses" in Poe, a negative version of transcendental aspiration. The self leaps into an unconscious beyond that it cannot control, but which beckons with its secret script.

Poe's inquiry into the instability of personal identity shapes much of his work. A variety of topics serve as its vehicle, including metempsychosis, reincarnation, doubles, and spiritual immortality. The interest is especially obvious and keen in the earlier tales and poems written most immediately under the influence of Poe's reading in Gothic fiction, British poetry, and idealist philosophy. In "Morella," a tale of the transmigration of soul from mother to daughter, the narrator-husband-father tells us of Morella's "profound" "erudition" in the "mystical

26. See Daniel Hoffman, *Poe Poe Poe Poe Poe Poe Poe* (New York: Anchor, 1972).

writings" of German literature. Meeting her "by accident," his soul
"burned with fires it had never before known; but the fires were not of
Eros," and he finds "tormenting" the "unusual meaning" and "vague
intensity" of his passions (CW 2: 229). Since Poe's epigraph comes from
Plato's *Symposium*, we can assume that "Eros" here means a sublimating
Platonic love that leads to the divine, and that the narrator begins by
repressing the explicitly physical aspect of his attraction to Morella's
person. But in his daughter's figure she returns, and he "shuddered at
its too perfect *identity*" (CW 2: 234) with Morella's.

Morella's "disquisitions" in "theological morality" cited the "wild Pan-
theism of Fichte . . . and above all, the doctrines of *Identity* as urged by
Schelling" (CW 2: 230–31).[27] The narrator summarizes:

> That identity which is termed personal, Mr. Locke, I think, truly defines
> to consist in the sameness of a rational being. And since by person we
> understand an intelligent essence having reason, and since there is a con-
> sciousness which always accompanies thinking, it is this which makes us all
> to be that which we call *ourselves*—thereby distinguishing us from other
> beings that think, and giving us our personal identity. But the *principium
> individuationis*, the notion of that identity *which at death is or is not lost forever*,
> was to me, at all times, a consideration of intense interest; not more from
> the perplexing and exciting nature of its consequences, than from the
> marked and agitated manner in which Morella mentioned them. (CW 2:
> 231)

Morella's "marked and agitated manner" captivates the narrator. The
troubled sublimity of her appearance inspires the arabesque or elevating experience that precipitates him into disaster. Her "manner" is her
style, and thus she embodies that "mesmerism" of language Poe finds
typical of romantic literature and German philosophy.

The prospect of immortality, of the repetition of characters, oppresses rather than exalts the narrator's soul: "Shall I then say that I
longed with an earnest and consuming desire for the moment of Morella's decease?" (CW 2: 232). The diction suggests her "decease" as a
substitute for coitus. The more she talked of spiritual immortality, the
more his repressed desires were thwarted, as she divorces body from
soul in quest of eternal identity. Her death would put an end to his
desire and prepare them for a spiritual union in death (that embrace

27. On the influence of German idealism upon American transcendentalism, see
Octavius Brooks Frothingham, *Transcendentalism in New England* (1876) (New York:
Harper, 1959), pp. 1–59. Most of that influence was secondhand. Few copies of Schelling
made their way into the United States, for example, and he was not translated into English
(says Frothingham) during this era.

in the tomb found from "The Visionary" to "Annabel Lee"). So her eyes become especially repugnant: "my soul sickened and became giddy with the giddiness of one who gazes downward into some dreary and unfathomable abyss" (CW 2: 231–32). His lust for her death is perverse, a fascination with what the abyss will reveal, even at the cost of that bodily organ that stands for the self. Those eyes (as Daniel Hoffman notes) are for him not the expressions of her "I" but displaced vaginas again, "her meaning eyes" inviting a glimpse into his own carnal nature, his place in a temporal order of determined creations. His sexual reading of her eye/I is defensive, for she is a woman who knows too much. Like the lakes and tarns throughout Poe's writing, those eyes are revisions into the romantic topos of the reflective pool, whose spring waters flow from the pond of Narcissus. The association of abyss, eye, tarn, and lake in Poe suggests the abysmal quality of self-reflection, for the view into the beyond gives back not a heightened vision of one's true self but a bottomless imagination of the otherness we find there.

In Egaeus's terms, the fetishized imagery of Poe's texts is produced by an *attentive* imagination that cannot turn its eyes from the primal scene of sexual difference; in a series of overdetermined tropological displacements, that imagination repetitively returns to what metaphysics considers a "frivolous" and "marginal" topic, and finds no conceptual apparatus equal to the task of permanently sublimating the difference of this scene into the vision of a true identity which would precede and transcend it. Typography, margins, letters, bodies, and the organs of gender escape the power of the philosophical man who would subject them to the history of a spiritual, abstract, timeless, and incorporeal truth.

Morella's gradual reappearance in her daughter is, like the death of Rowena in "Ligeia," a barely disguised wish fulfillment of the narrator's. He perversely christens his daughter with the dead woman's name: "What prompted me then, to disturb the memory of the buried dead? What demon urged me to breathe that sound . . . ? What fiend spoke from the recesses of my soul . . . ?" (CW 2: 235) Morella's transmigration turns into an allegory of the voice of the narrator's repetition compulsion.[28] The repetition compulsion is Freud's coinage for the unconscious reenactment in the present of ideas, relationships, or traumas from the past. The present self is literally made an actor in a drama authored by another, in this case the unconscious. Freud once hoped that such repetition might be worked over into remembrance, a revision that

28. See Freud, *Beyond the Pleasure Principle* (1920), *Standard Edition*, 18. My whole analysis of the staging of the disappearance of Poe's ladies reflects Freud's account of his grandson's game of *fort/da* (gone/there); see above, Chap. 3.

masters repetition and establishes the power of present narratives over past plots. In practice, the issue became "metapsychological" when Freud attempted to explain the repetition of unpleasurable experiences. He argued that erotic desire went beyond the pleasure principle in that its reproductive functions lead to change, rather than to the restoration of a past state. The repression enabling Freud's eros, however, is his exclusion of a human situation by the use of a biological tropology of "germ cells." This allowed him to make absent the most prominent and forbidding repetition compulsion in Freudian sexuality: the imagining of the sexual act as a return to the mother. The metaphor of the germ cell also erased the problem of sexual difference, and so removed the body of the mother from sight. (Recall that the patriarchal library in "Berenice" is also the death chamber of the mother and the place of Egaeus's birth.)

The narrator in "Morella" likewise hopes to cure and master repetition by recalling Morella's name, but what occurs instead is the involuntary dramatization of his own entrapment in a past fixation. Horror is redoubled when his original trauma before Morella's person and style is repeated with his daughter's transformation. The eternal identity of Morella turns into the terror of the past's tyranny over the present. The return of the repressed is immortality's dark double. The narrator's own identity comes undone as the repetition compulsion commands him to enact the script of the unconscious. The narration repeats the process, characteristically shrouding its content in a host of protestations of incomprehension and vagueness. The use of a first-person narrative, or of a nameless observer-double, allows Poe's stories to perform the discourse of a self beside itself, an articulation of "secret writings." We are drawn to interpret this discourse of the other that haunts the mystified accounts of these men driven to commit and confess acts for which their disturbed consciousness can ostensibly find no intelligible principle. We are tempted to become like Dupin, trying to restore the letter to its proper home.

The problem of identity in "Morella" comes out of Poe's reading in Locke's "Of Identity and Diversity," from *An Essay Concerning Human Understanding*.[29] Locke initially defines the *principium individuationis* as spatiotemporal noncontradiction, "it being impossible for two things of the same kind, to be or exist in the same instant, in the very same place; or one and the same thing in different places" (328). This is obviously not the case with such identities as Ligeia or William Wilson. Locke argues that if we define "identity of Man" as "one Organization of Life

---

29. John Locke, *An Essay Concerning Human Understanding*, ed. Peter H. Nidditch (London: Oxford University Press, 1975).

in several successively fleeting particles of Matter," then we shall "find it hard, to make an *Embryo*, one of *Years*, mad, and sober, the same Man, by any supposition that will not make it possible for *Seth, Ismael, Socrates, Pilate, St. Austin,* and *Caesar Borgia* to be the same man" (332). If we allow "the identity of Soul alone" to make "the same Man," then we fall into "the Notions of those Philosophers, who allow of Transmigration" (332). As this mix-up of souls and bodies would considerably confuse the Last Judgment, Locke sets out to redefine the relation between "Personal Identity" and the "Idea of a Man."

In the passage Poe paraphrases—or plagiarizes—in "Morella," Locke reduces the identity of man to a self that is noncontradictory, ever-present consciousness, without the play of unconscious forces: "When we see, hear, smell, taste, meditate, or will any thing, we know that we do so." So much for the "imp of the perverse," and for all those Poe protagonists driven by "no intelligible principle":

> For since consciousness always accompanies thinking, and 'tis that, that makes every one to be, what he calls *self;* and thereby distinguishes himself from all other thinking things, in this alone consists *Personal Identity,* i.e. the sameness of a rational Being; And as far as this consciousness can be extended backwards to any past Action or Thought, so far reaches the identity of that *Person;* it is the same *self* now it was then; and 'tis by the same *self* with this present one that now reflects on it, that the Action was done. (335)

It is this equation of self with a reflective consciousness both immediate and recollective that Poe's texts turn into an oddity. Even Locke recognized the times of heterogeneity in consciousness: forgetfulness, intoxication, the instances "when we say such an one *is not himself,* or is *besides himself*" (343). This unhappy anomaly he solves by simply excluding these fits of otherness from personal identity:

> If there be any part of its [the self's] Existence, which I cannot upon recollection join with that present consciousness, whereby I am now my *self,* it is in that part of its Existence no more my *self,* than any other immaterial Being. For whatsoever any Substance has thought or done, which I cannot recollect, and by my consciousness make my own Thought and Action, it will no more belong to me, whether a part of me thought or did it, than if it had been thought or done by any other immaterial Being any where existing. (345)

This self is a self-discourse, an uninterrupted narrative that shuts out anything violating the control of its self-representations. From the retrospective position of feminist criticism, this self is literally gendered;

the philosophical effort to construct an image of a rational being follows upon an identification with a masculine sphere of values and actions. This "Man" is a man, or would like to re-member himself as such through the mail system of a philosophy of psychological correspondence and exclusion. When Poe lifts the passage on the *principium individuationis* for "Morella," he switches the pronouns from "he" and "him" to "we" and "us." This substitution illustrates how the rhetoric of masculine sexual ideology masks the imposition and universalization of its own particular experience.[30] Poe's own identity as author is thus ensured by an abstraction that fabricates the passage as if it were his own private property. Locke's "self" defends against the influence of others, against thoughts or acts it cannot "own" and which do not "belong" to it. We are not surprised that Locke was the founding philosopher of private property, which of course could only belong to men (and which as a category of law often included the bodies of women).

Locke's self feels at home only in a discourse or consciousness that owns and disposes of its properties, and which is *essentially* not identifiable with anything or anyone outside the boundaries of its authorized entitlements. Political power as well depends on this possession of private property. The ordeals of Poe's narrators tell us much about the fallacy of equating "self" and "self-consciousness." Morella's "immortality" can be read as the action of the narrator's unconscious, and thus as a critique of the *principium individuationis* supposedly demonstrated by Morella's transmigration. His horror at her return is a fearful response to the "immortality" of an alien part of himself. That she—along with Ligeia, Berenice, Madeline, and Annabel Lee—is a woman implies an at least unconscious recognition that the other to Locke's rational man is woman.

The plot of "Morella" is typical of Poe: the death of a beautiful woman is the device that empowers the narrator's excursion into visionary consciousness.[31] The unmaking of his identity that follows proceeds in part from his implicit wish fulfillment, his "guilt" for her death. Poe often obscures this guilt by displacements into lament and adolescent melancholy, or occludes it by a rhetoric of arabesque frenzy. For example, in "Ligeia" the narrator's evident poisoning of Rowena (to enable

30. In an unfinished 1835 manuscript version of "Morella," Poe is obviously copying from Locke's text; he consistently uses "he" and "him" rather than "we" and "us" for the general pronouns here, and makes the switch only in the published versions. See *Collected Works*, 2: 226–27.

31. The thesis of Bonaparte's study is that this woman is always a sign of Poe's mother, Elizabeth Arnold, whose consumptive character is repeated in Poe's fictional heroines and in his marriage to his thirteen-year-old cousin, Virginia Clemm, whose main attraction seemed to be the certainty that she would die in the same style as his mother. See Bonaparte, *Life and Works*, pp. 222–23.

the "return" of the transcendentalist Ligeia) is presented as an opium dream of terror, in which the "angelic aspect" of Ligeia commits the fatal act. He has already cast Rowena into her "sudden illness" by surrounding her with the arabesque furnishings whose effect is the negation of mundane reality (Rowena's body).[32] The guilt of these men grows more explicit in Poe's career, into "The Fall of the House of Usher" and "The Black Cat." The lament for the lost lady gradually becomes the hysterical confession of her willful entombment or, in the poems, the delightful expression of necrophilia, as in "For Annie": "And I lie so composedly, / Now, in my bed, / (Knowing her love) / that you fancy me dead—" (CW 1: 459). The development of Poe's writings into confessional narratives includes his stories of revenge, of doubles murdered in an allegory of adultery and self-destruction. To understand these plots, we need to turn to the source for Poe's dead women and to the strange adaptation of this plot to Poe's theory of poetry.

Poetic Violence

Poe's war on plagiarism and his lifting of materials from other writers were defensive symptoms of his early anxiety of influence experienced under the spell of Coleridge and Byron. A wealth of criticism has disinterred many of Poe's sources, but none have followed Floyd Stovall's passing insight that Poe's "effort to be original" stirred a fanatic attempt "to eradicate all traces of influence" in his poetry. For my purposes, the key poet here is Byron and the central text his *Manfred*.[33] It provides Poe with many of his stock romantic devices, including of course the Byronic hero and the dead lady, as well as a simoon, ominous red lights, and a confession narrative. The relation of Byron's text to Poe's tells the tale of the subject of literary history as a psychological struggle for sexual identity and literary power. Manfred's tale, as Poe reads it, also becomes the story of the end of romantic and philosophical idealism.

Manfred's achievement of transcendental knowledge is haunted by his mournful remembrance of the dead Astarte. In an "all nameless

32. See Clark Griffith, "Poe's 'Ligeia' and the English Romantics," *University of Toronto Quarterly* 24 (1954): 8–25.

33. Floyd Stovall, "Poe's Debt to Coleridge," *University of Texas Studies in English* 10 (1930): 73. On Poe and Byron, see George H. Soule, Jr., "Byronism in Poe's 'Metzengerstein' and 'William Wilson,' " *Emerson Society Quarterly* 24 (1978): 152–62. Citations of *Manfred* are from *Byron*, ed. Jerome J. McGann (New York: Oxford, 1986), and are given parenthetically in the text.

hour" he knew her, and in that climax of his quest his "embrace was fatal." Manfred's double ("She was like me in lineaments"), Astarte dies ostensibly as a result of his Satanic, Faustian ambition: "The Tree of Knowledge is not that of Life." Doubtless Poe fixed on *Manfred* partly because of its incestuous plot and because his unconscious felt guilty for his own mother's death. His descriptions of Ligeia, Usher, and others mingle his own features with hers, as in mourning he introjectively identifies with her to immortalize her, destabilizing his own gender in the process. His ambivalent violence toward such composite figures expresses a profound struggle: a self-punishing guilt vies for supremacy with a desire for revenge against the mother who abandons him when she dies into a spiritual world.

"I loved her, and destroy'd her," wails Manfred. The implicit narcissism of his love, coupled with his otherworldly loneliness, intimates that the search for self-mastery may end in self-murder and the destruction of the other. Unable to demolish consciousness in forgetfulness or oblivion, he has Astarte conjured up in order to ask her forgiveness. She instead pronounces his doom, which works a curious effect on Manfred:

> If that I did not know philosophy
> To be of all our vanities the motliest,
> The merest word that ever fool'd the ear
> From out the schoolman's jargon, I should deem
> The golden secret, the sought 'Kalon,' found,
> And seated in my soul. (3.19–14)

The apparition of the dead accusatory Astarte brings a calm and truth the living lady never inspired. And yet that "If" casts doubt upon this ascension-through-death. His secure sense of guilt empowers at the end his resistance to the demand and his declaration: "The mind which is immortal makes itself/Requital for its good or evil thoughts,—/Is its own origin of ill and end" (3.4.129–31). This psychologizing of his fate turns guilt into the vehicle of truth and the self's identity. In his "crime," in the destruction of the apparently desirable presence, Manfred makes his vision of the "sought 'Kalon,' found." In Manfred's guilt the romantic dousing of the light of sense becomes the murder of the beautiful lady. The absence of the word, and of its transcendental center, is the precondition of Manfred's self and heroic text. The poem tells the tale of his compulsive remembrance, until Manfred returns to the tower where he and Astarte loved and she died, much as Poe and his Psyche will unconsciously find themselves suddenly at the tomb of lost Ulalume. Writing withdraws from immediate presence, displaces what is before it, eclipses (if it can) the old gods, and leaves the trace of a guilt for the necessary murder of former truths and texts.[34]

In "Byron and Miss Chaworth," Poe explicitly describes the advantages gained for the poetic imagination by the lady's absence. Although he acknowledges Miss Chaworth's charms, Poe concludes that it was "better" that "their intercourse was broken up in early life and never uninterruptedly resumed in after years":

> If *she* responded at all, it was merely because the necromancy of *his* words of fire could not do otherwise than exhort a response. In absence, the bard bore easily with him all the fancies which were the basis of his flame—a flame which absence itself but served to keep in vigor. . . . She to him was the Egeria of his dreams—the Venus Aphrodite that sprang, in full and supernal loveliness, from the bright foam upon the storm-tormented ocean of his thoughts. (CW 3: 1123)

This affirmation of the romantic visionary formula hardly seems applicable to the horrific figures of Poe's uncharneled ladies. An axiom like "I could not love except where Death/Was mingling his with Beauty's breath" (CW 1: 157) suggests the poet felt threatened by woman's presence. An "overdetermined" signifier, Poe's lady stands variously and often simultaneously for (1) the body, which the lady's presence excites, thus awakening the unconscious work of the instinctive other within the rational man; (2) the cultural inheritance (familial, national, European), which forms an influential other in the mind that dictates to the self; (3) truth as a metaphysical absolute; (4) the truths and beauties of past authors. If "supernal loveliness" requires the "death" of the other, then the ideals of truth, self, or originality depend on a repeated attention to what they seem to exclude. The same applies to the poet's revisions (or "murders") of his precursors. In fact, "supernal loveliness" is also the term Poe uses in "The Poetic Principle" for that transcendent beauty to which poetry vainly aspires. The "most entrancing" of "poetic moods" doesn't follow the "brief and indeterminate glimpses" of beauty, but rather from the "petulant, impatient sorrow at

---

34. In psychoanalytic terms, one could also read this as an allegory of male psychic separation from the mother. The boy negates his attachment to the presence of the body of the mother in order to establish an autonomous identity, and so as to enable the socially prescribed identification with the law and power of the father. The repetition compulsion displayed by Poe's texts is constantly refiguring this tale and suggests that the disappearance of his father and premature death and burial of his mother interrupted this process, which he now "completes" in fiction. Poe's identification with the feminine, exhibited by his tale's imagery and his taste in contemporary poetry, implies a "failure" to resolve the Oedipal crisis through the usual assumption of castration. Perhaps this wasn't such a bad thing.

our inability to grasp *now*, wholly, here on earth, at once and for ever," "a portion of that Loveliness" (SW 505). In other words, no past poet could have precluded this poet's vision; and besides, the failure to transcend inspires the best poetry.

In the preface to his first volume of poetry, the "Letter to B——," Poe attacks Wordsworth and Coleridge (though he ends by stealing, almost verbatim, the latter's definition of poetry). "He belittles their poetry," writes Stovall, "in order to persuade the reader that it has not influenced his own."[35] When Poe joins the debate over the American writer's originality, he does so in reference to the "established wit of the world . . . for it is with literature as with law or empire—an established name is an estate in tenure, or a throne in possession." Disparaging Wordsworth's supposed didacticism, Poe states: "He seems to think that the end of poetry is, or should be, instruction—yet it is a truism that the end of our existence is happiness" (SW 381). Removing truth from the center of writing and replacing it by "effect" (the correlative of arabesque elevations like opium or mesmerism) produces a poetics that disorders logocentric structures such as genealogy or literary history. Doing without truth, this rhetoric of effects casts writing into an abyss wherein we witness the disestablishment of proper forms and meanings. The maelstrom, the arabesquely furnished apartment, Dupin's library—these and other such derangements of reality are analogous to the space of writing itself, which likewise affects us deliriously in substituting its representations for our normal presences. The hysterical confession is also such a state. As a literary form it exemplifies how the telling of truth and the discourse of the other double each other. These spaces of representation provide the same perverse opportunities as those dark reflective waters that often occupy the center in Poe's poems and tales. They form a shadowy critical mirror of that idealism Poe sometimes indulged. In the review of Drake and Halleck, Poe extols "that evergreen and radiant Paradise, which the true poet knows, and knows alone, as the limited realm of his authority—as the circumscribed Eden of his dreams" (SW 395). Yet we find far different scenes in his work from the pastoralism he lauds, that of "the fair flowers, the fairer forests, the bright valleys and rivers and mountains of the Earth":

> My infant spirit would awake
> To the terror of the lone lake.
> Yet that terror was not fright—
> But a tremulous delight,

35. Stovall, "Poe's Debt," p. 73.

And a feeling undefin'd,
Springing from a darken'd mind.
Death was in that poison'd wave
And in its gulf a fitting grave
For him who thence could solace bring
To his dark imagining;
Whose wild'ring thought could even make
An Eden of that dim lake. (CW 1:85)

The strangest argument contending that the ideal's absence is poetry's law appears as "The Philosophy of Composition," Poe's supposed account of how he wrote "The Raven." The increasing prominence of the confession in Poe affects his criticism, too, so that this piece reads much like "The Black Cat" or "The Imp of the Perverse." Contradicting his former assertion that no "intelligible principle" governs our perverse actions, Poe in this essay gives an elaborate rationale for casting woman into the abyss. The opening references to Godwin and Dickens alert us that this is a murder mystery: the narrator of it turns out to be both culprit and detective. The critical voice ratiocinates with increasingly insane lucidity the modus operandi of a poetics whose "most poetical topic" is the death of a beautiful woman. This loss evokes "mournful and Never-ending Remembrance," the ultimate in Poe's elevating arabesque states of dissolution. The tension between the essay and the poem lies in the distinction between the lover-student's remembrance and the poet's recollection. Poe explains how willfully the student propounds his questions to the monologocentric bird. The student ends as intoxicated on "nevermore" as others are by drink, antique volumes, or the contemplation of arabesque tapestries. The raven perches on the bust of Pallas, reminding the student that the attainment of past wisdom, or the return of Lenore, is nevermore. This youth has a terrible case of Bloom's anxiety, reminded constantly of his belatedness, his loss of the Muse, and the probability that he will never attain (or regain) a philosophical, sexual, or literary Eden. (Not for nothing did Poe contrast his doctrine of mesmeric brevity to the "essential prose" lapses of *Paradise Lost,* as if his own "brief poetical effects" could hypnotize us into forgetting Milton's greatness.) Another parody of the transcendentalist, the student-lover is fanatic in his desire for the immortality of truth and beauty (Lenore).

The poet, however, claims a subtler idea of repetition. "The pleasure" of the poem's refrain, Poe writes, "is deduced solely from the sense of identity—of repetition" (SW 484). Originality is the constant topic of the essay, and here Poe sees his way to a literary "originality" that is not that of a single immortal identity: "I determined to produce continuously novel effects, by the variation *of the application* of the *refrain—the refrain* itself remaining, for the most part, unvaried" (SW 485). This principle holds for the combinatorial rhetoric of Poe's borrowings from literary tradition, high and low. The student's arabesque trance conjures, not the woman, but a death sentence for transcendentalism; Poe's critical account proceeds to confess the requisite erasure of the center, so that absolute repetition may be eluded. (Poe says he chose "Pallas" for its "sonorousness," and we note its homophonic resemblance to "palace" and "phallus," and thus to the haunting of the aristocratic, genealogical transmission of identities.) The eclipse of the light of sense in this case reveals a revision of the past, not a vision of the eternally present. If the eternal and immortal are repetitions, then the poet must control them if he is to establish his own identity. Yet the sorrowful spectacle in Poe's works usually shows protagonists controlled by repetitions, like the student compelled to repeat dead wisdom and dead loves.

Poe's claims to mastery in this essay remind us of the detectives and interpreters in his later work who seek sublimity in the decoding of mysteries. The skepticism of readers toward the "rational" explanation Poe gives of the composition of "The Raven" is well-founded when the dubious achievements of Dupin or Legrand are kept in mind. If the ratiocination of "The Philosophy of Composition" can be read as a defensive fantasy, then we may also speculate that these other geniuses are also perpetrating a hoax. Poe's essay, which begins by excluding the role of "accident" or of the unconscious from poetic creation, fabricates the identity of its own originality by the same repression that so evidently divides Poe's protagonists. But the mastery of speakers in Poe is undone by the whisperings of their doubles, those discourses of the other that irresistibly come to the "surface" when the text looks into the abyss of self-reflection. By creating himself through a poetic violence visited on the other, he makes violence integral to his structure of identity, and so builds his house on a cracked foundation. Given that all these arabesque states of mind in Poe are allegories of the act of writing, we can read in them the terror and fascination of the writer who knows (whatever that means) that writing dissolves his own identity, purloins his own character. What this mailman does is to put his character(s) in circulation. Do not his inevitable displacements and borrowings, and the unconscious figurations of himself in the work, make him yet another letter to be purloined in the reading game?

Purloined Power

As the double of the Minister D——, the Dupin of "The Purloined Letter" is both poet and mathematician. Although he resembles earlier

Poe heroes, his cool intuition of transcendent rationality now replaces the ecstatic state of revelation. The fundamental rule of mathematical calculation in this context is noncontradiction: integers must be identical to themselves. One must not occasionally be two or ten, else systematic combination of integers would prove nonsense. Nor must we inquire too closely into the hypothetical necessity of a zero for the system, lest we be drawn into interminable reflections on the interdependence of being and nothingness. The discrimination of identities, the routing of letters back to their homes or of aberrant crimes to their ordered place, is Dupin's primary activity. In "The Murders in the Rue Morgue," Dupin must solve a linguistic puzzle, for each witness to the murder of the women claims to have heard the criminal speak a different foreign language. When Dupin deduces that this was not a voice but the scream of an orangutan, and thus not the expression of a human passion or subjectivity, he becomes an accomplice to the allegorical repression of desire in language. According to this theoretical plot the orangutan gives us an alibi: the other is truly "other" and no part of ourselves. This may be a "correct" solution to the story's surface mystery, yet it is a very deluded explanation of the other within us that has unspeakable desires. The strength of Dupin's repression is measurable in the hyperbolic care he takes in solemnly incriminating the orangutan. That this animal could be identified with us is a possibility Dupin never entertains and is thus the one on which we are made to fasten. So obviously *outré* is this poor orangutan that readers who buy this explanation merely enact Dupin's own interpretive blindness. This hint of possible interpretive mastery on *our* part, however, for outsmarting Dupin, won't survive the more complicated exchange of identities in "The Purloined Letter."

Dupin's discourse on method in that tale concerns a schoolboy's victorious strategy in the guessing game of even and odd. The boy guesses his opponent's moves through "an identification of the reasoner's intellect with that of his opponent." The analytical reasoner turns himself into the object of scrutiny by becoming the other. "I fashion the expression of my face . . . in accordance with the expression of his, and then wait to see what thoughts or sentiments arise in my mind or heart, as if to match or correspond with the expression" (CW 3: 984–85). This purloining of character replays the romantic ideas of epistemological correspondence and sympathetic knowledge. In this game, the analytical player erases himself, takes the place of the other, and hopes to profit by the reflection (as indeed the Minister D—— hands over a check to Dupin for 50,000 francs). Yet we cannot be so simple as to assume a strict correspondence between surface expression and subjectivity, or to think that a binary calculus of reversals ("If he thinks that I think that he thinks . . ." etc.) will suffice. Poe puns mercilessly on "correspond," having Emerson (at least) in mind and cautioning against a too easy belief in the transmission of identities. Identification with another may be perilous if human subjectivity is heterogeneous or multiple. Which of the other's selves do we identify with, and with which one of our selves do we do it? Through identification we might take into ourselves the others within the other and deposit them unknowingly in our own unconscious (as we do all the time when we read). The complications of the story show up the fallacies of the method.

The "origin" of the story, however, as Derrida emphasizes, is in the usurpation of the King's authority and mastery by the Queen's presumed adultery.[36] The "phallogocentric" letter that circulates in the story demonstrates the wandering of meaning from its "proper" home. In restoring the letter to the Queen, Dupin does not return the letter to its proper place, for it can have none, not even where it is addressed, since it was improper in the first place. The power of the letter is generated by the absence of a univocal meaning and rests on a vulnerability to interpretation. This improper equivocality enables it circulation among purloiners who thus "correspond" with each other. The unrevealed "content" of the letter never concerns Dupin, for he has substituted a semiotic game of placement for the hermeneutic game of meaning. He will restore the letter to the Queen, and so restore the idea that it has a proper place, but he does so only through a systematic structuralist blindness that prevents him from reading its other addresses or his own displacement within the correspondence. Once more he mimics the Minister D——, who is "blinded" and loses the letter when Dupin's hired agents distract him with a staged disturbance in the street below, firing off a musket among a crowd of women and children. Dupin authors a violent primal scene to recapture the letter and thus hopelessly entangles himself in representations of transgression, castration, ejaculation, and dissemination. Dupin's dream of control is exquisitely expressed in his victorious pronouncement that "the pretended lunatic" who fired the shot "was a man in my own pay" (CW 3: 992). This triumphant scene, as Dupin narrates it, will within a page become an ironic commentary on Dupin's own blindness to the implications of the inscription he has left in the purloined letter's double, now stashed in its proper box above the Minister D——'s fireplace.

Dupin is a superficial reader. In deriding the Prefect for seeking the letter in depths or secret places he expresses his wish to avoid private

36. Jacques Derrida, "Le facteur de la vérité," *The Post Card: From Socrates to Freud and Beyond*, trans. Alan Bass (Chicago: University of Chicago Press, 1987), pp. 411–96. A portion of this essay also appears in *The Purloined Poe*, alongside the seminar by Jacques Lacan that Derrida deconstructs. Also reprinted there is Barbara Johnson's ingenious commentary on their dispute (pp. 213–51).

parts. Dupin keeps himself at a distance, theoretically, from abysses. He falls into one, however, through the reading of letters, because the acts of identification in interpretation require the displacement of our own identities and open up the possibility that the other within may engage in correspondences of an illicit, rather than rational or divine, kind with others elsewhere. In this textual maelstrom, reading turns into an arabesque excitement of the mind that may not result in apocalyptic characters but in the purloining of ourselves. Poe's own writings offer abundant evidence that the act of writing can precipitate disturbing and unwanted revelations, both within the text and within the mind of the reader.

Dupin suffers such a fate. At story's end, some perverse impulse prompts him to leave an incriminating signature within the "fac-simile" that he puts in the place of the repurloined letter. His desire for recognition stems from an old grudge with the Minister D——, and this inscription apparently announces Dupin's triumphant identity as the master. Simple, but odd. The signature quote, which takes the place of his proper name, is lifted by Poe from Crébillion's rewrite of the tragedy of the House of Atreus. As Riddel has keenly shown, that ancient revenge plot of adultery, theft, revenge, and cursed genealogy seems one that these Parisians are compelled to repeat. Dupin thus sends a letter to D——, but the "letters" belong to another writer. Dupin changes into a character from an old story, and it is unclear in reflection precisely who is writing who(m). Revenge is the parable of repetition par excellence, for its machinery dictates a binary choice of roles (victim or avenger) that reverse with each succeeding act, thus reducing the identities of the players to the script's tyranny. Dupin sacrifices his own identity and originality to produce an effect on the Minister D—— and thereby too becomes an odd letter needing interpretation and the probable victim of D——'s next move. Dupin wants to strike back for an "evil turn" done him by D—— in Vienna (of course), but we may surmise from Poe's purloining of the Atreus legend that Dupin has been acting all along in unconscious correspondence with a primal, ancient, internalized plot. "Nil sapientiae odiosius acumine nimio."[37] The primal scene here is represented as that "evil turn" in Vienna, a troping which other critics rightly guess to have a romantic content. If the Minister D—— first purloined a woman from Dupin in Vienna, Dupin's rescue of the Queen would put him back into the position of power or possession regarding the woman that he lost to D—— (the summary easily falls into psychomachia).

37. "Nothing is more distasteful to good sense than too much cunning." This, Poe's epigram fictitiously attributed to Seneca, may be applied best of all to Dupin himself.

Delivering the letter puts Dupin in the position of the male-man, in the place of the King, the Father, the Knower of the Truth. In this correspondence, Dupin sends a letter to himself. Addressed to his own narcissism, the letter gives him back the position of being (*lêtre*) male. The play of differences carried by the mail is then posted to and by the carrier of male identity. Derrida quotes the Littré dictionary to remind us that, in French, the mail is feminine: "Le *poste* ne diffère de la *poste* que par le genre."[38] (The genre of detective fiction may also be essentially male.) Derrida's critique of Lacan makes the same accusation: that the psychoanalyst plays the detective in the script of phallogocentrism:

> What does Dupin know? He knows that finally the letter *is found*, and knows where it must *be found* in order to return circularly, adequately to its proper place. This proper place, known to Dupin, and to the psychoanalyst, who in oscillating fashion, as we shall see, occupies Dupin's position, is the place of castration: woman as the unveiled site of the lack of a penis, as the truth of the phallus, that is, of castration. The truth of the purloined letter is the truth, its meaning is meaning, its law is the law, the contract of truth with itself in logos. (*The Post Card* 439)

According to Derrida, Lacan himself gets written into this tragedy when he seeks to revenge himself for the evil turn done to him by the queen of psychoanalysis, Marie Bonaparte. Lacan's seminar on Poe, like Freud's *Beyond the Pleasure Principle*, contains an allegory of disciplinary self-reflexivity: Lacan jockeys for position within the movement of psychoanalysis, assuming institutional power by taking hold of the letter of the law, playing *fort/da* with Queen Marie. That Lacan's rival is female, and thus that his double is the other gender, suggests again that woman is the deferred character put into the circulation of exchange by the mail/male system. Lacan becomes the double of the Minister D——, of the man of political power and intrigue, in that he is the agent of the Queen's lack. In purloining the truth of the letter of psychoanalysis and delivering it to himself, argues Derrida, Lacan repeats the ancient myth of phallogocentrism retold from Oedipus to Freud and beyond. The psychoanalytic movement remains that of the phallus: *fort/da*. Lacan now possesses, in dispossessing Bonaparte, the truth of the letter of Freud's legacy (*legs de Freud*).

Shoshana Felman champions Lacan's cause, explicating his remarkable superiority as compared to "the classical psychoanalytical treatment

---

38. Translation: "The 'post' in the sense of position differs from the 'post' in the sense of mail only by gender." See *The Post Card*, p. 421, n. 6.

of literary texts" exemplified by Bonaparte.[39] Like other overly enthusiastic poststructuralists, Felman confuses the deconstruction of reference
with the extreme claim "that the signifier can be analyzed in its effects
without its signified being known" (141). Lacan enables us to read
the return of purely nonreferential otherness where less sophisticated
readers (like Bonaparte) witness the repetition of "Poe's (sadonecro-
philiac) desire for his dead mother." Thus a useful caution against the
fallacies of the "biographical approach" becomes accomplice to yet one
more patriarchal *fort/da* of the mother's body (be it that of Bonaparte
or Elizabeth Arnold Poe). Lacan and Felman conspire to abstract the
historical construction of gender differences into the neutralized language of a signifying logic liberated from the contingencies of the
signified. In contrast to Felman's contention that Lacan's originality lies
in his refusal to "read the letter's hidden referential content," Derrida
insists that "in fact, we know what is in the note. Lacan indeed is obliged
to speak of and hold onto its meaning, at very least as that which
threatens the pact which constitutes the letter's meaning: the phallic law
represented by the King and guarded by the Queen, the law that she
should share with him according to the pact, and that she threatens to
divide, to dissociate, and to betray" (*The Post Card* 438).

In terms of psychoanalytic literary theory, one might challenge the
ridicule directed against Bonaparte and other "classical" critics who find
representations of the penis everywhere in literature by men. What if
the "literal" character of this psychoanalytic criticism brought us closer
to the "truth" about male writing than a semiotic abstraction of the
referent? Could not one see this repression of the masculine content of
psychoanalysis as another defense of the male system, so that a return
to the "naïveté" and "crudity" of Bonaparte's reading would be more
in accord with contemporary feminist criticism? This displacement of
woman from the history of psychoanalysis repeats, at the level of institutional politics, the erasure of her body performed by the dominance of
castration at the level of theory. As he had shown in his reading of
Freud's institutional politics of theory, Derrida here marks the irreducible overdetermination of the letter of Lacan's seminar by the auto-bio-
graphical framework of its articulation. Truth, power, and desire cannot
be sorted into different envelopes but are written in the margins (or
between/within the "legs") of each other's discourse. The return of the
subject of the history of address again shows up insofar as Poe, Dupin,
Freud, Bonaparte, Lacan, and even Derrida (as Barbara Johnson shows)
become the agents of enframing and inscription. Their singularity and

39. Shoshana Felman, "On Reading Poetry: Reflections on the Limits and Possibilities
of Psychoanalytical Approaches," in *The Purloined Poe*, p. 142.

historical position mark each of the letters they send and receive, though this does not restore them to the position of the Author in the theological or metaphysical sense.

For unless Dupin (and here's a wish fulfillment) is the author of the "original" purloined letter, the story ends with Dupin in a position of holding only the "truth" of the letter's endless circulation or with the sublimated ecstacy of his own apparent victory. If we read that "evil turn" as a symbolic castration of Dupin, we may understand how giving the phallogocentric letter back to the Queen revenges him. And this makes Derrida the double of Dupin, at least at this moment, in that each would restore woman to her power (Derrida is Bonaparte's agent): if there is a difference, and Barbara Johnson for one doubts it, it lies in the way Derrida opts for *la poste* over *le poste*, and so ensures the possibility that the mail carrier never arrives at his destination. What Dupin gains at story's end is the impotence of the Minister D——. Dupin's anticipatory enjoyment of the spectacle of the Minister's castration signals his occupation of both sexual positions assigned by the male system: he is a "man" insofar as he has won the Oedipal battle, and he is a "woman" insofar as he identifies with the Queen in her power. But again, despite this structural correspondence or androgyny, one should not mistake these positions for those of men and women, for the position of "woman" here is still defined in terms of the movement of the phallus. The only positions available here are those assigned by the movement of the properties of men.

The position of the male is not an essential one, but the product of the mail system, of the circulation of letters. In Lacan's terms, the Symbolic system addresses the subject in such a way as to designate his position. Man's "castration" must be assumed (as earlier we saw that the assumption of woman's absence was necessary if the dead letter of man was to reach its sublime destination). The power of letters lies in this capacity for assignation. "The Purloined Letter" might be called an allegory of the truth-of-power-as-castration, insofar as it demonstrates the coincidence of patriarchy and logocentrism in the structuring of the movement of the letter and its power. Whatever power the Queen holds, she holds only in sufferance, in terms assigned by the male system: her power is the power of castration, and to that extent it is never properly hers and always susceptible of theft. She only gets to play post-office. Women have no power in this system, though they may on occasion be its subjects.

CHAPTER SIX

Henry Adams: Outlaw Virgin

Historians undertake to arrange sequences,—called stories, or histories,—assuming in silence a relation of cause and effect. These assumptions, hidden in the depths of dusty libraries, have been astounding, but commonly unconscious and childlike; so much so, that if any captious critic were to drag them to light, historians would probably reply, with one voice, that they had never supposed themselves required to know what they were talking about.

—*The Education of Henry Adams*

Henry Adams plays an important role in representing the crisis of historicism at the end of the nineteenth century. Few agonized more seriously, or more parodically, over the breakdown of the major meta-narratives governing Western thought than did Adams. For Adams, the crisis of historicism would involve the subject and its desires in a catastrophic series of negative revelations, each of which would displace some key grounding concept of historiography, politics, religion, literature, philosophy, or science. Adams becomes an exemplary figure insofar as his texts exhibit the self-conscious collapse of the Hegelian model for historicism, in which history is narrated as the progressive, dialectical movement of Spirit's self-realization. The breakdown of this model, in Adams's case, is brought on by American political events that belie the myth that the nation-state embodies the organic unfolding of a people's spiritual development. Correspondent events in Adams's personal life and in his intellectual and social experiences produce similar moments in which the optimistic scenarios of the Enlightenment give way to the pessimistic declensions of modernity.

Adams looked to the Germans and the French for his historiographical theories, only to find them useless in accounting for General Grant, the Robber Barons, or his own wife's suicide. Turning to positivism and materialism, Adams likewise found their methods hopeless. Science, technology, and capitalism outrun the antique formulas of Newtonian physics; meanwhile the residual taint of Hegelian subjective idealism and teleological historicism in Marxism ill-suit Adams's experience of the American scene. Adams's desire as a writer, then, will be to address the crisis of historicism by making *himself* its subject. Of course this will mean the end of the subject of historicism, at least as far as Adams is concerned; both it and he will dissolve into the representational antics of his self-deconstructive style. The subject of Adams's *Education* can only center the history of his time by recording his sense of being absent from it.

Following Adams's own self-reflections, he is usually portrayed as a transitional figure between Victorianism and modernism, a man nostalgic for the order of eighteenth-century reason as he faces the anarchy of twentieth-century chaos. John Rowe positions Adams (and Henry James) directly as a forerunner of modernism (or even postmodernism) as he emphasizes Adams's subversion of the reigning conceptual terms of his era.[1] A more specific account of Adams's anxieties, however, might be put together by first placing his work within the particular story of the crisis of historicism in the nineteenth century, though this will inevitably involve some reductive generalizations. One must figure out how Adams's proposals and experiments in historiography embody, however allegorically, his reading of American culture in the post–Civil War era. This decoding of Adams's historical allegories will also have to take seriously his insistence that the subject of historiography (in the personal sense) cannot be written out of the subject of historicism. Adams skillfully adapts elements from the genre of autobiography to accomplish this double writing; this move invites a psychoanalytic interpretation of his historiographical method and opens up the question of how Adams enacts what I have called disciplinary self-reflexivity. Psychoanalysis will also prove useful in discussing the content of Adams's work, for the problems in cultural history that he often focuses on are those of the differing representations and powers of the sexes in contrasting nations and epochs. His masterworks, *Mont Saint Michel and Chartres* (1904) and *The Education of Henry Adams* (1907), bear more than a little resemblance to Freud's *Interpretation of Dreams* (1899) in their analytic concern with the historical character of sexuality (or the sexual character of history), as well as in their speculative use of materials from the author's life. While Adams did not create a new historicism in any (convincingly) programmatic fashion, the way he failed, and

1. See John Carlos Rowe, *Henry Adams and Henry James* (Ithaca: Cornell University Press, 1976); T. J. Jackson Lears, *No Place of Grace: Antimodernism and the Transformation of American Culture, 1880–1920* (New York: Pantheon, 1981); and Joseph G. Kronick, *American Poetics of History: From Emerson to the Moderns* (Baton Rouge: Louisiana State University Press, 1984).

succeeded, in critiquing the old historicism might be instructive to us today as we undergo a different crisis of historicism. A look back at Adams could clarify what the old historicism foundered upon, what brought it to ruin in Adams's case, and how the factors in its demise may continue to disturb attempts at making historicism new.

The Old Historicism

The distinctive character of nineteenth-century historicism, writes Maurice Mandelbaum, lies in the central role it accords to *development,* which then becomes the key to explanation and evaluation: "Historicism is the belief that an adequate understanding of the nature of any phenomenon and an adequate assessment of its value are to be gained through considering it in terms of the place which it occupied and the role which it played within a process of development."[2] Historical events cannot be read apart from the grand metanarrative of the developmental process informing them; this will also be a *progressive* story, having its roots in the Enlightenment and its ally in the metaphysical idealism of romanticism, which placed the story of spirit's coming-to-consciousness at the center of the historical pageant. It is not the individual changes, or even stages, that are the final subject of historicism, but the entity or essence subjected to historical development. The rejection of this developmental, teleological, and subject-centered model will, of course, be the hallmark of historical criticism under the sign of poststructuralism and will be particularly attacked by Foucault. Adams came to mock the theses of the old historicism and to offer instead a description of history as a discontinuous series of cultural formations oriented by desire and organized by symbols. The subject would remain at the center of Adams's historiography (at least through *Mont Saint Michel and Chartres* and the *Education*), but his history exhibited no development unless it were a comically progressive increase in complexity, bafflement, frustration, and sorrow.

Nineteenth-century historicism, borrowing a page from the neoclassicism of German comparative philology, made the nation-state into the subject of the historical process. As Mandelbaum summarizes it, historicism

held that the life of a people is a unitary thing, expressing itself in all laws and institutions, and in all artistic accomplishments; that this unity is

2. Maurice Mandelbaum, *History, Man, and Reason: A Study in Nineteenth-Century Thought* (Baltimore: Johns Hopkins University Press, 1971), p. 42.

achieved because of a unity of feeling which has grown through the traditions and inner needs of the people; and that such a unity of feeling is the
soul of the people. Thus the historian's task is that of grasping the inner
core of feeling which binds a people together and which manifests itself
in all of the accomplishments of that people; it is his aim to see the people
as a single, living, historical and history-making entity whose value must
be judged in terms of its own inner harmony, not in terms of a rational
and universal standard imposed upon it. (55)

Clearly Adams understood and shared this historicism, yet found it
wholly wanting when it came to representing or understanding the
experience of American modernity. The American nineteenth century
pivoted not on unity but on a Civil War, and precious little common
feeling joined the communities of the nation's competitive regions, or
the classes, races, and genders alienated from one another by the system
of industrial capitalism. In his work on the Middle Ages Adams employed the old historicism nostalgically, recomposing the emotional
coherence that built the cathedrals for Mary. *Mont Saint Michel and
Chartres,* however, depicts a society whose souls are at the mercy of
symbols, and where desire quickly becomes taken up and redirected by
the economics of exploitation. Adams's Middle Ages turn out to be an
allegory of America, and the task of the historian to reconstruct a usable
past in the form of an attractive symbol.

Though Adams studied Marx more seriously, and with more admiration, than did most late nineteenth-century American intellectuals, he
ultimately classified Marxism among the antiquated relics of the old
historicism. In the *Education,* Adams recalls how a visit to England's
"Black District" "made a boy uncomfortable, though he had no idea
that Karl Marx was standing there waiting for him, and that sooner or
later the process of education would have to deal with Karl Marx much
more than with Professor Bowen of Harvard College or his Satanic
free trade majesty John Stuart Mill."[3] The complacency and historical

3. Henry Adams, *The Education of Henry Adams,* in *Henry Adams: Novels, Mont Saint
Michel, The Education* [also includes poems], ed. Ernest Samuels and Jayne N. Samuels
(New York: Library of America, 1983) p. 786. Subsequent references are cited parenthetically as *Education.*
   The obstacles to Adams's conversion were practical and institutional as well as theoretical. In "The Tendency of History" (1894) Adams spelled out the sociopolitical consequences of adopting any scientific theory of history, including a Marxist one: "In whatever
direction we look we can see no possibility of converting history into a science without
bringing it into hostility toward one or more of the most powerful organizations of the
era. If the world is to continue moving toward the point which it has so energetically
pursued during the last fifty years, it will destroy the hopes of the vast organizations of
labor. If it is to change its course and become communistic, it places us in direct hostility
to the entire fabric of our social and political system. If it goes on, we must preach despair.
If it goes back, it must deny and repudiate science. If it goes forward, round a circle which

blindness of the "type bourgeois-bostonien" included their ignorance of Marx. "No one, except Karl Marx, foresaw radical change" after the events of 1848 (750). When at Harvard as a student (1854–58), recalls Adams, "he got little from Political Economy. He could not afterwards remember to have heard the name of Karl Marx mentioned, or the title of 'Capital' " (774). Had his teachers mentioned the book, it would have been a supreme feat of historical prescience, since Marx did not publish *Capital* until 1867. This passage is a joke on the American reader, presumably so ignorant of Marx that he would not catch the anachronism.

"Did you ever read Karl Marx?" inquired Henry Adams of Charles Milnes Gaskell in 1894; "I think I never struck a book which taught me so much, and with which I disagreed so radically in conclusion."[4] "By rights," Adams later observes of himself, "he should have been also a Marxist, but some narrow trait of the New England nature seemed to blight socialism, and he tried in vain to make himself a convert" (*Education* 925–26). The "conclusion" in Marx he objected to was the teleological notion of the inevitable victory of a classless and unalienated economy. While persuaded by Marx's argument that political economy determines the phases of history, Adams also knew that such a vision of order threatened, like scholasticism, to become a machine or to fall victim to that "insanity of force" at play in nature, human and physical. Adams's "dynamic theory of history" instead postulated a series of historical phases organized around an epoch's attraction to an ordering symbol, and he found in the Virgin his greatest example. The hypotheses of thermodynamics suggested to Adams a different kind of scientific materialism than Marx imagined, in which the "degradation" of civilization and policy followed the laws of entropy.

Adams began reading *Capital* in 1894, after the panic of 1893 and conversations with his brother Brooks on how systems of currency and trade might serve as the basis for calculating a science of historical change. In *Capital* Adams heavily annotates the early sections on "Commodities," "Money," and "The Rate of Surplus Value."[5] Here he would find Marx's genealogy of money: how history is a series of economic structures centered on more and more abstract terms of exchange, from barter to paper currency. Marx shows concepts and values to be

leads through communism, we must declare ourselves hostile to the property that pays us and the institutions we are bound in duty to support." See "The Tendency of History," in Henry Adams, *The Degradation of the Democratic Dogma*, with an introduction by Brooks Adams (New York: Macmillan, 1947), p. 129.

4. *Letters of Henry Adams, 1892–1918*, ed. Worthington Chauncey Ford (Boston: Houghton Mifflin, 1938), pp. 49, 248.

5. Ernest Samuels, *Henry Adams: The Major Phase* (Cambridge: Harvard University Press, 1964), pp. 139–40.

historically and systematically relative, and the theory of "commodity fetishism" unmasks the way desire invests in systems of exchange so as to realize value in reified forms—forms whose mystifications perpetuate and obscure the complicity of apparently logical truths with hidden powers. Capitalism's claim to authority through the principles of nature, freedom, individuality, rationality, and even divine sanction was exposed as an ideology covering the insanity of force at work in the wage-slavery of the mode of production. Marx's disclosure of how the circulation of money (what we might today call the discourse or text of political economy) produced reified notions that communist analysis might deconstruct resembles, with some qualification, Adams's discovery of nature and society's "pantomime" upon the death of his sister Louisa (see below). The dialectic of materialism and idealism issues in the apparent triumph of the former, though there remains the danger that materialism too may be a branch of metaphysics.

The gap between writing and history opens wider in Adams's work when he looks into the abyss between the sensible and the intelligible. Confronting the dynamos, X rays, and radium exhibits at the Great Exposition, Adams is confounded by the discontinuity between material forces and understandable forms, a discontinuity that casts into doubt the form of the material itself and thus any economics in the literal sense. "He had studied Karl Marx and his doctrines of history with profound attention, yet he could not apply them at Paris" (*Education* 1066). Historical materialism would not hold up if material itself were inconceivable by any logical economy and if the value of the relation between the sensible and the intelligible obeyed no designated law. The "new forces were anarchical," "parricidal in their wicked spirit towards science." Adams "lost his arithmetic in trying to figure out the equation between the discoveries and the economies of force. The economies, like the discoveries, were absolute, supersensual, occult; incapable of expression in horse-power" (1068) (recall Saussure's effort to harness the play of *fors*). Adams trembles at the prospect of a general economy of energy and exchange operating lawlessly "before" the appearance of matter and meaning and impossible to represent in itself. The old historicism sought the sublimation or sublation of the material in the intelligible (the sensible in the sensible). When the general economy informing matter will not abide by this restricted narrative—so that "Radium denied its God"—the translation of nature and objects into culture and ideas goes adrift from the start. Language, as the signifying use of material sounds and traces, likewise falters when the economy between sensory and truthful turns uncanny. Thus the operations of general economy defy denomination by the old logos, are "incapable of expression in horse-power."

Adams supplements *Capital*'s history of money through the economies of psychological attraction and symbolic force: the determinations
of exchange do not tell the whole story, since they leave out the crucial
factors of desire and signification. Money is a language of self-expres-
sion, its exchanges constantly mediating the construction of truth and
identities. Adams will sum up the lesson in "The Virgin and the Dynamo" when he describes the failure of the historian to find any principle of sequence for the interpretation of history. Discarding theories
based on great men, on society, on chronology, on economics, and on
ideas, Adams turns to the sequence of forces and finds they can only
be measured by their powers of attraction, which operate through great
distances:

> Clearly if he was bound to reduce all these forces to a common value, this
> common value could have no measure but that of their attraction on his
> own mind. He must treat them as they had been felt; as convertible,
> reversible, interchangeable attractions on thought. . . . The symbol was
> force, as a compass-needle or a triangle was force, as the mechanist might
> prove by losing it, and nothing could be gained by ignoring their value.
> Symbol or energy, the Virgin had acted as the greatest force the western
> world ever felt, and had drawn man's activities to herself more strongly
> than any other power, natural or supernatural, had ever done. (*Education*
> 1069–70, 1074–75)

This model allowed for the play of human desire in the course of
history, restored the play to the machine of determination, and made
of historical sequence a series of subjective experiences raised to the
level of communal autobiography. Values are accounted for not by
describing the objective sequence of material systems but by analyzing
the social subject's response to a historically specific symbolic system (an
institution taking both rhetorical and physical forms). This is a theory
of ideology which fits rather well with recent poststructuralist fusions
of Lacan and Marx, for it respects the forces of materiality even as it
locates the determinations of value in the economy of the subject's
mediated desires. In his fiction of the Virgin Adams posited a notion
of historical order as art and interpretation, rather than science or
epistemology, and so tried to free himself of the Manichaean choices
bequeathed him by Puritanism, rationalism, and orthodox Marxism.

The Self, the Truth, the Woman

In the final pages of *Mont Saint Michel and Chartres*, Saint Thomas
Aquinas serves as the final stand-in for Henry Adams's own quest to

"bridge the chasm between multiplicity and unity," a dilemma he called "the oldest problem of philosophy, religion, and science":[6]

> With practical unanimity, mankind rejected the dual or multiple scheme; it insisted on Unity. Thomas took the question as it was given him. The Unity was full of defects; he did not deny them; but he claimed that they might be incidents, and that the admitted Unity might even prove their beneficence. Granting this enormous concession, he still needed a means of bringing into the system one element which vehemently refused to be brought:—that is, Man himself, who insisted that the Universe was a unit, but that he was a universe; that Energy was one, but that he was another energy; that God was omnipotent but that man was free. The contradiction had always existed, exists still, and always must exist, unless man either admits that he is a machine, or agrees that anarchy and chaos are the habit of nature, and law and order its accident. (*Chartres* 685)

After the long imaginative journey back to the cathedrals of the Middle Ages, Adams's final chapters on Abelard, the mystics, and Aquinas make explicit the dialectical relation of the Medieval and the Modern, confirming our suspicion that the whole book has been less an objective account of Gothic and Norman art than a symbolic rendering of Adams's own spiritual autobiography. These last chapters are composed and revised while Adams reads intensely in the unsettling works of contemporary scientific philosophy, including Pearson's *Grammar of Science* and the work of Lord Kelvin and James Clerk Maxwell.[7] In both the waning of the Middle Ages and the entropy of the *fin de siècle*, Adams sees a failed quest for an Absolute to resolve contradictory oppositions into lawful unities. In the philosophy of history elaborated in *Chartres,* the identity of "Man himself" is an anomalous and troubled "element," less a center from which action radiates than a force-field subjected to the power of relentlessly conflicting energies.

The itinerary of Adams's education brings him, in the company of so many other nineteenth-century writers, to the twilight of the idols and the deconstruction of transcendental verities. As a consequence, personal identity, which is so dependent on its assumption of a secure place

6. Henry Adams, *Mont Saint Michel and Chartres,* in *Henry Adams,* ed. Samuels and Samuels, p. 621. Subsequent references are cited parenthetically as *Chartres.* Throughout I have adopted the editors' restoration of the original title typography; see p. 1219.

7. Samuels, *The Major Phase,* pp. 291, 305–7. Samuels's volume provides a comprehensive account of *Chartres*'s biographical context, compositional history, and principal themes. Two book-length studies, dependent on Samuels's work, are Robert Mane, *Henry Adams on the Road to Chartres* (Cambridge: Harvard University Press, 1971), and Joseph F. Byrnes, *The Virgin of Chartres: An Intellectual and Psychological History of the Work of Henry Adams* (East Brunswick, N.J.: Associated University Press, 1981).

in systems of social, political, religious, and even metaphysical order, will inevitably go adrift, decentered along with the other "texts" of the era. During his career as a professor and "scientific historian" Adams had been unable to sustain the balance between an objective reliance on original documents and a subjective ordering of history through literary devices.[8] His focus on the Virgin allowed him to explore his personal sense of history's inexplicability. "We do not," he wrote, "and never can, know the twelfth-century woman, or, for that matter, any other woman, but we do know the literature she created; we know the art she lived in, and the religion she professed. We can collect from them some idea why the Virgin Mary ruled, and what she was taken to be, by the world which worshipped her" (*Chartres* 537). This "we" is intentionally gendered as masculine by Adams's rhetoric: it is "we" historians, we men, who can never know woman. Is this another example of phallogocentrism, in which Woman is fetishized as an irrational mystery whose unknowability is part of her seductive design?[9] Is his fidelity to the Queen, like Dupin's, a ruse of patriarchy? Or is Adams genuinely attempting to value woman as something other than the negative mirror that returns speculative man to himself? If we follow Adams's footsteps to Chartres, we find him there seeking and worshiping Mary because her actions transgress the cosmic, moral, and judicial laws of the fathers. Salvation through Mary lies not in her ability to decide between order and chaos, law and accident, but in her absolution of man from the logocentric drive:

> Men were, after all, not wholly inconsequent; their attachment to Mary rested on an instinct of self-preservation. They knew their own peril. If there was to be a future life, Mary was their only hope. She alone represented Love. The Trinity were, or was, One, and could, by the nature of its essence, administer justice alone. Only childlike illusion could expect a

8. See William H. Jordy, *Henry Adams: Scientific Historian* (New Haven: Yale University Press, 1952), pp. 1–22.

9. "Woman seduces from a distance," writes Derrida, "and distance is the very element of her power. . . . This opening separation, this overture of a veiled proximity, gives rise to truth, from which woman is of herself separated. There is no essence of woman because woman distances and separates—as she diverges from and of herself. Abysmally, without end or ground, she engulfs and fundamentally distorts all essentiality, all identity, all propriety. Here, blinded and dazzled, somber philosophical discourse founders and is led headlong to its ruin. There is no such thing as the truth of woman, but this is because this abyssal divergence of and from the truth, this nontruth is 'truth.' Woman is but one name for this nontruth of truth" (translation modified). See Jacques Derrida, *Spurs: Nietzsche's Styles/Eperons: Les styles de Nietzsche*, trans. Barbara Harlow (Chicago: University of Chicago Press, 1979), pp. 48–51. For an astute commentary on the undecidability of "woman" in Derrida's texts, see Gayatri Spivak, "Love Me, Love My Ombre, Elle," *Diacritics* 14 (Winter 1984): 19–36.

personal favor from Christ. Turn the dogma as one would, to this it must logically come. Call the three Godheads by what names one liked, still they must remain one; must administer one justice; must admit only one law. In that law, no human weakness or error could exist; by its essence it was infinite, eternal, immutable. There was no crack and no cranny in the system, through which human frailty could hope for escape. One was forced from corner to corner by a remorseless logic until one fell helpless at Mary's feet. (*Chartres* 574)

Man turns for escape from the "remorseless logic" of the "One" to the significant form of Woman and her grace, to a power that displaces the Father and his commands. (And so, in fashion, the politics of the family are extrapolated to cultural history.) This allegory of Woman as a refuge from the truths of the patriarchs extends, moreover, beyond purely intellectual problematics and into the complex history of Adams's personal relations—familial and erotic.

Adams's search for a bridge between "multiplicity and unity" began, as the *Education* will tell us, in the contradictions of his youth: between Quincy's morality of Enlightenment rationalism and State Street's bourgeois capitalism; between an eighteenth-century polity of law and principle and a nineteenth-century democracy of bought votes and manipulated politicians; between New England's Puritan sensibility and the luxuriance of Southern sensuality; and between a career as a leader of the present order and one as a disorderly analyst of the present crisis of values. After deifying the Virgin's role as intercessor for the heretic in *Chartres*, Adams would cast these antinomies at the beginning of the *Education* under the general heading of paternal and maternal legacies, associating the paternal lineage with the logical quest for reason, truth, law, and the absolute and the maternal with that for sensation, imagination, and natural chaos. The theme is introduced in the long description of his grandmother Louisa, wife of John Quincy Adams:

> He never dreamed that from her might come some of those doubts and self-questionings, those hesitations, those rebellions against law and discipline, which marked more than one of her descendents; but he might even then have felt some vague instinctive suspicion that he was to inherit from her the seeds of the primal sin, the fall from grace, the curse of Abel, that he was not of pure New England stock, but half exotic. As a child of Quincy he was not a true Bostonian, but even as a child of Quincy he inherited a quarter taint of Maryland blood. (*Education* 737)

The entanglement of philosophical, social, and religious conflicts with the terminology of masculine and feminine—already evident in an early essay like "The Primitive Rights of Women" and in Adams's two novels—will be most elaborately explored in the structuring of *Chartres*, where the traveler begins with the masculine Norman architecture at Mont Saint Michel and the warrior verse of the *Chanson de Roland* before arriving at the feminine apotheosis of Mary at Chartres.

The symbolic significance of the Woman in *Chartres* as a relief from masculine imperatives has a number of autobiographical resonances. The Virgin Mary is commonly read as another monument, along with Saint-Gaudens's statute at Rock Creek Cemetery, to Adams's dead wife, Marian, who committed suicide in December 1885 by swallowing potassium cyanide from her photography kit. Completely absent from the *Education*, which passes over the years of marriage with a chapter simply titled "Twenty Years After," Marian haunts each of Adams's twin works like a ghostly muse and unspoken referent. The decentering undergone by Adams in the years following this shattering and inexplicable loss certainly fuels his increasingly intense and bitter quest for a saving absolute. Yet we must recognize the dangers of reduction here, and of inaccuracy, since the concerns of the *Chartres* obviously predate Marian's suicide, though Adams's account in the *Education* of his earlier years may be colored by the tint her death gave to his subsequent vision.

A case in point is the darkly absurd fate of Adams's sister Louisa in 1870, narrated in a chapter of the *Education* titled "Chaos." Thrown from a cab while on holiday in sunny Italy, she contracts tetanus: "He found his sister, a woman of forty, as gay and brilliant in the terrors of lockjaw as she had been in the careless fun of 1859, lying in bed in consequence of a miserable cab-accident that had bruised her foot. Hour by hour the muscles grew rigid, while the mind remained bright, until after ten days of fiendish torture she died in convulsions" (*Education* 982). It was "the last lesson—the sum and term of education":

> The first serious consciousness of nature's gesture,—her attitude toward life,—took form then as a fantasm, a nightmare, an insanity of force. For the first time, the stage-scenery of the senses collapsed; the human mind felt itself stripped naked, vibrating in a void of shapeless energies, with resistless mass, colliding, crushing, wasting and destroying what these same energies had created and labored from eternity to perfect. Society became fantastic, a vision of pantomime with a mechanical motion. . . . the idea that any personal deity could find pleasure or profit in torturing a poor woman, by accident, with a fiendish cruelty known to man only in perverted and insane temperaments, could not be held for a moment. For pure blasphemy, it made pure atheism a comfort. God might be, as the Church said, a Substance, but he could not be a Person. (*Education* 983)

No other episode in the *Education* so passionately expresses Adams's tutorial in cosmic senselessness: "Flung suddenly in his face, with the

harsh brutality of chance, the terror of the blow stayed by him thence-
forth for life, until repetition made it more than the will could struggle
with; more than he could call on himself to bear" (982). This "repetition"
is the book's most direct reference to Marian's suicide fifteen years
later. Of course it is impossible to gauge the degree to which Adams's
representation of Louisa's death is a displaced account of what Marian's
death had come to mean.[10] Likewise it would be impossible to exactly
measure the relation of these decenterings to Adams's experience of
chaos in the realms of politics and science and historiography, since the
economy of "repetition" in representation renders undecidable any
logic of cause and effect. What is apparent, however, is that the figure of
the Virgin in *Chartres* condenses a series of previous feminine energies,
restoring life to them and revising their relation to the problematic
of order and chaos. Within the binary machinery of masculine logic,
Woman's death meant meaninglessness and chaos; her revivification,
and that of Adams, would necessitate an overturning and displacement
of that logic. The binary value system of identity and difference, order
and chaos, man and woman, truth and illusion would have to be replaced by an economy or system of exchange radically other than that
of the merciless logic of the One. In Adams's account, Mary would
attract the energies and economic investments of her people precisely
because she offered them an alternative to the Father's Logos.

In *Mont Saint Michel and Chartres*, Adams carries his antipathy toward
a personal, paternal deity to its summation, one not without Oedipal
overtones. The *Education*, in fact, will begin with a comic portrait of
genealogical anxiety, of infant Henry born as "Israel Cohen" in Jerusalem, circumcised in the synagogue and "heavily handicapped" in the
race for life; the metaphor of circumcision wonderfully expresses the
ambivalent power of tradition to both empower and wound the son.
The Adams family legacy weighed heavily on him from his youth, when
even the gardener remarked that someday little Henry too would end
up president of the United States. Authority conceived thus in a line of
male descent was one of the commonplaces Adams's writings took pains
to undo, as he saw it undone in his own and others' life stories. Like
Hawthorne before him, he looked back upon a family history full of
national and symbolic importance, but seeming to decline as it came
closer to his own lifetime. While assisting in 1895 with his brother
Charles's biography of their father, Adams made the melancholy discov-

10. The accounts that Adams wrote at the time of his sister's illness and death, while
describing the experience as "in many ways the most trying and terrible days I ever had,"
do not express the apocalyptic bitterness and disillusionment contained in the passages
from the *Education*. See *The Letters of Henry Adams*, 3 vols., ed. J. C. Levenson et al.
(Cambridge: Harvard University Press, 1982), 2: 72–75.

ery that his father too felt an early sense of decay and morbidity.[11] America's, and the Adamses', decline could be dated from Andrew Jackson's victory in 1828, which displaced the last Adams president (John Quincy) with a figure of mob democracy and gold-bug expansionism.

Everything in politics, history, and personal affairs implied that the "track of the energy" led not simply from patriarch to patriarch, order to order, but by way of complex points of attraction and exchange, unaccountable without the force of woman. Woman might teach a lesson in how the reason of history tells the truth of desire rather than of logic. Henry Adams greatly admired the letters of his great-grandmother Abigail Adams, for example; they revealed a perspective on the revolution, diplomacy, and American life not apprehended by her male contemporaries. Abigail Adams's story, however, is known only to the few who have read her letters. Her life and thought remain in the shadow of her husband's historical fame. "The study of history," Henry Adams writes in the *Education,* "is useful to the historian by teaching him his ignorance of women; and the mass of this ignorance crushes one who is familiar enough with what are called historical sources to realize how few women have ever been known. The woman who is known only through a man is known wrong. . . . The American woman of the nineteenth century will live only as the man saw her; probably she will be less known than the woman of the eighteenth; none of the female descendents of Abigail Adams can ever be nearly so familiar as her letters have made her" (1042–43).

By inference, then, the *man* who is known only through men, and their orders, is known wrong too. After completing in 1890 *The History of the United States during the Administration of Thomas Jefferson and James Madison,* Adams seeks increasingly for a knowledge of women: more precisely, for an understanding of how men have been attracted to and become the instruments of the forceful energy of women. The woman who attracted Adams in the wake of Marian's death, and by all evidence throughout what he called his "posthumous existence," was Elizabeth Cameron, recipient of hundreds of Adams's voluminous letters and companion to his researches and thoughts. Ernest Samuels and others have traced the outlines of this frustrated affair, one felt more pressingly by Henry than by Elizabeth, and ultimately suppressed—or sublimated—by both.[12] She makes only one scant appearance in the *Education,* out of all proportion to her large role in his later life, an omission

11. Samuels, *Major Phase,* pp. 152–55.
12. Ibid., pp. 64–74; Mane, *Chartres,* pp. 75–76, 197; Byrnes, *Virgin,* pp. 68–87, 121–28, 162–68.

that recalls the excision of his years with Marian. Elizabeth and her daughter Martha may have inspired his love for the Madonna and child, but this surmise overlooks the character of his feeling for her, which made him both lover and supplicant. What we can assume is that his attraction to Elizabeth, added to the rebirth of Adams's senses during his travels in the South Seas, helped provide the energy for a renewed assault on the logic of the fathers and a fresh impetus to imagine a way out of the dualism and despair that characterized the period after Marian's suicide.

Adams's remark above (on the historian's "ignorance of women") refers to Mrs. Cabot Lodge: "For the moment he was rescued, as often before, by a woman." She "bade him follow her to Europe with the Senator and his two sons," where Adams continues the inquiry into the art, architecture, and women of the Middle Ages begun in 1893 after the financial panic and his work with Brooks Adams on *The Law of Civilization and Decay*. In Europe's past he reads, in the culture of another place and time, an interpretation of the riddle of nineteenth-century America and his alienated relation to it. When in 1892 Adams first began to plan a volume on his "Travels," including Asia and the South Seas as well as Europe, he described it to John Hay as "a sort of ragbag of everything; scenery, psychology, history, literature, poetry, art; anything in short, that is worth throwing in," and that would eventually include his own personal and philosophical anguish concerning the critique of metaphysics he saw enacted by science, by historical events, and by the deaths of Louisa and Marian.[13]

One "element which vehemently refused to be brought" into the scheme of unity was Adams himself, whose extreme self-consciousness and desire for independent identity would not allow him to be assimilated to any "machine," sociopolitical or theological. Yet his inherited and constitutional longing was for a vision of harmony joining individual, society, and nature in an orderly historical design. His metaphor of the machine and his discussion in the Aquinas chapter of the collapse of the dogma of organic unity exhibit *Chartres's* constant double focus: Adams will reflect, through a medieval mirror, on the passing away of nature as order's ground in the nineteenth century, when a capitalist political economy imposes its artificial values on things and science discovers a chaos of forces beneath the pantomimes (or reifications) of the physical universe. (However negative its direction, this account of America's fall belongs to the canonical historiography of the nation, as I described it in Chapter 4.) From his first essay on the "Gold Conspiracy" to his lengthy late letters on financial affairs, Adams reacts bitterly

13. Letter to John Hay, 9 January 1892, in *Letters*, ed. Levenson, 3: 599.

to the effects of American political economy as it displaces the moral
and philosophical order of the eighteenth-century rationalism represented by his family and the early nineteenth-century romanticism that
had hoped to salvage idealism. In writing the book on the Middle Ages,
Adams will create an allegorical commentary on his own age's rage for
scientific and mechanical order, its transformation of political economy
into an absolutist theology blind to its own relativism, and on his own
need to escape the systems of thought and society whose orders cost
more than they ever can repay. The Virgin's condemnation of the
money-changers in *Chartres* will give voice to Adams's own view of the
spiritual decline underwritten by finance capitalism since the Renaissance, and will mark the condensation of Adams's figure of the Virgin
with his figuration of himself.

Everybody's Autobiography

Adams put the finishing touches on the first edition of *Mont Saint
Michel and Chartres* in the early months of 1903 and sometime later
that year began composing the *Education*. The element of communal
autobiography underlying the conception of these intentionally corre-
lated volumes is suggested by a letter Adams wrote to Henry James
on 18 November, after "devouring" James's biographical study of the
expatriate sculptor William Wetmore Story:

> The painful truth is that all of my New England generation, counting the
> half-century, 1820–1870, were in actual fact only one mind and nature;
> the individual was a facet of Boston. . . . There was hardly a difference
> even in depth, for Harvard College and Unitarianism kept us all shallow.
> . . . *Type bourgeois-bostonien!* . . . God knows that we knew our want of
> knowledge! the self-distrust became introspection—nervous self-con-
> sciousness—irritable dislike of America, and antipathy to Boston. . . . So
> you have written not Story's life, but your own and mine,—pure autobiog-
> raphy,—the more keen for what is beneath, implied, intelligible only to
> me, and a half-dozen other people still living.[14]

Fusing self-figuration and cultural criticism, the textual "ragbag" of
Mont Saint Michel and Chartres belongs in an ironic manner to that genre
which Sacvan Bercovitch calls the "auto-American-biography," a text
that figurally composes the individual hero and the American nation in
a single history of exile and salvation. The "norms of spiritual biogra-

14. *Letters*, ed. Ford, p. 414.

phy" are projected rhetorically onto the history of the nation itself, while the individual identifies with America and becomes its representative *man*. This genre of personal narrative "reconstitutes national prophecy and spiritual biography as prophetic autobiography," and so "designates a comprehensive social-divine self-hood" that ultimately fulfills the promise of the forefathers."[15] Applying Erich Auerbach's theory of *figura* to Puritan typological thought, Bercovitch postulates a genealogical model of literary history that is also indebted to Harold Bloom's schema of the "anxiety of influence." Upon the American author, then, falls the burden of representing America in a double sense: the auto-American-biographer must both fashion a sacred national vision worthy of the forefathers' example *and* articulate a jeremiad against failures to fulfill the dream. The identification of individual with nation—creating a single Subject of History—means an inevitable doubling of the auto-American-biographer, whose castigations of the unregenerate country are matched in intensity only by self-doubts springing from an almost morbid habit of introspection. Auto-American-biography is a genre within the old historicism, but in Adam's hands the labor of the ironic sends negation beyond any redemptive hope and subverts the genre itself.

When Hawthorne opens "The Custom-House" at the beginning of *The Scarlet Letter,* he confesses to "an autobiographical impulse" which we must see informing the tale of Hester and Arthur as well as that of the Surveyor. We are reading the "A" that designates the autobiography of the New England Mind. It is hardly new to observe that this and other "classic" American texts—Emerson's essays, Thoreau's *Walden,* Melville's *Moby-Dick,* Whitman's *Leaves of Grass,* Twain's *Huckleberry Finn*—whatever their ostensible genres, are attempts at figuring a self for both individual and nation.[16] Indeed, the experimental or anomalous form of such texts, including *Mont Saint Michel and Chartres,* testifies to their place in a lineage of auto-American-biographies characterized by a radical uncertainty about individual and communal identities. The project of auto-American-biography might be considered, in Fredric Jameson's formula, both ideologically repressive (as it projects the life of a specific class onto the nation as a whole) and utopian (as it tries to imagine a community of equal souls).

What has perhaps been slighted in accounts of this tradition is how

15. Sacvan Bercovitch, *The Puritan Origins of the American Self* (New Haven: Yale University Press, 1975), pp. 106, 134–35.

16. The moment one tries to apply Bercovitch's schemas to texts from outside this region, class, race, and gender, the continuing ideological confusion of the category "auto-American-biography" will be starkly revealed. Is Kate Chopin's *The Awakening,* Ralph

each text fabulates a kind of reactionary utopia or "world elsewhere" as a romance resolution of contradictions wrenching the fabric of American sociopolitical and economic life. The chasm opening up between the auto-American-biographer and his nation, at least since the happy example of the industrious Ben Franklin, traces the individual's alienation from both inherited and contemporary modes of production, economic and intellectual. The children of New England's Calvinist theocracy find themselves steadily distanced from the growing power of the bankers, entrepreneurs, and traders who dominate Boston's State Street, and America's new city-center, New York. The sons and daughters of Hawthorne's "steeple-crowned progenitors" now belong to the enervated upper class of Boston's cultured and provincial elite, from which they feel as estranged as they do from the emergent lower class of laboring immigrants and the rising middle class of self-reliant businessmen. Those, like Whitman and Melville, born to the newer classes find themselves likewise unable to forge a secure link between the aristocratic orders of art and the chaos of a society where profiteering has replaced prophecy.

When Bercovitch extends his theory to Adams in *The American Jeremiad,* he finds the *Education* illustrative of this genre's continuity: "The distinctive quality of the *Education* is that it reverses all the effects of the jeremiad while retaining intact the jeremiad's figural-symbolic outlook. Adams is not a Victorian sage calling halt to a rampant industrial capitalism. He is a prophet reading the fate of humanity, and the universe at large, in the tragic course of American history."[17] Both *Chartres* and the *Education* resemble the jeremiads, since each is a declension narrative in which the children of modernity betray their forefathers' original strength of metahistorical purpose. But as Bercovitch himself sees, the figure of the fathers is not simply an idealized one: in *Chartres,* Normandy serves as an explicit metaphor of New England's Puritan past— a granitic severity and secure masculine faith—which the traveler leaves behind for Chartres's feminine artistry; in the *Education,* the twin legacies of Puritan self-denial and Enlightenment rationality are subject to the son's withering mockery. These books, in fact, go far toward deconstructing—and not just reversing—the terms of the jeremiad. The retreat from man's place in time and history that Bercovitch attributes to Adams's philosophizing underestimates, I think, how Adams's search

Ellison's *Invisible Man,* or Leslie Marmon Silko's *Ceremony* an "auto- American-biography"? See below, Chap. 7, for the contradictions Frederick Douglass faced in trying to transform the slave narrative into a representative American story.

17. Sacvan Bercovitch, *The American Jeremiad* (Madison: University of Wisconsin Press, 1978), pp. 194–97.

for universal laws ultimately fails *because* of its parodic fidelity to the Puritan and rationalist programs for decoding the work of reason in history and the self's identity with it. Adams *is* a Victorian sage bemoaning rampant industrial capitalism, an economy that declared itself the teleological tendency of history by virtue of the marketplace's metaphysical machinery and the "invisible hand" of its providence. To say that Adams's work "extols the national past while pointing steadily toward the cosmic void" misses the complexity of Adams's position. No simple recourse to history and the past is possible, for either radical or reactionary, until a more thorough analysis of what constitutes the subject and its history be pursued. Otherwise the agents of jeremiad risk merely repeating the formulas of the fathers (knowledge, progress, liberty) who also gave us capitalism (private property, economic imperialism, wage labor).

The classic form of the auto-American-biography as the prophetic history of saint and nation is sardonically twisted by Adams, who will fashion himself as outlaw and be blessed as such by the Queen of Heaven. In so doing he repudiates the ideology of the representative man, which enchained the individual to the machine of an American Logos. The auto-American-biography had been patriarchal from the start, a genealogy of righteous men wed to the sacred and unforgiving history of the Absolute. The Oneness of Truth was also its masculinity, and the transmission of knowledge found its image in the son's filiopiety, his repetition of the father's words and ways.[18] Woman, like the devil so often associated with her, tempted man to sex, relation, time, chance, difference, duality, chaos, and writing. Identification with woman disrupts the order of the fathers, allows the relativity of attraction and desire into the machinery of history, mixes truth with beauty. Adams's insistence on the return of the repressed woman in American culture symbolizes the return of what the philosophical orders of the fathers proscribed:

> Why did the gentle and gracious Virgin Mother so exasperate the Pilgrim Father? Why was the Woman struck out of the Church and ignored in the State? These questions are not antiquarian or trifling in historical value; they tug at the very heart-strings of all that makes whatever order is in the cosmos. If a Unity exists, in which and towards which all energies centre, it must explain and include Duality, Diversity, Infinity,—Sex! (*Chartres* 582–83)

---

18. On American filiopiety and self-representation, see Mitchell Robert Breitwieser, *Cotton Mather and Benjamin Franklin: The Price of Representative Personality* (New York: Cambridge University Press, 1985).

Church and State had turned against the Virgin, and ousted her from the center of culture, ever since the Renaissance, which brought the triumph of the Logos in the forms of scientific rationalism and finance capitalism. The tendency to see Western history as a long decline from the imaginative sensuality of the Middle Ages found its art-historical outlet in the Pre-Raphaelite movement, in which so many of Adams's friends participated and which sheds considerable light on the motives of his own medievalism.[19] The cult of the medieval, from Ruskin to Saint-Gaudens and LaFarge, developed explicitly out of the dissatisfaction of artists and intellectuals with the social and economic conditions of modernity, and with the artwork it produced. In the verbal texture of *Chartres* and the *Education* we find at once an intense representation of delight in the physical senses counterpointed to an equally strong and caustic intellectual asceticism. This dissociation of sensibility, this split between feeling and thought, is a carefully orchestrated theme in both of Adams's volumes and in the subtext of his self-figurations.[20] The erotic attraction of the Virgin entices the son to disobey his father's command to sublimation and long-term investment, pardoning his desire and inspiring him to create works more expressive of the principles of pleasure than those of Absolute Knowledge. Of course the Virginity of Mary and her position as Mother complicate this strategy quite considerably. It allows for the fulfillment of an Oedipal fantasy, of a return to immediate sensual gratification before the separation dictated by the Father's No, and it defers that forbidden dream, since the realization of the wish comes only in the work of art, and in a portrait of Woman as mother, not lover. A heavy load of guilt is still carried by the disobedient son, who seeks absolution from his Father's judgment at his Mother's feet. This complex ambivalence entailing desire and rebellion with guilt and a quest for pardon reflects back, from the Middle Ages, to Adams's own family romance, and to America's social autobiography in the nineteenth century.

Theorizing that history can only be read as a sequence of forces of desire, Adams contrasts his own attraction to Woman and Mother to America's ignorance, or repression, of her, except as a temptress to disease: "When Adams was a boy in Boston, the best chemist in the place had probably never heard of Venus except by way of scandal, or of the Virgin except as idolatry; neither had he heard of dynamos or

19. See Ernst Scheyer, *The Circle of Henry Adams: Art and Artists* (Detroit: Wayne State University Press, 1971).

20. Adams's orchestration of this theme is misread as a simple failure of feeling by T. S. Eliot in his review of the *Education*, where he asserts that "there is nothing to indicate that Adams's sense either flowered or fruited" ("A Sceptical Patrician," *Athenaeum*, 23 May 1919, pp. 362–63).

automobiles or radium; yet his mind was ready to feel the force of all, though the rays were unborn and the women were dead" *(Education* 1070). No one at school, complains Adams, had ever drawn his attention to the invocation of Venus in Lucretius or Dante. But if Woman could act as the center of cultural life, it was not merely out of sex appeal; the force of her attraction for Adams is inseparable from her power of maternity, her central place in an infinite reproduction of life and energy—a place now usurped by the mechanical mystery of the industrial dynamo:

> The Woman had once been supreme; in France she still seemed potent, not merely as a sentiment but as a force; why was she unknown in America? for evidently America was ashamed of her, and she was ashamed of herself, otherwise they would not have strewn fig-leaves so profusely all over her. When she was a true force, she was ignorant of fig-leaves, but the monthly-magazine-made American female had not a feature that would have been recognized by Adam. The trait was notorious, and often humorous, but anyone brought up among Puritans knew that sex was sin. In any previous age, sex was strength. Neither art nor beauty was needed. Everyone, even among Puritans, knew that neither Diana of the Ephesians nor any of the oriental Goddesses was worshipped for her beauty. She was Goddess because of her force; she was the animated dynamo; she was reproduction—the greatest and most mysterious of all energies; all she needed was to be fecund. *(Education* 1070)

Woman is the power that can vanquish death; she need only have a moment's help from man. The cruel slaughter of Louisa Adams Kuhn and Marian Adams at the hands of death (itself portrayed as a female deity in the passage on his sister's demise) is here imaginatively undone. The site of immortality is revealed as the fig-leaves are stripped away.

Adams's extraordinary passage, with its avid rediscovery of the mother's genitalia, recalls Freud's speculations on the consequences of the anatomical distinction between the sexes. For Freud the puzzled boy's glimpse of woman's uncanny difference remains a latent enigma until threats against his own treasured organ precipitate a retrospective confirmation of the "truth" of castration, and of woman as this truth. The truth of castration in turn reinforces the Father's No, the prohibition of the mother's body, the deferral of desire, the acceptance of symbolic substitutes, and the construction of personal identity as a socially regulated economy of libidinal investments. The little boy's identification of truth, and of the truth of his own sexual identity, with the absence or presence of the phallus inaugurates subjectivity under the authorization of the Father's Logos. Reduced to "penis envy," woman becomes the absence of truth—becomes madness, irrationality, the other—and her difference is covered over. The dis-covery of this difference threatens man, not because castration is a reality, but because it threatens to expose the unreality of castration, its fantastical construction, and the wholly speculative nature of male identity. Man's assumption of identity stems not from an original priority but from his negation of woman. Her difference marks the untruth of *his* truth, the artifice of his self-imagination. Woman tells the difference of every body's autobiography.

American culture, as Adams portrays it, is castrated and lacks women: "American art, like the American language and American education was as far as possible sexless" *(Education* 1072). American power increases in direct proportion to its acts of negation. The groundlessness, lack of principle, and sterility Adams identifies in his contemporaries are all indications that the power they wield comes at the cost of something essential. As the ultimate representative (though unelected) man of the nineteenth century, the "Henry Adams" of the *Education* reiterates this sense of lack in his monotonous refrain of personal failure, as if a demonic compulsion to repeat had taken hold of him and made his story the nation's fable. By its very repetition and dissemination, impotence becomes a kind of truth in the *Education:* like a fetish, it becomes a powerful force of attraction, a phantasmal center around which history is gathered. In so doing, it usurps the Logos, the Father's fetish, and does so in the name of the Mother, in whose image the son recognizes himself, another outlaw virgin.

Of course, Adams's worship of the maternal is also a reactionary fabulation designed to counter the century's deconstruction of organicism and woman's actual resistance to the mystical vocation of motherhood. "All these new women," as Adams describes them, are propelled out of the house by capitalism and into the social machine: "The woman had been set free—volatilised like Clerk Maxwell's perfect gas;—almost brought to the point of explosion. . . . In every city, town and farmhouse, were myriads of new types,—or type-writers,—telephone and telegraph girls, shop-clerks, factory hands, running into millions on millions, and, as classes, unknown to themselves as to historians" *(Education* 1126). Adams's celebration of the "superiority of woman" had been based on the character of Marian, Elizabeth Cameron, and other upper-class women whose freedom was economic as well as social, and who outshone their men in wit and moral sense. They succeeded, where the Daisy Millers failed, in creating, out of Gilded Age wealth and the leisure time provided by the sexual division of labor, a female type powerful enough to check the excesses of the nineteenth-century man, long since debauched by business and politics.

The quite unhistorical and rather romantic idealization of medieval women in *Chartres* portrays them as the agents of civilization correcting the childlike impulses of their warrior husbands; the lives of these courtly lords and ladies are, like the characters in Henry James's novels, playing out the contradictions of social life in America. But even the "superior women" of *fin de siècle* America are "failures":

> The cleverer the woman, the less she denied the failure. She was bitter at heart about it. She had failed even to hold the family together. . . . She had failed not only to create a new society that satisfied her, but even to hold her own in the old society of Church or State. . . . Never had the world known a more capable or devoted mother, but at forty her task was over, and she was left with no stage except that of her old duties, or of Washington society where she had enjoyed for a hundred years every advantage, but had created only a medley where nine men out of ten refused her request to be civilized, and the tenth bored her. *(Education* 1124–25)

If upper-class women failed to save society through the arts of persuasion, lower- and middle-class women failed, in Adams's eye, by being swept into society's dynamo and out of their natural place of power. They abandoned their organic place in the mode of reproduction and became the reified subjects ("type-writers") of capitalism's material and symbolic machinery:

> When closely watched, she seemed making a violent effort to follow the man, who had turned his mind and hand to mechanics. . . . He could not run his machine and a woman too; he must leave her, even though his wife, to find her own way, and all the world saw her trying to find her way by imitating him. . . . The woman's force had counted as inertia of rotation, and her axis of rotation had been the cradle and the family. . . . if her force were to be diverted from its axis, it must find a new field, and the family must pay for it. So far as she succeeded, she must become sexless like the bees, and must leave the old energy of inertia to carry on the race. *(Education* 1126–27)

The hegemony of industry capitalism over the means of production includes the reproductive unit, the family, and decenters it as woman moves into the work force, or stands helplessly by, making elegant conversation as business goes on as usual. She too is "sexless like the bees."

Adams's inability to conceive of woman in other than maternal figures indicates how deeply tied he remained to the culture of the Father. The organic culture of the family is offered here as prelapsarian antithesis, and symbolic antidote, to the modern machinery of social reproduction. A resentment and hostility toward modern (e)masculinity spurs Adams to an assault on the fathers, only to offer as alternative a metaphysical Maternity which once more identifies woman with her genitals, with her power to reproduce the image of Man's order and immorality: "Of all movements of inertia, maternity and reproduction are the most typical, and women's property of moving in a constant line forever is ultimate, uniting history in its only unbroken and unbreakable sequence" *(Education* 1123).

Henry and Marian Adams had no children. In Adams's library, reports Joseph F. Byrnes, was a copy of J. Marion Sims's *Clinical Notes on Uterine Surgery with Special Reference to the Management of Sterile Conditions.*[21] The various remarks in Adams's letters expressing indifference to childlessness seem, considering his worship of the Virgin, wholly defensive. The personal sense of sterility became compounded with the perception of an entropy in history, an "insanity" of disorder in nature, and with a heightened perception of finality and death. Mary would offer, as substitute mother, a reversal of history, as Adams could become the child he never had, and so thwart the patriarchal demiurge who, after torturing Louisa, would cut Adams off from the biological reproduction of his own identity. Identification with the Virgin would ironically preempt the Father through the Son's self-emasculation. Sexless as the bees, he could live a fantasy that would resolve the conflicts of society and sexuality through regression to a "oneness" that was not one.

Miracles for Criminals

Adams's thesis in *Chartres* is that the attractive power of the Virgin for the medieval world lay in her intervention between humanity and patriarchal judgment. Reading the stained-glass at Chartres, Adams deciphers "Our Lady's Promise of Paradise":

> She wielded the last and highest power on earth and in hell. In the glow and beauty of her nature, the light of her Son's infinite love shone as the sunlight through the glass, turning the Last Judgment itself into the highest proof of her divine and supreme authority. The rudest ruffian of the middle-ages, when he looked at this Last Judgment, laughed; for what was the Last Judgment to her! An ornament, a play-thing, a pleasure! a jeweled decoration which she wore on her breast! Her chief joy was to pardon; her eternal instinct was to love; her deepest passion was pity. (474–75)

21. Byrnes, *Virgin*, p. 25.

Staking out the thirteenth century as the transition from the "secure
rock foundation" of Norman absolutism to the corruption of society,
politics, and religion by commerce and finance, Adams sees the Virgin as
the people's symbolic resolution of their socioeconomic and theological
oppression. In this he generally follows the outline of Brooks Adams's
The Law of Civilization and Decay, adding the symbolic dimension to
Brooks's deterministic condemnation of usury capitalism. The Virgin
thus represents what nineteenth-century America, and Henry Adams,
lack and desire: a sanctified alternative to the laws of the fathers and
the bankers, and one in which the strict economy of labor and exchange
is replaced by a miraculous economy wherein the Logos of retributive
justice is silenced by love. Mary, says Adams, was "the *only* Court in
Equity capable of overruling strict law" (579). Her favors to the criminal,
the helpless, the reprobate, and the undeserving irked the orthodox
economists of salvation, who likewise frowned on her opinions about
usury: "She had very rudimentary knowledge indeed of the principles
of political economy as we understand them, and her views on the
subject of money-lending or banking were so feminine as to rouse in
that powerful class [the nascent bourgeoisie] a vindictive enmity which
helped to overthrow her throne" (586).

Identifying with the Virgin, Adams is empowered to write his allegorical jeremiad against Boston and State Street. By implication he becomes
the representative man of those weaker classes exploited by the paternal
order. Such a sentiment for the workers, however, was noticeably lacking in Adams's views on contemporary political affairs, in which his
hatred for the bankers was not matched by a support of the working
classes. (This anomaly characterizes a number of reactionary auto-
American-biographers whose estrangement from the elite also borrows
the elite's resentment of immigrant and laboring masses, from Thoreau
and Emerson to Eliot and Pound—and in significant contrast to Whitman.) Unable to disown the elitist legacy of eighteenth-century attitudes
on natural and intellectual aristocracy, and materially a participant in
the class interests of the bourgeois, Adams resolves his own ambivalent
situation only through the fiction of his oneness with the medieval
peasantry—a kind of political pre-Raphaelitism. Adams's jeremiad in
Chartres fulfills the imperative of the auto-American-biography, though
in doing so it also thwarts the apocalyptic plot of the form by negating
its teleological claim to the One Truth, since in the place of the Center
it puts a woman whose chief attraction is her suspension of the Law's
Truth. Thus Adams is spared the harsh judgment otherwise visited
upon him by his ancestral fathers, who would judge him a failure as
surely as Hawthorne's would have called him an "idler." His failure to
fulfill the promise of the Adams family is excused by the Virgin. His

symbolic identification with the people reverses Adams's own reactionary discomfort with the actual proletariat and grants him the representative status that eluded him in the politics and society of the nineteenth
century.

The construction of *Mont Saint Michel and Chartres* as a revision of the
auto-American-biography appears clearly in its opening chapter on
Normandy. The view from the Abbey Church there "recalls the coast
of New England. The relation between the granite of one coast and that
of the other may be fanciful, but the relation between the people who
live on each is as hard and practical a fact as the granite itself" (344).
The declension narrative artfully begins by a visionary scanning of the
landscape from Norman heights: "From the roof of the cathedral of
Coutances over yonder, one may look away over the hills and woods,
the farms and fields of Normandy, and so familiar, so homelike are
they, one can almost take oath that in this, or the other, or in all, one
knew life once and has never so fully known it since" (345). The return
to origins seeks the beginning of the spiritual history of both Adams
and America. In the shape of a gloss on the eleventh-century Church
Militant, Adams fashions a critique of his family's and nation's New
England foundations. (These genealogical concerns will of course be
echoed in the opening pages of the *Education.*) In a manner owing much
to Hawthorne's "Custom-House," Adams looks back ambivalently at
these stern, dogmatic warriors of God's Unity. Normandy becomes "the
pons seclorum, the bridge of ages, between us and our ancestors" (347).
He seems to narrate a lamentable decline from this masculine simplicity
of faith and will say later that "all Chartres is to be one long comment"
on what has been lost since the time of Mont Saint Michel. This simply
degenerative history, however, is belied by the chapter's language and
strategic function, both of which indicate the degree to which the Fall
is an uncanny tropological invention, a rhetorical device that conjures
the Origin into being, only to once more depart from it.

One of the attractions of this fabulated return to origins is its imaginative capacity to reverse time and entropy, restoring the old to youth
once more. Actual young people, says Adams, rarely enjoy the Norman:

They prefer the gothic, even as you see it here, looking at us from the
choir, through the great Norman arch. No doubt, they are right, since they
are young: but men and women who have lived long and are tired,—who
want rest,—who have done with aspirations and ambition,—whose life has
been a broken arch—feel this repose and self-restraint as they feel nothing
else. The quiet strength of these curved lines, the solid support of these
heavy columns, the moderate proportions, even the modified lights, the
absence of display, of effort, of self-consciousness, satisfy them as no other

art does. They come back to it to rest, after a long circle of pilgrimage,—
the cradle of rest from which their ancestors started. Even here they find
the repose none too deep. (349)

Tired of his posthumous existence, Adams circles back from age to
infancy as his pilgrimage returns him to the Norman home of those
who would become America's first pilgrims. This annihilation of self-
consciousness in a reunion with the cradle, however, serves only as the
first step in a new self-figuration, as the narrator-Uncle pursues the
itinerary of his rebirth and regeneration across the landscape of France,
from the men of Saint Michel to the women of Chartres. A closer
inspection of the impressive solidity at Saint Michel reveals that even
here the "repose" is "none too deep," that something essential is lacking—or too massively present—at the origin. In his overture to the
book, Adams represents his own lifelong wandering from the ways of
the New England fathers: in returning to Normandy–New England he
reverses his years of heresy, slumping exhausted at the foot of the
Archangel's militant figure. Yet strategically this is only a prelude to a
new errancy, as the journey from Saint Michel to Chartres repeats the
son's original departure from the father's ways. It is in the figural
repetition of this departure that *Mont Saint Michel and Chartres* traces
Adams's "autobiography." The repetition reverses the original sense
of guilt and nostalgia—even while giving expression to them—as the
narrator now leads his nieces and other errant readers down the same
disorderly path. The celebration of the Virgin, and Adams's identification with her, will justify his life of chaos and retrace the steps that
brought him—and the America he represents—from Norman/Puritan
militancy through the Woman's/Mary's grace to the ruin of philosophy
in Scholastic/Scientific indeterminacy.

The Fall from Unity, then, is a happy one, as it takes us from four
chapters on Normandy to nine chapters on the quite different spiritual
coherence inspired by women and symbolized by the Virgin (recall how
Hester Prynne had stepped from the Puritan prison-house and found
a wild rose). The passing of Norman–New England theocracy gains in
art and forgiveness what it loses in moral and philosophical security:
"The simple, serious, silent dignity and energy of the eleventh century
have gone. Something more complicated stands in their place; graceful,
self-conscious, rhetorical, and beautiful as perfect rhetoric, with its
clearness, light and line, and the wealth of tracery that verges on the
florid" (352). Like Hester at her needle, the Virgin will craft Gothic art
to her own fancy, and in that revisionary device Adams sees the emblem
for his own substitution of artful, self-conscious rhetoric in place of the
language of immutable laws. The descent from Norman to Gothic

retraces the line from Puritan faith to Gilded Age scepticism. In place of the Absolute, of the Truth and Order of the Fathers, comes the rhetorical fashioning of values self-consciously derived from human desire rather than divine scripture. Adams's lament for this Fall, however, coincides paradoxically with his eager espousal of its critical force. Like Hawthorne, he seeks the sympathy missing from the Word of the Fathers, and so insists on the need for the Mother as she who liberates the Son to be different. As Queen, the Virgin presides over a world that, like Henry Adams's nineteenth century, lacks any absolutes; it is precisely this absolution from choosing between Manichean fantasies of order and chaos that attracts Adams, whose spiritual and civic life is propelled by an inherited obligation to represent what is right. The Virgin embodies a general theory of relativity that sets aside the epistemological and social tribunals established by the inherited systems of history, theology, politics, and metaphysics: "What the roman could not express flowered into the gothic; what the masculine mind could not idealize in the warrior, it idealized in the woman; no architecture that ever grew on earth except the gothic, gave this effect of flinging its passion against the sky" (373).

The lesson Adams reads in the art and architecture of Chartres recurs when he turns to the role of women in medieval society, when "the superiority of the woman was not a fancy but a fact" (524). Here the Virgin's earthly emanations—Blanche of Castile, Eleanor of Guienne, Mary of Champagne—stand as allegorical commentary on the crisis of sex roles in Adams's own time. These shrewd, inspiring, and "masculine" ladies exercise in their epoch the civilizing function Adams had hoped the nineteenth-century American woman would perform for *her* warriors—the politicians, bankers, and industrialists who formed the nobility of the Gilded Age. Adams skips rather lightly over the evidently brutal physical and social subjugation of women in the Middle Ages; the "facts" about these queens and their female contemporaries are of less concern to Adams than expounding the meaning of various mens' legendary idealizations of them:

> We are concerned with the artistic and social side of life, and have only to notice the coincidence that while the Virgin was miraculously using the power of spiritual love to elevate and purify the people, Eleanor and her daughters were using the power of earthly love to discipline and refine the Courts. Side by side with the crude realities about them, they insisted on teaching and enforcing an ideal that contradicted the realities, and had no value for them or for us except in the contradiction. (536–37)

"For us," he observes, "the poetry is history, and the facts are false" (549). The many contradictions of this chapter include its fervent idealization of emasculation, as the fantasied power of the woman both signals and repeats the castration of the men. In the ensuing carnival of identities, the binary logic determining the distribution of male and female qualities breaks down. Adams quotes M. Garreau's argument that "a trait peculiar to this epoch is the close resemblance between the manners of men and women. The rule that such and such feelings or acts are permitted to one sex and forbidden to the other was not fairly settled" (524). Here the poetry of emasculation reverses the history of patriarchal rule, and we regress to a time when the play of differences between the sexes was still relatively free. The parable is indeed less historical than poetic and seems rooted more deeply in the history of Adams's psychology than in that of the Middle Ages.

One attraction of emasculation, of course, is the blow that it strikes at the potency of the father. The son exchanges his own masculine fetish for the relics of the Virgin, who supplements the ensuing lack with her powerful dispensation of grace. The Virgin's essential function comes to the fore in the climactic chapter on "Les Miracles de Notre Dame." The popularity of the legendary miracles Adams retells here depends on the Virgin's provision of grace to the poor, the old, the criminal, the unregenerate—and to her very unmasculine absence of pride:

> In no well-regulated community, under a proper system of police, could the Virgin feel at home, and the same thing may be said of most other saints as well as sinners. Her conduct was at times undignified. . . . She condescended to do domestic service, in order to help her friends, and she would use her needle, if she were in the mood, for the same object. . . . Mary did some exceedingly unconventional things, and among them darning Thomas A'Becket's hair-shirt, and the supporting a robber on the gibbet, were not the most singular. (580–81)

The economy of the Virgin's grace opposes that of a commodity system in which values and identities are determined by what they can be exchanged for on the open market. The Virgin's "illogical" dispensation of favors upsets the account books of salvation's authorities and their equation of social utility with eternal value: "Intensely human, but always Queen, she upset, at her pleasure, the decisions of every court and the orders of every authority, human or divine; interfered directly in the ordeal; altered the processes of nature; abolished space; annihilated time" (586). Adams's Virgin leads the revolt of the masses against the emergent bourgeoisie: "So Mary filled heaven with a sort of persons little to the taste of any respectable middle-class society, which has trouble enough in making this world decent and pay its bills, without having to continue the effort in another" (597). When the rising middle class finds there is no guaranteed return on their investment in the cathedrals, they cease to fund them. Commenting in an earlier chapter on the political economy of Mariolatry, Adams noted that "the *bourgeois* had put an enormous share of his capital into what was in fact an economical speculation, not unlike the South Sea Scheme, or the railway system of our own time." Once the bourgeois learned "that relics were not certain in their effects" and that "Mary herself could not certainly be bought or bribed," he closed his purse (431). The bourgeois, "satisfied that his enormous money-investment had proved to be an almost total loss," stood by astonished and plotted his revenge as Mary handed out favors to the commoners who invested their faith in her (432). A commodity economy of social and divine salvation will eventually cast the Virgin from Protestantism and make way for the marriage of Puritanism and capitalism. It is that ideology of logocentric orders, commodities, and identities which in turn drives Adams to seek an alternative, and symbolize it in the Virgin. The unpredictable efficacy of her grace counters the fetish of the father's law.

State, religion, politics, economy, and society appear to Adams as a hegemonic system of fixed identities dependent on a transcendental Logos or law that imposes a single interpretation on life's differences. Proper names and identities descend from their origin to form a kinship system that becomes the common matrix for determining social and philosophical proprieties. The opposition of order and chaos, along with all other binary oppositions, belongs to the system of logocentrism. The attraction of the Virgin's nonrational matrix lies in her promise to foil the determination of the Logos and frustrate domination:

Strict justice, either on earth or in heaven, was the last thing that society cared to face. . . . They longed for a power above law,—or above the contorted mass of ignorance and absurdity bearing the name of law,—but the power which they longed for was not human, for humanity they knew to be corrupt and incompetent from the day of Adam's creation to the day of the Last Judgment. They were all criminals; if not, they would have had no use for the Church and very little for the State; but they had at least the merit of their faults; they knew what they were, and, like children, they yearned for protection, pardon, and love. This was what the Trinity, though omnipotent, could not give. Whatever the heretic or mystic might try to persuade himself, God could not be Love. God was Justice, Order, Unity, Perfection; he could not be human and imperfect, nor could the Son or the Holy Ghost be other than the Father. The Mother alone was human, imperfect, and could love; she alone was Favor, Duality, Diversity.

. . . If the Trinity was in its essence Unity, the Mother alone could represent whatever was not Unity; whatever was irregular, exceptional, outlawed; and this was the whole human race. (583–84)

The "unity" of the Middle Ages is "not Unity," the Virgin no Center but an outlaw. She is a logos in the sense of a gathering of forces, but not in the sense of a divine paternal Word. For Adams the Virgin's cathedral is a refuge for the stubbornly human and imperfect, a place where the manacles of Platonism and the Great Patriarchal Chain of Being give way to the grace of Gothic realism. The cathedrals are thus also a respite from nihilism and chaos, since Mary's irregular economy unsettles the primacy of a system that had dictated a choice between mutually exclusive positions: "Without Mary, man had no hope except in Atheism, and for Atheism the world was not ready. Hemmed back on that side, men rushed like sheep to escape the butcher, and were driven to Mary; only too happy in finding protection and hope in a being who could understand the language they talked, and the excuses they had to offer" (574). Thus the itinerary of Adams's spiritual autobiography, begun in earnest through the figure of the heroine in *Esther*, ends here in the space imagination creates for its outlawed desires.

The final triad of chapters in the book, on the metaphysics and theology of Abelard, the mystics, and Aquinas are thus reduced in advance to hopeless shuttlings between merely logical antitheses, while human truth lies elsewhere, in the sequence of symbolic economies (a pattern of argument repeated in the matching three chapters concluding the *Education*). Indeed, as he brings his analysis of the Virgin to a close, Adams virtually completes his switch in identification from the Norman-New England fathers to the Gothic-Southern mothers until Mary and Henry seem indistinguishable: "Mary concentrated in herself the whole rebellion of man against fate; the whole protest against divine law; the whole contempt for human law as its outcome; the whole unutterable fury of human nature beating itself against the walls of its prison-house, and suddenly seized by a hope that in the Virgin man had found a door of escape. . . . She knew that the universe was as unintelligible to her, on any theory of morals, as it was to her worshippers, and she felt, like them, no sure conviction that it was any more intelligible to the Creator of it" (596).

Thus the symbolic figure of the Virgin turns out to be Adams's first major experiment in ironic self-fashioning. His reversal of the auto-American-biography projects prophecy into the past, finding in his version of the Middle Ages the principle—complexly symbolized by Mary—that America's future seems to lack. The outlaw characteristics he ascribes to the Virgin and her worshipers will be those given, in the

Education, to the rhetorical figure, spoken of always in the third-person, of "Henry Adams." "Henry Adams" of the *Education* will be the outlaw virgin of the nineteenth century, the noncenter of the text who nonetheless seems to attract all the forces of the era. "Henry Adams" will be but one name for the nontruth of truth. If the traditional auto-American-biographer has been, ideally, the representative man of the American Order, then the Adams of the *Education* becomes the representative man exactly insofar as he typifies the human realities that fail, or resist, being governed by the sociopolitical and philosophical economy of the American Order. Adams's failure to deliver the letter turns out to be his most powerful legacy.

CHAPTER SEVEN

American Literature and the
New Historicism: The Example
of Frederick Douglass

"What's happening here," I said, "a new birth of a nation?"
—Ralph Ellison, *Invisible Man*

Even seasoned observers of academic fashion may feel giddy observing the rise of something called the "New Historicism," especially as we had just grown accustomed to pronouncements—whether celebratory or derogatory—that there was no getting "beyond formalism." Like any label for a movement in criticism, "New Historicism" serves more as an indicator of associated tendencies than as the proper name for a specific or coherent school. Thus in line with the accounts of Brook Thomas and David Simpson, I shall use "new historicism" in a quite general sense rather than restrict it to the movement associated with Stephen Greenblatt (and consequently I shall drop the capitalization of the phrase).[1] Thomas and Simpson agree that what makes this return to history "new" is the influence of poststructuralism, which has undermined the premises of the old historicism as well as of the aesthetic formalism that was the other side of a singular theoretical coin. As a professional sign, the phrase "new historicism" often signals a negative reaction to the legacies of New Criticism, structuralism, and deconstruc-

---

1. Brook Thomas, "The New Historicism and the Privileging of Literature," *Annals of Scholarship* 4 (Summer 1987): 23–48; David Simpson, "Literary Criticism and the Return to 'History,' " *Critical Inquiry* 14 (Summer 1988): 721–47 (subsequent references are given parenthetically in the text). See also H. Aram Vesser, ed., *The New Historicism* (New York: Routledge, 1989). Stephen Greenblatt himself now prefers a different label from "new historicism." See his "Towards a Poetics of Culture," in Veeser, pp. 1–14, which offers a theory of "negotiation" in place of monolithic and determinist narratives of art's relation to capital.

tion, each of which is perceived, rightly or wrongly, as insufficiently responsible to something called "history" (or "politics" or "society" or even "reality"). Alternatives offered by new historicism include a return to empirical scholarship, revivals of the critique of ideology, studies of how material conditions determine writing and publication, research on gender, race, and class in the production of literature, and inquiries into the structural affinities of representational and social systems.[2] At its best, new historicism reminds us of issues we have forgotten or repressed, expands the canon we study, and provides new methods for literary and cultural interpretation. At its worst, new historicism is the old historicism or the old Marxism or the old sociology of literature or some confused mixture of these with current jargon and a bogus claim to the banner of political correctness.

As Judith Newton has shown, it is no accident that the revisionary return to history has paralleled the emergence of feminist, African-American, and postcolonial criticism.[3] Insofar as the old historicism centered the subject of development, teleology, and progress on the notion of the Spirit of Man, these critiques have decentered that historicism in demonstrating that the "Man" of History has usually been male, European, and middle- or upper-class. In various ways these movements have insisted on reading the intersection of the literary and the aesthetic with the historical and the political. Each in turn has been divided by its response to the poststructuralist revolt. The need to affirm the experience and identity of female, African-American, and non-European writers has, some argue, a priority over the philosophical deconstruction of identities and representations. Moreover, the anti-

2. When Simpson analyzes the "return to history" as a widespread phenomenon overdetermined by modern social and political events as well as by Continental theory, he underscores the often "reactive" character of poststructuralism's influence; that is, much of the work done under the heading of a new or renascent historicism bears the traces of a resistance to the critiques of mimesis, empiricism, and objectivity promulgated by poststructuralism. From this perspective I would include the "return to Marx" under the new historicist heading, even though Marxist criticism may often be distinct in its rejection of poststructuralism and in its political agenda. The popularity of such critics as Fredric Jameson suggests the preeminence of a poststructuralist Marxism and hence its possible coincidence of anxieties with the new historicism. For an important warning against the conflation of Marxism and new historicism, however, see Carolyn Porter, "Are We Being Historical Yet?" *South Atlantic Quarterly* 87 (Fall 1988): 743–86.
3. Judith Newton, "History as Usual?: Feminism and the 'New Historicism,'" *Cultural Critique* 9 (Spring 1988): 87–122 (reprinted in Veeser, *New Historicism*). "Feminist politics and feminist theory, then," she argues, "along with the black liberation movement and the new left, have helped generate the 'post-modern' assumptions about 'objectivity,' the construction of the subject, and the cultural power of representation currently identified with 'new historicism,' but they have articulated those assumptions in ways which are significantly different from what have become the more dominant, more fashionable, and the less politicized articulations" (99).

foundationalist character of poststructuralism is viewed as a disabling indulgence when it comes to the question of action. Meanwhile, mainstream critics increasingly turn to previously marginalized authors, such as Frederick Douglass, for examples that will illustrate the return of criticsm to history and politics, since such a choice already implicitly questions the aesthetic, ideological, and institutional criteria that have guided past literary scholarship. After a discussion of recent efforts to historicize criticism, then, I want to turn to the writings of Douglass, focusing principally on his *Narrative of the Life of Frederick Douglass, An American Slave, Written by Himself* (1845). Specifically I shall explore a kind of rhetorical criticism that will situate the historical and political dimensions of Douglass's work without sacrificing our contemporary sense that current deconstructions of representation make any "return" to history or politics as grounded positivities an illusory goal at best.

Douglass's new status as a canonical figure originates not only in his race and class, and not simply in his position as a historical-political actor as well as writer, but also in the kinds of texts he produced and in the way they came into being. If the point of new historical criticism is not simply to describe the (past) world, but to change it (and the present and the future), then we are likely to focus on authors and texts that undertook similar missions. Feminist, African-American, and postcolonial studies practice a moral criticism insofar as their choice of authors and modes of commentary are informed by value judgments concerning what is "good" socially and politically rather than just aesthetically. The author of three autobiographies, a novella, and hundreds of speeches, Douglass worked in genres that challenge our theories of aesthetic form and literary reference. Their didactic and political intentions underscore their determination by extraliterary forces; this strengthens their claim to reference and thus underwrites critical commentaries that wish to use Douglass's work to firmly link literature to past and present political agendas (and thus sometimes to tacitly reject the "textualism" of poststructuralism).

On the other hand, Douglass's character as a *rhetorician*, both as a producer of orations in public and as an author of texts in private, proves an obstacle to any theory of his texts' referentiality, since Douglass so consistently relies on conventional artifices of representation to achieve his persuasive effects. Douglass was the first to seize on himself for rhetorical purposes, the first to make an "example" of himself, before any of the critics got hold of him. Douglass is always already not an empirical or historical fact but a cultural figure inseparable from the mediating modes of production in his time (and our own). Ralph Ellison writes of the white minstrel player that "this mask, this willful stylization and modification of the natural face and hands, was imperative for the evocation of that atmosphere in which the fascination of blackness could be enjoyed, the comic catharsis achieved."[4] Douglass's mask was composed out of the dominant elements of white culture; he indulged his audience's fascination with moral as well as racial blackness in order to achieve his political catharsis. This original ventriloquism makes it impossible to fashion Douglass the example for any fixed interpretive system since the conditions of his performance transgress the binary opposition between object and representation, part and whole, or example and law. No historicism in the new or old sense can be founded on such an example of deconstruction. Although there may be sound reasons to offer Douglass as an example of how to fashion meaning and moral authority out of the suffering of history, one ought to be cautious about building too hasty a bridge between the critic's or reader's position and that of the exemplary subject.

These aporias or impasses between statements and their forms of representation in Douglass may be an opportunity, rather than a catastrophe, for an alternative "return to history." I would argue that historical understanding proceeds as an interpretive commentary on the specific character that this aporia between reference and representation takes *within* a particular work and *between* that work and the discourses and institutions that condition its production and reception. "Ideology" is but a name for the bridging devices (or tropes) required to suspend such aporia and so enable communication, understanding, and action. (In this sense there is no privileged critical position "outside" ideology, but then again no particular ideology has the power to control every instance of expression in a given culture.) Thus aporia is not the end of history but the occasion for its (re)production. This way of theorizing ideology draws on but complicates the "symbolic action" model for describing the text as a resolution of real social contradictions (a tradition running from Aristotle through Kenneth Burke, Northrop Frye, Lévi-Strauss, and Fredric Jameson).[5] The attempts of the text to resolve its *own* contradictions may not be simply conflated with a symbolic resolution of some set of "external" social or material conditions. Nor can the internal contradictions and ideological suspension bridges of other discourses be simply described as homologous to those of a contemporary literary text. Rhetoric directs its work simultaneously, and sometimes incoherently, toward both what it conceives as "internal"

4. Ralph Ellison, *Shadow and Act* (New York: Vintage, 1972), p. 49.
5. For a recent endorsement and application of this model, see Brook Thomas, *Cross-examinations of Law and Literature: Cooper, Hawthorne, Stowe, and Melville* (Cambridge: Cambridge University Press, 1987), pp. 6–7. While virtually impervious to poststructuralist theory, Thomas's new historicist reading of the intersections between literary and legal ideologies represents a formidable contribution.

formal or conceptual problems and what it represents to itself as the "external" conditions, forces, and persons it addresses.

We have seen that in the case of Henry Adams, the autobiographical subject self-deconstructs in reflections on the decentering of the Subject of History. Adams writes from the position of privilege, lamenting the passing of the gender, class, and race differences that enabled Western order, even as he ambivalently gives expression to the historical necessity of modernity's chaos. The autobiographies and other texts by Douglass, on the other hand, are written from quite different historical positions and utilize literary devices and conventions borrowed from very different traditions. Douglass writes/speaks from the position of the other, even as his rhetoric is designed to earn him an authority before the audience of the empowered Other. The crises of masculinity both experience, for example, contrast sharply: Adams was reacting to the hypermasculinity of Robber Baron capitalism and to the emergence of the New Woman, whereas Douglass's struggle to become a "man" took place within a racial institution of slavery that defined him as inhuman, and within a political and ideological discourse on abolition that allied the causes of feminism and antislavery. The empowerment of subjective agency is a chief theme in Douglass's work and a principal determinant of his rhetoric, whereas the language of Adams's *Education* bespeaks a subject of psychological lack and historical impotence.

In specific instances, then, the crossing of poststructuralism and deconstruction with the new historicism may result in the transformation and revival of rhetorical criticism. As such, rhetorical analysis needs to describe: (1) the set of discursive possibilities offered to the writer by the cultural archive; (2) the assumption within the text of a contemporary audience whose knowledge must both be used and resisted; (3) the projection within the text of a future audience constituted by its decipherment of the text; (4) the social, disciplinary, and institutional sites of the text's production and reception; (5) the figurations of subjectivity offered or deployed by the text; (6) the effects of self-reflexivity inscribed in the text; (7) and the possible contradictions between the text's cognitive, performative, didactic, aesthetic, psychological, and economic projects. In reading Douglass's rhetoric, and in particular the relation between his self-representations and the political movements of his time, I hope to sketch a mode of commentary that attends equally to history's dictates and language's powers; in questioning his texts' referential status I mean to deepen and disseminate, rather than dissolve, the political agenda to which his work belongs. In this I shall follow current African-American theorists who view the representational character of "racial" identity as opening a site for progressive historical struggle, one to be preferred over the paralyzing (and false) choice between affirming a socially constructed identity and nihilistically rejecting any self-naming at all. "Rhetoric" will become my word for this site, as well as naming a kind of commentary that situates textuality materially in the social moment, historical stage, and ideological drama of its (rhetoric's, the text's, the commentary's) production.[6]

Empowering History

Much theory and criticism of literature since the 1920s and 1940s—the period of Russian formalism, Prague structuralism, and New Criticism—has centered on one essential question: What *is* literature? (as Terry Eagleton's *Literary Theory: An Introduction* tirelessly reminds us). The major exception was Marxist criticism, which pursued the sociological or cultural contexts of literary production. As long as it remained within the orbit of orthodox Marxist theory, this tradition already knew the answer to the question "What is literature?" Literature is an expression of "ideology" in the pejorative sense. It is a cultural practice that mediates and signifies the actual social relationships and conditions of production, power, and technology, and does so in the masked interest of a ruling group. Opponents of "vulgar Marxism" contend that it never escapes the base/superstructure conception of the economy's determination of literature and so persists in theorizing the material world as a reality that could ground the study of the representations that reflected it. While some reflection theory doubtless informs much Marxist criticism, this characterization is simply untrue of the more sophisticated forms of literary-historical criticism fashioned by such theorists as Georg Lukács, M. M. Bakhtin, Walter Benjamin, or the members of the Frankfurt School. It is highly significant that almost none of the work of these critics received any attention in the United States prior to the 1960s, for this absence made the formalist case against Marxist criticism much easier to win and institutionalize.

During the 1930s in the United States, Marxism vied with the New Criticism for a position of predominance in literary criticism. This Marxism, however, was not of a very theoretical nature. It depended a good deal on positions coming out of the Soviet Union and later on the

6. On these and related issues, especially concerning reader-response theory, historical hermeneutics, and the institutional politics of discourse, see Steven Mailloux, *Rhetorical Power* (Ithaca: Cornell University Press, 1989). Mailloux's chapter "Cultural History and *Huckleberry Finn*" analyzes the historical conditions and political rhetoric informing Twain's representations of racism, and does so in a way similar to my reading of Douglass. See also Dominick LaCapra, *History and Criticism* (Ithaca: Cornell University Press, 1987), pp. 15–44, and Diana Fuss, *Essentially Speaking* (New York: Routledge, 1989).

writing of Trotsky. Its champions, such as V. F. Calverton and Granville
Hicks, did not produce work on a par with their European counterparts
nor with the complexity of their formalist rivals. Without rehearsing
the whole struggle and its sad conclusion, one can say that the defeat
of Marxist criticism in the United States nevertheless took with it the
only serious effort to answer another question fundamental to cultural
studies: "What *is* history?" No other compelling answer to this question
appeared from the 1940s to the 1970s, and in that absence interest in
"literariness"—in defining the special being of literature and of its
history, traditions, conventions, elements, and forms—prospered.
Whatever historical criticism occurred in literary studies continued the
tradition of the old historicism from the nineteenth century, unin-
formed by any serious questioning of either the ontology of representation or the politics of historical reconstruction. Meanwhile orthodox
Marxism turned out to be a disappointing recipe for political reform
and a stubbornly conservative and prescriptive theory for literature.
The ideology of Cold War anti-communism effectively prevented any
substantive dialogue between American literary theorists and the Western Marxism of European intellectuals, especially as American literary
criticism continued to indulge in a nationalist ideology that bought it
institutional and social legitimacy at the cost of intellectual and historical
blindness.

A number of forces have come together to change the situation over
the last 25 years. The impressive achievements of formalist criticism
exhausted certain kinds of analysis and demonstrated the limitations of
the school. Political upheavals during the 1960s in the United States
and Europe sent shock waves through higher education, beginning a
political reflection on the ends, or end, of education and intellectual
labor that today is still maturing, thanks in part to the arrival (and
anxiety) of the sixties' generation in positions of institutional authority.
Polemics on the crisis in education regularly noted the decline in students' knowledge of history, and Brook Thomas cites this rampant
"cultural amnesia" as a principal motivation for the new historicism and
a reason for its application in the classroom.[7] (The reactionary proposals
of Allan Bloom and E. D. Hirsch see the pedagogy of noncanonical
texts, historical revisionism, and ideological debate as the symptom of
decline rather than as the solution to it.) The provinciality produced by
New Critical methods was meanwhile attacked by structuralism and
deconstruction which, however indebted to formalism, were (or are)

7. Brook Thomas, "The Historical Necessity for—and Difficulties with–New Historical Analysis in Introductory Literature Courses," *College English* 49 (September 1987):
509–22.

interdisciplinary movements that produced studies that decoded the social production of meaning in culture, and so opened a door for the return of history and politics. Structuralism and deconstruction, both of whose origins also belonged to the 1960s, sprang from a European intellectual tradition in which Marxism had been a continuous and influential presence, so that the critical perspective on cultural history that they offered should not be a surprise. Their response to the questions "What is literature?" and "What is history?" were in many cases the same answer: texts, structures of signs, systems of codes, conventions of discourse, technologies of representation, institutions of cultural (re)production.

New historicism expresses both an acceptance and a rejection of these textualist answers, for it also borrows from other revisionary intellectual movements outside literary circles. In France members of the *Annales* school examined the ordinary, mundane, material, and institutional components of social existence rather than the grand narratives of great men, military adventures, or struggles for governmental power. In the United States a similar development was the rise of social history, often led by feminists, which challenged the traditional scope of the historical by concentrating on the anonymous lives and records of women, workers, slaves, and others who did not leave their stories in an authorized form. Like the women's movement, the civil rights movement forced a reassessment of American history and writing, prompting the manifestos on the Black Aesthetic and inspiring the contemporary renaissance in African-American cultural studies.

The work of Michel Foucault deserves special mention in this genealogy of the new historicism, for it has been widely influential, from Stephen Greenblatt's work on English Renaissance culture to Houston Baker's study of African-American discourse. Foucault, while denying he was a structuralist, contributed much to the critique of cultural representations by analyzing how such fields as economics, linguistics, and political economy were constituted as discourses with common conceptions and shared rules of practice, though their similarities could not be mistaken for the composition of an organic totality. His books showed how fields of knowledge were simultaneously techniques of representation, theories of epistemology, and modes of social organization. In extending his work to the medical clinic and the prison, Foucault made his critique more explicitly political, by underscoring the coincidence of knowledge with power. His last books, a multivolume history of sexuality, offered an even more radical critique of empirical notions of history, since here such natural physical realities as the body and its pleasures are also seen as defined within cultural discourses and representational techniques.

Edward Pechter notes that many new historicists have ignored Foucault's final theoretical reformulations about the nature of power—that it is heterogeneous, scattered, and interactive rather than simply a matter of a central authority dominating a system.[8] (This also implies the distinction between Foucault's discursive theory and orthodox views of the repressive function of ideology.) Foucault intends this as a final repudiation of Marxist political theory, one he arrives at through his own fascinating adaptation of Heidegger's meditations on Being, technology, and language. Pechter endorses Foucault's point and shows that much new historicism concentrates on the question of power as embodied by monarchs, fathers, or other traditional figures of authority. The panoptical (and sometimes paranoid) theses of Foucault's work on prisons can yield a reductive view of social history and power. Pechter rejects the new historicism insofar as it places the will to power at the center of its theory of history, and he sees this narrow vision as an unfortunate inheritance from the thematics of class struggle in orthodox Marxism. Equally disturbing to Pechter is the persistence of economic or social determinism in the new historicism, for he has little trouble showing that the movement constantly represents literary texts as ultimately conditioned and caused by an external power that governs representation, even (and perhaps more strongly) when that power itself cannot be represented.

As Carolyn Porter has pointed out, Pechter's assimilation of neo-Marxism to the new historicism contains numerous errors and tellingly reveals his own resistance to seeing history as the struggle of groups for power.[9] Foucault's late injunction that we must conceive of "power without the king," while well advising us to uncover where and how power takes place throughout the cultural scene, should not divert our attention from the fact that the king and the father quite often possess it and its technology. To say that power is everywhere can be as meaningless as to say that politics is everywhere. Derrida's phase of reversal—in which the hierarchy of two terms, one traditionally subordinated to the other, is overturned—must be insisted on, and persisted in, before we rush into disseminating or dissolving the opposition altogether. While the struggle for power may not be the only story in history, it may be one we ought to read more carefully before moving on to other

8. Edward Pechter, "The New Historicism and Its Discontents: Politicizing Renaissance Drama," *PMLA* 102 (May 1987): 292–303. See also Ihab Hassan, "Fictions of Power: A Note on Ideological Discourse in the Humanities," *American Literary History* 1 (Spring 1989): 131–42.

9. See Porter, "Are We Being Historical Yet?"

texts. This will be especially worth remembering in interpreting works by culturally marginalized subjects (such as Douglass).

David Simpson is also skeptical about applying Foucault to historical criticism. While Pechter ultimately wishes to return to humanism and *its* history, Simpson advises that we first pay closer attention to the obstacles that de Man, Derrida, Foucault, and others present to any historicism, humanist or materialist. Simpson contends that "assumptions about the identity of or difference between the analytic and the prescriptive [modes of historical criticism] have disabled the emergence of a comprehensive historical method" (727). This hermeneutic dilemma catches the critic between fabricating the past as an objectivity and constructing a past aligned with a narrative entailing and directing the present and the future. Entwined with this problem are those of subjective agency in history (and presumably in criticism) and the totality or nontotality of descriptive paradigms used in representing discourses or cultures. According to Simpson, the major figures of poststructuralism pose, and fall victim to, these quandaries: "For de Man there is no history at all. . . . Derrida offers a totalized past [Western metaphysics] and an unpredictable present-future; Foucault, a past frozen into local symmetries" (736–37). It is just this kind of simplistic account that I have tried to refute in my earlier chapters on Derrida and de Man. Nonetheless, the debate over the new historicism provides an opportunity to make good on the claim that deconstructive thinking can enable, rather than forestall, analysis of "how differences of interest might have combined in the emergency of events." In Douglass's case that analysis must focus on his performance as a political and rhetorical agent, for this is where he emerges as a historical subject.

But some new historicists question whether such a claim for poststructuralism simply repeats the deluded notion that literary modernism or formalist theory defamiliarize and expose the ideologies of language. From Bakhtin and Brecht through the New Criticism and deconstruction, texts are read as agencies of revolution, though for most critics and readers this remains a strictly paper tiger. Writing for the Berkeley new historicists, Catherine Gallagher asks: "Was it possible . . . that certain forms of subjectivity that felt oppositional were really a means by which power relations were maintained?" The effort of new historicists "was, and still is, to show that under certain historical circumstances, the display of ideological contradictions is completely consonant with the maintenance of oppressive social relations" (whether the agent of display is the text or the critic). Forms do not simply affirm or negate ideological institutions. In rejecting this binary schema, Gallagher offers a "third alternative in which the very antagonism between literature and ideology becomes, in specific historical environments, a powerful and socially functional mode of constructing subjectivity."[10] By attending to the play in Douglass between statement and rhetoric, we can see how the antagonism between literature and ideology may become an empowering way to construct a subjectivity that neither simply affirms nor negates the representational masks it puts on. Yet the historical record, along with the text's complexity, forbids concluding that Douglass's works were only a means to maintain oppressive relations. We are back now in a hermeneutic circle: is the text's subversive knowledge historically and formally verifiable, or is it the contingent product of the critic's interpretive method? Since I do not believe there is an outside to this circulating economy between history and interpretation, I am not inclined toward Gallagher's debunking of the debunkers. One can always demonstrate the complicity of an author, agent, or text in the resources of the culture; to conclude that this dooms any effort at resistance, or to stress repetitively this complicity rather than the text's struggle to make a difference, requires that one leave the circle and take sides. In a perverse extrapolation from deconstruction, this kind of new historicism takes the maxim "there is nothing outside of the text" to mean that a text, or culture, cannot differ from itself; it totalizes complicity until knowledge is again subjected to power, without a chance.

In sum, new historicism differs from the old historicism when (and if) it postulates theories of the historical that extend and correct the general critique of positivism, empiricism, chronology, causation, and representation proffered by structuralism and deconstruction. This general critique prevents us from assuming that we know what history is, where it takes place, who makes it, and whether history is ever distinct from the manner of its representations. At the same time, the study of representation is always in danger of lapsing back into a formalism that overlooks the social and institutional history of texts, as well as the power relations that inform all intellectual inquiry. Like the old historicism, the new historicism places the text among the events of its own time, reconstituting that context and deciphering the way in which history informs the practice of the text, and the way in which texts inform the practices of history. Unlike the old historicism, the new historicism disseminates the "context" of the text, proliferating a seemingly infinite series of discursive, material, and institutional histories that overdetermine the text. New historicism claims to have a new idea of what history *is*, both in terms of what objects we study and how self-conscious we are

10. Catherine Gallagher, "Marxism and the New Historicism," in Veeser, *New Historicism*, pp. 42, 44.

about the way we study them. It questions the "privileging of literature" even as it extends textualist ontology into the being of historicity itself. And it rejects models of historical totality even as it seeks to describe the culture formed by the specific competing and interactive material and discursive forces of the disparate subcultures. The contexts new historicism produces for the text, and the way it reads the relation of texts and contexts, should avoid the prejudices and errors and naïveté of the old historicism, especially its complacency about what properly belongs to history and its failure to question how its own agenda defines, retrospectively, the stories we authorize about the past.

Historicizing American Criticism

The Americanist school of new historicism, while responding to European schools, sees itself primarily as a revolution against what Carolyn Porter rightly called the "American ahistoricism" of such critics as F. O. Matthiessen, Richard Chase, R. W. B. Lewis, Leslie Fiedler, and Charles Feidelson.[11] Turning against the social progressivism of Parrington and away from the Marxism of the 1930s, this tradition of study applied the tenets of the New Criticism to the symbolism, language, and moral ambiguities of "classic American literature," a canon of works often consisting of the same familiar (white male) names: Hawthorne, Emerson, Thoreau, Melville, Whitman, Twain, James, and Eliot. These authors were usually portrayed as seeking aesthetic or psychological alternatives to life in society, an escapism still dominating the thematics of such brilliant books as Richard Poirier's *A World Elsewhere* and Leo Marx's *The Machine in the Garden*. In a pioneering study too often overlooked, H. Bruce Franklin traced the history of aestheticism and racism that produced this canon, including the textbooks and pedagogical attitudes supporting it.[12] Franklin's analysis of canon formation and his proposal that black slave narratives be placed at the center of American literary history acutely forecast the concerns of subsequent work on African-American and women writers. Franklin's main example is Douglass's *Narrative*. As we have seen in Chapter 4, Porter continued Franklin's argument by demonstrating that this critical tradition repeated, rather than analyzed, the alienation from society and economic

11. Carolyn Porter, *Seeing and Being: The Plight of the Participant Observer in Emerson, James, Adams, and Faulkner* (Middletown, Conn.: Wesleyan University Press, 1981). See also "New Americanists: Revisionist Interventions into the Canon," ed. Donald Pease, special issue of *boundary 2* 17 (Spring 1990).

12. H. Bruce Franklin, *The Victim as Criminal and Artist* (New York: Oxford University Press, 1978).

life represented by these authors, and so these critics missed the real and powerful historical dimensions of such texts.

The attempt to combine new historicism with ideology critique can be sampled in the collection edited by Sacvan Bercovitch and Myra Jehlen, titled *Ideology and Classic American Literature*.[13] What seems odd here is the retention of the "classic" canon: while the editors may have intended this ironically, or as a deconstructive reinscription, the vast bulk of articles treat the same expected figures and perform no substantive displacement of the notion of the "classic" that the title somewhat opportunistically exploits. The singular exception is an excerpt from Houston Baker's *Blues, Ideology, and Afro-American Literature* which treats the economics of slavery in Douglass's *Narrative*. Jehlen's introduction attempts to justify the use of "ideology" as a key term for the volume and proceeds through a rather awkward summary of the various definitions and uses of the term, until one wonders what—beyond its connotations of proper political skepticism—it could mean.

In his review of what he calls the "New Americanists," Frederick Crews observes that Jehlen's recourse to "ideology" in the pejorative sense, while it exposes the masking of political interests by aesthetic arguments, ultimately falls victim to its own binary logic. The New Americanists attack the ideological pretense that "great art must be decoupled from the struggle for social dominance." Aesthetic ideology "makes sense to them as a repressive strategy, a means of keeping the lid on divisive differences of interest such as those between slave masters and slaves, land clearers and those whose territory was thereby seized, and more recently between the purveyors of 'Americanness' criticism and the groups that find their traditions frozen out by that criticism".[14] Foucault and Crews notwithstanding, there remains a formidable dimension of truth in the repressive hypothesis, though not when it takes the form of a binary opposition between ideology and demystification. Poststructuralism begins, as it did for the Roland Barthes of *S/Z*, with the deconstruction of this opposition. Crews points out the contradiction involved when the methods used to debunk white male writers are cast aside in efforts to canonize and affirm formerly marginalized authors (though I sense I have more sympathy with this process than he does). In the case of such authors one should not lose sight of the interdependence of analytic and prescriptive historicism or of the fundamentally

13. Sacvan Bercovitch and Myra Jehlen, eds., *Ideology and Classic American Literature* (Cambridge: Cambridge University Press, 1986).

14. Frederick Crews, "Whose American Renaissance?" *New York Review of Books* 35 (27 October 1988): 74. For a critique of Crews, see Pease, pp. 1–37.

moral character of the premises for this kind of literary history. In other words, accusing others of having an ideology can become a way of avoiding the responsibility for justifying one's own ideology.

Nevertheless, Jehlen's essay "The Novel and the Middle Class in America" demonstrates the danger of too simply applying the repressive hypothesis in studying literature as an expression of ideology. The term "middle class" operates programmatically here without definition, as if nothing had occurred in social, political, or economic theory to disturb the confidence with which one could employ such a category. Jehlen asserts without evidence that "middle-class America *was* an integrated society . . . unlike nineteenth-century London and Paris" (129). Were the states of the Old and Deep South predominately "integrated" and "middle-class"? In what sense were the frontier towns of Ohio or Missouri or California "middle-class"? And where in this homogeneity do we fit the slaves or the Irish and Italian and Polish and German immigrants? And in what meaningful sense can we call Boston or New York "middle-class," whether in 1850 or 1950, without serious distortion? Is such a nomenclature even relevant when translated from Birmingham, England to Birmingham, Alabama? The notion of history at work here is at once vague and reductive, and often has recourse to the mimetic fallacy, as when Jehlen rehearses the tired accusation against Henry James that his work is not "socially encompassing," and that it "tacitly approved" bourgeois values (135). On the contrary, as my previous discussion of James tried to show, we are just beginning to learn to read the complex criticism offered by the "political unconscious" of his texts. The statement that "for James the coming of America offered at last the possibility of transcending both class and history" gets the story exactly wrong, as James's work everywhere labors to reinscribe the historical and social networks he found lacking in the transcendentalism he inherited. Jehlen's idea that the "principles of the bourgeois family, as the heart of middle-class ethics, are consistently upheld in American writing" borrows heavily from Leslie Fiedler and others and takes us spinning into accusatory generalities as clumsy in application as they are in formulation (141).

Here, as in many of the essays in the volume, the attempt to fuse literature, history, and politics occasions much violent yoking together, as when the nuclear freeze movement suddenly appears as a parallel to the Free Soil struggle in Jonathan's Arac's quite unconvincing treatment of "The Politics of *The Scarlet Letter*" (Crews also singles out this essay as particularly embarrassing). The tenuous quality of connection marking much of the new historicism stands out when Arac tries to situate the novel's hermeneutic indeterminacy in a political context:

Consider the problems of reading the letter in relation to the fundamental debates in the 1850s over the meaning of such documents of American life as the Declaration of Independence and the Constitution. As America left behind the directly "political" statements and actions of the Founders, the age of Clay, Webster, and Calhoun made "constitutional" questions a matter of "exegesis." All the fundamental questions of interpretation arose around these no less than around Hester's letter. Recall particularly that "adulterer" (or "adultery"?) is nowhere spelled out in Hawthorne's text, just as "slavery" is nowhere present in the Declaration or the Constitution. The authorial meaning of the Constitution, in particular, was deliberately "indeterminate" on the question of slavery, yet at a certain moment in American life a decision, and so a violation, was necessary. (260)

In the face of this "recall particularly" one thinks of the recurrent joke regarding the new historicism: that its motto could be "Coincidence? Perhaps!" The word "slavery" does not appear in the Constitution, but an effective fugitive slave clause was included as Article 4, section 2, which specifies that "No person held to service or labor in one state, under the laws thereof, escaping into another, shall, in consequence of any law or regulation therein, be discharged from such service or labor, but shall be delivered up on claim of the party to whom such service or labor may be due." (Franklin provides this citation as an epigraph to his study.) Most of Arac's points are better accounted for by the more usual consideration of the legacy of Puritan hermeneutics. "Exegesis" and "indeterminacy," the play between letter and spirit, had been an American preoccupation since the 1640s and found their first great literary expressions in Anne Bradstreet's "Contemplations." Likewise the background to the question of the individual's "right to decide the construction" of ambiguous letters has its chief source in Protestant Antinomianism and specifically (for Hawthorne) in Anne Hutchinson, not in contemporaries like Joseph Hopkinson or John Pickering. The adducement of such corrollary historical discourses is fascinating and informative, but quite often provides only a *sign*, rather than a real performance, of historicism. In fact, insofar as the new historicism earns its reputation through either the *terminology* of its discourse or the offering of empirical analogues as *references* to the historical, it operates far more as a *formalism* than many of its supposed antagonists.

    This formality of the historical also pervades Walter Benn Michaels's collection of essays, *The Gold Standard and the Logic of Naturalism*, which contends that "ideology" is a name for a nonexistent phenomenon.[15] Sponsored by Stephen Greenblatt as Volume 2 of a series dedicated

15. Walter Benn Michaels, *The Gold Standard and the Logic of Naturalism: American Literature at the Turn of the Century* (Berkeley: University of California Press, 1987).

to the "New Historicism," *The Gold Standard* reads a variety of texts, discourses, events, and conceptual problematics as characterizing a specific moment in American culture's ambivalent romance with the marketplace of capitalism. Michaels dissents from "the genteel/Progressive view of important works of art as in some sense transcending or opposing the market," a view he finds even in recent "oppositional criticism." Michaels condescendingly brushes aside such a description, or use, of literature for cultural criticism: "transforming the moral handwringing of the fifties and sixties first into the epistemological handwringing of the seventies and now into the political handwringing of the eighties does not seem to be much of an advance" (15, n. 16). With some glee he tries to show that works such as Charlotte Gilman's "The Yellow Wallpaper" epitomize, rather than demystify, the culture of marketplace consumption. Similarly, Michaels criticizes his own previous work on Dreiser (nonetheless reprinted as the opening chapter in the volume) for trying to assess "Dreiser's attitude toward capitalism: it depended on imagining a Dreiser outside capitalism who could then be said to have attitudes toward it" (19).

Michaels's version of the new historicism will then pursue what Simpson calls an "analytic" description of cultural totalities as it eschews any prescriptive reading of history's itinerary or, even worse (in his opinion), any indulgence in the problem of ethical and moral judgment. Michaels defines his project in explaining why he chose the term "naturalism," rather than "realism," for the period in question:

> Insofar as naturalism has been continually (and plausibly) defined as a variant of realism, it has been caught up in endless theorizing about the nature and very possibility of realistic representation: do texts refer to social reality? if they do, do they merely reflect it or do they criticize it? and if they do not, do they try to escape it, or do they imagine utopian alternatives to it? Like the question of whether Dreiser liked or disliked capitalism, these questions seem to me to posit a space outside culture in order then to interrogate the relations between that space (here defined as literary) and the culture. But the spaces I have tried to explore are all very much within the culture, and so the project of interrogation makes no sense; the only relation literature as such has to culture as such is that it is part of it. (27)

A number of fallacies are at work in this neopragmatist version of historicism. While Michaels rightly rejects a schema that makes "literature" the privileged "outside" to the nefarious determinations of culture, he does so by ignoring how texts are constituted by an often contradictory set of attitudes toward the heterogeneous archive that

composes the culture to which it belongs. It would be absurd to suggest
that a text, or an author such as Dreiser, contained no contradictions,
and Michaels's own readings everywhere show that they do. Michaels
might respond that such contradictions nonetheless belong to the "culture," not to some space "outside" it. Yet this transforms "culture," a
priori, into an organic totality that is all "inside" and no "outside."
Michaels must idealize the many events and discourses of the historical
period into the monolith of "the culture" in order to contain the question
of opposition "within" it, and so to tacitly disable "oppositional criticism." His own criticism, then, in adopting a variant of antifoundational
pragmatism, caricatures "culture" as a totality both organic *and* mechanical, since it automatically enforces its assumptions upon its subjects
without their having the capacity to resist it. There is truly a sophistry
in arguing that Dreiser (or the literary critic) cannot dislike or interro-
gate the culture to which he or she belongs; this would presuppose that
the culture exists as a single attitude or belief, whereas cultures are
uneven, changeable, and provisional associations of individuals, groups,
artifacts, and institutions, any one of which may provide the basis for
the evaluation or interrogation of the other. Michaels's dismissal of
moral, epistemological, and political problematics as so much intellectual detritus ultimately produces a theoretical position that is profoundly conservative.

Whereas Michaels's version of a poststructuralist new historicism provides no point for opposition and change, Russell Reising's neo-Marxist
resistance to poststructuralism provides him with all too many. In *The
Unusable Past: Theory and the Study of American Literature* Reising resumes
Carolyn Porter's argument and critiques the careers of major American
literary theorists after World War II. "The scenario," Reising writes,
"would look something like this: the avoidance or denial of overtly
political and economic issues in literary texts . . . functions as a strategy
which frees contemporary criticism from integrating social and political
issues into academic literary criticism."[16] This mise-en-scène, however,
continues to juxtapose the categories of the aesthetic, the political, and
the literary as if they were entities that could be separately defined and
then related one to the other. Reising's "Conclusion: The Significance
of Frederick Douglass" attempts to illustrate his thesis that "theorists of
American literature have failed adequately to approach American texts
in a specifically cultural and social context" (17). By placing Douglass
"within the mainstream" of what Matthiessen called "the American
Renaissance" Reising alters our sense of the literary canon and suggests

16. Russell Reising, *The Unusable Past: Theory and the Study of American Literature* (New
York: Methuen, 1986), p. 159.

a rehistoricized reading of figures such as Emerson, Thoreau, Hawthorne, Melville, and Stowe (269). But his analysis uses too many of the terms of traditional literary history—beginning with the dubious "American Renaissance"—and doesn't exactly spell out how to relate texts to their "material and historical context."

Rather than set aside the kind of hierarchical canon formation his book has criticized, Reising nominates Douglass "as a literary artist and thinker of the first rank" and argues that his *Narrative* "anticipates" many of the themes of the period's major figures, including that most ahistorical theme of "an individual's relationship with his community" (257). Yet there is no single community in Douglass's world, neither of whites (divided geographically and culturally) nor of blacks (whose disparate social formations exist only within prescribed limits). And when, if ever, Douglass becomes an "individual" is a major interpretive crux of his autobiographies, not a ground on which a reading can stand. On the contrary, one must read Douglass and other antebellum texts within specific discursive histories. These would include the legacy of eighteenth-century ideas of Enlightenment rationality and legal personhood; the dialogue of that legacy with romantic theories of genius and individuality; the correspondent rise of the moral psychology of sentiment and its emotional epistemology, which plays such a strong role in the literature of this period; the informing power of gender in the literary marketplace and its representations of social and moral realities; the formal conventions of slavery literature, pro and con, already popular in Douglass's time; and of course the relation of all these discourses to the rise of economic structures and social institutions that supported or were antithetical to them. Even a "Marxist" reading should never assume the isolate existence of "the individual" or "the community" in this period, but examine the crisis involved in the *invention* of both.

The Unusable Past does not establish the historical context in the above senses. Instead it demonstrates similarities between passages in Douglass and those in the works of canonical writers in order to situate Douglass "both within major thematics of the American Renaissance as well as within a proto-modernist tradition of literary practice" (266). This rather surprising thesis, which appears an extension of the school of Charles Feidelson, holds that the ironic puncturing of racist thought in Douglass's narrative constitutes a version of what the Russian Formalists called "defamiliarization." At the level of theory this is misleading, since the Formalists were concerned with altering automatized perceptions by increasing the artfulness of perceptual techniques, whereas Douglass—as Reising elsewhere shows—bases his rhetoric on appeals to empirical evidence (and, as I shall argue, on the discourse of sentimentality and the idealistic principles of Christian humanism), not on the kind of stylistic extravagance characteristic of a text like Thoreau's *Walden*. While the subversive troping of conventional representation is an important feature of African-American writing, it is not "proto-modernist" in any recognizable aesthetic sense. Indeed, in the twentieth century Ralph Ellison will complain that African-American writing suffers under the burden of a demand for realism, and Ellison advocates a modernism that bears striking resemblance to the programs of Feidelson and Trilling. The comparison of African-American (or women's) writings to canonical ones can certainly be useful, but not if the result is simply the inclusion of the marginal in the canonical or a reversal of privileges without a questioning of the terms of the hierarchy.

Poststructuralism and the African-American Text

How might one proceed to conduct a reading of Douglass that would be both literary and historical, rhetorical and political? Whereas Reising largely dismisses poststructuralism, a new generation of African-American critics, including Houston Baker, Hazel Carby, and Henry Louis Gates, Jr., are adapting the critique of representation to their readings of black literature and culture. According to Gates, "We urgently need to direct our attention to the nature of black figurative language, to the nature of black narrative forms, to the history and theory of Afro-American criticism, to the fundamental relation of form and content, and to the arbitrary relationships between the sign and its referent."[17] Gates builds on the arguments of Baker, Peter Walker, and Robert Stepto in rejecting any naive or politically reductive view of black autobiographical works as straightforward accounts of life, and his example is again Douglass.[18] The strategic revisions that went into the successive versions of his autobiographies show, in Gates's words, that "Douglass was demonstrably concerned with the representation in written language of his public self, a self Douglass created, manipulated, and transformed, if ever so slightly, through the three fictive selves he posited in his three autobiographies" (103). The portrait is considerably complicated by the personae orchestrated in Douglass's hundreds of recorded speeches, oratorical performances that took many liberties

17. Henry Louis Gates, Jr., *Figures in Black: Words, Signs, and the 'Racial' Self* (New York: Oxford University Press, 1987), p. 41.
18. See Robert B. Stepto, *From Behind the Veil: A Study of Afro-American Narrative* (Urbana: University of Illinois Press, 1979); Peter Walker, *Moral Choices: Memory, Desire, and Imagination in Nineteenth-Century American Abolition* (Baton Rouge: Louisiana State University Press, 1978).

with the facts and which alternately fashioned Douglass in the figure of the slave, the preacher, the criminal, the saint, the journalist, the worker, the revolutionary, the son, the father, and the prophet.

Other black critics, notably women, have expressed their disagreement with the work of Baker and Gates, citing Audre Lorde's maxim that "The master's tools will never dismantle the master's house."[19] As in the controversies between humanism and deconstruction or feminism and poststructuralism, the antiessentialism of recent theory is seen as a threat to the imperative need for an affirmative politics of identity. Each side, however, undertakes the common task of rewriting the history of African-American literature and asserting its power to resist the master's dictates. Such innovations in African-American criticism can assist in the radical rearrangement of historical and literary periods and their canonical contents, of ways of writing history and literary criticism, and of the very issues defined as constituting the essence of the story of American letters. In the realm of literary theory, however, this rewriting should not proceed on the basis of outmoded stereotypes of black writing as realistic, mimetic, descriptive, documentary, referential, or somehow intrinsically less literary and more political than white texts.

Though cautious about adopting the white man's critical theories, black feminist critics such as Hazel Carby are reopening the question of history and representation in their accounts of women in African-American writing. Carby cautions against the mimetic fallacy and any essentialist theory of black female experience or language:

> Language is accented differently by competing groups, and therefore the terrain of language is a terrain of power relations. This struggle within and over language reveals the nature of the structure of social relations and the hierarchy of power, not the nature of one particular group. The sign, then, is an arena of struggle and a construct between socially organized persons in the process of their interactions; the forms that signs take are conditioned by the social organization of the participants involved and also by the immediate conditions of their interaction.[20]

19. See Joyce A. Joyce, "The Black Canon: Reconstructing Black American Literary Criticism," *New Literary History* 18 (1987): 335–44, and " 'Who the Cap Fit': Unconsciousness and Unconscionableness in the Criticism of Houston A. Baker, Jr., and Henry Louis Gates, Jr.," *New Literary History* 18 (1987): 371–84; Houston Baker, "In Dubious Battle," *New Literary History* 18 (1987): 363–69; and Henry Louis Gates, Jr., " 'What's Love Got to Do with It?': Critical Theory, Integrity, and the Black Idiom," *New Literary History* 18 (1987): 345–62; Michael Awkward, "Race, Gender, and the Politics of Reading," *Black American Literature Forum* 22 (Spring 1988): 6–27; and Fuss, pp. 73–96.

20. Hazel V. Carby, *Reconstructing Womanhood: The Emergence of the Afro-American Woman Novelist* (New York: Oxford University Press, 1987), p. 17.

Linguistic power, then, is more than a negative or disciplinary agency: it establishes and sustains a social group's life and character. Language enables, posits, and persuades as well as oppresses. Carby's account does show the traces of a deterministic materialism in which signs are "conditioned by the social organization" while the conditioning of social organization by signs is passed over. Nonetheless, her argument marks a significant moment in African-American theoretical debate as well as in the general discussion of how to articulate the historical with the literary.

Baker and Gates share this view of language as a terrain of social struggle. In their work on Douglass they stress the dialectic of subjection and empowerment inherent in the African-American's achievement of literacy in his master's tongue. (Thus they provide a sometimes explicit allegory justifying their own use of the Euro-American masters' theoretical tools.) For the slave, the achievement of literacy is itself a political and even metaphysical revolution, since it defies the dominant culture's negative definition of her or his very human being. Slaves are defined as lacking civilization, reason, and the capacity for articulate expression; the equation of logos, soul, and being works to exclude the black from the category "human." In his 1855 autobiography, *My Bondage and My Freedom,* Douglass recalls that "I was generally introduced as a *'chattel'*— a *'thing'*—a piece of southern *'property'*—the chairman assuring the audience that *it* could speak."[21] The inherent antagonism between black speaker and white language means that a distancing, a revision, or a troping of language will always be fundamental to the "signifyin' " style of black discourse (Gates, *Figures* 48–54).

In *The Journey Back,* Baker describes the complex fate that awaited those black Americans who first sought to articulate their experiences of slavery in the New World. Robbed of their native culture, they had lost their tongue, their means of self-definition and expression. Thrust into an alien land, they had to learn the language of the oppressors, which they then would have to turn to their own purposes. Of the slave, Baker writes: "He first had to seize the word. His being had to erupt from nothingness. Only by grasping the word could he engage in the speech acts that would ultimately define his selfhood."[22] He would have to parrot, then parody, then talk back to his master's voice. For Baker and others, the *Narrative* of Frederick Douglass is the exemplary tale of this linguistic alienation; moreover, it foregrounds the achievement of

21. Frederick Douglass, *My Bondage and My Freedom,* ed. and with an introduction by William L. Andrews (Urbana: University of Illinois Press, 1987), p. 220. Subsequent references are cited parenthetically as *My Bondage.*

22. Houston Baker, *The Journey Back: Issues in Black Literature and Criticism* (Chicago: University of Chicago Press, 1980), p. 31.

literacy as the key to liberation. But Baker argues that because Douglass must adopt the rhetoric of the dominant culture—especially its Christian morals and sentimental psychology—in defining his experience, he inevitably misses the otherness of black life even as he represents it (36–37): "Had there been a separate, written black language available, Douglass might have fared better. . . . the nature of the autobiographer's situation seemed to force him to move to a public version of the self— one molded by the values of white America" (39). *The Journey Back* shows this estrangement increasing toward the close of the *Narrative*, and as overwhelming (and degrading) Douglass's subsequent autobiographical writings until he resembles none other than the Uncle Tomish Booker T. Washington, to whom Douglass has always been compared since the waning of his reputation in the 1870s and 1880s.

A theory of linguistic alienation, however, goes astray if it establishes the discussion by contrasting an authentically lived experience with its mistranslation or betrayal into language. The availability of a native language does not guarantee an unalienated speech or a mimetic transcription. Nor are such languages homogeneous in their cultural representations of lived experience. Since blacks had never lived as slaves in America before, they of course could have had no language for this life, no native "terms of order" for the experience. Had they been able to perpetuate their African languages and cultures, they might have had a nonwhite rhetoric to figure their experience, but then they would not in that case have *had* the experience, for slavery meant precisely the cultural expropriation and transformation of a people. Douglass had no choice but to draw on the cultural archive of white society and then transform his materials rhetorically. Baker characterizes Douglass's appendix on Christianity as trying to justify his status as a true Christian. Yet the appendix continues Douglass's assault on the institutional and political practice of Christianity in the United States, keeping strictly to the policy of Garrisonian abolitionism in its harsh critique of the role of religion in the slave states. The "true" Christianity Douglass endorses is a *figure* for a morality quite other than that of the professedly "true" Christians of the United States, North and South. In taking up their rhetoric and their religion, he inserts an otherness into both, gives voice to the hypocrisies and flaws within them, and thus puts an alien discourse serviceably to work for the black experience.

In *Blues, Ideology, and Afro-American Literature,* Baker heads in a more poststructuralist direction, though this is combined with cultural anthropology and a strong dose of neo-Marxism. He now includes discussions of black women's writing, yet curiously without the eye for their self-reflexivity that we might expect. In his discussion of Harriet Jacobs's *Incidents in the Life of a Slave Girl* Baker focuses on the economics of

slavery in black women's lives, but he does not address that text's gendered revision of the black scene of writing.[23] When Jacobs teaches
herself to read, it only provides a new occasion for her master's sexual
harassment: "He frowned, as if he were not well pleased; but I suppose
he came to the conclusion that such an accomplishment might help to
advance his favorite scheme. Before long, notes were often slipped into
my hand. I would return them, saying, 'I can't read them, sir,' 'Can't
you?' he replied; 'then I must read them to you.' He always finished the
reading by asking, 'Do you understand?'."[24] Whereas Douglass represents literacy as the road to freedom, Jacobs narrates a dialogical scene in
which her empowerment is immediately subordinated to the seduction
scheme: she must read the master's words, the language of patriarchy.
Jacobs foregrounds her own text's revisionary stance toward the tradition of epistolary romances and seduction novels that were the favored
books for many women of her time. According to Jacobs's allegory, the
letters forced on women readers and writers at least since *Clarissa* have
been the story of their rape.

Jacobs repeatedly dramatizes the role of reading and writing in
her struggle. *Incidents* depicts the black woman either as a resisting
reader or as a writer of disguised and subversive texts, like those
letters she writes from her garret and has posted by friends in the
North so as to entice her master to undertake fruitless journeys to
recapture her. At the end of the book the escaped Linda (Jacobs's
autobiographical protagonist) receives another letter, reproduced
graphically in the book almost as if to insist on this text's relation to
epistolary fiction. It is signed and purportedly written by her mistress's
brother, and answers her plea for freedom with a request that she
return. The correspondence of slavery with seduction is spelled out by
this letter, which reinforces the text's dissemination of the difference
between the lives of black slave women and their Northern sisters.
Jacobs is by now a fully resisting reader capable of seeing through
the duplicity of the mail/male system. She recognizes the style, the
character, of the author as none other than that of her old master.
"Verily, he relied too much on 'the stupidity of the African race' "
(172). *Incidents*, as Franklin and Carby show, deploys the rhetoric of
the "cult of true womanhood" and its literary tradition but teaches
the reader to decipher the oppressive character of that discourse.

    23. Houston Baker, *Blues, Ideology, and Afro-American Literature* (Chicago: University
of Chicago Press, 1984), pp. 50–59.
    24. Harriet Jacobs, *Incidents in the Life of a Slave Girl: Written by Herself*, ed. Jean Fagan
Yellin (Cambridge: Harvard University Press, 1987), p. 31.

Thus the referential realism of Jacobs's autobiography is enframed by a highly self-conscious rhetorical and literary deconstruction of the discursive conditions that determine her position.

The new historical and economic concerns of Baker's *Blues* show too when he once more makes Douglass his example. Now he calls the *Narrative*'s rhetoric a "palimpsest" in which a deeper level belies the figurations offered at the surface. "The tones of a Providentially oriented moral suasion," he argues, "eventually compete with the cadences of a secularly oriented economic voice" (43). Baker reads the "economic coding" in Douglass as a tale of the expropriation of "surplus value" in Marx's sense. He attributes this knowledge to Douglass himself, who now turns out to be anything but an Uncle Tom or Booker T.: "Douglass heightens the import of this economic coding through implicit and ironic detailing of the determination of general cultural consciousness *by commerce*" (45). Douglass "has arrived at a fully commercial view of his situation" by the latter half of the book, says Baker, and despite Douglass's idyllic representation of New England's commerce Baker finds him slyly subverting this traffic by the very act of writing and selling his story: "The nineteenth-century slave, in effect, *publicly* sells his voice in order to secure *private* ownership of his voice-person" (50). As a salaried spokesman for Garrison's American Anti-Slavery Society, Douglass turns surplus value toward the cause of liberation. (The happy rise of Douglass through literacy to lecture fame, authorship, his own newspaper, and a national audience should be compared to Harriet Jacobs's struggle even to find a publisher for her book, which suffered a century of skepticism about its authenticity and lingered in powerless obscurity.)

Baker's new reading of Douglass leaves two important questions in its wake. First, is the representation of surplus value in Douglass's *Narrative* a sign of the author's knowledge or a trace of documentation, that is, a trace of the real that *we* make apparent by recourse to Marxist theory? Second, does the *Narrative* unfold progressively toward an "ultimate convergence" in this knowledge, or do the economic and moral codes operating in Douglass's rhetoric more often run at cross-purposes or into aporias that no narrative or history can totalize? A comparison to another autobiography of antebellum America, Thoreau's *Walden*, might be of use here. *Walden* could be considered—historically as well as theoretically—as another escaped slave's narrative. The opening chapter on "Economy" skillfully uses the diction of business metaphorically, undoing the denotational and alienating value system that money and its powers enforce. "But men labor under a mistake," Thoreau writes, when materialist objectivity and possessiveness rule their perceptions.[25] They undertake Herculean labors in order to acquire and maintain properties. It is in this context that Thoreau writes: "I sometimes wonder that we can be so frivolous, I may almost say, as to attend to the gross but somewhat foreign form of servitude called Negro Slavery, there are so many keen and subtle masters that enslave both north and south. It is hard to have a southern overseer; it is worse to have a northern one; but worst of all when you are the slave-driver of yourself" (4). It is a point made earlier by Emerson in his "Lecture on the Times," and one feels compelled to point out the luxury of the observation for these two white men of privileged New England.[26] Yet the power of Thoreau's language to abstract extravagantly—to play and pun and generalize—allows his text to articulate a critique of capitalism in a way strikingly different from Douglass's text.

Like the transcendentalists, Douglass represents individual emancipation of the soul as the heart of the quest for freedom, relegating economic and political issues to the margins. The reliance of the *Narrative* on the rhetoric of religious and moral truth actually works to preclude a wider study of slavery's historical dimensions; Thoreau, by virtue of his style, ties slavery North and South to a myriad of economic, philosophical, social, scientific, and literary events in his age. As Douglass speaks of his experiences in the South, and in the Maryland shipyards and in Nantucket, his criticism of racial and working-class conflicts always stress the religious and the moral over the monetary, eliding or obscuring the essentially capitalist nature of the slave industry. When Douglass introduces the story of his resistance to the overseer Covey, he declares: "You have seen how a man was made a slave; you shall see how a slave was made a man."[27] I shall return later to this crucial chapter and its 1855 revision, but here the important point is the transcendentalist cast of Douglass's "glorious resurrection" after the fight: "My long-crushed spirit rose, cowardice departed, bold defiance took its place; and I now resolved that, however long I might remain a slave in form, the day had passed forever when I could be a slave in fact" (*Narrative* 81). It is difficult to see the difference between this declaration and Thoreau's insistence that the essence of slavery lies in the individual's failure to enact a radical program of self-conception or self-reliance. Douglass portrays slavery as a psychological or moral "fact" and rele-

25. Henry David Thoreau, *Walden and Civil Disobedience*, ed. Owen Thomas (New York: Norton, 1966).

26. Ralph Waldo Emerson, "Lecture on the Times," *Works*, 22 vols. (Boston: Houghton, Mifflin and Company, 1883), 1: 266–67.

27. Frederick Douglass, *The Narrative and Selected Writings*, ed. Michael Meyer (New York: Random House, 1984), p. 75. Subsequent references are cited parenthetically as *Narrative*.

gates its economy to mere "form." His identification of freedom with economic self-determination leads, as many have noted, to the complicity of his discourse with the laissez-faire capitalism that had produced slavery in the first place.[28]

Later in the book Douglass confronts the economics of slavery more directly when he hires his time out at the shipyard. The introduction of wage labor into the schema of slavery makes the expropriation of the value of the slave's labor easier to recognize, since it appears in the ready representation of coinage: "I was now getting . . . one dollar and fifty cents per day. I contracted for it; I earned it; it was paid to me; it was rightfully my own; yet, upon each returning Saturday night, I was compelled to deliver every cent of that money to Master Hugh" (*Narrative* 104). Douglass calls this expropriation by "power" a kind of "piracy," but he does not expressly see any analogy between wage labor per se and the expropriation of the value of the slave's labor. It is in regard to this moment, I think, that Baker overstates his case for Douglass's knowledge. The partly feudal and relatively primitive character of Southern slavery as a mode of production dictates that the subject it produces will perceive private property as a desired, if currently prohibited, goal. Slavery, as the alienation of the body itself, is especially likely to produce discourses that privilege the sanctity of private property. Since the overt design of the *Narrative* is based on the acquisition of freedom and the ownership of one's own body, Douglass's argument tends to merge quite neatly with the emergent social formation of American capitalism and its thinking about private property. Only from the standpoint of a different historical moment, or from within the subjectivity of a different class relation to capital, will private property appear to be itself an alienating notion, as it is for Thoreau. "Private property" for Douglass is an attractive notion; its contradictory implications in his text illustrate Jameson's "dialectic of ideology and utopia" rather than Gallagher's sense that complicity only reproduces oppression.

When Douglass arrives in New Bedford after his escape, he contrasts its "proofs of wealth" with the squalid conditions characteristic of the South, polemically reversing the common portraits offered by proslav-

28. William Andrews argues that Douglass goes from being a chattel slave to being the political slave of Garrison, and that only in the 1850s with the writing of *My Bondage* does Douglass liberate himself. Whether this is true or not, the representation of Douglass's quest for freedom in Andrews remains personal and psychological rather than economic or political. This is probably more the fault of Douglass's own contradictions than of his critics. See Andrews, "The 1850s: The First Afro-American Literary Renaissance," in Andrews, ed., *Literary Romanticism in America* (Baton Rouge: Louisiana State University Press, 1981), and *To Tell a Free Story: The First Century of Afro-American Autobiography, 1760–1865* (Urbana: University of Illinois Press, 1986), pp. 214–39.

ery writers. In New Bedford, "every man appeared to understand
his work, and went at it with a sober, yet cheerful earnestness, which
betokened the deep interest which he felt in what he was doing, as well
as a sense of his own dignity as a man" *(Narrative* 116). These pages
could be compared to Thoreau's harsh description of economic labor
at the outset of *Walden,* where the enslavement of the body to material
ends leads to "mean and sneaking lives" of corruption, "trying to get
into business and trying to get out of debt, a very ancient slough,
called by the Latins *aes alienum,* another's brass" (4). Thoreau's punning
perception of the alienation inherent in labor under capitalism contrasts
sharply with the teleology of freedom and manhood in Douglass. Situated historically, this difference may be thought of in terms of the
unevenness of development separating white economics from black.
Never having worked through to the stage of wage labor, Douglass
cannot be expected to theorize the contradictions awaiting the worker
at that next turn in the dialectic. Thoreau, on the other hand, from the
standpoint of a laboring middle class now being subordinated to mass
industrial capitalism, and thus threatened with the loss of a purely
private or individual control over production and market value, is positioned to speak about a different phase in the history of political economy and its subjects.

This brief comparison of Douglass and Thoreau suggests that the
intersection of language and history can be read through a kind of
rhetorical analysis that combines a poststructural critique of hermeneutics and representation with a constant attention to the text's conditions
of production. *Walden* and the *Narrative* were not books produced by
artists in tortured seclusion writing only to themselves or posterity. They
were didactic, performative discourses designed to make a difference
in the public affairs of their culture. They worked, sometimes self-
consciously and sometimes not, with the modes of representation informing the communities of their time.

The Rhetoric of the Historical Agent

In rhetorical terms, Douglass's *Narrative* can be situated in the literary
histories of the sermon, the political stump-speech, the sentimental
novel, the slave narrative, and the reform lecture among others. The
"realism" of Douglass's text is not simply mimetic but owes much to the
required style and topoi of these genres. Often ghostwritten by white
abolitionists, pamphlets telling the tales of escaped slaves countered the
"master's moonlight and magnolias portrait of slavery" with their own
stock story, a "dramatic, sometimes starkly horrifying, and hard-hitting

eyewitness account of human bondage from the vantage point of one of its victims."[29] Douglass drew on the devices of these stories for his public orations, which often lasted more than two spellbinding hours.

Douglass began speaking at abolitionist meetings in 1841, three years after his escape, and literally became an agent of Garrison's American Anti-Slavery Society. As a speaking subject, Douglass becomes the agency through which the literary and social ideologies of his time speak, and his autonomy is consistently undermined by his role as agent. Yet as Baker and Gates argue, Douglass's mastery of the master's tongue transforms him from the dictated subject of ideology into the agent of historical (and literary) change. Douglass's texts, then, are exemplary in that their subject is neither a predetermined automaton of the social Symbolic nor an autonomous self freely creating its world. The metaphor of agency suggests rather that the subject occupies a dynamic historical position in which he or she may at once be the medium for ideology's reproduction and the device for its undoing. For the Symbolic cannot reproduce itself without agents, and this dependence creates a supplementary relation of ideology to agency that opens up the space for a difference (though not for any imaginary liberation of "free will").

The first version of the *Narrative* was not published until 1845, some four years after Douglass became an agent. It is tempting to see the *Narrative* as the polished public version of an address delivered many times during those years as Douglass repeated the heartfelt truth of his former life. In *My Bondage and My Freedom* Douglass himself maintains that "during the first three or four months, my speeches were almost exclusively made up of narrations of my own personal experience as a slave" (360–61). Critics often repeat Douglass's story of how his white abolitionist friends Foster, Collins, and Garrison pressured him to stick to this simple narrative, avoid abstract pronouncements, and pepper his eloquence with "a *little* of the plantation manner of speech" (361– 62). According to Douglass, writing after his bitter break with the Garrisonians in the early 1850s, the dramatic and largely empirical style of the book is partly a result of the censorship he suffered on the podium. As an escaped slave his job was to witness his suffering objectively, not to assume the authority to speak *in principle* or as an *authority*, for this even his largely white abolitionist audience would not accept. "It did not entirely satisfy me to *narrate* wrongs; I felt like *denouncing* them" (361–62). Thus the predominance of "verisimilitude" over "abstract and reflective" knowledge in the *Narrative* of 1845 is not the result simply of its unified argument for a materialist epistemology, as Reising

29. William Loren Katz, ed., *Five Slave Narratives* (New York: Arno Press, 1968), pp. xviii–xix.

would have it. Rather, it indicates the formal limitations of the slave narrative genre and its site of production.

Yet the matter is not quite this simple. John W. Blassingame argues that "Douglass exaggerated the restrictions placed on him during his first months," for "white abolitionists advised him *not* to give the details of his slave experience for fear that he might be recaptured. The private letters of white abolitionists and news accounts published between 1841 and 1845 furnish little evidence to support Douglass's assertion."[30] In fact from the start Douglass spoke on a wide range of general topics and denounced slavery, Christian hypocrisy, and Northern racism.[31] Douglass's speeches, like the *Narrative* and his subsequent autobiographies, framed their illustrative episodes and examples with lengthy passages of exhortation, ridicule, and denunciation. While the reliability of these early newspaper transcripts is questionable, one finds in them little of the plantation speech and self-humbling Douglass purportedly adopted.

In October of 1841 the *Pennsylvania Freeman* published the first extant account of Douglass's rhetoric. In it he does begin with a confession of embarrassment, a resolution to tell of his bloody personal experience in slavery, and introduces his often to be repeated story of how Thomas Auld quoted from the Bible as he whipped Douglass's lame cousin Henny. He concludes, however, with this blunt statement: "Emancipation, my friends, is [the] cure for slavery and its evils. It alone will give to the south peace and quietness. It will blot out the insults we have borne, will heal the wounds we have endured, and are even now groaning under, will pacify the resentment which would kindle to a blaze were it not for your exertions, and, though it may never unite the many kindred and dear friends which slavery has torn asunder, it will be received with gratitude and a forgiving spirit" (*Papers* 1.4). What Douglass may have resented in retrospect was the relative generosity of this rhetoric, which spoke in the voice of a cautious abolitionism that hesitated to condemn its audience. Yet if the bitter sarcasm that would later characterize Douglass's best writing and speeches is absent in these lines, the seeds of its growth appear a bit later in the paragraph when Douglass turns to the topic of Northern racism: "The northern people think that if slavery were abolished, we would all come north. They may be more afraid of the free colored people and the runaway slaves going South. We would all seek our home and our friends, but, more than all,

30. John W. Blassingame, ed., *The Frederick Douglass Papers*, Series 1, 3 vols. (New Haven: Yale University Press, 1979): 1: xlviii. Subsequent references are abbreviated *Papers* and cited parenthetically by volume and page.

31. See Waldo E. Martin, Jr., *The Mind of Frederick Douglass* (Chapel Hill: University of North Carolina Press, 1984), pp. 22–23.

to escape from northern prejudice, would we go to the south. Prejudice against color is stronger north than south; it hangs around my neck like a heavy weight" *(Papers* 1.5).

Editorial accounts frequently mentioned the force of Douglass's sarcastic oratory, and the published speeches from the period 1841 to 1845 show Douglass fully in command of various rhetorical postures as he speaks on a wide range of issues. In the *Herald of Freedom* of 16 February 1844, editor Nathaniel P. Rogers reported that Douglass "began by a calm, deliberate and very simple narrative of his life," including numerous incidents later represented in the *Narrative.* Rogers found it "interesting all the while for its facts, but dullish in manner . . . though I discerned, at times, symptoms of a brewing storm." Douglass "closed his slave narrative, and gradually let out the outraged humanity that was laboring in him, in indignant and terrible speech. It was not what you could describe as oratory or eloquence. It was sterner, darker, deeper than these. It was the volcanic outbreak of human nature long pent up in slavery and at last bursting its imprisonment. It was the storm of insurrection. . . . He was not up as a speaker—performing. He was an insurgent slave taking hold on the right of speech, and charging on his tyrants the bondage of his race" *(Papers* 1.26–27). Of course Douglass *was* "up as a speaker—performing." His skill lay in *impersonating* a *natural* eloquence, so as to link the antislavery cause to the eternal moral truths of the human heart (obscuring the economic and political dimensions of slavery). This naturalization of his oratory would in effect make Douglass more palatable, since it effaced his capacity for cultural education and thus made him, as a black man, more a thing of nature than of culture.

On 6 May 1845, just prior to the publication of the *Narrative,* Douglass addressed the Twelfth Annual Convention of the American Anti-Slavery Society in New York City's Broadway Tabernacle. He previewed the contents of the book and gave the most complete account yet of his past. The second half of Douglass's speech, however, went on to discuss crucial issues involving the principles and strategies of the abolitionist movement, and to mock the North for its connivance in the return of fugitive slaves:

> The people at the North say—'Why don't you rise? . . .' Who are these that are asking for manhood in the slave, and who say that he has it not, because he does not rise? The very men who are ready by the Constitution to bring the strength of the nation to put us down! You, the people of Massachusetts, of New England, of the whole Northern States, have sworn under God that we shall be slaves or die! And shall we three million be taunted with a want of the love of freedom, by the very men who stand

upon us and say, submit, or be crushed? . . . You say to us, if you dare to
carry out the principles of our fathers, we'll shoot you down. . . . Wherever
I go, under the aegis of your liberty, there I'm a slave. If I go to Lexington
or Bunker Hill, there I'm a slave, chained in perpetual servitude. I may
go to your deepest valley, to your highest mountain, I'm still a slave, and
the bloodhound may chase me down. *(Papers,* 1.32–33)

It was the success, inventiveness, confidence, linguistic power, and
complexity of his speeches that prompted doubts about Douglass's claim
to being an ex-slave, a suspicion that finally motivated the writing of
the *Narrative* in order to invent and establish the personal authenticity
audiences required for a speaker who ranged so far into public issues
usually restricted to educated white men. The often-praised "simplicity"
of the *Narrative* and its concentration on "personal" experience are thus
the result of political and rhetorical decisions and the pressures of the
historical situation, not the spontaneous outburst of an untutored soul
or the product of an unmediated "realism."

   The rhetorical genealogy behind the *Narrative* helps account for the
variable quality of its style, which in fact often departs from the simple
dramatic accounting of incidents and spirals into melodrama, sarcasm,
ridicule, and denunciation—all characteristics widely found in Douglass's speeches and in the rhetorical genres from which he borrows.
This occurs most frequently in the context of religious hypocrisy, an
issue that Garrison had emphasized. "A great many times have we poor
creatures been nearly perishing with hunger," he writes, "when food in
abundance lay mouldering in the safe and smoke-house, and our pious
mistress was aware of the fact; and yet that mistress and her husband
would kneel every morning, and pray that God would bless them in
basket and store!" *(Narrative* 64). Douglass's tendency in the *Narrative*
to move from autobiography to statements of principle may be traced
in the following passage, which is demonstrably indebted to his many
speeches of the early 1840s castigating religion as the bulwark of slavery:

   I assert most unhesitatingly, that the religion of the south is a mere covering
   for the most horrid crimes,—a justifier of the most appalling barbarity,—
   a sanctifier of the most hateful frauds,—and a dark shelter under, which
   the darkest, foulest, grossest, and most infernal deeds of slavery find the
   strongest protection. Were I again to be reduced to the chains of slavery,
   next to that enslavement, I should regard being the slave of a religious
   master the greatest calamity that could befall me. *(Narrative* 85)

Whatever its calculated realism and horrifying detail, the *Narrative* is
full of a metaphorical and hortatory rhetoric typical of its period and
at variance with the claim for the simple verisimilitude of the text. The

constant use of Christian diction and imagery, as in the famous passage about how the fight with Mr. Covey signals Douglass's "resurrection" from slavery, is one example, as is the repeated characterization of Covey as a "snake." Despite Douglass's outbursts against the hypocrisy of Christianity, his rhetoric everywhere utilizes the terms of his oppressors as he invokes the diction and imagery of Christianity. What de Man might call the aporia between denunciatory statement and figurative language here might be accounted for by the public nature of Douglass's project. His real audience was most often not fellow blacks, but curious whites, newspaper reporters, and the powers that be in Washington. He could not extend the implications of the hypocrisy of Southern Christians to the North without endangering his cause, though in his speeches he sometimes crossed the line. Nor could he find a handle for his revolutionary purposes without engaging the moral epistemology of his audience, which was rooted in Christian texts and ethics. He appealed, quite frankly, to the transcendental character of Christian principles in a war against a very political and historical foe.[32]

The religious and moral tropology of Douglass's rhetoric, then, creates a dynamic interchange between ahistorical principles and historical institutions and practices. His recourse to transcendental concepts is reflected also in the sentimental rhetoric of the book, which has bothered many readers (as has, at least until very recently, the sentimental power of that nineteenth-century women's fiction to which Douglass is indebted). Like Hawthorne in his discourse of "sympathy" in *The Scarlet Letter* or Stowe in her sublime rhetoric of maternal love in *Uncle Tom's Cabin*, Douglass manipulates eighteenth-century ideals of sentimental morality and nineteenth-century political romanticism in protesting the inhumanity of slavery. Michael Meyer's introduction to his edition of Douglass cites as example the page and a half on Douglass's "poor old grandmother" whose years of faithful service to her master yield only ingratitude as she is turned out to die. Douglass depicts, in stock melodramatic terms, the "dim embers" of her "desolate" hearth and the crushing "gloom" as she faces the impending "grave" without her family's comfort: "She stands—she sits—she staggers—she falls—she

32. Martin seems to take Douglass's rhetoric at face value when he describes Douglass as combining "Christian and natural rights elements" with "an instinctive belief in the inviolability of human freedom." Abolitionism "was rational, or enlightened, as well as intuitive, or romantic. It exemplified the basically consistent Enlightenment and romantic notions of man's innate goodness" (*Mind* 20). My point is that Douglass's degree of adherence to these discourses cannot be separated from their rhetorical utility; I doubt that even Douglass was always in control of the difference. Douglass's *experience* certainly contradicted the thesis of "man's innate goodness" even as he appealed to that notion as an enabling *figure* for abolitionist persuasion. And his belief in freedom's "inviolability" was a thoroughly historical, rather than "intuitive," creation.

groans—she dies—and there are none of her children or grandchildren present, to wipe from her wrinkled brow the cold sweat of death, or to place beneath the sod her fallen remains" *(Narrative* 60–61).

Such scenes recall popular antislavery engravings of the antebellum period which similarly focused on slavery's violations of hearth, home, and family. Meyer denigrates the passage as overwritten and heavy-handed, and significantly (and negatively) aligns it with the "sentimental romances" of the era *(Narrative* xviii–xix). Such an evaluation is based on an aesthetic and mimetic, rather than rhetorical, reading. Even the literal or referential sense of this story, so long and often used by Douglass, may be doubted. According to Dickson J. Preston, Douglass knew by 1849 that his grandmother had been taken from her "desolate hut" by Thomas Auld and given a place in the master's kitchen.[33] Though he called some of his remarks on Auld "unjust and unkind," Douglass reprinted the passage about his grandmother verbatim in the 1855 *My Bondage and My Freedom,* and included as an appendix an 1848 letter to Auld repeating the claim that his grandmother had been "turned out like an old horse to die in the woods" *(My Bondage* 269). He did not include his second open letter to Auld (1849), which apologized for some of his remarks.

It is the semiotic and allegorical uses of such passages as *emblems* of slavery that we must examine. The calculated appeal of Douglass's passage is *not* to a historical fact or political position but to an emotional and moral verity—the sanctity of the family and of the mother—thus aligning antislavery rebellion with the powerful conventions of domesticity. As in his ambivalent use of Christian ethics against Christian hypocrisy, here Douglass uses the family against slavery, scarce suggesting (as Jacobs does) that the paternalism and property relations at the heart of the slave system might also play a part in the oppressive construction of domestic relations. The connection between slavery and feminism, in fact, was at this moment being forged by various reform figures, including Douglass himself, making this aporia all the more puzzling and powerful.

The ahistorical and apolitical character of Douglass's rhetoric in his 1845 autobiography should be understood within the context of the debate over the strategies of abolitionism in this period. The debate between Garrisonians and radicals played an important role in shaping some of the *Narrative*'s most important passages, as can be seen from changes Douglass made in later years when he turned against Garrison and advocated a political and military solution to the "slave question."

33. Dickson J. Preston, *Young Frederick Douglass: The Maryland Years* (Baltimore: Johns Hopkins University Press, 1980), pp. 229–30, n. 10.

The Garrisonian position which Douglass accepted in the 1840s (though evidently with some doubts) emphasized "the strategic value of moral suasion and the importance of altering public consciousness. He fully adopted the Garrisonian doctrine of immediate and unconditional emancipation of the slaves as a moral and Christian duty."[34] But this moral and voluntarist abolitionism stressed the dissolution of the North's ties to the slave states rather than any active communal, public, or political assault on the institution of slavery. It denounced the Constitution as a "pro-slavery" document incapable of bringing about any change, and Garrison called on his followers to cease voting. The Garrisonian position of nonresistance did not call for a political intervention by the present government against the slave states and did not advocate the use of military force. In these principles radicalism and moderation were linked as white Northerners were offered a chance to wash their hands of an evil set apart from themselves. Above all, Garrisonianism urged *moral persuasion* as the essential tactic of the abolitionist cause. It would be through argument and *example* that slavery was overthrown.

Thus it was the function of escaped witnesses like Frederick Douglass to inspire *feelings* of horror, shame, and guilt rather than to urge overt political or military measures. The rhetoric of the *Narrative*, along with the reading lesson at Mrs. Auld's, suggests the validity of the Garrisonian position; the fight with Mr. Covey, however, belies that message and contains the seeds of Douglass's later break with Garrison, for he will come to believe that a real physical struggle against the slave powers—like his friend John Brown's—is the only real solution.[35] Eric Sundquist sees this as a progressive change, embodied in the rebellious identification of Douglass with the revolt of Madison Washington recounted in Douglass's 1853 novella "The Heroic Slave" and culminated by the identification of Douglass with the Founding Fathers throughout *My Bondage and My Freedom*.[36] While this is a plausible reading, it transforms a reiterated contradiction in Douglass's work into a gradual evolution, ignoring the recurrent citations of Washington and of the Revolutionary Fathers in Douglass's speeches since the early 1840s. The psychological cast of Sundquist's new historicism, like that of Peter Walker, pays too much attention to Douglass's search for fathers and manhood and too little to the political conditions of his rhetoric. In contrast, Waldo Martin finds that from early in the 1840s Douglass "deemphasized the Garrisonian doctrine of nonresistance. . . . Having been compelled to resort

34. Martin, *Mind*, p. 22.
35. See Franklin, *Victim*, pp. 18–22.
36. Eric Sundquist, "Frederick Douglass: Literacy and Paternalism," *Raritan* 6 (1986): 108–24. See also Robert Stepto, "Storytelling in Early Afro-American Fiction: Frederick Douglass' 'The Heroic Slave,' " *Georgia Review* 36 (Summer 1982): 355–68.

to violence in self-defense and to assess the viability of violence as a strategy for slave emancipation and black liberation, on a personal as well as ideological level, Douglass understood and personified resistance."[37] The conflict between the primacy of moral suasion and the necessity of violent resistance, then, belongs to the original structure of Douglass's rhetoric in the 1845 Narrative and informs the contradictory tropes, episodes, statements, and self-figurations of his work.

How does the reading lesson with Mrs. Auld construct its allegory of the text's rhetorical theory? When Mr. Auld forbids his wife to continue Frederick's education, he justifies the injunction by saying: "If you give a nigger an inch, he will take an ell. A nigger should know nothing but to obey his master—to do as he is told to do. Learning would *spoil* the best nigger in the world" (*Narrative* 49). What we might not hear here is something Douglass's contemporaries could scarcely ignore, which is what Mr. Auld does *not* say. He does not say, as public racist discourse of the period would dictate, that Mrs. Auld's efforts are futile because of Frederick's innate biological inferiority. In the privacy of this conversation Mr. Auld does not bother to repeat the standard rhetoric, bolstered in the antebellum period by the growth of a "racial science" of Negro incapacity, childishness, or animality, as advocated by Dr. Samuel Cartwright and others.[38] Rather, Auld speaks frankly in terms of power, and the not-so-subtle lesson Douglass learns is the old truth that knowledge and power are interdependent. Literacy, the passage implies, is the route to freedom.

The evaluative distinction between public and private discourse that grounds the truth claims of this lesson, however, cannot be stabilized or sustained by a text that everywhere depends on rhetorical conventions for its force of persuasion. While the *personal* and historical experiences of Frederick Douglass seem to operate as the guarantors of the text's validity, the rhetoric of the text abstracts him to fashion his truth as a *representative* figure. So James McCune Smith, in his introduction to *My Bondage and My Freedom,* will say that Douglass "is a Representative American man—a type of his countrymen" (17). Douglass achieves this typological status through his reliance on the transcendental rhetoric of Christianity and the allegorical devices of sentimental humanism, without which his story would remain merely the isolate experience of a single individual. Here also, as Baker argues, is the danger for Douglass, since the specificity of his black tale gets whitewashed in the effort to

37. Martin, *Mind,* p. 24.
38. See, for example, Harriet Wilson's 1859 novel *Our Nig: or, Sketches from the Life of a Free Black* (New York: Random House, 1983) where Mrs. Bellmont asserts that "people of color" are "incapable of elevation" (30).

become the "Representative American man." But a difference remains, in that the problems of literacy and resistance are not the same for the black slave and the white abolitionist. While Douglass gives voice to Garrisonian pacifism, his text speaks of the black subject's necessity and right of revolt. In this specificity his message ceases to be universally representative, because the black man's freedom entails an actual struggle against the power of the white.

Having taught himself to read despite Auld's prohibition, Douglass finds in *The Columbian Orator* a published dialogue in which a thrice-escaped slave debates his master, and "the conversation resulted in the voluntary emancipation of the slave on the part of the master" *(Narrative* 52). This lesson provides an allegory of the Garrisonian position: "The moral which I gained from the dialogue was the power of truth over the conscience of even a slaveholder" *(Narrative* 53). A subsequent episode, however, flatly repudiates this moral. Beaten senseless by the slave-breaker Covey, Douglass flees back to Thomas Auld to argue his case. "My legs and feet were torn in sundry places with briers and thorns, and were also covered with blood," he recalls, his martyrdom a type of Christ's: "In this state I appeared before my master, humbly entreating him to interpose his authority for my protection." Auld's response was that Douglass probably "deserved it" and must go back to Covey *(Narrative* 77–78). Auld will not sacrifice his investment. So much for the liberating powers of representation. This scene immediately precedes the climactic fight with Covey, a juxtaposition that implies Douglass's early dissent from Garrison's advocacy of nonresistance. Douglass carefully portrays his resistance as defensive and walks a very fine line here rhetorically. The episode is no simple recollection, but an allegory advocating slave revolt to blacks while signaling the requisite pacifism to whites. "He can only understand the deep satisfaction which I experienced," writes Douglass, "who has himself repelled by force the bloody arm of slavery. . . . I did not hesitate to let it be known of me, that the white man who expected to succeed in whipping, must also succeed in killing me" *(Narrative* 81). Is any white man, then, in a position to "understand" Douglass?

In 1855 Douglass expands and revises this key chapter for *My Bondage* and again Meyer finds it "less successful" and too didactic *(Narrative* xxvii). Read allegorically, however, the revision reveals what the "directness" and "simplicity" of the *Narrative* obscured.[39] On his way back from Auld's to Covey's, Douglass runs into another slave, Sandy Jenkins.

39. For a thorough discussion of how *My Bondage* revises the *Narrative,* see Andrews, *To Tell a Free Story,* pp. 214–39. Andrews argues that Douglass turns away from the paternalism and individualism of the *Narrative* to the affirmation of black heritage and community in *My Bondage.*

Sandy convinces Douglass to carry a magical root that will supposedly protect him from any whipping by a white man. "The root," observes Baker, "does not work. The physical confrontation does." In the *Narrative* this signifies a "displacement of Christian metaphysics by African-American 'superstition' " and "the inefficacy of trusting solely to any form of extrasecular aid for relief (or release) from slavery" *(Blues* 47). In context the significance of the root is even more specific, as Frederick returns to find Covey on his way to Sunday meeting. The Sabbath puts off his whipping for only a day. Antisabbathism was another of Garrison's tenets. The Sabbath is equated here, through the root, with superstition. This is made very clear when Douglass writes, "I suspected, however, that the *Sabbath,* and not the *root,* was the real explanation of Covey's manner" *(My Bondate* 148). The incident accords with Douglass's entire polemic against relying on American Christianity for one's secular salvation. Yet it also implies that the doctrine of moral suasion might itself be a superstition, that the difference between the hypocrites and the Garrisonians, like the difference between Sandy and Mr. Covey, might be less than one imagined.

The revisions of 1855 make these subversive twists more decipherable. Sandy is called a "genuine African." "Now all this talk about the root," Douglass recalls, "was, to me, very absurd and ridiculous if not positively sinful" *(My Bondage* 147). The past tense allows Douglass both to flatter his audience's piety and to indicate a possible change in his disparaging attitude. "It was beneath one of my intelligence," he writes, "to countenance such dealings with the devil, as this power implied. But, with all my learning—it was really precious little—Sandy was more than a match for me. 'My book learning,' he said, 'had not kept Covey off me,' (a powerful argument just then), and he entreated me, with flashing eyes, to try this" *(My Bondage* 147). The primary scene of Douglass's "book learning" was his reading of the *Columbian Orator.* According to Sandy's criticism, Douglass's belief in the liberating power of the white man's language was a superstition. Only by holding on to a symbol of his African roots—to a different "divination" of his situation—can Douglass be saved. This in turn means that while the doctrine of moral persuasion may be a fit belief for white abolitionists, it is of no use to black slaves whose lives are otherwise rooted. If, as Peter Walker and Sundquist argue, Douglass's texts appear to express a desire to achieve the status of white manhood, this desire runs alongside a countermemory of genuine African roots and thus of a difference that can not be brought to light in the white man's language.

"My religious views on the subject of resisting my master," writes Douglass, "had suffered a serious shock. . . . I now forgot my *roots,* and remembered my pledge to *stand up in my own defense*" *(My Bondage* 148–

49). The referents of "roots" include Douglass's "book learning," and beyond that his roots in Garrisonian abolitionism, and, deeper still, his roots in slavery's expropriation of the slave's cultural legacy and the consequent fettering of the slave's ability to fight (and speak) back. Douglass's split racial genealogy, like his split allegiances to white abolitionism and black resistance, riddle his rhetoric with contradictions and reversals, as forgetting one tangle of roots means recalling another. "*I was resolved to fight,*" he now writes, "as though we stood as equals before the law. The very color of the man was forgotten" *(My Bondage* 149). This assertion plays to the humanism of white abolitionism and comforts the audience as it erases the different color of the speaker before them, who is thus uprooted from blackness. In another reading, however, for Douglass to forget Covey's color means that he forgets the *significance* accorded to it by slave discourse and the state apparatus that supports it. Or he remembers its roots in prejudice, power, and the arbitrariness of categories like "black" and "white."

Douglass is "compelled to give blows, as well as to parry them," when Covey's cousin Hughes attempts to tie his hand. When the battle ceases to be of two individuals and becomes a social act of enforced bondage, the situation and strategy change: "I was still *defensive* toward Covey, but *aggressive* toward Hughes," who receives a sickening blow *(My Bondage* 149). To the refusal of fellow slave Bill to help Covey Douglass now adds a new scene as Caroline, a slave forcibly made into a "breeder" by Covey, appears and ignores Covey's pleas for aid. "We were all in open rebellion," recalls Douglass *(My Bondage* 151). The rhetoric he adds to the 1855 conclusion puts a primacy on force and power: "A man, without force, is without the essential dignity of humanity. Human nature is so constituted, that it cannot *honor* a helpless man, although it can *pity* him; and even this it cannot do long, if the signs of power do not arise" *(My Bondage* 151). While these revisions obviously reflect the kind of militant support of slave revolt expressed in "The Heroic Slave," they operate as rewritings that elicit the repressed in the *Narrative,* and in abolitionism, that concern the "signs of power." "Humanity," "nature," and "man" are signs in a terrain of struggle over properties: Douglass now asserts the rights of a black difference in appropriating the force and meaning of these signs. In rereading his own earlier version of the Covey fight, he remarks its events as "signs of power," an emblem scene in the history of abolitionism and of the discursive fight that will culminate in the Civil War.

Baker's *Blues, Ideology, and Afro-American Literature* proposes to mix the Marxism of Jameson with the poststructuralism of Foucault to advance a new heremeneutic for African-American criticism:

The emergence of conditions for Afro-American literary history is a function not only of an enlarged perspective but also of the "method" of history
itself. Moving beyond the explicit levels of discourse, the archaeology of
knowledge seeks to discover organizing or formative principles of discourses that it evaluates. . . . If historical method consists in cataloging
elements, then all histories are, at least theoretically, open-ended—the
possible inclusions, limitless. In practice, histories are always limited by
ideology. . . . The ideological orientation foregrounded for "Afro-American literary history" under the prospect of the archaeology of knowledge
is not a vulgar Marxism, or an idealistically polemical black nationalism.
. . . Rather than an ideological model yielding a new "positivism," what
interests me is a form of thought that grounds Afro-American discourse
in concrete, material situations. Where Afro-American narratives are concerned, the most suitably analytical model is not only an economic one, but
also one based on a literary-critical frame of reference. (25)

In accord with Baker, I have focused my reading on the economy of
Douglass's rhetorical modes of production, convinced that in this case
such a method best combines the insights of materialism and literary
theory. An archaeology of Douglass's rhetoric displays its overdetermination by the material conditions of his life, the legacies of African
experience, the political circumstances of his speech and writing, the
psychological character of his attitude toward symbols of authority, the
literary devices of romanticism and sentimentalism, the philosophical
diction of the Enlightenment, and the language of Christian humanism.
While each of these institutions of representation contributes to the
history of Douglass's texts, they do not together form a single "ideology"
or narrate an epochal totality. To write Douglass's history within the
confines of any one of them would be, as Baker notes, both an inevitable
temptation and an interpretive limitation.

Rhetoric, as I have construed it, may name the process of struggle,
adjustment, resolution, and disruption between such heterogeneous
representational institutions. In this case, rhetoric is also a means by
which racial difference—marked by the hyphen in "African-American"—receives its various determinations. (One might say that the strategic choice of the name "African-American" underscores this histori-
cal-differential character of a people's identity rather than
denominating it as a timeless essence.) In this sense, rhetoric cannot be
identified with "ideology." Ideology rather names those provisional
moments of suspension when the economic transactions among these
forces yields a balance, a surplus value, or breaks the conceptual bank.
Within a text, for example Douglass's, an ideology of form such as
"heroic individualism" may negotiate the contradictions between economic and psychological registers, papering over the collective charac-

ter of political economy and the social nature of subjectivity. While this mystification may borrow its tropes from previously articulated ideological forms within an available cultural archive, it may also generate possibilities of contradiction between the text and the archive. And here the difference of "race," as an always-to-be-determined character rather than an essence, upsets the balance. Douglass's heroism both borrows the language of Christian humanism, placating his audience and whitewashing his story, *and* subverts that humanism insofar as its rhetorical construction depends on maintaining the speculative difference between Euro-American "civilized humanity" and its "barbarian other."

Thus it would be erroneous to interpret Douglass's invocation of humanistic discourse as only ideological in the negative sense—that is, as a maneuver of complicity that allows just a bit of rebellion before recovering power in the name of the hegemonic forces of control. The practice of that discourse, historically, by Douglass, reinscribes a difference that white hegemony cannot efface. As a speaking subject, Douglass constantly trades on the shock value of his eloquent literacy, on the *irony* of his appearance and speech. Dialectically, one cannot *understand* Douglass without recognizing his humanity, and to recognize his humanity is to transform the history and category of the "human" as his era conceives it. This process unfolds even if, and as, Douglass the man mediates this effort through other desires that condition it— his desire to recover the authority and love of the father, his desire to accede to white society and power, his desire to be recognized as a "man" in the gendered sense. Recalling Baker and Gates on the black speaker's always-already alienated relation to white language, one can argue that the black subject makes a space for opposition within ideology by just opening his or her mouth. (Unless readers, like the Dupin of *Murders in the Rue Morgue*, insist on hearing only the screams of a beast.) Even if the intention were to espouse the ideology, as it is with Douglass when he indulges the rhetorics of entrepreneurship, individualism, and sentiment, the mode of production and the subject's material life in history generate ironies that divide the totality of expression against itself. The force of the hyphenated difference marking "African-American" language cannot forever be contained by the ruses of ideology. Using the distinction formulated by David Simpson, I think we need both an "analytic" historicism (which attends to the description of the various archival registers of representational forces and their material conditions of production) and a "prescriptive" historicism (which will utilize such findings to reconstruct alternative narratives for social and literary history). The interpretation of the African-American difference involves the reader in decisions about the ends of criticism. We move in an ethical as well as a hermeneutical circle, for the values that motivate analysis find their end in the moral narratives that result, which in turn motivate other analyses that inevitably challenge their antecedents.

The study of African-American culture can mobilize the difference of race to undo the limits of history, ideology, and rhetoric. The African-American experience of slavery and oppression dictates that we cannot neglect factoring material conditions into the history of ideas and literature (on either side of the hyphen); moral and ethical considerations likewise motivate the interpretive process, while also demanding a different relation between the reading subject and the speaking subject than had once obtained under the sway of aesthetic humanism. The difference of race continually prompts a reminder of one's *own* particularity, one's own marginality, one's own construction by a limited rather than total history. As one deciphers the rhetorical-institutional history of race difference, a perception of ideology in its repressive mode gives way to a reading of ideologies in their representative functions, which include acts of affirmation, establishment, and progressive empowerment, even as these may require the troping translation from one ideological or social idiom into another (as Douglass translates terms from white discourse into the language of his own liberation). Once rhetoric becomes a method for analysing the *process* by which history unfolds through the struggles *within* and *between* discourses, the possibility of changing history (past, present, and future) through rhetoric becomes an understandable, practical, and responsible proposition.

CHAPTER EIGHT

Hegel and the Dialectics of American Literary Historiography: From Parrington to Trilling and Beyond

Instead of writing history, we are always beating our brains to discover how history ought to be written.

—Hegel, *Philosophy of History*

The assertion of Hegel's importance for an understanding of American literary criticism and historiography should come as no surprise. Underlying most standard theories of American literature one can detect Hegel's thesis that the "History of the world is none other than the progress of the consciousness of Freedom," though in its appearance one must see that the "History of the World is not the theatre of happiness."[1] The correspondences between Hegel's philosophy of history, with its emphasis on self-consciousness, and American literary histories stem in part from their common beginnings. Both rewrite the legacy of Christian historiography, especially as regards the immanence of Providence, the dialectic of good and evil, and the salvational teleology governing the unfolding of individual and national destinies. Both recast Protestant pietism and millennialism through the mediation of Enlightenment epistemology, the political revolutions in France and America, and the quarrel of idealism with materialism in the age of science, capitalism, and urban industrial development. But Hegel's theory of history will come down to future generations in Europe most often through its Marxist revision. In the United States, the thematics and dialectics of literary historiography will privilege the terms of Puri-

1. G. W. F. Hegel, *The Philosophy of History*, trans. J. Sibree (New York: Dover, 1956), pp. 19, 26.

277

tanism, transcendentalism, and romanticism, though these too belong
to a cultural tradition of idealism in which Hegel remains a central
figure. My concern is both with Hegel's actual influence, as in the case
of Trilling, and with what the difference between Hegelian dialectics
and American oppositional criticism can teach us. In keeping with
Derrida's double reading of Hegel—as both the final exemplar of metaphysics and the end of the line of logocentrism—I shall be arguing
that American criticism has been both too Hegelian and not Hegelian
enough.[2]

American criticism has been too Hegelian in constructing models
based on oppositional schemas that tend to become formal rather than
historical, and that concentrate on consciousness as the central term of
cultural study. It has been insufficiently Hegelian in not realizing the
critical power of dialectics as a method for undoing reified cultural
categories, and it has overlooked the potential for the deconstruction
of representation that Derrida has exploited in his reading of Hegelian
speculation.[3] The modern use of dialectical terms in American literary
historiography often lapses into static contradictions, having lost faith
in the teleology of Spirit and exhibiting little of the philosophical rigor
or cultural breadth of Hegel's dialectical speculation. The result is a
dehistoricizing of dialectic and a separation of the aesthetic from the
psychological, the philosophical, and the political. Dialectic reverts to
schemas of binary opposition, and aesthetics takes refuge in formalism.
As we shall see, the work of Lionel Trilling played a crucial role in the
formal and psychological redefinition of dialectic. Both Mark Krupnick
and Russell Reising have recently argued that Trilling emptied dialectic
of its original force and, as part of his reaction to Marxism, offered
instead a formula for stasis, equilibrium, and tragic impotence.[4] This
reaction was not only Trilling's, since he inadvertently epitomizes the

2. While Derrida's reading of Hegel is spread throughout his *oeuvre*, see in particular
Of Grammatology, trans. Gayatri Chakravorty Spivak (Baltimore: Johns Hopkins University
Press, 1976), chap. 1; "From Restricted to General Economy: A Hegelianism with Reserve," *Writing and Difference*, trans. Alan Bass (Chicago: University of Chicago Press,
1978), pp. 251–77; "The Pit and the Pyramid: Introduction to Hegel's Semiology,"
Margins of Philosophy, trans. Alan Bass (Chicago: University of Chicago Press, 1982), pp.
69–108; and *Glas*, trans. John Leavey, Jr. (Lincoln: University of Nebraska Press, 1986).
3. Fredric Jameson's Preface to *Marxism and Form: Twentieth-Century Dialectical Theories
of Literature* (Princeton: Princeton University Press, 1971) points out that American literary
Marxism from the 1920s to the 1960s had almost no contact with the Hegelian movement
of Western Marxism initiated by Georg Lukács and variously developed by Theodor
Adorno, Max Horkeimer, Walter Benjamin, Herbert Marcuse, and Jean-Paul Sartre.
Jameson's concluding chapter, "Toward Dialectical Criticism," remains a brilliant explica-
tion of Hegel's importance for literary theory.
4. See Mark Krupnick, *Lionel Trilling and the Fate of Cultural Criticism* (Evanston:
Northwestern University Press, 1986), pp. 156–59, and Russell Reising, *The Unusable Past:
Theory and the Study of American Literature* (New York: Methuen, 1986), pp. 93–107. See

dehistoricizing of criticism that came in the wake of the 1930s, despite his general effort to use literary commentary to criticize contemporary culture.

While Krupnick and Reising accurately pinpoint the tendency in Trilling toward seeing culture in terms of static oppositions, they overlook his constant engagement with the unsettling dialectic between self-consciousness and writing. This dialectic, with its incessant negation of the truths of culture and its decentering of the writing subject, continued to play an important part in Trilling's work right on up through his chapter on Hegel in *Sincerity and Authenticity* (1972). This dialectic of the subject of writing may be the most truly Hegelian aspect of Trilling's work. It is of interest to criticism today since it involves a recurrent resistance to writing by a self that nevertheless repeatedly recognized the representational status of consciousness and the subject. Trilling's repression of literary theory was representative of much of the humanist scholarship in his time (and in current resistances to theory), but his essays and books also demonstrate the dialectical return of writing despite (or because of) every effort to negate it. This makes a reassessment of Trilling an opportune place to measure both the predominance of metaphysical paradigms in American literary studies *and* the degree to which a deconstructive approach to representation can return us to historical thinking.

A Nation of Contradictory Spirits

Trilling's encounter with Hegel must be understood as part of a tradition in American literary historiography dating back at least to Van Wyck Brooks and Vernon Parrington. In their canonical collection, *Theories of American Literature,* Donald Kartiganer and Malcolm Griffith even titled the first section "American Literature as Dialectic." For their epigraph they chose this famous and highly influential paragraph from Trilling's *The Liberal Imagination:*

> A culture is not a flow, nor even a confluence; the form of its existence is struggle, or at least debate—it is nothing if not a dialectic. And in any culture there are likely to be certain artists who contain a large part of the dialectic within themselves, their meaning and power lying in their contradictions; they contain within themselves, it may be said, the very

_____

also Daniel T. O'Hara, *Lionel Trilling: The Work of Liberation* (Madison: University of Wisconsin Press, 1988), for a sustained theoretical reading of Trilling's ambivalences as a kind of "ethics of impersonation."

essence of the culture, and the sign of this is that they do not submit to
serve the ends of any one ideological group or tendency. It is a significant
circumstance of American culture, and one which is susceptible of explanation, that an unusually large proportion of its notable writers of the nineteenth century were such repositories of the dialectic of their times—they
contained both the yes and the no of their culture, and by that token they
were prophetic of the future.[5]

Reacting against Parrington's account of American literary history as
the dialectic of liberal and conservative, Trilling self-consciously used
the diction of Hegel and Marx to make Hawthorne and Henry James
into the forerunners of the infinite dialectical complexity of the modernist mind. This philosophy of literary history casts the writer in the role
of Spirit, as a self-consciousness that lives and transcends the contradictions of the national experience. A psychological Hegelianism locates
the struggle for unity in the individual self, in contrast to the social
resolution emphasized by American Marxists of the 1930s.

Kartiganer and Griffith follow Trilling's lead in narrating the story
of American literature and its historiography as a series of binary oppositions leading to unavoidable tragedy. Their introductory comments
highlight a loose but recognizable concept of dialectic in the work of
such critics as Brooks, Perry Miller, Richard Chase, A. N. Kaul, Leo
Marx, Richard Poirier, R. W. B. Lewis, and Roy Harvey Pearce. The
"common practice" of such critics, they note, "has been to discuss American life and literature in terms of tension and polarity, to view our
culture as essentially an expression of radical oppositions." These "un-
reconciled forces" receive various names in different versions, including
"the New World vs. the Old, America vs. Europe, liberal vs. conservative,
agrarian vs. technological, the individual vs. the community, the private
imagination vs. cultural convention—ultimately man, or Man, vs. all
the apparatus, natural and civilized, which make up his splendid if
necessarily resistant environment."[6] Students of Hegel will rightly object
that this list confuses mere opposition with the highly specific structure
of necessary negation that characterizes Hegelian dialectics. Certain
terms associated with the New Criticism, such as "tension" and "polar-

5. Lionel Trilling, *The Liberal Imagination: Essays on Literature and Society* (1950), The
Works of Lionel Trilling (Oxford: Oxford University Press, 1981), p. 9. Subsequent
references are cited parenthetically as LI. Trilling's critique of Parrington first appeared
as "Parrington, Mr. Smith and Reality," a review of Bernard Smith's neo-Marxist *Forces
in American Criticism* (*Partisan Review*, 7 [January/February 1940]: 24–40); this passage on
culture as dialectic was added during revision for the book.

6. Donald M. Kartiganer and Malcolm Griffith, eds., *Theories of American Literature*
(New York: Macmillan, 1972), p. 28.

ity," become the abstracted metaphors for terms that in their original context had considerable philosophical, historical, and political weight.

In tracing the sources of the American "tendency toward dialectical thinking" back to German romanticism, Kartiganer and Griffith never mention Hegel or Marx or even Parrington. Instead they cite the "Kantian recognition of the split between mind and world." "Through subjectivism," they explain, "through imagination and art, man could recognize all those antinomies that blocked a rational approach to knowledge, and yet embrace them in an imaginative structure enabling the human mind to survive in what might very well be an actual chaos" (28). Here one detects the aesthetic Kantianism advocated by René Wellek and Cleanth Brooks and underlying much of the New Criticism. The experience of chaos and disunity is defined as a psychological problem that can be resolved through aesthetic and perceptual devices, rather than as a response to material, social, or political circumstances whose alteration might allow the "human mind to survive." Kartiganer and Griffith, quite conventionally, go on to nationalize the achievement of harmony and order out of tension and opposition: it is a capacity of the "European mind," while in America the dialectic yields no synthesis. Echoing Richard Chase, they define the Americaness of American literature as a willingness to live in irreconcilable contradictions, as "a perpetual argument of persistently antithetical positions" (29). A tale of eternal conflict replaces the historically specific experiences of contradiction making up American history. Such psychological and aesthetic emphases, especially as they privilege vision or perception over the mediation and negation of writing, indicate that the enervation of dialectic in "tension" or "opposition" also involves a fundamental resistance to the temporality and history of representation.

A quite different account of dialectic, and of its role in history and cultural works, can be produced by a look back to Hegel's texts. Stated briefly, the dialectic of Hegel's *Philosophy of History* presents the realization of the Idea in space as Nature, in time as Spirit. These realizations necessarily entail the self-negation or self-differencing of the Idea as it seeks its potential through the materiality of spatial and temporal existence. (This differing from itself of the Idea in its materialization will, of course, later spur deconstructive allegories of writing that subvert the metaphysical claims of representation.) The end of the dialectic is self-subsistence, unity, and freedom from external determination. For Hegel the dialectic of materialism and idealism is guided by the teleology in which Spirit achieves Freedom through History. Thus temporality as mere sequence becomes the time of a narrative, the story of the emergence of the self-consciousness of Spirit. The dialectical stages of self-consciousness in history, moreover, have political consequences as Spirit seeks to realize its potential as Freedom, moving from merely individual liberties to the organic unity of necessity and will when the Spirit of the People and the State conjoin at history's end. Hegel's speculative political anthropology declares that for the Orientals "one is free," the despot; for the Greeks and Romans, "some are free," the ruling class; for us moderns, beginning with the Germanic peoples, "man, as man, is free" (18). The sequence of political institutions reflects the stages of this dialectic, wherein freedom becomes the end (in both senses) of the world-historical process. Aesthetic, political, psychological, and philosophical oppositions are reconciled by this process when contradiction is read as an internal negation requiring the revision of the terms and institutions themselves.[7]

The dialectics of American literary historiography are usually cast in terms of the thematics of freedom and often reduced to a particular impasse in the relation of the individual to the powers of social, cultural, or political determination. This relation bears directly on how such concepts as "freedom," "nature," and the "individual" itself are defined. Now the conclusion that an irreconcilable split separates matter from spirit, man from nature, or the self from society was anathema to Hegel, who saw such dualisms as catastrophic notions inherited from Rousseau's romanticism. In Hegel's view there is no "state of Nature" in which "mankind at large are in the possession of their natural rights with the unconstrained exercise and enjoyment of their freedom":

> The perpetually recurring misapprehension of Freedom consists in regarding that term only in its *formal*, subjective sense, abstracted from its essential objects and aims; thus a constraint put upon impulse, desire, passion—pertaining to the particular individual as such—a limitation of caprice and self-will is regarded as a fettering of Freedom. We should on the contrary look upon such limitation as the indispensable proviso of emancipation. Society and the State are the very conditions in which Freedom is realized. (41)

For Hegel, freedom apart from society and the state, or nature conceived as original freedom, was an anthropological fiction and logical impossibility. Only in the narrative of the historical dialectic by which

---

7. Hegel places America beyond this dialectical sequence, however, because in his version of the frontier thesis America's abundant geographical space combines with the absence of Old World institutions to eliminate the political contradictions necessary for the development of a culture and spirit of freedom. Freedom in nature is primitive, "for a real State and a real Government arise only after a distinction of classes has arisen. . . . America is therefore the land of the future, where, in the ages that lie before us, the burden of the World's History shall reveal itself" (*Philosophy of History*, pp. 85–86).

practice seeks to achieve the Idea, and thus Freedom, does the individual come to the Truth of Self-Consciousness and of its Being.

The self's rejection of society, culture, and the determinations of history, on the other hand, is recounted by American literary historians as the salient and quite un-Hegelian truth of American literature, from Trilling and Fiedler to Poirier and Bercovitch. In such mythologies an eighteenth-century individualist liberalism persists, propped oddly by a romantic metaphysics of nature, perception, intuition, and expression. The judgment of irreconcilability masks an a priori definition of nature, liberty, and the soul as existing somehow outside the determinations of culture, society, and language. As critics join Huck Finn in lighting out for the territories, freedom turns into an indeterminate state rather than appearing as the concrete negation of particular historical conditions. This flight from history usually involves a resistance to or repression of writing, of textuality in the general sense, insofar as writing comes to stand preeminently for the mediating powers of culture. Such resistance can appear either in the form of an aestheticism that imagines art's defensive independence of history or as a realism that fails to reflect on the historical character of its own modes of representation and production. At the level of politics these metaphysical strategies truncate the practical dialectic of idea and realization that informs social change; at the level of hermeneutics they foreclose the text around binarisms rather than reading the historical and representational contradictions that produce them. Freedom is thus doomed, by metaphysics, to be always already a paradise lost, and history of no use to the writing—or the making—of the future. While Hegel argues that "Society and the State are the very conditions in which Freedom is realized," the antinomian Liberal Mind sees itself as the "opposing self," ideally "beyond culture," and thus ultimately uninterested in altering the conditions of the State. Formal and aesthetic scenarios effect a state of organic psychological or artistic harmony in which the Idea realizes its potential for Freedom through symbolic representations.

Hegel himself had begun the *Phenomenology* with a critique of Kant, intuitionism, and aestheticism. Kant did not resolve the antinomy between empiricism and idealism; the opposition between consciousness and the thing-in-itself remained intact. The result, writes Hegel, was a renewed enthusiasm for the sublime, for an "immediate knowledge of the Absolute, religion, or being," which is the "opposite of the form of the Notion." Hegel describes the predicament of philosophy in terms that will be repeated for the next 150 years:

> Spirit has not only lost its essential life; it is also conscious of this loss, and of the finitude that is its own content. Turning away from the empty husks,

and confessing that it lies in wickedness, it reviles itself for so doing, and now demands from philosophy, not so much *knowledge* of what it *is*, as the recovery through its agency of that lost sense of solid and substantial being. Philosophy is to meet this need, not by opening up the fast-locked nature of substance, and raising this to self-consciousness, not by bringing consciousness out of its chaos back to an order based on thought, nor to the simplicity of the Notion, but rather by running together what thought has put asunder, by suppressing the differentiations of the Notion and restoring the *feeling* of essential being: in short, by providing edification rather than insight. The 'beautiful,' the 'holy,' the 'eternal,' 'religion,' and 'love' are the bait required to arouse the desire to bite; not the Notion, but ecstasy, not the cold march of the necessity in the thing itself, but the ferment of enthusiasm, these are supposed to be what sustains and continually extends the wealth of substance.[8]

Hegel's commitment to the labor of the negative, to "the differentiations of the Notion," would in theory distinguish his dialectic from the stale antinomies or dogmatical choices posited by philosophy's stalemate between mind and matter, idealism and empiricism. His *Aufhebung* or sublation would not be a suppression of differences but their activation and preservation in real achieved harmonies. Thus there is doubtless a Hegelian strain in even the vulgar dialectics of American literary historiography and criticism, which posit themselves against the absolutisms of scientific and political representations. But when Derrida argues that Hegel is the last philosopher of the book and the first philosopher of writing, he means to trace an *other* labor of the negative in Hegel which does not contribute to the profit of the Notion. The concepts of truth, speech, presence, time, space, memory, consciousness, and the state in Hegel can only be posited through the simultaneous deployment and repression of representation. In giving philosophy over to the "differentiations of the Notion," Hegel opens up the textuality of ontological and epistemological terms and so becomes the first philosopher of writing, of a writing without end, of speculative representation without object or foundation. Yet in continually closing up these differences into metaphysical concepts, Hegel remains the last philosopher of presence, totality, truth, the mind, the book, and the state. Indeed, the difference between a dialectical Hegelianism constrained by harmony and a disseminated Hegelianism without reserve is difficult, if not impossible, to read. That difference or undecidability, however, may be similar to the one that haunts the dialectics of American literary historiography, in which the commitment to irreconcilable contradictions

8. G. W. F. Hegel, *Phenomenology of Spirit*, trans. A. V. Miller (New York: Oxford University Press, 1977), pp. 4–5.

seems also, at another level, to perpetuate certain fixed and metaphysical oppositions. In each case the history *of* writing spurs a reflection
upon it which both activates the differentiations of ideological notions
and attempts to erase representations of temporality through various
figures that transcend them.

"Americanness" has itself served as precisely one such figure, used to
order and foreclose the differences of American literary history into a
narrative that almost parodies the *Phenomenology,* as in each successive
stage of its experience the "American mind" posits and negates itself in
ever more complex realizations of its Spirit. In this process the spectacle
of differentiation or radical opposition masks a drama of exclusion as
well, this time of such "empirical" others as Native Americans, women,
and blacks. The absorption of American tensions and polarities into a
series of psychological conflicts implicitly sets up a model in which a
single homogeneous consciousness becomes the reality of America—a
consciousness most distinctly white, male, and usually middle- or upper-
class. Speaking of the tropes of the millennium and the "New Jerusalem"
in American literary historiography, Houston Baker speculates that a
"secularized Hegelian version of the framework implied by traditional
American history would claim that the American *Volkgeist* represents
the final form of absolute Spirit on its path through history. . . . Similarly, the world triumph of an absolute literary creativity finds its ground
properly prepared in the evolutionary labors of American writers."[9]
This narrative, argues Baker, requires an original exclusion of the
deportation and slavery that made Armageddon, rather than the New
Jerusalem, the figure for American history in African-American discourse. Baker also analyzes how the black's "scene of writing," in which
instruction in the master's language both empowers and reenslaves the
writer, makes any forgetting of representation impossible and dooms
any unitary account of American literary evolution. In this context
Henry Louis Gates, Jr. has discussed Hegel's racism and the effects of
the master/slave dialectic on images of writing in African-American
literature.[10] Judith Fetterley, Nina Baym, and many other feminist critics have demonstrated as well the unsuitability of canonical accounts
of American literary history when it comes to women writers.[11] The

9. Houston Baker, *Blues, Ideology, and Afro-American Literature* (Chicago: University
of Chicago Press, 1984), p. 20.

10. Henry Louis Gates, Jr., *Figures in Black: Words, Signs, and the "Racial" Self* (New
York: Oxford, 1987), pp. 19–21.

11. Nina Baym, "Melodramas of Beset Manhood: How Theories of American Fiction
Exclude Women Authors," in *The New Feminist Criticism,* ed. Elaine Showalter (New York:
Pantheon, 1985), pp. 63–80; Judith Fetterley, *Provisions: A Reader from Nineteenth-Century
American Women* (Bloomington: Indiana University Press, 1985).

differences of racial or ethnic or sexual experience and textuality interrupt the metaphysical sublimation of the American writer's conflicts and
leave decipherable marks that cannot be located within the traditional
opposition. While there is some danger that the empiricism enabling
such critiques will again repress textuality and fall back on essentialized
concepts of race or class or gender, it is equally possible that they will
open up the history of writing in America by exposing the false dialectics, metaphysical readings, and cultural agendas that have governed
our literary histories. One cannot promulgate a model in which figuration determines politics, or in which material interests determine figuration: rather the economy regulating the exchanges between figuration
and reference, meaning and determination, will have to be charted in
a given case without recourse to metaphysics and with a methodological
self-reflexivity that mediates the ideological values of one's critical
project.

The Liberal Mind

The influence and uses of Hegel in American literary historiography
have been long-standing and various, direct and indirect, and this chapter means only to sketch a part of the story. In doing so it lapses
partially into historicism of an undeconstructed kind, as it locates the
(mis)reading of Hegel within the frame of the quarrel between an
American Marxism and American New Criticism, as if the complexities
here were locally determined rather than inherent in the representational issues at stake. This historical schema, moreover, slides over the
question of actual influence, since few of the critics under discussion
(other than Trilling) actually read Hegel with any seriousness. On the
first count I would respond that I do not mean to suggest that the
Marxism/New Criticism debate determined the reception of Hegel, or
vice versa, but that this debate and that reception belong to a single
"history" whose place, character, and importance we have yet to read.
On the second count, I would say that the structures of conception and
writing that I trace and describe here belong to a "history" that cannot
be limited to the notions of authorship, intention, and influence, though
these no doubt have their local appearances there. One can only gesture
vaguely toward the whole body of poststructuralist thought to justify
such a mode of historical reading. A diagram of Hegel's American place
must be multidimensional, then, partly because of his double role both
as a source of ideals for American writers and as a source of themes
and analytical methods for theorists of American literature. Beyond

this still rather empirical complexity lies the horizon in which the texts of Hegel and those of America (literary, historical, theoretical) participate in the "same" general economy of representations concerning "history" and "literature."

The direct influence of Hegel on the generation of New England transcendentalists appears to have been minimal.[12] A standard account by one of the younger participants, O. B. Frothingham, dwells at length on Kant, Fichte, and Jacobi, but dismisses Hegel. In 1876 Frothingham writes that Hegel's speculation "was scarcely known thirty-five years ago, and if it had been, would have possessed little charm for idealists of the New England stamp."[13] Frothingham's influential chapters on the German roots of American transcendentalism stress the development of Idealism out of the quarrels between Realism and Nominalism, spiritualism and materialism, and portray the philosophies of faith, intuition, and "sublime egoism" in Jacobi and Fichte as the true sources of New England transcendentalism. In Kant as well he finds a pietistical individualism that recovers moral and ethical duty as the practical consequence of the vision of pure reason. (This will be important in regard to the social and political reformism so central to New England transcendentalism.) In Hegel, by contrast, Frothingham finds a conservative and counterrevolutionary philosopher who has "struck hands with church and state in Prussia." Frothingham speaks caustically of the subordination to authority he finds in Hegel's system, for it clashes with the radical Protestant and antinomian strains of New England transcendentalism. Frothingham's one-dimensional attack makes no mention of dialectic or the labor of the negative. Unlike the Emerson of the "Divinity School Address," writes Frothingham, Hegel "was more orthodox than the orthodox; he gave the theologians new explanations of their own dogmas, and supplied them with arguments against their own foes. . . . The ideal elements in Hegel's system were appropriated by Christianity, and were employed against liberty and progress" (44–45). Whatever the merit of this reading of Hegel, it helps explain the absence of much reference to him in contemporary documents of transcendentalism, as well as in subsequent movements in American intellectual history. (There was, of course, a flourishing Hegelian school in St. Louis during the late nineteenth century, but American philosophy took the prag-

12. For background see René Wellek, "Emerson and German Philosophy," in his *Confrontations: Studies in the Intellectual and Literary Relations between Germany, England, and the United States during the Nineteenth Century* (Princeton: Princeton University Press, 1965), pp. 187–212.

13. Octavius Brooks Frothingham, *Transcendentalism in New England: A History* (New York: Harper, 1959), p. 43.

matic and analytic turn and forgot Hegel until the recent revival of
Continental speculation.)[14] Frothingham's reading suggests that one
should ask whether modern Hegelian interpretations of transcendentalism or America's literary history supported the antinomian spirit or
"were employed against liberty and progress."

Obviously the American destiny of Hegel cannot be separated from
readings of Hegel's politics and his perceived usefulness for programs
of American cultural or social reform. In Europe it was Marx, however,
who played the key part in addressing Hegel's legacy, representing his
own work as the rehistoricization and materialist correction of Hegel's
dialectical system. Much of the modern revival of Hegel in France, in
fact, is attributed to the Marxist commentary offered in Alexander
Kojève's *Introduction to the Reading of Hegel*, which had a profound
influence on phenomenology, structuralism, and deconstruction.[15] (It
should be noted, however, that Kojève himself drew upon Husserl and
Heidegger extensively.) In the United States of the latter nineteenth
century the impact of Marx was relatively minimal, especially among
literary intellectuals and critics. Henry Adams wistfully wrote that he
should have been a Marxist, but his disillusionment with dialectics of
consciousness, evolution, and progress, along with his lingering ties
to the *ancien régime*, foreclosed that option. More important than the
discourses of Marxism was the continuing development of an American
liberalism that borrowed themes from European socialist thought. The
specific events of American historical experience—the conquest of the
native land, the absence of monarchical and feudal relations, the establishment of slavery, the rapid industrialization of production, the domination of representative government by commercial interests, the heterogeneous mass culture derived from disparate European and Asian
sources—created a particular crisis of capitalism and its social formation
by the end of the century.

In the Progressive movement this crisis was addressed by a return to
Jeffersonianism in a doomed reaction to the emergent hegemony of
urban factory life and the steady decline of the economic and political
power of small-town and agricultural America. The dialectical terms,
then, that appear in the literary criticism of Brooks and Parrington, the
founders of modern American literary historiography, come out of this

14. The main reference work detailing the impact of German philosophy on
American writers is Henry A. Pochmann, *German Culture in America, 1600–1900* (Madison:
University of Wisconsin Press, 1957).

15. Alexander Kojève, *Introduction to the Reading of Hegel*, trans. James H. Nichols, Jr.,
ed. Allan Bloom (New York: Basic Books, 1969). These transcripts are of Kojève's lectures
delivered from 1933 to 1939 at the Ecole des Hautes Etudes.

era. As in the period of transcendentalism, the Hegelian strain in their work comes modulated through theories of individual consciousness, social reform, and in response to contemporary historical events. Kartiganer and Griffith quote at length from Brooks's 1915 manifesto, *America's Coming of Age*, which recasts the conflict between idealism and materialism as the tragic flaw of American culture. In a phrase that will in turn give Parrington the title for his own study, Brooks writes that "from the beginning we find two main currents in the American mind running side by side but rarely mingling." On the one hand is the spiritualism and transcendentalism running from Edwards to Emerson and beyond; on the other is the "catchpenny opportunism" and mercantile pragmatism running from Benjamin Franklin to the Gilded Age and into "the atmosphere of contemporary business life."[16]

The work of differentiation and self-negation *within* bourgeois criticism turns into an opposition *between* antinomies as Brooks's backward glance projects American cultural history as an eternal recurrence of binary opposition. Brooks's famous essay "On Creating A Usable Past" will then be able to narrate the appearance of Progressive critical consciousness as the necessary resolution of the quarrel between idealism and materialism that has shaped American life. This places the writer—creative or critical—in the position of embodying this knowledge and his consciousness at the "end" of American history. At the same time the labor of creating, of writing, a past to ground the consciousness of the present inevitably subverts the authority of the present claim to knowledge and once more entangles consciousness in the temporality/textuality that engenders it. The psychologization of contradiction increases throughout Brooks's career until he suffers a nervous breakdown—while trying to write a study of Emerson. Spiritualism and organicism will emerge as the prevailing discourses in his massive literary history, *Makers and Finders: A History of the Writer in America, 1800–1915*. As its five volumes appeared between 1936 and 1952, however, Brooks's novelistic portraits of the spiritual lives lived by writers in particularized historical locales proved unsatisfactory to both materialists and formalists. Marxist criticism had already insisted on a strictly economic rereading of the dialectic in American literature, and New Criticism had already begun to produce a formalist redaction of it as well.

The various schemas dominating theories of American literature during the first three decades of the twentieth century centered on the quest of the Liberal Mind. Brooks and Parrington were most influential

16. The quotes are from Van Wyck Brooks, *America's Coming of Age* (New York: Huebsch, 1915), pp. 9–10.

in this regard, establishing the various opposing terms in which the progress of the American self would be narrated.[17] The politics of the Progressive era would underwrite the teleology of the Liberal Mind, which would reach back to Jefferson and the Enlightenment for principles that might justify a reformist critique of capitalism, urbanism, and modernity. Unfortunately, Woodrow Wilson turned out to be the Liberal Mind in its political incarnation, bequeathing an imperialist war abroad and a systematic repression of immigrants, pacifists, and dissenters at home. (Wilson's justifications of the Ku Klux Klan are quoted verbatim in D. W. Griffith's *The Birth of a Nation* (1915). John Dewey and the "war liberals" would support Wilson, leaving only Randolph Bourne, Charles Beard, and a few radical voices to cry in the wilderness.

Nationalism would continue in the 1920s and 1930s to exercise a powerful and usually reactionary influence on American literary scholarship, as the American Liberal Mind began to identify itself with the telos of the Western Spirit. Caught up ambivalently in these developments was Parrington, a midwest Populist who would dabble in Marxian socialism and write the first important interpretive history of American literary culture of the modern period. *Main Currents in American Thought* (1927–29), however, already showed the strains of balancing the Populist and Marxist agendas. As a Jeffersonian Parrington opposed governmental intervention and longed for a lost agricultural economy; under the influence of Marxian socialism his individualist response to capitalism had to give way to the models of economic determinism proffered by figures like Beard. Parrington's work, despite his Pulitzer prize, seemed destined for immediate supersession, because Marxists on the Left found him antiquated and humanists on the Right found him reductive, and this before the New Criticism emerged to systematize the intrinsic study of literature.

Main Currents in American Thought was arguably the most influential work of American literary historiography produced in the modern period. It narrated the story of America, from the Puritans to the Robber Barons, as an unfolding dialectic of pointedly political proportions. Parrington's famous statement in the Foreword to the first volume establishes the dichotomies: "The point of view from which I have endeavored to evaluate the materials is liberal rather than conservative, Jeffersonian rather than Federalistic; and very likely in my search I

17. On the politics of Parrington's historiography, especially the contradiction between his Populist and Marxist tendencies, see Richard Hofstadter, *The Progressive Historians: Turner, Beard, Parrington* (New York: Knopf, 1968), pp. 349–436. See also Peter Bellis, "Vernon Parrington," in *Modern American Critics, 1920–1955*, Dictionary of Literary Biography, vol. 63, ed. Gregory S. Jay (Detroit: Gale Research Co., 1988), pp. 210–20.

have found what I went forth to find."[18] He sought a past usable for the purposes of bolstering the cause of the Progressive movement as it faced the new economic and political challenges of the 1920s. The Liberal Mind becomes the hero of Parrington's *Bildungsroman* as it does successive battle with reactionary Puritan theologians, mercantile Federalists, and the various spokesmen of conservatism he aligns with the rise of capitalism and industrialism in the nineteenth century. (Parrington's original title was *The Democratic Spirit in American Literature*.) Transcendentalism will be but one of the major moments of the Liberal Mind Parrington celebrates. An evolutionary philosophy of spirit imbues his conviction that "to enter once more into the spirit of those fine old idealisms, and to learn that the promise of the future has lain always in the keeping of liberal minds that were never discouraged from their dreams, is scarcely a profitless undertaking" (xiii). Yet the dreams of that mind, as shown in *The Great Gatsby*, were inseparable from the profiteering romance of capitalism (see above, Chapter 4).

While Parrington's flaws are well-known, it is less often observed that he could be a subtle practitioner of dialectical thought, both in handling the relation of representation to modes of production and in describing the necessary negation of idealism by material conditions (and vice versa). Parrington's opening summary of transcendentalism avowedly borrows Frothingham's schematic opposition of idealism and materialism, only to later abandon Frothingham's emphasis on the primacy of intuitionism and spiritualism. Instead he delineates the determining dialectic of transcendentalism and social or cultural criticism:

> Communing with the ideal rarely begets complacency; the actual seems poor and mean in comparison with the potential. Hence the transcendentalists, willingly or not, were searching critics of their generation. . . . In the midst of a boastful materialism, shot through with cant and hypocrisy and every insincerity, fat and slothful in all higher things, the critic proposed to try the magic of sincerity, to apply the test of spiritual values to the material forces and mechanical philosophies of the times. His very life must embody criticism; his every act and word must pronounce judgment on the barren and flatulent gods served by his countrymen. . . . Here was a revolutionary business indeed, that the critic was proposing to himself; and the calm serenity with which he set about it was disconcerting.[19]

18. Vernon L. Parrington, *Main Currents in American Thought*, vol. 1, *The Colonial Mind, 1620–1800* (New York: Harcourt, Brace, and World, 1927), p. vii.

19. Vernon L. Parrington, *Main Currents in American Thought*, vol. 2, *The Romantic Revolution in America, 1800–1860* (New York: Harcourt, Brace, and World, 1927), pp. 377, 379.

Parrington's position has been convincingly developed in Anne C. Rose's definitive study, *Transcendentalism as a Social Movement, 1830–1850* (New Haven: Yale University Press, 1981).

This last remark on the revolutionary business of the critic was, as Parrington might admit, a bit of self-projection. One wonders whether Parrington was the Fitzgerald, the Nick Carraway, or the Gatsby of historiography? Still, whereas Van Wyck Brooks's schema followed Frothingham's in displaying idealism and materialism as tragic antagonists of a timeless quarrel, Parrington's narrative revivifies the power of idealism and refurbishes its reputation as an agency of cultural criticism. The language of a logical or dialectical historical progression is heard in his "begets," "hence," and reiterated "must." Materialism calls forth its own negation in idealism, which out of this origin is compelled to negate materialism in turn. Historical determinism subtly corresponds to the will of the spirit in shaping the calling of the critic.

Hegel's description in *The Philosophy of History* of world-historical individuals, such as Caesar, sheds some light on Parrington's figuration of Emerson:

> It was not, then, his private gain merely, but an unconscious impulse that occasioned the accomplishment of that for which the time was ripe. Such are all great historical men—whose own particular aims involve those large issues which are the will of the World-Spirit. They may be called Heroes, inasmuch as they have derived their purposes and their vocation, not from the calm, regular course of things, sanctioned by the existing order; but from a concealed fount—one which has not attained to phenomenal, present existence—from that inner Spirit, still hidden beneath the surface, which, impinging on the outer world as on a shell, bursts it in pieces, because it is another kernel than that which belonged to the shell in question. (30)

The world-historical individual is *not* the determined emanation of material cultural circumstances, *not* the representative man or spirit of a particular age. Instead his inner spirit belongs organically to another development, and his bursting forth is from a kernel of the Idea quite different from the origin from which the shell of mundane history springs. The inner Idea that determines the Hero is none other than Freedom, which is why his relation to circumstance is one of resistance, negation, and the will to power. In the case of Caesar, who is only a man of action and not a philosopher, the world-historical individual is an agency but not an instance of self-consciousness. Emerson's antinomian self-reliance moves him closer to the philosopher's achievement, though his effort to realize the freedom of his self-knowledge brings him once more into dialectical conflict with materiality, experience, and fate.

In taking seriously the economic and political registers of materialism in transcendentalist discourse, and in emphasizing the involvement of the transcendentalists in various oppositional social movements, Parrington's history is a salutary reminder of much that was obscured by the formal, symbolic, and psychological readings of the "American Renaissance" that prospered after 1940. Parrington's portrait shows Emerson as a hero driven by dialectic into becoming the conscience of the nation and the natural heir of Jefferson. After surveying Emerson's views on democracy, commerce, and the state, Parrington's chapter becomes even more self-reflexive in the admission that Emerson "rejected the economic interpretation of politics," though as "a child of the romantic revolution he understood quite clearly how the waves of humanitarian aspiration broke on the reefs of property rights, how economic forces were in league against the ideal republic" (387). This admission made, Parrington proceeds to argue that while Emerson could not "accept the theory of economic determinism," his essay on "Politics" deals at length with the "philosophy of property" and its contemporary effects.

"Politics" is the only Emerson essay quoted in any substance during Parrington's chapter on Emerson. (He does quote the journals frequently.) Of course it is the "property" and "material" of Emerson's *writing*, of his styles and forms of representation, that Parrington himself fails to discuss in formulating the economics of Emerson's transcendentalism. *Main Currents* had begun by rejecting "belletristic" literary history (a reference to Barrett Wendell), and here the repression of writing in the service of a profitable allegory of critical conscience yields a caricature of Emerson's work. Although Parrington can cite Emerson, he can't read him. The resistance to "economic determinism" turns out also to be an allegory of the resistance to textuality as "Emerson" is separated from his writing and made into a figure in Parrington's story of the Liberal Mind. Emerson, as Harold Bloom has reminded us, worried much about how representation determined the fate of the subject and conditioned its experience. The dialectic of individual and society in transcendentalist discourse should not be separated from the dialectic of the subject and the text, for both such oppositions are engineered by the same metaphysical strategy and result in similar repressions of writing and history. In Parrington's chapter on Emerson this becomes clear as Parrington avoids the return to individualism and the primacy of the soul in Emerson's discourse, bravely ending instead with his opposition to slavery and his action on behalf of "justice, truth, righteousness." Emerson's liberalism, like his philosophy of authorship, rejected determinism in basing reformation on the original power of the independent soul of virtue and self-reliance. When treated thematically, this move produces a very nondialectical conceptual opposition of determining circumstance and liberated selfhood which runs throughout Emerson's prose and many commentaries on it. Parrington's recourse to such a thematic reading truncates the dialectic of Emerson's style and reduces him to the figure of the liberator, a strategy which evades rather than negates (in the Hegelian sense) the material conditions of literary or social production.

Thus the materialism of late nineteenth-century America ensures the doom and alienation of the Liberal Mind, and the heir to Jefferson and Emerson becomes Henry Adams if not Parrington himself. Yet even here Parrington appears ready with a new dialectical turn. The defeat of transcendentalism will set the stage for the critical realism of a new middle-class ideology that might, as Brooks had dreamed, formulate an internal and hence transformative critique of late nineteenth- and early twentieth-century America. *The Romantic Revolution in America* ends with this prophecy:

> In the world of Jay Cooke and Commodore Vanderbilt, the transcendental dream was as hopelessly a lost cause as the plantation dream. . . . A new age had come and other dreams—the age and the dreams of a middle-class sovereignty, that was busily surveying the fields of its future conquests. From the crude and vast romanticisms of that vigorous sovereignty emerged eventually a spirit of realistic criticism, seeking to evaluate the worth of this new America, and discover if possible other philosophies to take the place of those which had gone down in the fierce battles of the Civil War. What form this critical spirit assumed, and what replies it returned to the strident challenge of the time, are questions not to be answered here. (465)

Parrington did not live to furnish the answers. His unfinished third volume appeared posthumously, an ironic twist for a literary history so teleologically conceived as the evolution of the Liberal Mind toward its present regenerative fulfillment. The Pulitzer prize accorded Parrington signaled the acceptance of his economic emphases as the 1920s ended, while the individualism and liberal politics of his narrative ensured a warm reception from most literary intellectuals. Parrington's fate in the 1930s, however, belied his prophecy. Marxism took up the mantle of the waning Progressive movement and won the allegiance of the dominant portion of the literary and intellectual Left in America. From their standpoint Parrington's work, though grounded in the concepts of economic production and class struggle, remained insufficiently materialist. On the other hand, the rise of literary theory and the beginnings of the New Criticism would bury Parrington's work with the observation that it was a history of everything but literature. The victory of this latter movement came with the publication in 1941 of F. O. Matthiessen's *American Renaissance,* which begins by explicitly appropriating the democratic political nationalism of Brooks and Parrington and then subordinating it to the New Criticism's concern with language, style, and tragic vision. While Matthiessen's effort to remember writing often yields good results, his work is finally undone by an allegiance to T. S. Eliot's logocentric nostalgia for a language that would unite the word with the Word. (Matthiessen, of course, had written first on Eliot, and Eliot's postlapsarian thesis concerning the "dissociation of sensibility" underwrites the theoretical program of *American Renaissance.*)

The turn against the Liberal tradition in American literary historiography was also signaled by the rise of Perry Miller, who set out to save the Puritans from the castigations of Brooks and Parrington. (Brooks had punningly titled his 1908 study of America *The Wine of the Puritans.*) In 1940 Miller published "From Edwards to Emerson," a polemical piece of revisionary historiography in which the genealogy traced by Brooks and Parrington is put to different uses. Miller writes as American literary Marxism and the Progressive school are under siege, and his purpose is to show the insufficiently dialectical character of economic determinism. He questions the consensus in "contemporary criticism" that believes that "ideas are born in time and place, that they spring from specific environments, that they express the force of societies and classes, that they are generated by power relations."[20] He disparages the

20. Perry Miller, "From Edwards to Emerson," in Kartiganer and Griffith, *Theories,* p. 326. The essay also appears in Miller's *Errand into the Wilderness* (Cambridge: Harvard University Press, 1956). It first appeared in the *New England Quarterly* in December 1940.
    This essay is one of two by Miller included by Kartiganer and Griffith. (He is the only critic so honored.) Their volume reprints his "Errand into the Wilderness" as its prologue. This canonizing move is motivated, one surmises, by the nationalism and teleological dialectics of Miller's historical vision, which must have been welcome in the 1950s. He dwells, in New Critical fashion, on the "ambiguity" of the word "errand," its "double meaning." The nation, on the one hand, is like an "errand boy" or a husband who "must run an errand for his wife," or on the other hand "the runner of the errand is working for himself" (*Theories* 12). Historical fulfillment and national identity become the achievement of a self-reliant male consciousness who embodies God's will in his own Spirit. The dialectic between obedience and creative will repeats those of Europe and America, tradition and the individual talent, and—prefiguring Leslie Fiedler—woman and man. As the dialectical ambiguity oscillates to emasculate the will of the Puritan, the "problem of his identity" is psychologized. Rather than a conflict with "stones, storms, and Indians," it becomes a search for the new American mission. Having emptied the native land of its inhabitants and natural integrity, and having imagined the blankness of their own social context, they "were left alone with America," wondering if they were men enough for the job. There is a trace here of Parrington's complaint that "our literary historians have labored under too heavy a handicap of the genteel tradition—to borrow Professor Santayana's happy phrase—to enter sympathetically into a world of masculine intellects and material struggles" (*Colonial Mind* xii).

presentist perspective in which "Emerson becomes most vivid to us when he is inscribing his pungent remarks upon the depression of 1837, and Thoreau in his grim comments upon the American blitzkrieg against Mexico." Admitting that transcendentalism was a response to "commercial times," Miller strongly objects to accounts (such as Frothingham's) that trace the origins of its philosophy to European or Asian sources. Was theirs not a "natural reaction" for "descendents of Puritans and Quakers"? Miller tacitly rejects Parrington's version of the historical dialectic as a quarrel between various imported liberalisms and conservatisms. Instead he finds the essence of the dialectic within the single structure of Puritan consciousness and theology itself: "At the core of the theology there was an indestructible element which was mystical, and a feeling for the universe which was almost pantheistic; but there was also a social code demanding obedience to external law, a code to which good people voluntarily conformed and to which bad people should be made to conform" (325, 328, 331).

The dialectical historiography running through his two-volume *The New England Mind* is evident here: the internal contradiction between Puritanism's spiritual core and rational shell determines the stages from Edwards to Emerson. Miller finds himself writing a history of ideas, and he must stop to admit that "I am guilty as Emerson himself if I treat ideas as a self-contained rhetoric, forgetting that they are, as we are now discovering, weapons, the weapons of classes and interests, a masquerade of power relations" (337). Yet he immediately drops this politico-critical rhetoric in arguing that Emerson and Fuller led careers that disobeyed the laws of economic determinism, which should have made them the spokespersons for "respectable, prosperous, middle-class Boston and Cambridge" (337, 339).

Miller's argument sets up a very un-dialectical notion of economic determinism as a straw man and is in this regard less sophisticated than Parrington's observation of how transcendentalist social criticism grew out of its idealism. Miller cannot rejoin the history of ideas with the history of economics since he is committed to seeing ideas as the representations of willing subjects rather than as parts of an always already material signifying practice. His own position as an antagonist to Marxist historiography and as an apologist for nationalist mythologizing also dictates a reimposed binarism of idealism and materialism; otherwise he would have to undertake a more unsettling reflection on the economic, political, and historical determinants of his own thoughts as a spokesman for respectable, prosperous Boston and America.

Matthiessen's and Miller's arguments were enabled in part by the major turn against Parrington and against Marxism in the career of

Lionel Trilling.[21] Trilling had begun, in the 1920s and early 1930s, as an aspiring novelist and cultural critic writing from within the New York Jewish intellectual circle formed around *The Menorah Journal*. Trilling's position as an "other"—Jew, Freudian, Marxist—was explicitly cited during the attempt to fire him at Columbia in the early thirties. Trilling undertook his own assimilation, however, in writing a dissertation on Matthew Arnold, which became the book that got him tenure. Arnold was the English critic who symbolized the identification of the Man of Letters with the Subject of History. This identification attracted Trilling because it placed the marginalized writer and thinker at the center of intellectual and cultural history, and indeed made him its embodied consciousness. One source, then, of the contradictions in Trilling's work will be the tension between his desire for assimilation to this abstract position of authority within Anglo-European high culture and the traces of his allegiance to an "otherness" that prompts the rebellions of the opposing self.

Trilling's 1940 essay "Parrington, Mr. Smith, and Reality," which was later revised as "Reality in America," the lead essay of *The Liberal Imagination*, argued that the Left view of literature, history, and politics offered a simplistic mind-versus-reality dualism. While acknowledging Parrington's preeminence and the importance of "his informing idea of the economic and social determination of thought," Trilling attacks the mimetic fallacy that structures Parrington's way of relating aesthetics and politics. Trilling's Parrington believes that "reality" is "one and immutable," "wholly external," an object that the artist reflects by constructing an artifact that corresponds to it. "It does not occur to Parrington," he writes, "that there is any other relation possible between the artist and reality than this passage of reality though the transparent artist" (LI 4–5). Like others, Trilling finds that Parrington's rejection of the "belletristic" amounts to a refusal of mediation—of writing itself. Yet Trilling's formula again erases writing by making the mind of the artist (rather than language itself) the agency of negation and mediation. Trilling's future interest in Hegel's *Phenomenology* is foreshadowed here by the decidedly psychological bent of his own aesthetics, in which the mind-versus-reality dualism becomes a largely internalized psychological dialectic.

Passing over Parrington's "most cherished heroes, Jefferson and Emerson," Trilling defends Hawthorne's "questioning of the naive and often eccentric faiths of the transcendental reformers." Trilling praises

21. See Gregory S. Jay, "Lionel Trilling," in Jay, *Modern American Critics*, pp. 267–89. A few passages of the present chapter first appeared there in different form.

the realism of the "man who could raise those brilliant and serious doubts about the nature and possibility of moral perfection, the man who could keep himself aloof from the 'Yankee reality' and who could dissent from the orthodoxies of dissent and tell us so much about the nature of moral zeal."[22] In the original essay, the example given is *The Blithedale Romance;* its excision in the book version allows Trilling's sentence to fall in general terms on the leftists and dissenters of the 1930s. At this point he also adds the passage on culture as dialectic and the artist as the consciousness of social contradictions. As with Parrington, the description of the artist appears to be a sketch of the critic's situation and vocation as well, here of the modernist critic confronting the end of the Liberal dream.

A decade and a second World War separate Trilling's first attack on liberalism from the shape his views take in *The Liberal Imagination.* In the Preface Trilling describes the "paradox" afflicting the mind of modern liberal critics and artists. While liberalism begins in the emotional imagination of "variousness and possibility" in life, the "organization" of liberalism as a political or cultural ideology inevitably (if unconsciously) imposes limitations. In Hegelian terms, the realization of the Idea in practice negates its original form (the Idea of Freedom) and thus provokes the dialectical criticism of "naive and eccentric reformers" by the Hawthornes and the Trillings. In his deep suspicion of liberalism's hope "to organize the elements of life in a rational way," Trilling displays the same Populist resistance to the institutions of government and society that Parrington had felt. The modernist "tragic vision" Trilling offers in the wake of liberalism's paradoxes and failures focuses on the view that "the world is a complex and unexpected and terrible place which is not always to be understood by the mind as we use it in our everyday tasks." Set against the background of the war, the Holocaust, and Hiroshima and Nagasaki, these rather deceptively simple words take on considerable resonance. The special cognitive virtue of the literary, according to Trilling, is its dialectical power to reopen the complexities foreclosed by ideologies. Trilling's version of Cleanth Brooks's thesis, in "The Language of Paradox," that contradiction is the essence of the literary, appears here to unite literary, psychological, and moral theory.[23] Criticism should "recall liberalism to its first essential

22. Trilling, *Liberal Imagination,* pp. 8–9. Trilling expands these points influentially in his "Hawthorne in Our Time," *Beyond Culture: Essays on Literature and Learning* (1965), The Works of Lionel Trilling (Oxford: Oxford University Press, 1980), pp. 155–80.

23. Cleanth Brooks, "The Language of Paradox," in *The Well Wrought Urn* (New York: Harcourt, 1947), pp. 3–21. For Brooks "the language of poetry is the language of paradox," so that while "the tendency of science is necessarily to stabilize terms, to freeze them into strict denotations; the poet's tendency is by contrast disruptive" (3, 9). In

imagination of variousness and possibility, which implies the awareness of complexity and difficulty." Literature has a "unique relevance" in criticizing the liberal imagination because it is the human activity that most fully and precisely renders that awareness. Trilling posits his literary theory as more dialectical, more attuned to difference, than that of the Left's dogmatists, so that one might see here a strong return to the labor of the negative in writing. On the other hand, tropes such as the "imagination" and "awareness" restore a Kantian or aesthetic psychology to the position of a center of consciousness that can contain "the fullest and most precise account" of contradiction, thus recuperating the "differentiations of the Notion" in a spiritual and timeless rather than materialist and historical narrative.

There are few explicit references to Hegel in *The Liberal Imagination.* In "Freud and Literature" Trilling mentions the enthusiasm of Hegel and Marx for Diderot's *Rameau's Nephew* in a passage that serves as the germ for *Sincerity and Authenticity.*[24] Trilling turned increasingly to Freud as well as Hegel during the 1940s and 1950s in order to find a model for the psychological dialectics he wished to substitute for what he saw as the mind-versus-matter dualisms in Marxism and liberalism. Hegel's presence, however, looms larger than Freud's in the volume's final essay on "The Meaning of a Literary Idea." The literary idea is not a referential reflection or timeless proposition. Rather, "the very form of a literary work" is "a developing series of statements": "Dialectic, in this sense, is just another word for form, and has for its purpose, in philosophy or in art, the leading of the mind to some conclusion" (LI 266). But "in our culture," argues Trilling, "ideas tend to deteriorate into ideology," which explains the hostility toward ideas on the part of even the most sensitive readers and critical theorists (LI 269). Some of these, like René Wellek and Austin Warren, respond to ideological reading by turning to "purely aesthetic values." Here Trilling parts

---

"Wordsworth and the Paradox of the Imagination," Brooks explains that these disruptive "ambiguities" and "contradictions" spur the work of the "synthesizing imagination," so that poet and reader unite in a single act of aesthetic cognition superior to the referential discourse of science or the propositional discourses of religion, morals, or politics (147). The similarities between *The Liberal Imagination* and *The Well Wrought Urn* deserve extended reflection.

24. It can be surmised that Trilling's reading of Hegel began in the late 1930s as a result of his friendship and team-teaching with historian Jacques Barzun at Columbia, where their colloquium on modern culture included Diderot's *Rameau's Nephew.* In 1943 Barzun dedicated *Romanticism and the Modern Ego* (New York: Little, Brown, 1943; 1947) to Lionel Trilling. In a note on Hegel, Barzun confesses guilt for the "vulgar error" of previously representing Hegel as "a Prussianizer *à outrance*" and source of modern fascism. Against the "recurrent epidemics of anti-Heglianism" he prescribes an "inoculation" of "reading or re-reading" *The Philosophy of Right* and the *Phenomenology* in order to clarify the meaning of *The Philosophy of History.* Apparently Trilling undertook the treatment.

company with the New Criticism in insisting that the dialectic of literary ideas can have "the authority, the cogency, the completeness, the brilliance, the *hardness* of systematic thought" (LI 272). In support, he quotes from the introduction to *The Philosophy of History*, in which Hegel states that "grammar, in its extended and consistent form, is the work of thought, which makes its categories distinctly visible therein."[25] In the coming decades Trilling will increasingly adapt the teleology of historical self-consciousness in Hegel to his own diagnoses of the modern spirit and its literature, though he mutes the millennialism of Hegel and the revolutionary hope of Marx with the tragic stoicism he finds in Freud. Hegel's recognition that the form of grammar coincides with the work of thought implies an inseparability of consciousness and language which will be exploited by deconstructive readers of Hegel. The consequences of this inseparability, however, will produce as many ambivalences in Trilling's texts as they do in Hegel's.

Opposing Selves

As a theorist of literary history, Lionel Trilling was principally concerned with describing the character and qualities of modernism, and his theory of modernism is entangled in his reactions to Hegel, Freud, and Marx. Trilling wanted to develop moral and psychological accounts that would complement or displace the aesthetic and political readings of modernism offered by New Critics and Marxists. This view of modernism would be American insofar as the "tragic" complexity of contemporary ethical and cognitive problems was a direct result of the rise and fall of the Liberal Mind and its literature. The individualist strain in American cultural politics, which had produced the ambivalence in Parrington between a desire for the reform of institutions and a desire for freedom from all determination, yields in Trilling the idea of the "opposing self," an idea that at first seems to come from Freud. This subject will also significantly be a troping of the Marxist economic explanation of "alienation" and thus not surprisingly involve a return to Hegel's thinking on the topic, specifically in the chapter on "Self-Alienated Spirit" and culture in the *Phenomenology*.

In the 1955 Preface to *The Opposing Self* Trilling defines the "distinguishing characteristic" of the modern self as "its intense and adverse imagination of the culture in which it has its being." He deliberately substitutes "culture" for "society" in order to extend the dialectic to the

25. The quote appears in Hegel, *Philosophy of History*, p. 62.

individual's relation to the entire range of a tradition's legacies—textual, psychological, moral, material, and institutional. Drawing on Freud as well as Marx, Trilling theorizes the "indignant perception" of the modernist as a view turned toward the "unconscious portion of culture." The specter of determination, the haunting figure that threatens the self's freedom, inhabits not simply the machinery of external institutions or historical formations, but lives within every aspect of culture as well as within the self or subjectivity. "Men began to recognize the existence of prisons that were not built of stone, nor even of social restrictions and economic disabilities," he writes. Drawing on Freud's notion of the superego as internalized social determination, Trilling describes how the "newly conceived coercive force required of each prisoner that he sign his own *lettre de cachet,* for it had established its prisons in the family life, in the professions, in the image of respectability, in the ideas of faith and duty, in (so the poets said) the very language itself."[26]

The metaphor of the *lettre de cachet* and the final reference to "language itself" are enormously suggestive. They imply that the dialectic of the subject is inextricably a matter of language and of writing, and that the historical process is itself carried on within the legacies, practices, and institutions of textuality. The prison-house of language, one might say, is glimpsed here as coercive determination. Cultural history cannot be separated from writing, and hence the substitution of "culture" for "society" effectively acts here as a remembering of representation if not a return of the repressed. To play on Hegel, "history ought to be written" rather than theorized as a referent whose ontology lies outside language. Any attempt to use writing as a technique for overcoming determination and thus achieving a dialectical transcendence or Hegelian *Aufhebung* is doomed from the start; each new letter is a re-mark of history, materiality, contingency, and otherness. The struggle to achieve subjectivity or freedom through language can only produce more letters, further disseminating the "differentiations of the Notion" and entangling the Spirit in the historical matter of textuality. The *lettre de cachet* must be purloined from the cultural archive, and the authority of its signatory becomes undecidable. Who signs for freedom? the letter or the spirit? history or the subject? writing or desire? determination or chance? In French the *cachet* is not only a seal, stamp, or character, but also the sign of genius and of achieved subjective expression: *son style a un cachet particulier.* The stamp that seals writing's difference, says the dictionary, also marks the *lettre de cachet* as an "arbitrary

26. Lionel Trilling, Preface to *The Opposing Self* (1955), The Works of Lionel Trilling (Oxford: Oxford University Press, 1980), n.p. Subsequent references are cited parenthetically as OP.

warrant of imprisonment."[27] The plight of the modern self is that of a desire for freedom that nevertheless cannot forget its determination by writing, or that may even suspect the determination of this desire and this dialectic by "language itself."

According to Trilling's Preface, the "best account of the strange, bitter, dramatic relation between the modern self and the modern culture is that which Hegel gives in the fourth part of his *Philosophy of History*." Trilling uses Hegel to set Marx back on his feet by arguing that Hegel's discussion of "alienation" properly centered on psychological, moral, and aesthetic phenomena (rather than politics or economics). But in Hegel's chapter on alienation in the *Phenomenology* the forces of state power and of wealth are explicitly incorporated into a dialectic of consciousness (thus sparking Marx's argument for a dialectic of historical materialism). Trilling's version of alienation, like the tragic vision spoken of so frequently by American critics in the period after the 1930s, constitutes a teleological dialectic "which the modern self contrives as a means for the fulfillment of its destiny" in a pain the self incurs as a "device of self-realization." This self-realization requires rendering judgments on the quality rather than the fact of an act: "Not merely the deed itself, [Hegel] said, is now submitted to judgment, but also the personal quality of the doer of the deed. It has become not merely a question of whether the action conforms to the appropriate principle or maxim of morality, but also of the manner in which it is performed, of what it implies about the entire nature, the *being*, of the agent." In other words, style is the man.

Hegel's text becomes a pretext in Trilling for affirming the ontological reality of the "performed" self, the written subject, who thus recovers from the inauthenticity of repetition and the impotence or errancy of action. Hence Hegel "brought together the moral and the aesthetic judgment" and "made the aesthetic the criterion of the moral." The threatened disappearance of the modern self intimated by the passage on the *lettre de cachet* is remedied in this paragraph by postulating an ontological and referential determination of writing by selfhood. Whereas the fact or "deed," the mark of writing, may be the work of cultural history, the manner or stylus "implies" "the entire nature, the *being*, of the agent." Style is freedom, choice, and responsibility, and Trilling can thus theorize the cohesion of the moral and the aesthetic judgment. To do this, he must smuggle back into the equation a binary

27. *The New Cassell's French Dictionary*, rev. Denis Girard (New York: Funk and Wagnall's, 1962), entry on *cachet*, 118. Of the many texts of Jacques Derrida bearing on these metaphorics, one might begin with *The Post Card: From Socrates to Freud and Beyond*, trans. Alan Bass (Chicago: University of Chicago Press, 1987).

opposition between "deed" and "manner," "act" and "quality," history and writing, which his own previous argument has rendered groundless. The liberation of the free aesthetic/moral subject from the determinations of history is accomplished by an a priori fiat that arbitrarily establishes the very differences that are supposed to be determined later by the deliberations of judgment. Needless to say, the political consequences of separating the judgment of deeds from the judgment of their quality are enormous, especially in an era when the destiny of the Liberal Mind led it to contemplations of Auschwitz and Hiroshima.

The essays of *The Opposing Self* chart the "duality" or "dialectic" of "spirit and matter," "form and force," art and common fact in various writers. Each of the analyses, as is typical with Trilling, becomes an opportunity to address contemporary quarrels in criticism and culture, here the fate of individuality, politics, and literature in the post-World War II era of middle-class normality. The only Americans included are Henry James and William Dean Howells. The quite extraordinary essay on Howells and his style is pervasively Hegelian in its terms and argument. Trilling characterizes Howells's bourgeois mind as an "unhappy consciousness," and he seeks to redeem Howells for our interest by seeing the dialectic between "the conditioned" and "life as pure spirit" in his work. The distinction between act and quality Trilling finds in Hegel is here utilized to restore respect for the "way of life, of quality of being" represented by Howells. The mundane world of Howells should not be judged aesthetically but rather celebrated as "social witness" and "loving wonder at the fact that persons of the most mediocre sort somehow manage to make a society."

Trilling counters this democratic humanism to the "revolutionary" Marxists who condescend to Howells's "genteel" critique of capitalism; Trilling sympathetically situates Howells's allegiance to the ordinary within a tradition stretching back to Wordsworth, whose gentility and orthodoxy are rehabilitated by a similar argument elsewhere in the volume. Howells's place in the American canon, moreover, is ensured by the assertion that a Hegelian dialectic is peculiar to the nation's history: "From one point of view, no people has ever had so intense an idea of the relationship of spirit to its material circumstances as we in America now have. . . . Yet it is to be seen that those conditions to which we do respond are the ones which we ourselves make, or over which we have control, which is to say conditions as they are virtually spirit, as they deny the idea of *the conditioned*. Somewhere in our mental constitution is the demand for life as pure spirit" (OP 79). This demand, says Trilling, informs the views of those Americans who find hope in the dream of a Communist society in which the conditioning determinations of materiality wither away with the ascendency of the people's spirit. Howells's

insistence on mundane matters offers a corrective, for it reminds us
that "much in our dull daily lives really does make a significant part of
man's tragic career on earth." In contrast,

> when we yield to our contemporary impulse to enlarge all experience, to
> involve it as soon as possible in history, myth, and the oneness of spirit—
> an impulse with which, I ought to say, I have considerable sympathy—we
> are in danger of making experience merely typical, formal, and *representa-*
> *tive,* and thus of losing one term of the dialectic that goes on between spirit
> and the conditioned, which is, I suppose, what we mean when we speak of
> man's tragic fate. We lose, that is to say, the actuality of the conditioned,
> the literality of matter, the peculiar authenticity and authority of the merely
> denotative. (OP 82)

The cunning of Trilling's dialectic may leave the reader a bit confused
at this point. Hegel's terminology led us to expect Howells to emerge
as the embodiment of the oneness of the Bourgeois Mind, which will
find its historical destiny in the conformity of the 1950s. And indeed
he does so appear, though at the cost of his freedom. Trilling turns
away from the typical, the formal, and the representational in an effort
to recover the "authenticity" of material life and of the "merely denota-
tive." This would appear to be a nostalgia for a life outside language
and *its* conditioning powers, for a life beyond culture. Yet Trilling
quickly insists that to lose these material facts is to lose the facts of spirit,
for the conditioning forces of actuality are none other than the cultural
forms made by men themselves in the practice of their ideas. What one
recovers through Howells, then, as through Arnold or Wordsworth, is
not a natural material world outside language or beyond culture; rather
it is an argument for the value of the cultural tradition inhering in the
mundane quality of life lived by the middle class. Trilling's unease
with the formal radicalism of modern literature coincides here with his
distrust of modernism's attack on the spirit of the middle class. Where
the opposing self had once found authenticity in expressing its alienation from the bourgeoisie, it now finds it in adopting an adversary
relation to the culture of modernism and the politics of the Left.

The cultural and political turmoil of the 1960s severely tested Trilling
as he struggled to understand the alienation of the New Left and the
attack on humanism coming from European critical theory, which was
using Hegel in ways Trilling had not anticipated. The result was *Sincerity*
and Authenticity (1972), a speculative discussion of the dialectic informing
the development of the modern self since the Renaissance. Like Trilling's previous volume, it traced the conflict between the socialized personality and the autonomous individual, though now with references

to Raymond Williams, Claude Lévi-Strauss, Lucien Goldmann, Walter Benjamin, Nathalie Sarraute, Michel Foucault, and Jacques Lacan, when few established American literary intellectuals had read these thinkers. Although Trilling continues to resist a purely structural approach to selfhood—whether economic, linguistic, or psychoanalytic—fearing that it weights the case too far in the direction of determinism, he nevertheless shows a capacity to balance notions of the will and its artistic forms with a deep understanding of the history and ideological mechanisms that inform them, and his recourse to Marx here is more explicit—and more sympathetic—than it had been since the 1930s. It is Hegel, however, who again provides Trilling with the fundamental terms of his argument and who is the subject of the key chapter "The Honest Soul and the Disintegrated Consciousness." Hegel's world-historical dialectic will enable Trilling to universalize the American quest for freedom and selfhood, and so to negate American literature and modernism in a dialectic that would contain and surpass them.

In the manner of Williams and Foucault, Trilling undertakes an archaeology of "sincerity" and "authenticity" as terms of moral consciousness and forms of textual representation, beginning with Polonius's "To thine own self be true" and ending with R. D. Laing's advocacy of madness as an authentic rejoinder to the insanity of the reigning culture. Sincerity may be defined as "the avoidance of being false to any man through being true to one's own self." Sincerity is social, moral and theatrical. This theatricality dooms it to its modern devaluation, since we are quick to see the incongruence between feeling and avowal. Iago's "honesty" is the foil to Polonius's sincerity, itself enmeshed in a dubious and self-serving rhetoric. For Trilling, the breakdown of any cultural consensus of moral values makes sincerity almost impossible, for there is no faith in the public creed to which the self subscribes: "Which is not to say that the moral temper of our time sets no store by the avoidance of falsehood to others, only that it does not figure as the defining purpose of being true to one's own self." The gap between the self and its representations can no longer be closed by protestations of sincerity: "In short, we play the role of being ourselves, we sincerely act the part of the sincere person, with the result that a judgment may be passed upon our sincerity that it is not authentic." The cult of authenticity, which informs the sublime, romanticism, and much of the modernist avant-garde, arises as a reaction against the consciousness of "dissimulation," which is often associated with the artifices of culture. "Society" appears, argues Trilling, when culture becomes the primary audience for the self's definition, displacing God and the monarchy. Citing the invention of mirrors by the Venetians as well as Lacan's thesis on the "mirror stage," Trilling sees that the "individual" comes into being as the subject of representation. The example is Rousseau, but the lesson is for all modernity: "His conception of his private and uniquely interesting individuality, together with his impulse to reveal his self, to demonstrate that in it which is to be admired and trusted, are, we may believe, his response to the newly available sense of an audience, of that public which society created."[28]

In his chapter on Hegel, Trilling returns to the remarks on Diderot's *Rameau's Nephew* that appear in the section of the *Phenomenology* on the "self-estranged" (or self-alienated) spirit in culture. Hegel here tracks the dialectic in its historical guise, as the forms that self-consciousness passes through in its relation to culture as state power, culture as wealth, and culture as language. Both state power and wealth are the products of alienation, whereas language is simultaneously the enactment and transcendence of self-estrangement. The feudal monarch receives the estranged selfhood of his vassals in the form of obedience, so that ultimately he can say "L'Etat c'est moi." The wealth received by the nobility in turn represents their alienated essence, only now in the form of a thing. The nobility of service passes dialectically into base cynicism and the language of flattery, and wealth passes from the representation of noble being into the representation of the self's estranged essence. The witty and satirical talk that pervades this culture expresses its alienation in the form of wit—of a negativity that cynically gives voice to the hollowness of the culture and its dependence on power, servitude, and hypocrisy. Diderot's dialogue of the *philosophe* with Rameau's mimic Nephew captures, for Hegel, the dialectic overturning the eighteenth-century culture and portends its revolutionary transcendence.[29]

Language in the form of speech, Hegel insists in the *Phenomenology*, has an essential role throughout these dialectical reversals. In speech self-consciousness comes into existence as "something for others" (as

28. Lionel Trilling, *Sincerity and Authenticity* (Cambridge: Harvard University Press, 1972), pp. 9, 11, 25. Subsequent references are cited parenthetically as SA.

29. In his commentary on this section of the *Phenomenology*, Jean Hippolyte (seeing partly through Marx's eyes) stresses Hegel's allusions to the stages of French aristocracy and its lacerated end in the Revolution, a background reinforced by the citations of Diderot. Revolution is the inevitable result of this torn consciousness; like Rameau's Nephew, the spirit in revolt speaks the language of demystification, at once disintegrating the pretensions of the cultural world and, in its own self-condemnation, achieving a transcendence (or *Aufhebung*) of its alienation by returning to itself in the language of laceration. It knows itself as alienation and thus returns to itself, preparing the way for a new set of dialectical phases (of faith and intellect) as self-consciousness pursues a world of absolute freedom beyond *this* world of culture and alienation. See Jean Hippolyte, *Genesis and Structure of Hegel's "Phenomenology of Spirit"*, trans. Samuel Cherniak and John Heckman (Evanston: Northwestern University Press, 1974).

Daniel O'Hara uses the theories of Harold Bloom in tracing what he calls the "outrageous misreading" of Diderot and Hegel performed by the anxious and defensive Trilling; see O'Hara, *Lionel Trilling*, 247–74.

state power and wealth had been the representation of self for others). But whereas in "every other mode of expression" the self "is absorbed in some concrete actuality," in speech it attains transcendence through a grammatical *Aufhebung* that cancels and preserves its existence:

> Language . . . alone expresses the 'I,' the 'I' itself. This *real* existence of the 'I' is, *qua* real existence, an objectivity which has in it the true nature of the 'I.' The 'I' is this particular 'I'—but equally the *universal* 'I'; its manifesting is also at once the externalization and vanishing of *this* particular 'I', and as a result the 'I' remains in its universality. The 'I' that utters itself is '*heard*' or '*perceived*'; it is an infection in which it has immediately passed into unity with those for whom it has a real existence, and is a universal self-consciousness. (308–9)

The content of the "I," however, may be negative, as in the "witty talk" of those like the Nephew who give voice to this alienated "I." But "only as self-consciousness in revolt is it aware of its own disrupted state, and in thus knowing it has immediately risen above it." All moral and cultural content is negated: "The positive object is merely the *pure 'I' itself*, and the disrupted consciousness *in itself* this pure self-identity of self-consciousness that has returned to itself" (321). This dialectic will yield either the Left Hegelianism of Marx and Lukács, in which the masses are identified as the "I" of history, or the right Hegelianism of much of modernism, in which the alienated "I" engages in a ceaseless revolt against culture. Jean Hippolyte comments that the "decent soul of the philosopher cannot adapt itself to such a perpetual reversal of values. Indeed, Hegel too often tries to evade the consequences and the logic of his own dialectic" (413). For Trilling the "I" 's entanglement in language and representation promises no accession to absolute freedom but only a further determination and disintegration of the will. Rather than being taken as the proper target of negation, culture for Trilling becomes the possibility of a sincere or authentic "I," though this once more, dialectically, costs the "I" its freedom.

According to Trilling, Diderot presents us with an honest and sincere *Moi* who confronts in the Nephew an alienated figure whose "social being" is "a mere histrionic representation." "Mimetic skill" is the "essence of his being" as he apes all the social roles: "There you have my pantomime; it's about the same as the flatterer's, the courtier's, the footman's, and the beggar's." The modernity of the Nephew, however, lies in the truth of his pantomime as it exhibits the inauthenticity at the heart of the theater which is society. He becomes an image of the antihero and of the self Trilling elsewhere celebrates: "he figures not only as an actual person but also as an aspect of humanity itself, as the

liberty that we wish to believe is inherent in the human spirit, in its
energy of effort and its limitless contradictions." This leads immediately
to the Hegelian Spirit whose power of negation is the dark but authentic
experience producing cultural criticism and self-knowledge. While we
harbor our nostalgia for "the archaic noble vision of life" embodied by
Diderot's *Moi* or Austen's "idyllic" England, no such life without negation is open to us. Instead there is only "culture," Hegel's (and Arnold's)
Bildung, an "exigent spiritual enterprise" in which self-negation and
social transformation are caught up in interminable dialectics. Art itself,
which requires representation and thus the confining dictates of a social
audience, corrupts the self with its theatrical seductions. "Literature is
an accomplice in the social betrayal," and thus the move within art to
defy the bourgeois audience, after Nietzsche, with a Dionysian assault
upon its very conventions. "The astonishing performance" of the pantomime, quoted with such delight by Hegel, "proposes the idea which
Nietzsche was to articulate a century later, that man's true metaphysical
destiny expresses itself not in morality but in art." As if drawing back
from the postmodern implications of his argument, Trilling turns again
to Austen's *Mansfield Park,* where the condemnation of "amateur theatri-
cals" recalls us to the dream of a life of sincerity beyond representation
(SA 31–33).

Trilling's hostility to Hegel's reading of *Rameau's Nephew* turns on his
assertion that Hegel sides completely with the revolt of the Nephew and
loses sight of the value of the nobility of Diderot's *Moi.* Explicating the
stages of the dialectic of alienation in Hegel's chapter, Trilling describes
how the noble passes from obedience and identification with the state
into the language of flattery, baseness, and an assertion of freedom:

> Between the intentions of the base self and its avowals there is no congru-
> ence. But the base self, exactly because it is not under the control of the
> noble ethos, has won at least a degree of autonomy and has thereby fulfilled
> the nature of Spirit. In refusing its obedient service to the state power and
> to wealth it has lost its wholeness; its selfhood is 'disintegrated'; the self is
> 'alienated' from itself. But because it has detached itself from imposed
> conditions, Hegel says that it has made a step in progress. . . . The 'honesty'
> of Diderot/*Moi,* which evokes Hegel's impatient scorn, consists in his whole-
> ness of self, in the directness and consistency of his relation to things, and
> in his submission to a traditional morality. Diderot/*Moi* does not exemplify
> the urge of Spirit to escape from the conditions which circumscribe it and
> to enter into an existence which will be determined by itself alone. (SA 38–
> 39)

Trilling's Diderot/*Moi* sounds suspiciously like his William Dean Howells. The interpretation he offers of *Rameau's Nephew* and his response

to Hegel's commentary on it are shaped, I believe, to suit Trilling's critique of the cultural dialectic between tradition and revolution in his own era. He criticizes what he sees as Hegel's permissive support for the rebellious Nephew because it seems to authorize an attitude that will eventuate in the countercultural radicals of the 1960s who lacerated the self-consciousness of Columbia University. Trilling disparagingly quotes Hegel's conclusion to the chapter, in which "self-consciousness in revolt" leads to the dialectical return of self-identity. He remains unpersuaded by Hegel's argument that the Nephew's parodic panto-mime leads to an authentic new stage of consciousness. The Nephew stands for writing or representation gone mad, beside itself, endlessly negating and subverting the identities propagated by the norms of his culture. Trilling's preference for Diderot/*Moi* suggests a desire to con-trol the labor of the negative: both language and cultural self-conscious-ness in Hegel threaten to unleash a history of differentiation that will not submit to any "traditional morality." In contrast, the figures of Austen, Wordsworth, and Arnold preside over the conviction in Trilling (and in T. S. Eliot) that the antidote of tradition should be prescribed for the modernist disease of excessive self-consciousness.

Sincerity and Authenticity brings the story of Hegel and American liter-ary historiography full circle. The dialectical schema that had begun in Hegel as a world-historical phenomenon became nationalized in the context of American critical writing, adapted and made specific to the destiny of the nation. Trilling's return to Hegel projects American dialectics back onto the scene of the history of the Self in the West, as one can see in those few passages that touch upon American writers. A later chapter discusses Emerson's *English Traits* and repeats the cliché that "the American self can be taken to be a microcosm of American society, which has notably lacked the solidity and intractability of English society." The dialectic of material determinism and spiritual freedom, or of writing and the self, passes through the dialectic of "Tradition and the Individual Talent" to become a national opposition: "The Hegelian terms which I touched on earlier bear upon the difference between the two nations [England and America]. Americans, we might say—D. H. Lawrence did in effect say it fifty years ago—had moved into that historical stage of Spirit which produces the 'disintegrated' or 'alienated' consciousness." Emerson's warm response to English traits "must" be ascribed to "the archaic intractability of the English social organization: the English sincerity depends upon the English class structure" (SA 113–14). Back in America one would only find Melville writing *The Confidence Man* or Huck and Jim fighting to retain their sincerity in the face of the King and the Duke and all the masquerades of society. (Trilling later mentions Melville's "Bartleby the Scrivener" as evidencing

the total inauthenticity of the social world.) Trilling's reference to Lawrence clearly indicates that this account falls within the mainstream of
American literary histories that have taken up Hegelian dialectics as
their themes.

But Trilling cannot long remain content with sincerity. The power
of the negative remains a function inherent in cultural history per se,
so that any recourse to a tradition will entail some dialectic with anarchy
and the indeterminate "differentiations of the Notion." When he takes
up Marx's rewriting of Hegel's notion of "alienation," specifically in
Marx's 1844 manuscripts, Trilling likes the humanism of *this* Marx and
the pathos with which he expresses man's loss of his authenticity. What
Trilling doesn't like is the economic determinism that stipulates that
"Money, in short, is the principle of the inauthentic in human existence"
(SA 124). In light of this observation, Marx is being truer to Diderot
and Hegel than is Trilling since the dialectic of wealth and self-consciousness is an essential ingredient in *Rameau's Nephew*. (As Trilling
knows, Marx sent Engels a copy of Diderot's book with an enthusiastic
note.) For Trilling, inauthenticity is rather the essential condition of
social existence; in society the self exists and has freedom only by virtue
of the pantomime of representation, the agreement to participate in
the spectacle of a tradition's script. The worlds of Diderot, Austen, and
Arnold give birth to the alienated practices of Stendhal, Joyce, and
Conrad. Hegel and American literary history bequeathed to Trilling
the search for an authenticity that would not be conditioned by the
social, and in his final chapter on Freud he imagines he has found it,
though the tale is every bit as tragic as Ahab's or Huck's or Gatsby's.

"The Authentic Unconscious" offers a version of Freud as a resolving
figure of the dialectics haunting Trilling. He notes the decline of narrative in contemporary literature and ties it to the death of the past for
the modern deracinated self: "It bears upon the extreme attenuation
of the authority of literary culture, upon the growing indifference to
its traditional pedagogy; the hero, the exemplary figure, does not exist
without a sharp and positive beginning; the hero is his history from his
significant birth to his significant death." Trilling's "hero" is the self,
whose birth and death his volume traces. The word "hero" rings hollow
in the late 1960s, since it requires either a shared communal goal or a
radical belief in the power of the individual. As structuralist terminology
suggests, the heroic self will be replaced by the "subject," an entity who
always functions within and is defined by a system from which there is
no "beyond." Trilling recognizes this lesson in his defense of Freud
against Sartre, when he points out that the theory of the superego,
especially as its implications are spelled out in *Civilization and Its Discontents,* lodges the culture within the self, and vice versa, so that the self

is always doomed to perform for a symbolic Father or social audience that has been internally incorporated: "The virtually resistless power of this principle of inauthenticity is the informing idea of Freud's mature social theory." Freud's book "may be thought to stand like a lion in the path of all hopes of achieving happiness through the radical revision of social life" (SA 150–51).

The argument now takes some surprising turns as Trilling seeks to capture for Freud the mantle of authenticity. Unlike a rational conscience, the superego institutes a "largely gratuitous" and harsh sense of guilt, felt not for a deed done but for the repressed wish of "aggression against a sacrosanct person, originally the father" (SA 152). While the superego makes civilization possible, the price is "deplorable irrationality and cruelty." Moreover, "although it was to serve the needs of civilization that the superego was installed in its disciplinary office, its actual behaviour was not dictated by those needs; the movement of the superego from rational pragmatic authority to gratuitous cruel tyranny was wholly autonomous" (SA 154). Thus the superego achieves that autonomy the self dreamed of, an authenticity which as "a given of biology" becomes a force not susceptible to social reform or corruption. The superego is beyond culture. Freud has postulated a "flagrant inauthenticity" within the self: "Man's existence in civilization is represented as being decisively conditioned by a psychic entity which, under the mask of a concern with social peace and union, carries on a ceaseless aggression to no purpose save that of the enhancement of its own power" (SA 154). Power, not spirit, appears as the teleology of self-consciousness. Ironically, this irrational Fate becomes the origin of man's authentic will, the necessity or Ananke that inspires his oppositional being in a world where cosmic and theological absolutes have expired: "Freud, in insisting upon the essential immitigability of the human condition as determined by the nature of the mind had the intention of sustaining the authenticity of human existence that formerly had been ratified by God" (SA 156). What Trilling once called the "tragic" appears here as the irreconcilable dialectic of will and negation, something that goes on within the self and within society, not simply in the adversarial relation between them. The separation of the superego from its function as representative of society removes the conflict from history, makes it mythic and universal, and so restores a vision of primal essences liberated from the pantomimes to which human existence seems otherwise doomed.

In American literary histories since the 1970s, the speculative terms and narratives dominating works from Brooks and Parrington through Trilling are now subject to critique, either by poststructuralists who elaborate deconstructions of Hegelian thematics or by feminists, African-Americanists, and new historicists who reject the totalizing cultural and political psychology of the previous models. It would take another essay entirely to analyze these developments in light of current rereadings of Hegel. Suffice to say here, by way of prospect, that the current antimony between the literary and the historical in much critical writing has its correspondence to the opposition of writing and being in Hegel. Poststructuralist readings of Hegel call us back to remember the work of representation in his text, and so to defer the transcendence or *Aufhebung* his dialectics recurrently posit. Derrida's notion of *différance*, and his other inconceivable "concepts" maneuver to displace dialectics with a power of the negative that no *Aufhebung* can account for. This reactivates and reinscribes the terms of dialectical opposition in ways that recover their "history," though history now thought beyond the categorical opposition of representation and reality. Much of the current return to history in American criticism has failed to attend to the relevance of this lesson, offering versions of the historical which are quite conventional in their assumptions of what the historical *is* or how and where it might take place. Trilling's *agon* with Hegel anguishes over the death of the subject of literary history, in every sense of the phrase. Efforts to move past the antinomies of his criticism, and of the tradition he belonged to, require a thinking of the dialectic of the literary and the historical that does not subordinate itself to either a deterministic narrative of the subject's subordination to Power or an idealistic tale of the achievement of an Absolute Freedom for Consciousness. It can only be historical, and political, if it remembers that history is a way of being that cannot simply be referred to. Our responsibility is rather to rewrite it, though it cost us our "I" 's in the process.

CHAPTER NINE

The Subject of Pedagogy: Lessons in Psychoanalysis and Politics

> Has that which our praxis engenders the right to map out for itself necessities, even contradictory ones, from the standpoint of truth? This question may be transposed in the esoteric formula: *how can we be sure that we are not imposters?*
> — Jacques Lacan, *The Four Fundamental Concepts of Psycho-Analysis*

> *Once again: Who is we?*
> — Adrienne Rich, "Notes towards a Politics of Location"

In previous chapters I have been analyzing the function of the subject as an organizing notion in theories of literature, psychology, politics, history, and culture. In formulating or disciplining these discourses, the metaphor of the subject has been an active agent in delimiting their scope, their inclusions and exclusions, their conceptual frameworks and institutional destinies. I have tried to work through the subject, in various of its (dis)guises, rather than accede either to exaggerated accounts of its disappearance or to hortatory claims for its imperative ascendency. With Habermas I would agree that none of the attempts to think the other of reason have escaped the theoretical framework of the subject, but against him I would also argue that an escape into "communicative rationality" would only repeat the misprisions and exclusions of previous discourses on the subject.

The decentering of the subject will not be accomplished, once and for all, by philosophical argument or textual practice only, though these have their necessity and value. An analysis of the politics of the subject as it has represented itself demonstrates that its power and its hegemony owe much to its abstraction from the historical specificity of its site of production, that is, its masking of how the subject of Western humanism has been modeled on the historical class of Euro-American heterosexual males of the middle and upper classes. Even the proletarian subject of history, in the work of Marx and Lukács, does not escape this formative bias. In the future, the problem of the subject will be thought through a more rigorous attention to the multiple determinants that position historical agents, and through a dialogue with the other that resists the condescending obscurantism of "identification" as well as the exploitative colonialism of appropriative "understanding."[1] A progressive cultural politics of the subject will have to abandon the desire lived out tragically by Lionel Trilling in his attempts to assimilate himself to the Arnoldian subject who stood at the center of the Western tradition. That is not a position to which students or teachers should continue to aspire, and indeed we should be dedicated to examining historically the past consequences of how that subject position has been occupied. The institutional emblem of Trilling's desire was the Great Books course he continued to teach at Columbia, and which represented the Subject Who (or Which) One is Supposed to Know. The revolution now under way against the hegemony of the Eurocentric canon, then, belongs also to the critique of the subject advanced by literary and critical theorists who otherwise may not recognize their alliance with feminist, African-American, or postcolonial activists. Nonetheless the dislocation of the subject is now an important event in curriculum and teaching, as it has been in theory, and so it is fitting to conclude this book with some reflections on the subject of pedagogy.

Many who try to make sense of Lacan's published seminars conclude that these pedagogical performances are indeed the work of an imposter, some Wizard of Id feigning knowledge behind an array of obscure musings and baffling flights of fancy. This author, we suspect, doesn't *know* what he's talking about. It would be ludicrous, it seems, to suggest that Lacan's work could be of any use in devising a philosophy or praxis of teaching, presuming that pedagogy requires, first of all, an instructor certain of his subject. This requirement evidences what Lacan calls the demand for the "subject who is supposed to know" (*sujet supposé savoir*), a demand every teacher has felt in the classroom (a space, in fact, constituted by this demand). It is the most exacting and intractable imposition that teaching and its institutions put upon an instructor, and the one which must be analyzed and resisted if education is to be something more than socialization or consumption. This demand is the essence of the "transference" that structures the classroom experience,

1. For a suggestive account of such a dialogical relation to the other, see Tzvetan Todorov, *Mikhail Bakhtin: The Dialogical Principle*, trans. Wlad Godzich (Minneapolis: University of Minnesota Press, 1984), pp. 94–112.

in which the teacher is called to assume the authorized position of the subject who is supposed to know.

In her account of the pedagogical implications of recent work in psychoanalysis and feminism, Constance Penley observes that "the student, like the child with the parent, is almost *clairvoyant* when it comes to understanding the desire of the Other and how best narcissistically to mirror what the Other desires."[2] Since the structure of the pedagogical performance is its own primary lesson, more readily and more permanently learned than any subject matter, this transference effectively stymies critical thinking by inculcating a relationship of identification instead of analysis. The deluded teacher identifies with the imago of mastery, whereas the student identifies with the imago of lack. The transference fixes the positions of knowledge rather than questioning their assumptions or displacing their privileges. Lacan's disruptions of the position, or subject, of knowledge graphically foreground and deflect the effects of the transference. "This pedagogical approach," explains Shoshana Felman, "which makes no claim to total knowledge, is, of course, quite different from the usual pedagogical pose of mastery, different from the image of the self-sufficient, self-possessed proprietor of knowledge, in which pedagogy has traditionally featured the authoritative figure of the teacher."[3] Teachers *are* imposters, though no more so than their students, and education ought to disclose the structures and articulate the consequences of the postures we have assumed or imposed. "Who does not know," asks Lacan, "that one may not wish to think?—the entire universal college of professors is there as evidence."[4] Lacan moves disciplinary self-reflexivity into the theater of the absurd; his performance pieces are a kind of Brechtian pedagogy that alienates the audience of education.[5]

One thing our traditional pedagogy has not wished to think—under the influence of a historically Eurocentric, abstract, and metaphysical "humanism"—is how our material locations as bodies function in the

2. Constance Penley, "Teaching in Your Sleep: Feminism and Psychoanalysis," in *Theory in the Classroom*, ed. Cary Nelson (Urbana: University of Illinois Press, 1986), p. 133.

3. Shoshana Felman, "Psychoanalysis and Education: Teaching Terminable and Interminable," *Yale French Studies* 63 (1982): 34–35.

4. Jacques Lacan, *The Four Fundamental Concepts of Psycho-Analysis*, ed. Jacques-Alain Miller, trans. Alan Sheridan (New York: Norton, 1977), p. 234.

5. For a suggestive account of the aesthico-political problem of the audience, from Brechtian estrangement to postmodern performance art, see Herbert Blau, "Receding into Illusion: Alienation, the Audience, Technique, Anatomy," *New German Critique* 47 (Spring/Summer 1989): 93–117. This forms part of Blau's *The Audience* (Baltimore: Johns Hopkins University Press, 1990), which also treats Lacan at some length (see especially chaps. 2 and 3).

production, reception, and interpretation of cultural works. These would include situations of geography, nationality, race, class, gender, sexual orientation, social caste, and those other multitiple determinants that constitute what Adrienne Rich calls the "politics of location," a politics long dominated by the white male subject.[6] Has *this* subject been displaced by Lacanian psychoanalysis, which theorizes positionality through an algebra of familial and semiotic terms abstracted from any historical specificity? Lacan's dislocutions of the master's voice ventriloquize an other who is colorless, sexless, indeterminate, and so hardly more than a specular negation of a self always in place. Felman is right to argue that "Teaching, like analysis, has to deal not so much with *lack* of knowledge as with *resistances* to knowledge" (30), but she fails to explain what motivates and informs such resistances. There is a politics to the location of the reader's resistances which must be taken into account. This chapter thus first surveys how psychoanalytic theories of the subject's position have been brought to bear on the pedagogical scene and then turns to the interpretive politics entailed by Faulkner's "A Rose for Emily," which despite its popularity as a reading lesson may still have something to teach us about how "we" decipher the social text.

Dis-Locutions of Mastery

In *Reading Lacan,* Jane Gallop specifies from the start the paradoxical position of the reader who sets out to write, to teach, about Lacan. "I have come to believe," she confesses, "Lacan's text impossible to understand fully, impossible to master."[7] This lack of mastery, however, turns out to be the most illuminating reading lesson taught by Lacan, since it calls into question the "phallic illusions of authority" inherent in traditional readings in which the critic occupies the position of the "subject who is supposed to know." Gallop takes up an/other position in reframing the poststructuralist double bind according to Lacanian and feminist perspectives:

> What does it mean to invoke authority in order to legitimate an attack on authority? This ambiguity, I believe, is what promises the most. To speak without authority is nothing new; the disenfranchised have always so spoken. Simply to refuse authority does not challenge the category distinction between phallic authority and castrated other, between "subject presumed

6. Adrienne Rich, *Blood, Bread, and Poetry: Selected Prose 1979–1985* (New York: Norton, 1986), pp. 210–32.

7. Jane Gallop, *Reading Lacan* (Ithaca: Cornell University Press, 1985), p. 20.

to know" and subject not in command. One can effectively undo authority
only from the position of authority, in a way that exposes the illusions of
that position *without renouncing it,* so as to permeate the position itself with
the connotations of its illusoriness, so as to show that *everyone,* including
the "subject presumed to know," is castrated. (21)

Gallop's awkward position recalls the proviso of Derrida (cited in my
Introduction) that deconstructions always work from the "inside" of
structures "in a certain way" that derails both their operation *and* the
critic's reading of it. For Gallop this means a shift from reading (or
writing) as "interpretation" to analysis as engagement in the "transference": "Interpretation is always the exercise of power, while transference is the structuring of that authority. To analyze transference is to
unmask that structuring, interrupt its efficient operation" (27). The
unmasking of the pedagogue, then, will entail the exposure of his
posts—of the positions enabling his speech, of the truth his place assumes, of the power informing the effectivity of his representations, of
the address that directs our reception of his letters. As Gallop argues,
this unmasking will not, however, be an exhibition that presents the
nudity of knowledge behind the false appearances of disguise; rather
it will initiate an economy or rhythm between truth and illusion, imposition and solicitation, masquerade and its mockery. Yet as some feminists
have argued, Gallop's presumption that "everyone" is subject to castration appears to acquiesce to a male imposition that universalizes an
anxiety that actually belongs only to a minority of the population.

The *Oxford English Dictionary* defines "imposter" as "one who imposes
on others; a deceiver, swindler, cheat; now chiefly, one who assumes a
false character, or passes himself off as some one other than he really
is." After deconstruction, we may be less sure than ever of the difference
between a subject's performance and what "he really is." In the theater
of the classroom, the pedagogue relies constantly on the actor's and
rhetorician's arts. A teacher produces the effect of authority through a
repertoire of gestures, attitudes, postures, promises, excuses, inflections, allusions, and tones. These are not "false," as opposed to "true,"
representations, and they do communicate valued information. But one
recognizes that in pedagogy, as in literature, meaning consists as much
in the *how* of the medium as in the *what* of the message. The pedagogical
"medium" embodies a kind of split: the teacher's authority—like that
of the priest—comes from the position itself and tends to operate regardless of what a particular self lacks in the way of knowledge. The
imposter, says the *American Heritage Dictionary,* is "a person who deceives
under an assumed identity." As Lacan will help us to see, the identity
or subjective position that the teacher assumes is one undertaken be-

cause of the student's demand, and as part of a larger superstructure of institutional arrangements of power and thought. Both teacher and student are subject to pedagogy, and in tracing this subjection we can detect the political stakes at risk in the scene of instruction.

Gregory Ulmer's chapter on Lacan's "post(e)-pedagogy" argues that "one of the chief lessons of Lacan's discourse for a nonmagisterial pedagogy is its exploitation of linguistic and symbolic devices, addressing the class in the poetic mode of evocation as well as in the scientific mode of assertion."[8] In recalling Lacan's own performances, Catherine Clément writes:

> In form Lacan's teaching was entirely in keeping with the purest traditions of the French university. . . . But we had the exquisite sensation of tasting the forbidden fruit of a rhetoric that attacked our teachers precisely where our teachers bored us, with their classicism, their humanism, and their endless repetition. . . . Sentences flew like arrows toward their prey. After a long arc of periods they would suddenly tear open a bleeding wound. Sometimes they would turn somersaults of esoteric allusion before homing in on their target. Lacan spoke as the hawk flies, circling about an idea before grabbing it in a lightning swoop.[9]

Of course sometimes he missed, boredom spread, or his rendition of the iconoclastic prophet became too Mosaic. While his rhetoric remained subversive, the form and site of the lecture, the *leçon*, retained him in the position of the master, as did the implication of his hermetic speech. The rebellious students of May 1968 challenged Lacan, and in later years devoted followers grew tired of his puns, charts, and topological graphs. Future feminist critics would look askance at his flying arrows and bleeding wounds. Yet there remains an enchantment in this sorcerer who makes our self-delusions and antithetical desires his subject, and who constantly dramatizes the impossibility of his own role, taking Descartes's self-doubt to a radical extreme and often identifying his own speech with that of "hysterical" women.

When Lacan sets out in *The Four Fundamental Concepts of Psycho-Analysis* to systematize his teachings, he posits a central question: "What is the analyst's desire?" (9). As Ulmer notes, this self-reflexiveness suggests the postmodern quality of Lacan's thought, and the way in which Lacan will subvert his own authority, role, and speech acts. The function of the analyst's desire will be crucial to Lacan's rethinking of "transfer-

8. Gregory Ulmer, *Applied Grammatology: Post(e)-Pedagogy from Jacques Derrida to Joseph Beuys* (Baltimore: Johns Hopkins University Press, 1985), p. 213.
9. Catherine Clément, *The Lives and Legends of Jacques Lacan*, trans. Arthur Goldhammer (New York: Columbia University Press, 1983), pp. 12, 14.

ence." The entry on "Transference" by Laplanche and Pontalis emphasizes how the concept developed in Freud's thought, from a general
category for displacements of affect to a specific description of events
occurring between patient and analyst in the therapeutic situation itself.[10] "What are transferences?" asked Freud in his study of Dora:
"They are new editions or facsimiles of the tendencies and phantasies
which are aroused and made conscious during the progress of the
analysis; but they have this peculiarity, which is characteristic for their
species, that they replace some earlier person by the person of the
physician."[11] Quite often, according to Freud, the analyst is cast in the
position of the father; his theory of the Oedipal complex recasts the
"transference neurosis" as he focuses on the unconscious resistances
working through the transference and linked to primal familial and
sexual relationships. But what is the *analyst's* desire, and how does it
affect Freud's reading of Dora? Critics of the Dora case have pointed
out the self-serving quality of Freud's theory.[12] By imposing the transference on Dora, Freud masks "the tendencies and phantasies" of his
own psyche as he struggles with Dora's resistance toward patriarchal
oppression, which concludes with her walking out on Freud's analysis,
leaving him in *hermeneuticus interruptus*. Such readings, ironically, confirm that in writing the patient's case the analyst becomes the analysand
of his own text, and so testifies unwittingly to the dislocation of the
position of the subject who is supposed to know.

When Lacan rereads the Oedipal complex in terms of the Father's
No and Name, he changes the sense of the transference, since now the
relation to the father is seen in terms of the subject's assumption of a
position in respect to the Symbolic order presided over by the discourse
of the Father. It is the *desire* of the Father toward which the subject must
be oriented, and which the subject incorporates through the socialization process of the Oedipal complex and its resultant Symbolic order.
It is Lacan's theory of the Symbolic that attracts critics who would link
its account of positionality to specific empirical categories for individuals
(sexual, racial, economic, etc.) and so make the Symbolic the base of the
social text. While Lacan's notion of desire radically subverts the idea of
the empirical (the Real is always impossible for Lacan), and so thwarts an
easy correspondence between psychoanalytic and sociological positions,

10. Jean Laplanche and J. B. Pontalis, *The Language of Psycho-Analysis*, trans. Donald
Nicholson-Smith (New York: Norton, 1973), pp. 455–62.
11. Sigmund Freud, *Fragment of an Analysis of a Case of Hysteria* (1905) in *The Standard
Edition of the Complete Psychological Works of Sigmund Freud*, ed. James Strachey, 24 vols.
(London: Hogarth Press, 1953–74): 7:116.
12. See Charles Bernheimer and Claire Kahane, eds., *In Dora's Case: Freud—Hysteria—
Feminism* (New York: Columbia University Press, 1985).

his reading of the Symbolic remains suggestive for an archaeology of those historic places to which we find ourselves assigned.

In the transference, then, it is not that the patient "loves" or "hates" the analyst, but that the patient defends herself (and the analyst) by desiring and offering what the Other (the analyst) desires (unless, as in Dora's case, she literally abandons the scene). In the case of Anna O.— "let us drop this story of O. and call her by her real name, Bertha Pappenheim" (157)—Lacan reads her "nervous pregnancy" *not* as a symptom of her own desire but as a *sign* of the analyst's, Josef Breuer's, own anxiety:

> [W]hy is it that we do not consider Bertha's pregnancy rather, according to my formula *man's desire is the desire of the Other,* as the manifestation of Breuer's desire? Why do you not go as far as to think that it was Breuer who had a desire for a child? I will give you the beginning of a proof; namely that Breuer, setting off for Italy with his wife, lost no time in giving her a child. . . . But let us observe what Freud says to Breuer—*What! The transference is the spontaneity of the said Bertha's unconscious. It's not yours, not your desire, it's the desire of the Other.* I think Freud treats Breuer as a hysteric here, since he says to him: *Your desire is the desire of the Other.* (157–58)

We can say of Freud what Clément says of Lacan: "He didn't know how truly he spoke" (51). For Freud's words should be addressed to Bertha—and have been transferred here to Breuer, thus, says Lacan, revealing Freud's desire as well: "the whole theory of the transference [before Lacan] is merely a defence of the analyst," whose desire might then be excluded from calculations of the patient/subject's speech or symptoms (158). As a reading lesson, this passage is representative of Lacan's revision of Freud. Lacan deciphers a self-reflexive structure, hinged on the desire of the analyst, which undoes the manifest level of a case or theory and discloses an/other signifying economy. This is "reader-response" theory with a vengeance and should make every textual analyst a bit more wary when the symptoms of the work appear to be pregnant with an intrinsic meaning. For Lacan, the primal scene of psychoanalysis is still the analysis of the transference, but now this demands a reading not just of the patient/subject's unconscious, but of its involvement in the unconscious of the analyst as well, and a study of the situation that determines the utterances of both parties. The analyst becomes not only a reader of another subject but also a subject to be read, though not simply in his or her own acts or words; the analyst also is split, and the figures of the analyst's desire appear symbolically in the unconscious of the patient who positions herself through an interpretation of the analyst's desire. Hence the "authorship" of selves and utterances in such a scene is thoroughly intersubjective; the author-ity of the analyst ceases to be merely personal since it assumes a position within that Symbolic discourse which is inseparable from the authorized text of sociocultural formations. The primal scene of the transference actively repeats the primal scene of the subject's constitution through the family's primal scenes, and these, in turn, are inevitably a part of a society's way of reproducing the proper positions of desire, gender, authority, and speech.

Instructional Positions

How, then, should we analyze the pedagogical primal scene? While it is tempting, especially for those of us who are teachers, to see the pedagogue as master analyst and the student as confused analysand, this rigid and hierarchical characterization belies the mobility of instructive positions (and as the Dora case suggests, repeats the gendered connota-tions of the student/teacher hierarchy). "Teacher" and "student," like "analyst" and "analysand," should be thought of as metaphors of the dis-positions of power and knowledge rather than as fixed empirical categories. The problem with ideological and institutional practice is that it represents the "subject who is supposed to know" as only a *person*, as the unity of a body and a position, rather than as a floating function of discursive scenes. The deconstruction of such identifications of sub-jectivity, however, should not blind us to the fact that the Symbolic cannot function without its agents, who may be located in very histori-cally specific bodies.

In "Writers, Intellectuals, Teachers," one of the first Lacanian medita-tions on pedagogy, Roland Barthes questions our traditional notions of the performative positions of pedaogy's *mise-en-scène:* "How can the teacher be assimilated to the psychoanalyst? It is exactly the contrary which is the case: the teacher is the person analyzed."[13] Barthes makes the correspondence between teacher and patient by picturing the lec-turer as someone whose speech before an audience inevitably betrays itself:

> Imagine that I am a teacher: I speak, endlessly, in front of and for someone who remains silent. I am the person who says *I* (the detours of *one, we,* or impersonal sentence make no difference), I am the person who, under cover of *setting out* a body of knowledge, *puts out* a discourse, *never knowing*

13. Roland Barthes, "Writers, Intellectuals, Teachers," in *A Barthes Reader*, ed. Susan Sontag (New York: Hill and Wang, 1983), p. 382.

how that discourse is being received and thus forever forbidden the reassurance of a definitive image—even if offensive—which would *constitute me.* In the *exposé,* more aptly named than we tend to think, it is not knowledge which is exposed, it is the subject (who exposes himself to all sorts of painful adventures). (382)

Yet that "exposé" and "adventure" of the teacher's discourse remain subject to the transference—in all its psychological, institutional, and political senses—which constrains the drift of speech in order to produce the truth of a discipline. The pedagogue, in fact, must labor in his dis-position to incite the shift whereby the student assumes the place of the analyst. Barthes acknowledges this modernist double bind of his pedagogy in advocating a "writerly" classroom speech that borrows its principles of defamiliarization from the performances of Brecht. On the one hand (and in line with Lacan), Barthes can observe that "when the teacher speaks to his audience, the Other is always there, *puncturing* his discourse" (383). On the other hand (and also *à la* Lacan), he also affirms the necessity of the speaker's self-wounding, of the production of a lack in speech through a self-resistant style. Pedagogical discourse (spoken or written) must not attempt to communicate clearly since that would be a traffic in stereotypes. The teacher ought to be *paradoxical,* to undertake a critique that would call its subject into crisis, and to utter "a language *which is not forgetful of itself*" (389).

Barthes seems to underestimate how this very performance, however, like Lacan's own, may only reinforce the student's sense of the teacher's mastery. The transferential character of the pedagogical scene dictates that we "work through" (to use Freud's language) the teacher-student relation rather than imagine we can utterly suspend it. The historically, politically, and institutionally given positions of pedagogical practice do effectively put the teacher in the analyst's position of knowledge/power and the student in the patient's position of lack, despite the theoretical and practical problems with this correspondence. (This seems particularly true during "discussion" periods, office hours, and when papers are graded.) The stress on a revolution in language would appear to repeat the modernist confusion of linguistic with political upheaval, and to invite the same kind of split between "high" and "mass" culture that so debilitated modernism.

Of course the student, unlike the patient, may not initially enroll in a course or come to a teacher to resolve a personal crisis, though such a need may enter into the pedagogical relation rather quickly. Conventional pedagogy is objective rather than intersubjective. The student comes to acquire knowledge, both of what things are and of how they are to be known. Objectives and information are communicated between independent persons engaged in a profitable economic exchange. The contracted psychoanalyst, in contrast, intends to teach the patient speculatively and subjectively. The analyst seeks above all to disclose the work of the patient's unconscious, and so to change the patient's reading of herself and to alter her relation to the production of her symptoms, utterances, and behaviors. The teacher, however, would not normally be thought of as offering students an educational disclosure of their unconscious thought processes or an exposé of the pedagogue's own lack of mastery.

Yet I want to argue that the systematic bringing to discourse of unconscious thoughts, and of resistances to thought, is the primary task of teaching, recognizing (with Barthes) that this task must be turned back upon the pedagogue's unconscious as well. Our difficulties in teaching ourselves or our students to think consciously often stem from a failure to engage and verbalize the unconscious conceptual grammars of which we, and our students, are the subjects. These grammars, in turn, compose the structures of life we inhabit, our historical positions, so that self-critical discourse means a soliciting and mapping of the locations from which we speak and the effect those locations have on what we can articulate. Psychoanalysis teaches that ignorance "is not a passive state of absence—a simple lack of information: it is an active dynamic of negation, an active refusal of information" (Felman 29–30). That refusal, as Rich argues, comes not out of some abstract need for identity but from the politics of identity incumbent upon subjects by the place they inhabit materially as well as psychically.

There is a "pedagogical unconscious," then, informing the educational performance, and what we resist knowing is intricately tied to our constitution and location as social subjects. It is this structure of resistance that the student already "knows" yet still needs to "learn": the teacher, like the analyst, doesn't know the content of this unconscious but serves as an occasion for its articulation. (Here and below, I shall use "teacher" and "student" both to indicate empirical categories *and* to mark discursive positions within the pedagogical scene that any given individual might at some moment occupy regardless of his or her institutional status.) Freud found that, in analysis, simply *telling* a patient about the facts of his or her case did no good; unless the network of resistances and defenses is broken, such information falls on deaf ears. Most students and teachers relive this lesson daily in the classroom. Whether by teacher or student, the full speaking of the truth of a position seems to have no effect, other than to reconfirm the positions of the auditors. As long as the student continues to occupy the same position in relation to the information involved—a position in which the student "knows" by virtue of identification with the position of the teacher as the subject who knows—then there is no knowing in any productive sense.

The teacher, like the analyst, will have to conduct sessions that bring unconscious concepts, defenses, and desires into the realm of discourse, argument, and performance. Students may then discover how what they don't know that they think prevents them from knowing or thinking something else. The puzzling dialectic of blindness and insight that de Man traced in the work of the best critics holds true for the novice as well: the point of view that allows for a perception also prevents another perspective. A classroom exercise in which the specific values of disparate interpretive frameworks are tested does not lead to an ultimately homogeneous total interpretation offering "the" meaning of the work, or to a vacuous relativism in which all meanings are equal. Instead we can teach the "partiality" of knowledge—its incompleteness and its dependency on ethics and values. Such a lesson places the demand for criticism on the interpreter, and it answers the call to responsibility by disclosing the pedagogical unconscious as a structure of investments— an ideological discourse, if you will—which both enables and restricts verbal or written expression.

The presiding humanist position in most classrooms projects a kind of "common vision" as the end of interpretation: what counts at bottom is the universal truth common to all men [sic], and the way to get to that truth is through a transcending of one's own particular interests. This explains in part why the New Criticism was such a popular and successful mode of pedagogy, since it disciplined the reading subject to an impersonal brand of aesthetic and moral commentary that was utterly blind to its own cultural idiosyncracy. A dis-locational pedagogy, on the other hand, begins by asking readers to conceive of the partiality of their positions, to analyze how their historical condition frames their responses. At the outset we ought to remember our differences rather than obscure them under a humanist banner that only serves the cause of a hegemonic minority who have made the Symbolic their own agency.

If pedagogy simply transmits knowledge units, it never questions these unconscious epistemological and political discourses and so never enables the student to think critically. A pedagogy of the unconscious must dislocate fixed desires rather than feed us what we think we want to know. Unfortunately, this means that the teacher's task is to make the student upset or ill (which we often do unknowingly anyway). Where the (American) psychoanalyst seeks to stabilize a shattered self, the pedagogue should hope to unsettle the complacency and conceptual identities of the student. Education becomes subjective in the sense that the student realizes and experiences his or her existence as a being subjected to various discourses, including that of the teacher. The disturbance that ensues includes the split between the self-as-subject and the subject-of-knowledge, since the latter comes into being in skeptical reflections on the former—even to the point of finally doubting the value of such reflection. Like psychoanalysis, education can only begin with self-doubt, and its disciplinary self-analyses should be interminable.

As long as the problematic of authority and positions remains caught up in the student/teacher relation, however, there is always the danger that the "subject of certainty" will reappear, now disguised as the skeptic who is presumed to know the difference between knowledge and its other. One way to complicate the transference (in which the position of authority/knowledge oscillates forever between teacher and student) is by including the text within it. "In the relation of transference," observes Gallop of our usual reading positions, "the critic is no longer analyst but patient" (30). Rather than portraying the critic as the subject presumed to know the meaning of the text, Gallop describes how the reader presumes the authority of the text—supposes that the text knows the truth about itself and is centered in a subjectivity whose coherence guarantees the comprehensibility of the text. The reader transfers authority onto the text the way the patient transfers saving knowledge to the analyst. The double play of Gallop's title—*Reading Lacan*—lies in her resistance to this transference, in her counterpresumption that the text doesn't know all that it's talking about. Reading *à la* Lacan, in a Lacanian style, means opening reading to textual effects unauthorized by any certain subject (like the signifying effects of dreams, parapraxes, or the typographical errors in Lacan that Gallop herself analyzes [175–77]). Her speculations, like Derrida's, cannot be returned to any authoritative sender: they are de-sendered modes of analytically addressing the text, and they play with the de-sendering of the signifying effects produced in reading.

The Fathers Know

How do Lacanian approaches to pedagogy differ from other well-known psychological or even Freudian ideas about teaching? The answer emerges partly from considering the pedagogical implications of the essential points developed by Lacan in his rereading of Freud. These are by now fairly familiar, even if only as slogans such as "the unconscious is structured like a language" (20). The self is analyzed by Lacan as a phenomenon of language, as a *subject* that comes into being through the assumption of positions offered to it by cultural discourses: "in so far as we are the subject who thinks," says Lacan, "we depend on the field of the Other, which was there long before we came into the

world, and whose circulating structures determine us as subjects" (246).
Lacan's summary of his theory is worth quoting in full:

> The unconscious is the sum of the effects of speech on a subject, at the
> level at which the subject constitutes himself out of the effects of the
> signifier. This makes it clear that, in the term *subject* . . . I am not designating
> the living substratum needed by this phenomenon of the subject, nor any
> sort of substance, nor any being possessing knowledge in his *pathos*, his
> suffering, whether primal or secondary, nor even some incarnated logos,
> but the Cartesian subject, who appears at the moment when doubt is
> recognized as certainty—except that, through my approach, the bases of
> this subject prove to be wider, but, at the same time much more amenable
> to the certainty that eludes it. This is what the unconscious is. (126)

The genesis of subjectivity begins with the fabricated difference between the sexes, which is not biologically determined. Juliet Mitchell
and Jacqueline Rose explain that sexual identity "is something enjoined
on the subject" by that master of signifiers, the Name and No (and
Know) of the Father (*le nom-du-père*), which prescribes identity in symbolic terms according to the presence or absence of its token: the phallus.[14] This legislative imposition underscores the Father's own lack,
however, so that phallocentric discourse will always be uncertain and
riven by its own desire: "Sexuality belongs for Lacan in the realm of
masquerade" (43).

It is quite possible, says Lacan, even inevitable, for the subject to
appear before its identity is recognized: "Remember the naive failure
of the simpleton's delighted attempt to grasp the little fellow who declares—*I have three brothers, Paul, Ernest and me*. But it is quite natural—
first the three brothers, Paul, Ernest and I are counted, and then there
is I at the level at which I am to reflect the first I, that is to say, the I
who counts" (20). In understanding ourselves, it is always a matter of
which I counts. ("And so," writes Rich, "even ordinary pronouns become
a political problem" [224].) Here Lacan demonstrates that the subject
of numerical calculation is not identical with the subject who reflects on
this operation. This heterogeneity or split within the subject will be a
constant theme in Lacan's work, as is his insistence that the subject
functions as in grammar, that is, relative to the discursive or calculational
structure it inhabits at some given level—there being many such levels
at work in the self. These various determinations cannot be totalized in
some dark vision of the self as a completely conditioned creature, how-

14. Juliet Mitchell and Jacqueline Rose, eds., *Female Sexuality: Jacques Lacan and the
"école freudienne,"* trans. Jacqueline Rose (New York: Norton, 1982), p. 40.

ever, precisely because the subject's enunciation of any one position necessarily obscures or represses others. As in the relation between the unconscious and a slip of the tongue, an incalculable play is also at work in the signifying of the subject: "It is always a question," warns Lacan, "of the subject *qua* indeterminate" (26).

The theoretical displacement of the independent self by the (in)determinate subject occurs in various brands of poststructuralist thought, and thus in part explains the appropriation of Lacan's work by overtly political critical schools such as feminism and Marxism. The reception of Lacan in England, for example, was principally among Marxist critics, who followed the French philosopher Louis Althusser in adapting Lacan's ideas about the unconscious to a new semiotic model of how ideology structures subjectivity.[15] These developments were ably demonstrated in Rosalind Coward and John Ellis's *Language and Materialism.*[16] "Ideology," they wrote, "is conceived as the way in which a subject is produced in language able to represent his/herself and therefore able to act in the social totality, the fixity of those representations being the function of ideology" (2). The semiological argument that no natural bond links signifier to signified now joins up with the Marxist argument that ideology represents fabricated "truths" as "natural" or "divine" certainties:

> Meaning, then, is no longer a matter of a pre-given, arbitrary relation between signifier and signified, but rather the fixing of the chain of signifiers to produce a certain meaning. . . . What emerged was a need for a theory of the production of the positions by which the chain of signifiers becomes attached to a specific signified, and what is demanded is a theory of the process and positions occupied by the subject in relation to language and ideology. (7)

In the lexicon of deconstruction, various instances of "logocentrism" work to fix the "chain of signifiers to produce a certain meaning," and so the undoing of the "arbitrary relation between signifier and signified" is essential to the critique of ideology. When a signifier like "black" has certain signifiers tied to it, like "unknown," "evil," "mysterious," "irrational," "false," "lustful," and so forth, the political as well as semiotic consequences of the signified thus fixed are considerable. The interpretation of literary characters, then, will involve tracing the signifiers fixed to a name, and disclosing what ideological discourses provide

15. Louis Althusser, "Freud and Lacan," in *Lenin and Philosophy,* trans. Ben Brewster (London: New Left Books, 1971), pp. 189–219.
16. Rosalind Coward and John Ellis, *Language and Materialism: Developments in Semiology and the Theory of the Subject* (London: Routledge, 1977).

the materials for these characterizations. Such was the method of Roland Barthes in *S/Z*, that parody of pedagogy, in which the signifiers
of femininity are found attached to a castrato, and the ideological
certainties hinging on the absolute difference between male and female
yield to deconstruction. This dissemination of positions, Barthes shows,
includes those social and class structures which Balzac so meticulously
scrutinizes in this little tale about art, desire, storytelling, and capitalism.[17] Barthes' compelling use of Lacan to revise his own earlier Marxist
version of semiotics implies, however, a critique of any position that
would see the subject as some natural entity now alienated by the ruses
of capitalism, or which would offer the semiotic critique of ideology as
a way toward a true politics (and reading) beyond ideology or free
of the impositions of a historic location. The danger of the Marxist
appropriation of Lacan lies in the temptation to see "politics" in a
transcendental sense as the final term or ultimate end of psychoanalysis,
pedagogy, or literary criticism. That would indeed put an end to all
three. Rather than terminate these discourses by imposing an a priori
idea of politics upon them, one wishes to discern where and how politics
takes place for each, and what politics informs the relations between
them. In each case one ought to consider politics as a *supplement* (in
Derrida's sense) to these discourses, and vice versa, so that none arro-
gates to itself a position of mastery. To see something called "politics"
as the last horizon of critical theory would be to simply repeat the
Hegelian narrative of the Subject arriving in time at Absolute Knowledge, a story that would cancel all our recent reading lessons about the
unconscious and the textuality of our histories.

Yet a Lacanian pedagogy cannot avoid the political if its primary
concern is with articulating how particular texts subject us to specific
meanings. Likewise, the first step in any literary pedagogy ought to
teach how meaning is unnatural and constructed, and this cannot help
but unsettle the security of our ordinary perceptions and values. To
experience how one's truth is indissociable from a social position may
prompt alarm, defensiveness, or even shame when the consequences of
that perspective are unfolded. The difficulty most students experience
in interpreting literary texts is a powerful if indirect consequence of
their socialization as ideological subjects. When you have been trained
to see the truth about certain relations—such as those between the poor
and the rich, men and women, or "whites" and "blacks"—as natural or
god-given, as events rather than signs, it is very hard to engage in
interpretive acts in which you must assume a critical position toward
the very workings of representation. Again, the resistance is not so

17. Roland Barthes, *S/Z*, trans. Richard Miller (New York: Hill and Wang, 1974).

much in the "content"—students can easily be taught to repeat liberal platitudes—as in the students' struggle against opening interpretation to an undecidability that threatens the politics of their identity. A student prefers "knowing" the "new truth" about social relations to the more dangerous experience of making interpretations and value judgments in the absence of either historical or transcendental verities.

It should be stressed that this has nothing to do with "pluralism" or "relativism," with which most students and teachers are all too comfortable. Pluralism implies a set of personal points of view that can happily coexist in the larger transcendental framework of tolerance and liberal humanism. Pluralism encourages students to ask "Why isn't *my* interpretation just as good as yours, or anyone else's, if there is no one right interpretation?" The answer is that it isn't *your* interpretation, but a reading effect produced by the operation of a trans-personal method oriented by a social position (tell *that* to your freshmen!). A psychoanalysis of pedagogy also means its de-personalization insofar as the Symbolic is a cultural discourse; different interpretations must be seen, not as parts of a whole truth or as compatible differences of opinion, but as contradictory and often mutually exclusive conflicts between heterogeneous positions of value and of knowledge.

In fact, students will respond with relief when they grasp that the multiple meanings of a literary text are not the product of some inscrutable genius on the part of the author or the teacher, but can be arrived at through the practical application of specific interpretive frameworks—through working to occupy *other* subjective positions. Early in my introduction to literature, I list the major critical methods on the blackboard; in the course of the semester, we frame our interpretations of various works by reference to the particular method we are now employing. Are we doing a biographical interpretation of "Prufrock"? A historical or political or Marxist reading of *Heart of Darkness*? Are we utilizing the theories of psychoanalysis in deciphering "Young Goodman Brown," and if so what strengths and weaknesses can we expect in our reading? How will a feminist approach to Shakespeare's *Othello* change our choice of characters to study or our interpretation of the themes of jealousy, revenge, and marital violence? The teacher of freshmen or sophomores should provide students with basic information about these major approaches to literature and help them learn how to apply them. Their skill and responsibility as readers are directly dependent on this acquisition of the various methods of criticism.

These methods, however, cannot be adopted without a simultaneous analysis of the reader's historically given position, and of the resistances between that position and the ones produced by the method. The anxiety and confusion produced when men try to read as feminists is only one of many examples. What psychoanalysis teaches is that the adoption of a method is also the assumption of a position, one with consequences we may not always foresee. Resistance to a specific method entails resistance to the position it offers, or defense of the one it endangers, and so debates over critical methods quickly become discussions of assumptions, beliefs, and values. Such discussions rightly belong in the earlier stages of instruction in literature and writing, beginning in high school and the first year of college, for they establish the necessary principles and procedures for sophisticated cultural literacy. Critical theory should not simply be an advanced course for majors, but an integral part of our entire approach to pedagogy, curriculum, and the design of educational institutions. And insofar as such a pedagogy necessitates reading from an/other's point of view, it underscores the need to make multicultural study the foundation for educational practice.

Students will often repeat the cliché that we must "read between the lines" or "look for the deep meaning" when doing interpretations. I tell them that such well-intentioned metaphors are misguided nonsense. There is nothing between the lines but blank whiteness, nothing beneath the page but more pages. Our task is rather to work with the words on the surface, to make these words signify newly to us by placing them in an/other interpretive context. One student recently expressed her frustration (a common one) with Joyce's *Dubliners*, saying that she got nothing from it, that it didn't *mean* anything to her. This led quite nicely into a discussion of how literary meaning doesn't exist like a scoop of ice cream to be spooned and swallowed. It has to be produced actively by the reader, and so the class began a discussion of how we go about making meaning happen while we read. What kinds of things must we stop to notice, and how do we make those things mean something to us? Is there a reason, historical or ideological or personal, why we at first can't "see" something which the later adoption of a critical perspective suddenly brings into focus? How much about the positions of religion, class, and gender in Joyce's Ireland do we need to know for *Dubliners* to mean something for us? In a given situation (a play, a football game, a barroom seduction, a presidential news conference), what are the materials out of which meaning is being made, and by what common rules? Is the structure of discourse conscious or unconscious, and what is the relative position of the participants in relation to the powers at work and values at stake in this production of meaning?

Reading in Black and White

The isolation of signifying elements is traditionally the province of formalist criticism, which specifies (after the New Criticism) that we

note point of view or imagery or metaphor in our analysis. The interpretation of these elements, the making of meaning out of them, then
depends on the context or method of interpretation we apply to them.
Thus we can easily see why a signifying element—like the figure of
the father in Faulkner's "A Rose for Emily"—has so many different
meanings. Do we interpret him historically as a metaphor of Southern
manhood? Psychologically as the cause of Emily's neurosis? In a feminist
context as a symbol of the patriarchal repression of freedom and desire?
Do any of these meanings seem more comprehensive than the others
in accounting for the other signifying elements of the text? What procedures would we follow in testing the significance of these interpretations
or in trying to tie them together? The political version of Lacanian
interpretation appears peculiarly well-suited to Faulkner's texts, in that
they so demonstrably involve the positional conflicts of masters and
slaves, aristocrats and rednecks, patriarchs and sons and daughters in
anguished narratives that dramatize our historic choices of what and
how to value.

My choice of example, however, somewhat belies the simplicity of my
model, since it is the critical framework that dictates which signifying
elements we notice and interpret. Would I, in the absence of psychoanalysis or feminism, stop and ponder at such length that paternal, immov-
able body blocking Emily's access to society and sexuality? And how will
these perspectives affect my decision as to whether this Emily (like Emily
Dickinson) is a madwoman in the attic or a victim of patriarchal culture?
These are questions that students can, and should, learn to ask. "A Rose

Whereas a conventional psychological reading might emphasize Miss
Emily's "insanity" or "hysteria," a Lacanian one would focus on her
position in a community of structuring institutions. As Judith Fetterley
has shown, " it is a story of a woman victimized and betrayed by the
system of sexual politics," or in Faulkner's own words the tale of a young
girl "brow-beaten and kept down by her father, a selfish man who didn't
want her to leave home because he wanted a housekeeper."[18] Miss
Emily's position is most graphically represented in a reminiscence of
the primal scene of her spinsterhood: "None of the young men were
quite good enough to Miss Emily and such. We had long thought of
them as a tableau; Miss Emily a slender figure in white in the background, her father a spraddled silhouette in the foreground, his back
to her and clutching a horsewhip, the two of them framed by the back-
flung front door" (437).

My choice of example, however, somewhat belies the simplicity of my
model, since it is the critical framework that dictates which signifying
elements we notice and interpret. Would I, in the absence of psychoanalysis or feminism, stop and ponder at such length that paternal, immov-
able body blocking Emily's access to society and sexuality? And how will
these perspectives affect my decision as to whether this Emily (like Emily
Dickinson) is a madwoman in the attic or a victim of patriarchal culture?
These are questions that students can, and should, learn to ask. "A Rose

18. Judith Fetterley, *The Resisting Reader: A Feminist Approach to American Fiction*
(Bloomington: Indiana University Press, 1977), p. 35; Frederick L. Gwynn and Joseph
Blotner, eds., *Faulkner in the University* (New York: Vintage, 1959), p. 185.

for Emily," in its final Gothic nightmare of repression and necrophilia, spells out a tale of the Name-of-the-Father as a prohibition and perversity of desire, and Emily's murderous union a symbolic resolution of her feminist outrage and erotic longing. But what complicates our reading is the realization of the multiple and contradictory subject positions of the characters as well as of ourselves as historically located interpreters.

The narrative point of view in "A Rose for Emily" puts "us" in a strange position. It is "out town," and our position toward Emily is initially that of the narrator and the community. They are the subject who is supposed to know, but this posthumous narrative turns on their lack of knowledge—a lack that leads to a corpse and to what Emily's life has lacked. Pedagogically, an analysis of this narrative temporality must pose certain questions: why is this tale told after the fact? what gap in the town's knowledge of Emily does the narrative set out to bridge? how is the inquisitive structure of this detective narrative analogous to an act of voyeurism, and part of the town's long-standing prurient curiosity toward Emily? is the narrator's gaze essentially male, and if so in what position does that put the reader? An effort to interpret the lack of knowledge which motivates this narrative, then, will open up discussion of the correspondences between the represented themes and characters of the story, on the one hand, and the possible modes of representation and reception on the other.

What the narrator and the town don't know is the answer to Freud's famous question: "What do women want?" In prescribing that woman's desire must be desire for the phallus, as Colonel Sartoris and Emily's father do, the patriarchal subject writes of his own lack, projected as the "castration" of woman, which returns to haunt him in the poisoned figure of Emily's lover, Homer Barron. This none-too-subtle name signifies the lack of love in Emily's house and the sterility of ancient patriarchal structures. Fetterley brilliantly summarizes the tale's conclusion:

When the would-be "suitors" finally get into her father's house, they discover the consequences of his oppression of her, for the violence contained in the rotted corpse of Homer Barron is the mirror image of the violence represented in the tableau, the back-flung front door flung back with a vengeance. Having been consumed by her father, Emily in turn feeds off Homer Barron, becoming, after his death, suspiciously fat. Or, to put it another way, it is as if, after her father's death, she has reversed his act of incorporating her by incorporating and becoming him, metamorphosed from the slender figure in white to the obese figure in black whose hair is "a vigorous iron-gray, like the hair of an active man." She has taken into

herself the violence that thwarted her and has reenacted it upon Homer
Barron. (42–43)

As Faulkner shows in "The Bear," man's desire to own and control
nature, women, and other races becomes the desire for death, for the
end of his own lack. In acting out the Lacanian formula that desire is
always the desire of the Other, Emily revenges herself by identifying
with man's desire, by incorporating the Father, by giving him what he
wants—death. In penetrating Emily's house to discover the truth about
her, our male narrator actually dramatizes the truth of male desire in
an anxious discourse that discloses the castration fear signifying man's
own lack. To ask what Emily wants seems, with Freud, almost inconceivable, and it is her point of view, her position, which becomes the most
difficult, and necessary, for us to occupy. And this can be no simple
identification, since, as Penley argues, "each individual 'exists' only as
a nexus of various and *sometimes contradictory* subjectivities which are
legislated or assumed, either consciously or unconsciously" (144). As a
subject of racial and regional and class discourses, the figure of Emily
is more than a "woman," and so the reader must resist a reading that
is "only" feminist.

Here, then, is where we discover the color blindness of Fetterley's
interpretation, for in incorporating her father's desire Emily adopts
a subjective position—that of the racist patriarchal master—which in
fact has been a constitutive part of her character all along. Emily is
not simply the feminist subject (or victim), as Fetterley's reading often
implies (its motto could be "Spinsterhood is powerful!"); Emily is
also, contradictorily, identified with the enforcers of subjection, as a
train of imagery and incident shows. Her fate's connection to the
Civil War is indicated by her burial site "among the ranked and
anonymous graves of Union and Confederate soldiers."[19] Questions
about her position in the town lead not only to her prisonlike house,
but to the strange details that link her fate to those of the blacks.
We learn, for example, that she is a "sort of hereditary obligation
upon the town" since "that day in 1894 when Colonel Sartoris, the
major—he who fathered the edict that no Negro woman should
appear on the streets without an apron—remitted her taxes" (433).
The date suggests a coincidence of Miss Emily's oppression and the
advent of the Jim Crow laws. This parenthetical aside functions like
a slip of the tongue to disclose what Faulkner is often at pains to
explore—the fundamental analogy between the patriarchal subjection

19. William Faulkner, "A Rose for Emily," in *The Portable William Faulkner*, ed. Malcolm
Cowley (rev. ed. 1967; New York: Penguin, 1977), p. 433.

of women and blacks, condensed in the image of that dictated apron which is "fathered" by Sartoris, and which simultaneously signals racial, sexual, and class differences with a fig-leaf-like coverup.

Although Fetterley quotes the same passage, she never, from her white liberal feminist point of view, sees that the woman is black, nor does her reading ever mention the other blacks in the story. In discussing Emily's shadowy "Negro" servant (whose race she doesn't notice either), Fetterley sees his domestic work as an upsetting of sexual stereotypes, when in fact it is principally a perpetuation of racial and class roles, a social structure also embodied by the house Emily presides over. The servant's name is Tobe, a punning appellation that echoes Hamlet in signifying the black man's split being and the deferred futurity of his achievement of any authorized subjectivity. Such subjection is literally the business of Homer Barron, a construction company foreman who, like the plantation overseer, disciplines the "niggers and mules and machinery" (438). Although he is a Yankee, Barron actually perpetuates that racial and class patriarchy associated with the South, as Faulkner pointedly indicates: "The little boys would follow in groups to hear him cuss the niggers, and the niggers singing in time to the rise and fall of picks" (439). The class snobbery of Emily's disdainful townsfolk, who deride her romance, reflects their own defensive repression of the fact that the master's power depends on, and is embodied in, the work of the overseers and slaves. Their condemnation of Emily's affair suggests their own desire to sustain the delusory differences of race and class at precisely the historical moment when such differences—and the identities they uphold—are crumbling: the imposition of the Jim Crow laws institutes segregation as the ideological and administrative antidote to the abolition of slavery. Distancing himself from the past, the narrator scrupulously uses the nominal "Negro" for the manservant, who ages with Emily and disappears at her death. Perhaps liberated, Tobe's fate remains obscure, as is characteristic of Faulkner's apocalyptic representations of the black race's future at the end of novels such as *The Sound and the Fury, Absalom, Absalom!,* and *Go Down, Moses.*

Emily Grierson, then, presents a hermeneutic puzzle. As feminist subject her story speaks of a revolutionary subversion of patriarchy: as herself a figure of racial and class power, Emily also enacts the love affair of patriarchy with its own past, despite all the signs of decline and degradation. She is a split subject, crossed by rival discourses. What the text forces us to think, then, is the complex and ironic alliance between modes of possession and subjection, desire and ownership, identity and position. As Rich points out, the concept of patriarchy cannot be posited as the sole location or cause for cultural criticism:

The white radical feminist is confronted by the analysis by women of color of simultaneity of oppressions. For women in whose experience—and in whose theory, therefore—sex, race, and class converge as points of exploitation, there is no "primary oppression" or "contradiction," and it is not patriarchy alone that must be comprehended and dismantled. ... [T]he woman trying to fit racism and class into a strictly radical-feminist analysis finds that the box won't pack. The woman who seeks the experiential grounding of identity politics realizes that as Jew, white, woman, lesbian, middle-class, she herself has a complex identity. (xii)

Readings from the standpoints of the subject's various locations in cultural history will each yield a different gloss on the text, and we will be hard put to totalize them or reconcile their contradictions. This puzzle also arose when I was teaching Alice Walker's *The Color Purple*. There it was black men, rather than white women, who were split by contradictory subject positions. In terms of race, they were subjected to white power, as prizefighter Buster Broadnax is helpless to aid Sophia when she is beaten by the police for slugging the mayor's wife. In terms of gender, the black men subject their own women to physical and sexual violence which occurs in rough proportion to their own social and economic emasculation. In terms of class, black men and women have a common experience of exploitation that they fight against together. In terms of history and geography, blacks in the South and blacks in Africa confront each other to discover that their common oppression by white colonial imperialism does not necessarily guarantee their mutual understanding or solidarity as a unifiable cultural group. No single point of view can forge these disparate contradictions into a totality with a single locatable cause.

While we all give lip service to the unity of form and content, we cannot systematically identify or link them in the absence of a critical method for doing so. The death of literary study begins when students start memorizing terms like "personification" and "catharsis" with no sense of their intellectual, psychological, historical, or ideological functions. When I taught Melville's "Benito Cereno" in my "Literature and Composition" course, we centered our formal analysis on the question of point of view, a stock term in the critical vocabulary. But Melville's argument is that point of view is constituted by the perspectives dictated by one's place in racial, economic, legal, and class structures. Captain Delano's blindness to the reality of events on board the San Dominick, which the students found unbelievable, cannot be explained as a clever technique on the author's part to heighten suspense and achieve artistic excellence. Such a formalist or aesthetic explanation is hollow, and the students will quite correctly voice dissatisfaction with it.

Melville's story forces us to consider the sociocultural construction of our points of view, which in Delano's case forbids him to see the possibility of courage or heroism on the part of blacks, much less the possibility of a slave revolt. As Carolyn Karcher has shown, "Benito Cereno" is "an exploration of the white racist mind and how it reacts in the face of a slave insurrection."[20] Even in his New England liberalism, Delano is never able to see events from the slaves' point of view, and this displays the essence of the bad faith that makes racism and slavery possible. I brought into class information about Melville's historical period, his views on slavery, the role his father-in-law played in enforcing the Fugitive Slave Law—though these materials only buttressed what could be clearly read in the structure of the story. The class's final assignment was to imagine that Babo, the leader of the revolt, had changed his mind at the trial and decided to tell his tale. They were to write Babo's speech, in the first person, telling the story from his point of view, thus analyzing Melville's method and reenacting it, since they would now have to do what Delano never did—identify with the condition and voice of a black man. This put the "politics of location" into pedagogical practice.

It is somewhat ironic, in light of the largely ignorant attacks made upon poststructuralist thought by left- and right-wing spokesmen, that we discover the imperative to *ethics* as a major consequence of Lacan's work. I often open the first sessions of introductory courses with a discussion of what value, if any, lies in these required literature classes. What knowledge do they offer to justify their imposition? Traditionally, literature has been listed among those "humanities" whose acquisition marks the civilized man. It consisted of a body of objects for digestion, and a set of vague but comforting generalities about human life—a sort of post-Arnoldian (or, for Americans, post-Trilling) source of maxims to replace religion. No one should be surprised, then, that when poststructuralism takes on the transcendental signifieds of Western culture, it earns the wrath of "humanists," who preserve the light during the twilight of the gods. What Marx, Nietzsche, Saussure, Lacan, Derrida and others suggest, instead, is a pedagogy of production rather than consumption, in which education is a practice in the performance that makes knowledge.

What I tell my students, then, is that the worth of humanities courses lies precisely in the degree of their refusal of a technological, quantitative, absolutist, or correspondence model of truth. Here, on the contrary, is a laboratory for discovering the rules by which truths have

20. Carolyn Karcher, *Shadow over the Promised Land: Slavery, Race, and Violence in Melville's America* (Baton Rouge: Louisiana State University Press, 1980), p. 128.

been produced, the value systems these truths have supported, and the historical consequences of such discourses and institutions. It is an opportunity to debate meanings and values, and once students overcome their initial fright the response is usually one of relief and excitement, since American pedagogy has largely abandoned critical thought out of its obesiance to vocationalism or its tired allegiance to banalities that bore even the instructors who repeat them. Interpretation brings together the production of meaning with the production of values, discloses their inseparability, and places the subject in an *ethical* situation. For the literary critic, the description of the formal and technical devices by which meaning is produced cannot be divorced from seeing the imposition of subjective positions and value structures these devices prescribe, and so an education in conventions merges irresistibly with the recognition of ideologies.

In an age when the natural and social sciences have developed highly sophisticated theoretical models, vocabularies, and procedures, literary criticism regularly confesses with some embarrassment that it doesn't know what it is doing, though this admission often takes the form of defensive assertions that the rigorous intellectual analysis of artworks is somehow a violation of their mystery and virtue. Northrop Frye summed up the problem in 1951, but the resistance to theory has continued to prevent us from putting his argument into practice:

> Every organized body of knowledge can be learned progressively; and experience shows that there is also something progressive about the learning of literature. Our opening sentence has already got us into a semantic difficulty. Physics is an organized body of knowledge about nature, and a student of it says that he is learning physics, not that he is learning nature. Art, like nature, is the subject of a systematic study, and has to be distinguished from the study itself, which is criticism. It is therefore impossible to "learn literature": one learns about it in a certain way, but what one learns, transitively, is the criticism of literature. Similarly, the difficulty often felt in "teaching literature" arises from the fact that it cannot be done: the criticism of literature is all that can be directly taught.[21]

Our job in the classroom, then, is to teach criticism, and this ought to be the fundamental principle underlying the construction of the syllabus, the arrangement of readings, the direction of discussion, and the assignment of papers. Any other approach is likely to degenerate into sermonizing, impressionism, or aimless chitchat. Worse, it may deterio-

---

21. Northrop Frye, "The Archetypes of Literature," in *Twentieth-Century Literary Criticism*, ed. David Lodge (New York: Longman, 1972), p. 477.

rate into an Oedipal entertainment, in which identification with or hostility toward the instructor as the Subject Who Knows dominates classroom practice. Through a psychoanalytic and political analysis of pedagogy, we can better resist the oppressive liberal myth that aesthetic education in the Western Classics is a progressive and value-neutral exercise. Unfortunately, we have gone on too long ignoring the fine line that separates cultural appreciation from cultural fascism. The dislocation of the privileged pedagogical subject (the middle-class white male of Western Europe and North America) could open up a multicultural teaching in which every body is supposed to know.

Index

Library of Congress Cataloging-in-Publication Data

Jay, Gregory S.
    America the scrivener : deconstruction and the subject of literary
history / Gregory S. Jay
        p.   cm.
    Includes bibliographical references.
    ISBN 0-8014-2386-4 (alk. paper). — ISBN 0-8014-9610-1 (pbk. :
alk. paper)
        1. American literature—History and criticism—Theory, etc.
2. Criticism—United States. 3. Deconstruction. I. Title.
PS25.J39   1990
801'.95'0973—dc20   90-1801